FROM THE VULGATE
TO THE VERNACULAR

Four Debates on an English Question c. *1400*

The use of the vernacular language for scriptural citation was a central issue for the followers, sometimes called Lollards, of John Wyclif. It was an issue which aroused considerable academic interest, especially in Oxford where the first complete translation of the Bible seems to have originated. The matter was in some sense decided in 1409, when archiepiscopal legislation was passed to severely restrict the making and possession of new translations of the Bible except under episcopal licence. The four texts that are presented here, three in Latin and the fourth in English, derive from the academic debate which immediately preceded this decision. Two of the Latin texts, written by a Franciscan, William Butler, and a Dominican, Thomas Palmer, are wholly hostile to the idea of translation. The other, the longest and most perceptive, edited here for the first time, was written by a secular priest of impressive learning, Richard Ullerston, whose conclusions ran in the other direction. The English text, which is anonymous, draws on Ullerston's while adapting and augmenting it. Together, these texts preserve the most detailed discussions of translation and the theory of language that survive from late medieval England.

This volume provides editions and modern translations of these four texts, together with a substantial introduction explaining their context and the implications of their arguments, and encouraging further exploration of the perceptions of the nature of language that are displayed there.

BRITISH WRITERS OF THE MIDDLE AGES
AND THE EARLY MODERN PERIOD 7

Edited by

JAMES P. CARLEY
York University
Pontifical Institute of Mediaeval Studies

ANNE HUDSON
University of Oxford

†RICHARD SHARPE
University of Oxford

JAMES WILLOUGHBY
University of Oxford

STUDIES AND TEXTS 220

FROM THE VULGATE TO THE VERNACULAR

Four Debates on an English Question c. *1400*

Edited and translated by

ELIZABETH SOLOPOVA,
†JEREMY CATTO,
and ANNE HUDSON

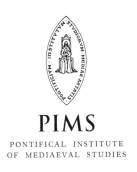

PIMS

PONTIFICAL INSTITUTE
OF MEDIAEVAL STUDIES

Bodleian Library

UNIVERSITY OF OXFORD

Library and Archives Canada Cataloguing in Publication

Title: From the Vulgate to the vernacular : four debates on an English question c. 1400 / edited and translated by Elizabeth Solopova, Jeremy Catto, and Anne Hudson.

Names: Solopova, Elizabeth, editor, translator. | Catto, Jeremy, editor, translator. | Hudson, Anne, 1938– editor, translator. | Pontifical Institute of Mediaeval Studies, publisher. | Bodleian Library, publisher.

Series: Studies and texts (Pontifical Institute of Mediaeval Studies) ; 220. | British writers of the Middle Ages and the early modern period ; 7.

Description: Series statement: Studies and texts ; 220 | British writers of the Middle Ages and the early modern period ; 7 | Includes bibliographical references and indexes. | Original texts in Latin with parallel English translation; critical matter in English.

Identifiers: Canadiana (print) 20200246976 | Canadiana (ebook) 20200247328 | ISBN 9780888442208 (hardcover ; PIMS) | ISBN 9781851245635 (hardcover ; Bodleian Library) | ISBN 9781771104081 (PDF)

Subjects: LCSH: Bible – Translating – England – History – To 1500. | LCSH: Bible. English – Versions – History – To 1500. | LCSH: Translating and interpreting – England – History – To 1500.

Classification: LCC BS455 .F76 2020 | DDC 220.5/20094209024–dc23

Published in North America by the Pontifical Institute of Mediaeval Studies, 59 Queen's Park Crescent East, Toronto, Ontario, Canada M5S 2C4 (www.pims.ca).

Published in Europe, including the United Kingdom, by The Bodleian Library, Broad Street, Oxford OX1 3GB (www.bodleianshop.co.uk).

© 2020
Pontifical Institute of Mediaeval Studies
59 Queen's Park Crescent East
Toronto, Ontario, Canada M5S 2C4
www.pims.ca
MANUFACTURED IN CANADA

Contents

TEXTS AND TRANSLATIONS

Acknowledgements

Any book is the outcome of collaboration. The collaboration involved in the present case has been particularly extensive and long-lasting. Work on the editions that follow here was begun by Anne Hudson around 1970, when the anonymous determination in ÖNB MS 4133 was transcribed; a few years later the author, date and place of the text became known from a binding fragment in Gonville and Caius College in Cambridge; these findings were published, and the account excited interest widely, but not to the extent of identifying a second editor. Only around forty years later Elizabeth Solopova saw and urged the importance of an edition of this text, and of a handful of other shorter texts on the same subject; she offered to collaborate. When completion of the edition seemed feasible only after a long investigation, the two of us invited Jeremy Catto to help; Jeremy's expertise in fourteenth- and fifteenth-century academic persons, structures and authorities was perceived as a valuable reinforcement, and the outlines of the edition, together with specification of the person(s) responsible for each part, were finalized. Jeremy contributed with even more enthusiasm than had been expected: he volunteered to produce the modern translations of all the Latin material. Though it had been clear for some time that Jeremy's health was declining, his death on 17 August 2018 came as a brutal shock; only around two weeks before this, he had urged the submission of a complete draft of the whole to the present publisher.

The remaining editors cannot supply acknowledgements to those whom Jeremy would have thanked, but they can give absolute priority in their own gratitude to Jeremy as a collaborator. He would have been a valued participant in the rather obscure manœuvres that ensued before final publication, not least because of his own commitment to a realistic evaluation of a past time—he was without doubt a 'sense for sense' and not a 'word for word' scholar.

The work on the edition has been supported by generous grants from the British Academy and the Leverhulme Trust Small Research Grants programme, and from the Ludwig Humanities Research Fund of New College, Oxford, awarded to Elizabeth Solopova. These grants funded travel to libraries, as well as an international conference, 'Translation Theory and Practice in the Later Middle Ages: the Bible and Beyond', held in Oxford in September 2019. Work on the edition progressed in parallel, and was informed and inspired

by research towards a new edition of the Wycliffite Bible, supported by a three-year grant from the UK Arts and Humanities Research Council (2016–19) awarded to Elizabeth Solopova and Anne Hudson. The scale of the work on the 'Ullerston' group of texts is put in perspective in comparison with the vast Wycliffite Bible project—we hope this edition will be seen as an outrider of that more ambitious enterprise.

We are indebted to many libraries, especially the Bodleian Library, the home of all three of us; the Österreichische Nationalbibliothek, Vienna; Trinity College, Cambridge; Gonville and Caius College, Cambridge; Merton College, Oxford; and the Pierpont Morgan Library in New York. To select friends and colleagues for particular thanks is hard, and for the most part we baulk at doing it, but we are particularly grateful to the Revd David Thomson, former bishop of Huntingdon, for his very sensitive checking and improving of the texts and notably the translations, to Prof. Andrew Kraebel for advance sight of his latest book and help with the Vienna manuscript, and to Prof. Christina von Nolcken for her generous hospitality in London. We are grateful to the two anonymous readers appointed by the Pontifical Institute of Mediaeval Studies, for their careful reading of our work and for many useful suggestions. Especial thanks are due to James Willoughby, who has acted as copy-editor for the whole—a thankless task, but without James's kindness and good judgement completion would have been impossible. As this book goes to press, we record our sadness and shock at the news of the sudden death of Richard Sharpe, founding member of the guiding committee of this series published by the Institute.

We are grateful to the Österreichische Nationalbibliothek, Vienna; the Master and Fellows of Gonville and Caius College, Cambridge; the Master and Fellows of Trinity College, Cambridge; and the Warden and Fellows of Merton College, Oxford, for permission to publish photographs.

Elizabeth Solopova
Anne Hudson

List of Plates

(following page cxxxvi)

1. Vienna, Österreichische Nationalbibliothek, MS 4133, fol. 195r, Richard Ullerston's determination, opening page.

2. Vienna, Österreichische Nationalbibliothek, MS 4133, fol. 207v, Richard Ullerston's determination, final page.

3. Cambridge, Gonville and Caius College, MS 803/807, fragment 36, recto, Richard Ullerston's determination.

4. Cambridge, Gonville and Caius College, MS 803/807, fragment 36, verso, Richard Ullerston's determination.

5. Cambridge, Gonville and Caius College, MS 803/807, fragment 36, verso, ultra-violet image, Richard Ullerston's determination.

6. Cambridge, Trinity College, MS B. 15. 11, fol. 43r, Thomas Palmer's determination.

7. Oxford, Merton College, MS 68, fol. iii^v, added table of contents with William Butler's determination listed as an addition underneath the main table, probably in a different contemporary hand.

8. Cambridge, Trinity College, MS B. 14. 50, fol. 26r, *First seiþ Bois.*

Abbreviations

Add.	Additional (in manuscript shelfmarks)
AL	*Aristoteles Latinus*, Union académique internationale, 25 vols (Rome 1951–)
Bale, *Catalogus*	John Bale, *Scriptorum illustrium maioris Brytannie, quam nunc Angliam & Scotiam uocant, catalogus*, 2 vols (Basel 1557–9; repr. Farnborough 1971)
Bale, *Index*	*Index Britanniae scriptorum: John Bale's Index of British and Other Writers*, ed. R. L. Poole & M. Bateson (Oxford 1902; repr. with introduction by C. Brett & J. P. Carley, Cambridge 1990)
Bekker	*Aristotelis opera*, ed. Immanuel Bekker, Preussische Akademie der Wissenschaften, 5 vols (Berlin 1831–70) [Bekker numbers are provided when references to Aristotle's works are identified in notes to texts]
BL	London, British Library
Bodl.	Oxford, Bodleian Library
BRUC	A. B. Emden, *A Biographical Register of the University of Cambridge to 1500* (Cambridge 1963)
BRUO	A. B. Emden, *A Biographical Register of the University of Oxford to AD 1500*, 3 vols (Oxford 1957–9)
c.	*circa*
CA	*S. Thomae Aquinatis Catena aurea in quatuor evangelia*, ed. A. Guarienti OP, 2 vols (Turin & Rome 1953) [cited by volume, page and column]
CBMLC	Corpus of British Medieval Library Catalogues, 1– (London 1990–)
CCCM	*Corpus Christianorum, Continuatio medievalis*, 1– (Turnhout 1966–)
CCSL	*Corpus Christianorum, Series Latina*, 1– (Turnhout 1953–)
CHB2	*The Cambridge History of the Bible*, 2: *The West, from the Fathers to the Reformation*, ed. G. W. H. Lampe (Cambridge 1969)
Constantiense	*Magnum Oecumenicum Constantiense Concilium*, ed. H. van der Hardt (Frankfurt 1700)
Coxe	H. O. Coxe, *Catalogue of the Manuscripts in the Oxford Colleges*, 2 vols (Oxford 1852) [note that each college's listing is separately paginated]
Deanesly	M. Deanesly, *The Lollard Bible* (Cambridge 1920; repr. 1966)

Denis	J. N. C. M. Denis, *Codices manuscripti theologici bibliothecae Palatinae Vindobonensis latini*, 2 vols (Vienna 1793–1800)
DML	*Dictionary of Medieval Latin from British Sources* (Oxford 1975–2013)
Doctors in English	A. Hudson, *Doctors in English: a Study of the English Wycliffite Gospel Commentaries* (Liverpool 2015)
Dove, *EAEB*	*The Earliest Advocates of the English Bible: the Texts of the Medieval Debate*, ed. M. Dove (Exeter 2010)
Dove, *FEB*	M. Dove, *The First English Bible: the Text and Context of the Wycliffite Versions* (Cambridge 2007)
DVSS	John Wyclif, *De veritate sacrae scripturae*, ed. R. Buddensieg, 3 vols (London 1905–1907)
EETS	Early English Text Society, Original Ser. 1– (London & Oxford 1864–); Extra Ser. 1–126 (London 1867–1935); Supplementary Ser. 1– (London & Oxford 1970–) [volumes without prefix are in the Original Series, those prefixed ES or SS are in the Extra Series or Supplementary Series respectively]
EHR	*The English Historical Review*, 1– (London 1885–)
ESWB	*The Wycliffite Bible: Origin, History and Interpretation*, ed. E. Solopova (Turnhout 2016)
EV	Earlier Version of the Wycliffite Bible
EWS	*English Wycliffite Sermons*, ed. P. Gradon & A. Hudson, 5 vols (Oxford 1983–96)
FM	Forshall and Madden, editors of *WB*
fol.	folio
fols.	folios
Friedberg	*Corpus iuris canonici*, ed. E. Friedberg, 2 vols (Leipzig 1879–81; repr. Graz, 1959)
FZ	*Fasciculi zizaniorum magistri Johannis Wyclif cum tritico: ascribed to Thomas Netter of Walden*, ed. W. W. Shirley, RS 5 (1858)
G&C	Cambridge, Gonville and Caius College
GO	*Glossa ordinaria*, quoted from *Biblia latina cum glossa ordinaria: Facsimile Reprint of the Editio Princeps Adolph Rusch of Strasburg 1480/81*, ed. K. Froehlich & M. T. Gibson, 4 vols (Turnhout 1992)
GP	*General Prologue* to the Wycliffite Bible (no. 1 in Dove, *EAEB*)
HUO	*The History of the University of Oxford*, ed. T. H. Aston & others, 8 vols (Oxford 1984–94)
IPMEP	*Index of Printed Middle English Prose*, ed. R. E. Lewis, N. F. Blake & A. S. G. Edwards (London 1985)

James, *Gonville*	M. R. James, *A Catalogue of the Manuscripts in the Library of Gonville and Caius College, Cambridge*, 3 vols (Cambridge 1907–14) and Supplement (1914)
James, *Trinity*	M. R. James, *The Western Manuscripts in the Library of Trinity College Cambridge: a Descriptive Catalogue*, 4 vols (Cambridge 1900–1904)
JTS	*The Journal of Theological Studies* 1–50 (Oxford 1899–1949); new ser. 1– (Oxford 1950–)
LALME	*A Linguistic Atlas of Late Mediaeval English*, ed. A. McIntosh, M. L. Samuels, M. Benskin, 4 vols (Aberdeen 1986)
LB	A. Hudson, *Lollards and their Books* (London 1985)
Leland	J. Leland, *De viris illustribus*, ed. and trans. J. P. Carley, with the assistance of C. Brett, *De viris illustribus: On Famous Men* (Toronto & Oxford 2010)
LV	Later Version of the Wycliffite Bible
Lyndwood	W. Lyndwood, *Provinciale* (Oxford 1679; repr. Farnborough 1978)
MED	*Middle English Dictionary*, ed. H. Kurath, S. M. Kuhn & others (Ann Arbor, MI, 1952–99; http://quod.lib.umich.edu/m/med/)
MWBO	E. Solopova, *Manuscripts of the Wycliffite Bible in the Bodleian and Oxford College Libraries* (Liverpool 2016)
NCHB2	*The New Cambridge History of the Bible*, 2: *From 600 to 1450*, ed. R. Marsden & E. A. Matter (Cambridge 2012)
NIV	*The Holy Bible: New International Version* (London 1978)
NT	New Testament
ODCC	*The Oxford Dictionary of the Christian Church*, ed. F. L. Cross & E. A. Livingstone, 3rd edn (Oxford 1997)
ODNB	*Oxford Dictionary of National Biography* (printed version Oxford 2004, online version updated)
OED	*Oxford English Dictionary* (printed version Oxford, reissued 1933, online version updated)
ÖNB	Vienna, Österreichische Nationalbibliothek
OT	Old Testament
PG	J.-P. Migne, *Patrologia Graeca*, 161 vols and index (Paris 1857–66)
PL	J.-P. Migne, *Patrologia Latina*, 271 vols (Paris 1844–55); Index, 4 vols (Paris 1864)
PR	A. Hudson, *The Premature Reformation: Wycliffite Texts and Lollard History* (Oxford 1988)
QCA	Oxford, The Queen's College Archives
Riverside Chaucer	*The Riverside Chaucer*, ed. L. D. Benson & others, 3rd edn (Boston, MA, 1987)

RP	*Two Revised Versions of Rolle's English Psalter Commentary and the Related Canticles*, ed. A. Hudson, EETS 340, 341, 343 (2012–14)
RS	Rolls Series, 99 vols in 259 (London 1858–1911, 1964)
SC	*A Summary Catalogue of Western Manuscripts in the Bodleian Library at Oxford*, 7 vols (Oxford 1895–1953; repr. 1980) [cited by no.]
Sharpe	R. Sharpe, *A Handlist of the Latin Writers of Great Britain and Ireland before 1540* (Turnhout 1997)
Somerset, *Dialogues*	*Four Wycliffite Dialogues*, ed. F. Somerset, EETS 333 (2009)
Stegmüller	F. Stegmüller, *Repertorium Biblicum medii aevi*, completed by V. Reinhardt, 11 vols (Madrid 1950–80) [cited by number]
STWW	A. Hudson, *Studies in the Transmission of Wyclif's Writings* (Aldershot 2008)
T	prefixed to a number refers to item number(s) of Wyclif's Latin works as listed in Thomson, *Wyclyf*
TCC	Cambridge, Trinity College Library
TCD	Dublin, Trinity College Library
Thomson, *Merton*	R. M. Thomson, *A Descriptive Catalogue of the Medieval Manuscripts of Merton College, Oxford* (Cambridge 2009)
Thomson, *University and College Libraries of Oxford*	R. M. Thomson, *The University and College Libraries of Oxford*, CBMLC 16, 2 vols (London 2015)
Thomson, *Wyclyf*	W. R. Thomson, *The Latin Writings of John Wyclyf* (Toronto 1983)
Vulgate	*Biblia sacra iuxta Vulgatam versionem*, ed. R. Weber & others, 5th edn (Stuttgart 2007)
WB	*The Holy Bible . . . Made from the Latin Vulgate by John Wycliffe and his Followers*, ed. J. Forshall & F. Madden, 4 vols (Oxford 1850; repr. New York, NY, 1982)
Wells Rev.	*A Manual of the Writings in Middle English, 1050–1500*, ed. J. E. Wells, J. B. Severs, A. E. Hartung, P. G. Beidler, 11 vols (New Haven, CT, 1967–2005)
Wilkins	*Concilia Magnae Britanniae et Hiberniae*, ed. D. Wilkins, 4 vols (London 1737)
WLP	*The Works of a Lollard Preacher*, ed. A. Hudson, EETS 317 (2001)
Wogan-Browne	*The Idea of the Vernacular*, ed. J. Wogan-Browne & others (Exeter 1999)
WS	Wyclif Society Publications (London 1883–1921)

Introduction

The first complete English translation of the Bible, made from the Vulgate, was produced in the last quarter of the fourteenth century and was from an early date associated with John Wyclif and his followers. Notwithstanding that all English versions of the biblical text itself were entirely uncontroversial, the hierarchy of the English church, and notably a sequence of three archbishops of Canterbury (Courtenay 1381–96, Arundel 1396–7, 1399–1414, and Chichele 1414–43), regarded biblical translation into English as unacceptable. In the *Constitutions*, drafted in 1407 and promulgated in 1409, Archbishop Arundel forbade the making or use of translations produced from the time of Wyclif or later, unless both the version and owner were episcopally approved. Despite the continued validity of the ban until the Reformation, the Wycliffite Bible became the most widely disseminated medieval English work, surviving in over 250 complete and partial copies.

Work on the scrutiny of available Latin texts, and on the translation and revision of the English versions, seems to have been concentrated in Oxford, and in Oxford there seems to have been some academic interest, beyond the central circle of translators, in the theoretical issues raised by the work. Was it legitimate to translate the Bible into various vernacular languages, and if not, why were some vernaculars unacceptable? Can meaning be preserved in translation without loss and alteration, and what makes this possible? Considering that the Vulgate was circulated in a variable and imperfect form, and was itself a translation from languages inaccessible to most fourteenth-century scholars, was it an adequate basis for new translations? Who should undertake the task of translation and what would be the intellectual, social and political consequences of such a move? As will be demonstrated below, these and similar questions were debated in Latin and English, in academic and pastoral contexts, and by practising translators in prefaces to their works. The four texts edited here, however, are either a direct outcome of a debate that took place in Oxford during the academic year 1400–1401, or a result of its more distant influence. On the evidence of the introductory words of one of the treatises, Richard Ullerston's university determination, two doctors at Oxford devoted the entire time of their series of lectures during that academic year to the topic of the legitimacy of biblical

translation. Ullerston's treatise is a literary version of a determination on this subject, probably based on lectures and academic exercises that took place in the same year.

Ullerston argues in favour of the legitimacy of English translation from an orthodox perspective; he is known as the author of other works, from which he appears as a reformist but not a Wycliffite. He offers a carefully balanced case that sees the value of translation even while acknowledging its problems. The second treatise, by the Franciscan William Butler, is a literary version of his *principium*, a lecture given on inception as a doctor of theology, in which he responds to Ullerston, a more senior master. The third work, by the Dominican Thomas Palmer, also takes the literary form of a determination on the same topic. It may not be a record of a real *quaestio disputata*, an academic exercise in which an opponent and a respondent presented arguments, and a presiding master determined the question, but it may be based on lectures to clergy, perhaps at the schools of St Paul's or at Palmer's own priory, the London Blackfriars. Both Butler's and Palmer's contributions are unequivocally hostile to the use of the vernacular for biblical texts. The final text edited here, an English treatise known by its opening words as *First seiþ Bois*, is a free adaptation of Ullerston's determination with significant abbreviation as well as the addition of new material. Though none of the works refers directly to what we now call the *Wycliffite Bible*, as a complete and recent English translation, made almost certainly by Ullerston's and Butler's colleagues at Oxford, that was in all likelihood the ultimate inspiration for the debate. Whereas Ullerston's and Butler's treatises, and probably Palmer's contribution as well, were written at a time when translation of the Bible was not prohibited or seen as necessarily heretical, *First seiþ Bois* most likely postdates Arundel's *Constitutions*. The Latin works discuss translation as primarily an academic issue, in a tone that is relatively moderate and even at times light-hearted in Butler's case, in the spirit of the festive tradition of a *principium*. Palmer's treatise, however, possibly due to its somewhat later date, reflects the hardening of attitudes to translation, while in *Bois*, little is left of Ullerston's reasoned impartiality, even though it was probably written by an author whose background was not radically different from that of Ullerston's or Butler's.

The texts' importance and distinctiveness resides in the fact that they preserve the most detailed discussions of different aspects of translation that survive from late medieval England. The only earlier English author who produced comparable work on this subject is Roger Bacon, whose views on translation are discussed and partly refuted by Ullerston. Ullerston's treatise is by far the longest and

most learned, but all the texts make observations about the nature and status of vernacular languages, the value of different versions of the Bible, the history of biblical translation, its principles and methods, the form in which Christian doctrine should be disseminated, the difficulties translators face and the strategies they employ. Access to vernacular versions and their authorization by the church are also debated, but what is probably the most unique aspect of these works is their detailed treatment of theoretical issues around translation. Ullerston in particular advances a sophisticated linguistic appreciation, quoting an impressive range of authors and offering observations on a wide variety of topics.

All texts edited here have been known for a long time, but their modern histories differ considerably. Only two of them, the treatises by Butler and Palmer, have previously been published; Ullerston's determination is printed here for the first time. For many years it was available to scholars in the form of photocopied transcripts and translations, and black and white images of the only complete manuscript, currently in Vienna. A full transcript with identification of authorities and a translation was made by Anne Hudson and Dr Valerie Murray in 1970–71. In 1972 Neil Ker handed over to Anne Hudson another transcript of Ullerston's work made independently by Marthe Dulong, to be used if it proved helpful; the date of the copying, its instigation and motive are unclear.[1] All these materials were the starting point in our work; their comparison was helpful in catching errors and raised many queries, some reflected in the notes to texts. At least in so far as the evidence currently stands, neither Ker nor Dulong knew of the Caius fragment, and hence the connection of the determination with Ullerston. This came to light as a result of a discovery made by Anne Hudson, who identified the fragment as containing the final part of Ullerston's determination. The colophon on the fragment helped to settle the question of the text's authorship, as reported in her article 'The debate on Bible translation' published in 1975.

The knowledge of the pieces by Butler and by Palmer has a longer history, as is shown by the evidence of John Bale and John Leland discussed in the following chapter. The first to print both texts,

---

[1] Thanks are due to Dr Martin Kauffmann for his attempt to find relevant evidence on either in the archive of Ker papers in the Bodleian Library, Oxford: Marthe Dulong appears to have been based in London and Paris (not Vienna), and to have been interested in biblical prologues in medieval Parisian manuscripts; she evidently knew Neil Ker's family well, at least during the period 1960–75. Nothing, unfortunately, has come to light on Neil Ker's knowledge of Ullerston's determination beyond his consultation of its Vienna manuscript: Österreichische Nationalbibliothek has a record that he had access to the manuscript in 1955.

though without translation and with only minimal notes, was Margaret Deanesly in her study *The Lollard Bible* (1920), pp. 401–18 (Butler) and 418–37 (Palmer).[2] In default of a facsimile, anyone interested in the material has naturally used Deanesly's text.[3] Deanesly was also the first to produce a modern edition of *First seiþ Bois*; her knowledge of this work, derivative of Ullerston's, came from her reading of Denis's catalogue of medieval manuscripts in the Österreichische Nationalbibliothek in Vienna.[4] Deanesly was aware of Ullerston's treatise, but there is no evidence that she had seen the Vienna manuscript herself.

The late Mary Dove edited in her posthumously published book, *The Earliest Advocates of the English Bible* (Exeter 2010), the vernacular defences of translation, but, as reviewers have observed, included none of the Latin reactions to the material, an omission that somewhat invalidates her title. Their publication is long overdue and the current edition aims to fill this major gap in medieval English scholarship.

In a book dedicated to translation, it is fitting to give a brief characterization of the translations printed here facing the Latin texts. The task was to produce fluent translations reflecting stylistic nuances of the Latin works, rather than to translate as literally as possible. Translations of biblical quotations usually follow the King James Version, to maintain their stylistic distance from the authors' own text, unless the versions used by the authors differ significantly from versions that underlie the KJV. This seemed to us to be a good solution, considering that translations are printed side by side with the Latin originals, offering the reader an opportunity to resolve any queries readily. Since Dove, in the collection mentioned above, printed an edition of *First seiþ Bois* based on all surviving manuscripts, we felt that a full new edition was not required, but we included for

---

[2] A reprint of Deanesly's book appeared in 1966 with a very short 'prefatory note' by the author (pp. [vii–viii]) and 'Errata for Volume I' (pp. xxi–xxiii). A few corrections relate to the texts and background to the treatises of Butler and Palmer, but there is no change to the attribution or context of the debate.

[3] R. Hanna in 'Richard Rolle's *Incendium amoris*: a prospectus for a future editor', *Journal of Medieval Latin* 26 (2016), 221–61, gives a critical account of Deanesly's edition of Rolle (Manchester 1915) and points out the lack of systematic training in the necessary editorial skills she had had by that early stage of her career—her work on Butler and Palmer was published only five years later.

[4] J. N. C. M. Denis, *Codices manuscripti theologici bibliothecae Palatinae Vindobonensis latini*, 2 vols (Vienna 1793–1800), 1. cols 842–8. Denis's brief quotations, which certainly go back to the specific medieval text, are traceable to Thomas Tanner, *Bibliotheca Britannico-Hibernica* (London 1748), to which Denis refers. Entries in Tanner are: for Ullerston, col. 740; for Butler, col. 114; for Palmer, col. 571; the sources of information are mostly Leland and Bale.

the convenience of the reader a text based on the only two surviving complete medieval copies. Considering how closely the two works, Ullerston's determination and *First seiþ Bois*, are related and how difficult their comparison was previously, we felt that the reader would be assisted by the inclusion of this text.

In these introductory chapters we aim to explain the context and individuals involved, to provide details about the biography and other works of the three named scholars, to offer a discussion of the structure of each text and the literary form of the Latin works, and to give an account of the participants' views on language and translation. The chapter 'The Four Treatises: Significance and Scholarship to Date' explains the reasons for academic interest in the treatises, as well as for their neglect, and gives an account of previous scholarship, including the early-modern period. Since the argument in all works relies heavily on citations from classical and medieval authorities, the chapter 'Authorities Cited in the Texts' offers an overview and observations on the authors' knowledge and use of the earlier tradition; references to the Bible and authorities are also explicated in the texts and commentary notes (see below, 'Note on Editorial Practice'). The chapter 'The Participants' Knowledge of Earlier Translations into Vernaculars' offers a brief summary of biblical translations into vernaculars as mentioned by the participants, and discusses the possible sources of their knowledge. Since precedent is important for all authors, and the knowledge of earlier translations by Ullerston is impressive, while some of his claims are unusual or less easily identifiable, we felt that the reader would benefit from this additional background material. The chapter 'The Views on Translation in Late Middle English Texts' compares opinions expressed in the Latin works to those found in Middle English discussions, including the *General Prologue* to the *Wycliffite Bible*. Since comments on translation most commonly occur during this period in prefaces to translated works, we felt that such an overview could be of benefit in placing the debate in its contemporary context, and in giving a better sense of the uniqueness of the texts edited here. We are very aware that what is offered here is undoubtedly only a first contribution to the research that these texts deserve and make possible, and we hope that the edition will instigate and facilitate new discussions around the numerous aspects of these works that have to remain outside the scope of this volume.

[ES]

II. THE FOUR TREATISES: SIGNIFICANCE
AND SCHOLARSHIP TO DATE

The three Latin texts, which together form the focus of the present volume, relate to the question of the legitimacy of translation of the Bible from the Latin of the Vulgate text to the vernacular. From its earliest stages Christians had recognized that their history was based on translated writings; the story of Acts 2 where 'every man heard them (Peter and the apostles) speak in his own language' dramatizes the dilemma faced by every evangelist in passing on central history and its crucial beliefs in a variety of tongues.[5] The further complication that the religious language of the Jews was Hebrew, a language far beyond the acquaintance of almost all ancient and medieval Christians, was recognized by the ubiquity of Jerome's translations of the Old Testament. This problem of the believers' linguistic variety but credal singularity has many implications. One case, limited in its range but interesting for those concerned with medieval English by the end of the first decade of the fifteenth century, came to be associated closely with the increasing hostility of the English clerical hierarchy to the ideas and followers of John Wyclif. Wyclif's ideas questioned many of the theological and especially ecclesiological views of contemporary accepted orthodoxy and have been seen to anticipate later reformist opinions. How closely the writers of each of the three tracts edited here associated translation with Wyclif will be considered below.[6] But it is clear that all placed some stress on the issue of linguistic legitimacy: for all of them, though in differing ways, the question of linguistic feasibility is of lesser significance than the question of its authorization—the crucial matter is not a linguistic problem but a political one. All three tracts reflect academic modes of procedure, though with varying clarity; two of them (those by Ullerston and by Butler) claim to originate in Oxford, though the third may be the product of a Dominican school where similar modes of discussion were commonplace.[7]

---

[5] For this question see *The Early Text of the New Testament*, ed. C. E. Hill and M. J. Kruger (Oxford 2011); *The New Cambridge History of the Bible*, 2: *From 600 to 1450*, ed. R. Marsden and E. A. Matter (Cambridge 2012); and H. A. G. Houghton, *The Latin New Testament: a Guide to its Early History, Texts and Manuscripts* (Oxford 2016) and bibliography there.

[6] For an account of the situation, concentrating on the academic world of the period, see J. Catto, 'Wyclif and Wyclifism at Oxford, 1356–1430', in *HUO* 2: *Late Medieval Oxford*, ed. J. I. Catto & T. A. R. Evans (Oxford 1992), 175–261; for an introduction to wider issues in Wycliffite or Lollard history see A. Hudson, *The Premature Reformation: Wycliffite Texts and Lollard History* (Oxford 1988).

[7] A useful summary of the standard of education available in late medieval England,

Enquiry into this discussion can begin with the participants. John Leland, the noted sixteenthth-century antiquary, commented in his entry for arguably the most perceptive and intelligent of the three, 'Richardus Vllerodvno nondum tam aperte mihi cognitus quam optarem' ('I am not yet as well acquainted with Richard Ullerston as I should like to be').[8] Leland might have extended his comment to include both William Butler and Thomas Palmer, both of whom appear in his *De uiris illustribus* even more briefly than Ullerston; only for Butler is there any connection made with a debate on biblical language.[9] John Bale, Leland's more assiduous follower, repeated Leland's warning about Ullerston in his *Catalogus*, acknowledging its source in Leland; how much more than Leland he knew about any of them will emerge as uncertain.[10] Both critics provided titles of some works by each of the three, in some cases with an incipit: for Ullerston and Palmer neither title nor incipit suggests that the texts here could be in question. For Butler, however, Leland reports (c. 480) that he has read that Butler wrote a determination against the translation of sacred scripture into the vernacular. The immediate source of this information may have been Bale. In his *Index* (p. 119) Bale records under Butler's name a text on that subject with the incipit *Vtrum sacre scripture canon pro vulgari*; Bale there claims the manuscript he had seen was in the collections of The Queen's College, Oxford.[11] This information is repeated in the *Catalogus* (1. 536), though Bale's location could be a confusion of the lost Queen's manuscript with the surviving book in Merton College (see the description of Oxford, Merton College, MS 68 below). The incipit may well have been correct, but the loss of the opening of Butler's work in the one surviving copy in Merton does not permit its verification.

with particular reference to the Dominican order, can be found in W. J. Courtenay, 'The London 'studia' in the fourteenth century', *Medievalia et Humanistica*, new ser. 13 (1985), 127–41.

  [8] John Leland, *De viris illustribus: On Famous Men*, ed. and trans. J. P. Carley with the assistance of C. Brett (Toronto & Oxford 2010), 692–3, c. 491.

  [9] Butler, 684–5, c. 480; Palmer, 690–91, c. 488.

  [10] John Bale, *Scriptorum illustrium maioris Bryttannie . . . catalogus*, 2 vols (Basel 1557–9), 1. 536 for Butler; 540 for Palmer; and 572 for Ullerston. Only Ullerston appears in Bale's *Summarium* (Wesel 1548), fol. 188r. We are indebted to James Carley for discussion of the bibliographic relation of Leland to Bale, a relationship which is apparently more fluctuating and less assured than earlier criticism has allowed. It is possible that Carley's wider enquiry will clarify this particular case.

  [11] John Bale, *Index Britanniae scriptorum: John Bale's Index of British and Other Writers*, ed. R. L. Poole & M. Bateson (Oxford 1902; repr. with introduction by C. Brett & J. P. Carley (Cambridge 1990)), 119; no copy now survives at Queen's, but see below for the possibility that Bale's information was correct when he wrote.

Although the issue debated by these three tracts remained in question through the sixteenth century and beyond, later bibliographers
do not seem to have pursued the information provided by Leland
and Bale. In particular, Ullerston's work on translation, arguably by
far the most perceptive of the three, seems to have been entirely
unknown to the bibliographers.[12] As attested at present, each of the
three tracts survives only in a single complete, or near complete,
copy; two of these (Butler's in Merton 68, Palmer's in Cambridge,
Trinity College, MS B. 15. 11) were written in England (albeit the
scribe of Palmer's names himself as Cornelius Oesterwik, of English
residence, but not English by birth), but the copy of Ullerston is in
a Bohemian hand, and by 1585 was in the Imperial Library in Vienna
where it remained.[13] The late eighteenth-century cataloguer of that
collection correctly identified the English origin of the text, but the
anonymity of the Vienna manuscript casts its usual obscurity and
lack of interest over the work.[14]

None of the references mentioned so far to any of the three tracts
associates any of them explicitly with Wyclif, or with the legislation to
control and suppress vernacular scriptures in England.[15] Study of the
Wycliffite translation of the Bible was revolutionized by the edition
of the two main versions of its text by Frederic Madden and Josiah
Forshall that appeared in 1850 from the Oxford Clarendon Press in
four volumes.[16] It is amazing that, within their detailed, if somewhat
confusing, introduction to the *WB* texts, the editors show knowledge
of Butler's text and also of Ullerston's work, albeit the latter only
in its anonymous state. Their source of information for Ullerston
was Denis's catalogue of the Vienna manuscripts: given the pressure
that the editors were under in the final couple of years before the
belated publication, it is remarkable that they should have picked up
this detail from the catalogue to a library far away from their usual
enquiries.[17] After the appearance of FM's edition of *WB*, the first

[12] The most useful of modern bibliographical listings covering these three is R. Sharpe, *A Handlist of the Latin Writers of Great Britain and Ireland before 1540* (Turnhout 1997), 757 (Butler), 674 (Palmer), 516–17 (Ullerston).   [13] See below, pp. cxvii–cxviii.

[14] Denis, 1. 842–7. For a summary of the complicated story of the transmission of Bohemian manuscripts to the Imperial Library, see A. Hudson, 'The survival of Wyclif's works in England and Bohemia', in her *Studies in the Transmission of Wyclif's Writings* (Aldershot 2008), no. xvi, 29–41.

[15] For the divided critical reaction to this translation see most recently the essays in *ESWB* and, from a perspective that many will feel unnecessarily sectarian, H. A. Kelly, *The Middle English Bible: a Reassessment* (Philadelphia, PA, 2016).

[16] Details of the production of the edition are in A. Hudson, 'Editing the Wycliffite Bible', in *ESWB*, 453–62, and 'The making of a monumental edition', in *Rosarium amicitiae: Essays in Honor of Christina von Nolcken*, ed. S. Butler, forthcoming.

[17] See FM 1. xxxiii, footnote t. In addition to the records of his official activities, kept

serious enquiry into the background to the *WB* translation came seventy years later in *The Lollard Bible and Other Medieval Biblical Versions* by Margaret Deanesly (Cambridge 1920, reprinted with a few modifications 1966).[18] In Appendix II, 'Documents', Deanesly printed Butler's and Palmer's treatises from the two single known manuscripts; she there also claimed that the English *First seiþ Bois* derived from parts of the Latin text found in ÖNB MS 4133. Deanesly had consulted Denis's extracts and summaries from his catalogue, but did not extend his material with further extracts of her own. Disliking as usual the anonymity of the Vienna text, she claimed through a series of complicated and unconvincing arguments that its writer was John Purvey; Purvey had previously been asserted as closely involved with the *WB* work, and indeed with almost any text of Wycliffite sympathies, English or Latin.[19] Purvey, whose academic qualifications appear, judging from his absence from Oxford or Cambridge university records, to have been minimal, is consequently a highly improbable originator of the sophisticated and scholarly text here. Later critics, however, for the most part accepted Deanesly's attribution even if they expressed doubts. Deanesly also argued (pp. 299–303) that Peter Payne was the English Wycliffite who took the text to Bohemia. Payne's education, and his commitment to Wycliffite causes, cannot be doubted. He also certainly fled from hostile enquiries in England to Bohemia, where he became an important leader in Hussite activity; but this journey was some fifteen years later than the 1401 date of the debate here. It is possible that he could have acted upon an earlier concern and been responsible for transmitting Ullerston's text, but direct evidence for this is lacking.[20] The reliability of Deanesly's transcription of both Butler's and Palmer's

---

in the British Library, Madden also left a very detailed diary account of his daily concerns that is now Bodl. MSS Eng. hist. c. 140–182. Only when all these sources are available in searchable editions will it be feasible to give a firm statement about the trail of evidence which led him and Forshall to Denis's work.

[18] Deanesly's 1966 note, pp. vii–viii, and the list of errata, xxi–xxiii, explains the process, but does not allow for certainty of detail. We have used throughout this 1966 edition. For further discussion, see R. Hanna, 'The transmission of Richard Rolle's Latin works', *The Library*, 7th ser. 14 (2014), 313–33, and 'Richard Rolle's *Incendium amoris*'.

[19] The legend of Purvey is surveyed in A. Hudson, 'John Purvey: a reconsideration of the evidence for his life and writings' in *Lollards and their Books* (London 1985), 85–110. Since the writing of that paper Maureen Jurkowski's discovery of evidence for Purvey's involvement in the Oldcastle Revolt of 1415, and the confiscation of nineteen books from his possession, in 'New light on John Purvey', *EHR* 110 (1995), 1180–90, has somewhat changed our view of Purvey's education and possible involvement in the organization of work on *WB*.

[20] The most adequate recent biography of Payne (adequate, interestingly, because of its author's linguistic coverage) is by F. Smahel in *ODNB* (2004).

texts is sometimes questionable: she was working at a date prior to the availability of cheap photography, and from indications in her footnotes she was not always helped in her access to the relevant manuscripts.[21]

The situation concerning the three Latin tracts edited here changed, however, with the publication in 1975 of the finding of the fragment that is now Cambridge, Gonville and Caius College, MS 803/807, fragment 36.[22] This is a binding fragment, badly damaged on its verso, but certainly identifiable on its recto with the end of the Vienna tract (from lines 2043–2117). Most importantly, the verso contains a colophon provided by the scribe: *Explicit tractatus Magistri Ricardi Vllerston d[octoris in theologia] de tran[slacione] sacre scripture in vulgare editus ab eodem Oxon' a[nno] domini 1401.*[23] The form of this colophon is very close to that found concluding a better attested work by Ullerston, and, as will be discussed below, there seems no reason to question its reliability. Quite apart from its statement of authorship, the colophon locates and dates a debate, and in so doing associates it closely with the text by Butler (see below). As a result of the clarification afforded by the G&C fragment, historians and literary critics in publications from 1975 onwards have shown renewed interest in the full contents of the Vienna text.[24]

Circulation of any of these three determinations would not from present knowledge seem to have produced many copies. Only a single manuscript of each survives, and in the case of Butler's even that is now acephalous, though, as pointed out above, confusions in Bale's material may suggest the existence of a second copy in Oxford. The Caius fragment testifies more usefully to a second copy, one that may be assumed to have been originally complete, of Ullerston's work; this was an English copy. The Bohemian transcript of Ullerston's determination raises many questions: it appears as the final item in a manuscript, with four longer items preceding it; though written by

---

[21] See Deanesly, 399–438.

[22] Documented in A. Hudson, 'The debate on Bible translation: Oxford 1401', first published in *EHR* 90 (1975), 1–18, and reprinted in *Lollards and their Books* (London 1985), 67–84.

[23] Doubt about the identity of the final digit was acknowledged in the 1975 paper (*LB*, 75); a new ultra-violet image printed here does not entirely resolve the question—the dilemma is that no other numeral seems more likely. Though not absolutely clear, the final digit seems to be '1' rather than '7' which would have been similar in this script to an upside down 'v'. For a suggestion that the final digit is '7' see Kelly, *The Middle English Bible*, 53–4.

[24] For instance see R. Copeland, *Pedagogy, Intellectuals and Dissent in the Later Middle Ages: Lollardy and Ideas of Learning* (Cambridge 2001), esp. 115–20.

a new scribe and codicologically independent, it must have belonged to the volume in the fifteenth century when the volume was assembled in its present binding, and may have been part of the original collection of Wycliffite and Hussite materials assembled by an early owner, Paul of Slawikowicz.[25] Considerable care was taken in the correction of its text, and in the revision (not always either accurate or helpful) of its structure; so detailed are some of the corrections that they must have been made against a second copy (probably also English, like the main scribe's exemplar); proper names and transliterations of English words are careful.

The migration of the manuscript to Vienna occurred at the persuasion of Kasper von Nydbruck in 1557: his collection of Bohemian manuscripts that might influence the religious complexion of the imperial court was assembled at that time from Bohemian sources. What is now Vienna, Österreichische Nationalbibliothek, MS 4133 was one of those borrowed and, following von Nydbruck's unexpected early death with no will provided, the collection was forfeited permanently to the emperor.[26] In the catalogue of the library of the College of the Bohemian Nation in Prague, dated 1461, appears an entry 'L26 Item tractatus Magistri Richardi de translacione sacre scripture in wlgare ydiomate'.[27] It seems a reasonable conjecture that the surname of the Master Richard was Ullerston. Less persuasive is the possibility that ÖNB MS 4133 had previously been L26 itself in that same catalogue: Ullerston's text is the last item in the extant manuscript, and would on its own seem unlikely to attract a cataloguer's attention; the other items, longer as well as earlier in the whole, would seem to demand prior attention. Crucially, from ÖNB MS 4133, how would a Christian name be deduced, but no surname in either catalogue or manuscript? Even if we accept the identity of the cataloguer's text, we should almost certainly deduce that L26

[25] For details of the Slawikowicz association see the description of the manuscript below. Bohemian transcriptions of Wycliffite texts are by no means uncommon: see the recurrent information in Thomson, *Wyclif*; A. Hudson's additions and extensions in *STWW*, Appendix ii; and A. Hudson, 'From Oxford to Bohemia: reflections on the transmission of Wycliffite texts', *Studia Mediaevalia Bohemica* 2 (2010), 25–37.

[26] Recently this migration has been surveyed by I. von Morzé, 'Illuminierte Wyclif-Handschriften der ÖNB aus dem Nachlass des Kaspar von Niedbruck', in *Art in an Unsettled Time: Bohemian Book Illumination before Gutenberg*, ed. M. Studničková & M. Theisen (Prague 2018), 170–81.

[27] See the recent *Catalogi librorum vetustissimi universitatis Pragensis*, ed. Z. Silagiová, CCCM 271 (2015), 98; the text is not identified by the editors. The recent survey by Šmahel of Hus's interests in language, spelling, indexing and even biblical translation (see *A Companion to Jan Hus* (Leiden 2015), 370–409) should encourage further investigation of possible contacts between Ullerston's determination and similar later reformist works in Oxford and in Prague.

was a second, separate copy. This, of course, raises the possibility that more copies may still appear in old Bohemian collections: as an unattributed text of (by late medieval standards) modest length, possibly without a title (as in ÖNB MS 4133) and with distinctive English authorities and claims, it would be easy for Ullerston's text to remain unidentified by a central European cataloguer, even if the English-speaking equivalent should with current electronic resources have a better chance of recognizing the tract.[28]

So far no mention has been made of the single vernacular text included in the present volume. The relation of this Middle English text is to Ullerston's determination only—there seems no connection beyond the most general subject-matter with Butler's or with Palmer's. But there are immediately striking similarities of argument, authorities cited and historical details recalled between Ullerston and *First seiþ Bois*. The nature of the connection and the position of the English tract in the debate will be discussed below.

Two of the Latin treatises here (Ullerston and Butler) are dated by their scribes or a subsequent medieval annotator as written in 1401, following discussion of the issues in the Oxford schools. No such plain dating is available for Palmer (or for the English text). But only Palmer mentions the group, *Lollardi* (see lines 156.105 and 164.245) who came to be most closely associated in England with late medieval demands for the free availability of scripture in English. Interestingly, however, Palmer uses the term only twice, both in fairly neutral contexts and neither apparently requiring comment or interpretation. Given this neutrality, and in the light of further evidence discussed below (pp. xlii–xlv), it seems probable that Palmer's tract also dates from the first few years of the fifteenth century.[29] The dating that seems most probable thus falls before the publication of Arundel's *Constitutiones*, issued at the Council of Oxford in 1407 and confirmed in 1409.[30] No named, or descriptively identifiable, group is specifically mentioned as favouring translation; no legislation against the rendering of scripture in the vernacular is specified. This should be stressed, especially for Butler and Palmer: citation of papal or archiepiscopal restriction of such translation would surely be strong evidence that anyone supporting Arundel's prohibition would mention. William Lyndwood's commentary on Arundel's legislation, written between

---

[28] We can report, however, that a search with the online resource In Principio produced no results.

[29] C. Linde in her paper 'Arguing with Lollards: Thomas Palmer, O.P. and *De translatione scripture sacre in linguam barbaricam*', *Viator* 46 (2015), 235–54, urged an earlier date for Palmer's text; see discussion of this below, pp. xlii–xlv.

[30] The Constitutions are printed by Wilkins, 3. 315–19.

1422 and 1430, within twenty years of the Constitutions' issue, makes clear the extreme effects intended—*de libro sive libello, ut scilicet textum sacrae scripturae in tali libro vel libello applicet*—not only the whole Bible or books from it required the approval specified, but even brief scriptural citations.[31]

Arundel's Constitutions as a whole were directed primarily towards the episcopal authorities of the southern province, and especially to those with responsibilities in the academic world of the universities, notably Oxford.[32] Any translation from the time of Wyclif onwards required the scrutiny of properly qualified and placed ecclesiastics to guarantee its orthodoxy. The requirement of such a guarantee was obligatory for its intended owner. But no guidance was apparently given, at least in writing, of how these requirements were to be satisfied. Presumably the heads of Oxford colleges or halls, charged with the scrutiny of each student in their care every month could make enquiries—but, even in the defined context of an Oxford college or hall, how was the acceptability or otherwise of any text to be established? The provision of a list of acceptable and unacceptable readings, namely the list of quotations from Wyclif's Latin writings to be condemned that was made a few years later, leading to the 1411 list of 267 quotations, suggests such a 'recognition kit' must have been considered.[33] In its absence all vernacular versions of scripture come to be suspicious and, save in the case of the politically untouchable, by the orthodox to be avoided. Such an outcome was, of course, entirely acceptable to Arundel.[34] And the more general terms of the prohibition may explain why in trials of Lollard suspects in the late fifteenth and early sixteenth centuries, ownership of vernacular scriptures is often an incriminating factor, but very rarely the only factor, in the case against a suspect. Overall, however, the vagueness of the Constitutions' terms was probably a stronger deterrent than more clear-cut examples would have afforded. Arundel's legislation remained in force

[31] William Lyndwood, *Provinciale* (Oxford 1679; repr. Farnborough 1968), 286. See C. R. Cheney, *Medieval Texts and Studies* (Oxford 1973), esp. 158–84; also B. E. Ferme, *Canon Law in Late Medieval England* (Rome 1996), esp. 43–54.

[32] For the target of Arundel's Constitutions see N. Watson, 'Censorship and cultural change in late-medieval England: vernacular theology, the Oxford translation debate, and Arundel's *Constitutions* of 1409', *Speculum* 70 (1995), 822–64; responses to this paper have been many and various in their outlook, but the book *After Arundel: Religious Writing in Fifteenth-Century England*, ed. V. Gillespie & K. Ghosh (Turnhout 2011), exhibits a selection.

[33] See A. Hudson, 'Notes of an early fifteenth-century research assistant, and the emergence of the 267 Articles against Wyclif', *EHR* 118 (2003), 685–97, reprinted *STWW*, § XIII.

[34] For the (non-)observance of the restrictions, see most recently M. Jurkowski, 'The selective censorship of the Wycliffite Bible', *ESWB*, 371–88.

until 1529,[35] by which time other vernacular versions were becoming available—these new translations could, through their printed form, gain a much wider circulation, but also, because the techniques of print allow for multiple identical copies, new legislation was both feasible and necessary.[36]

Many of the issues and questions so far outlined will be discussed in more detail and with further references in the sections that follow, but this outline may indicate the context in which the texts edited here should be placed. The importance of the tracts, and especially of Ullerston's, can hardly be overemphasized. Discussions of language, its structure, its relation to senses, physical and mental, the ways in which it conveys (or obstructs) meaning, would seem to be almost inevitable in the medieval period in western Europe when any educated person would certainly have been aware of the coexistence of at least two, often three and occasionally more languages. Yet, turning to the position in England, only very rarely is comment made on the juxtaposition of Latin with English and French. Our access to the discussion of linguistic diversity is doubtless limited: Chaucer did not need to gloss the Man of Law's description of Custaunce's speech as 'a maner Latyn corrupt', but expected his audience to find the expression individualizing.[37] The importance of semantics to any biblical exegete is overwhelmingly apparent—but only a few commentators such as Grosseteste turn regularly from the ubiquitous Latin to the parallel Greek, let alone Hebrew, wording. Ullerston's interest in these matters extends beyond the individual words to the structure of language, and how meaning can be conveyed by different methods in different tongues—questions such as what are the implications, if any, of the claim that English is closer to Greek than is Latin because Greek like English has a definite article, but Latin none (58.1056–7). Ullerston certainly had read some Grosseteste texts, along with others on language by Roger Bacon; intriguing but unclear is whether he also knew the text we call the *General Prologue* to the *Wycliffite Bible*: that text reveals a comparable concern with some problems of linguistic translation.[38] Ullerston has been understood as entirely orthodox in his theological opinions,

---

[35] See *PR*, p. 489 and n. 267.

[36] For various views of the differing challenges of manuscript and print, see the papers in *The Uses of Script and Print, 1300–1700*, ed. J. Crick & A. Walsham (Cambridge 2004), several of which urge that the importance of the introduction of print in the success of sixteenth-century reformed religion has been exaggerated.

[37] The Man of Law's Tale, *Riverside Chaucer*, 94, l. 519.

[38] See further discussion in the section below, 'The Views on Translation in Late Middle English Texts'. For the date and outlook of the *General Prologue* see *ESWB*, 147–9, 233–6.

the *General Prologue* is more radical. But, as more work is done on the penumbra of short texts associated with *WB*, and on the myriad cases where the two versions of the *WB* differ in their rendering, we should wonder whether such concentration should, in place of such a simple dichotomy, rather be turned to the more complicated and conflicting concepts of meaning and linguistic structure of which Ullerston shows himself so aware.[39]

The alert reader will have noted the frequency in this section that discussion of the involvement of The Queen's College, Oxford has been mentioned. Contacts between Wyclif and Queen's are of many kinds, from records of two improvements to Wyclif's accommodation in the college,[40] to the loan of money against a copy of Wyclif's *De mandatis*.[41] Henry Bryt, fellow of Queen's 1403/4, was one of three owners of Cambridge, Gonville and Caius College, MS 337/565, probably the second most important surviving English manuscript of Wyclif's Latin works (in bulk and variety of content Cambridge, Trinity College, MS B. 16. 2 must take first place, but its texts are notoriously unreliable in their readings).[42] But interest in radical ideas, and especially in the justification of Bible translation existed at Queen's before Ullerston's provable involvement in 1401. As will be explained in detail below, the translator John Trevisa's association with the college seems to have begun in 1370; more importantly, he was one of the southerners involved in the troubles over the election of a provost. When those troubles were concluded, it emerged that a considerable collection of books had been removed and were to be restored: these books were specified, and it is clear that many of them would have been of value to anyone involved actively in translation or interested in the subject.[43] Trevisa obviously fits into that description, with his own translations and especially the *Dialogue between a Lord and a Clerk* dedicated to Lord Thomas of Berkeley *c.* 1378.[44]

[39] See below, 'The Participants' Views on Language and Translation'.

[40] QCA, Long Rolls, 2.P.12, 2.P.23 and 2.P.27, dating from October 1363 to 1380.

[41] See N. R. Ker, 'Wyclif manuscripts in Oxford in the fifteenth century', *Bodleian Library Record* 4 (1953), 292–3.

[42] For details see A. Hudson, 'Wyclif's Latin sermons: questions of form, date and audience', in *STWW*, § VI.

[43] Details of Trevisa's life can be found in *BRUO* 1903–1904, and in more detail in D. C. Fowler, *The Life and Times of John Trevisa, Medieval Scholar* (Seattle, WA, 1995). The list, with important information about the books, is now available in Thomson, *University and College Libraries of Oxford*, 1236–40 (UO82); several volumes (e.g. Higden and Lyra) anticipate the use made of them in the texts edited here; the presence of incipits confirms the validity of the claims about the removal and restoration of the books.

[44] Trevisa's works and their survival in manuscripts are conveniently listed in D. C.

The recent catalogue of the medieval manuscripts at Queen's College does not apparently confirm the possibility of interest at the college in translation either in general terms or in particular Wycliffite regard. There are two copies of *WB*, MS 369 of the New Testament in EV and MS 388 of the entire translation in LV; neither is likely to have been in Queen's before the modern period.[45] But there is yet another source of information that tells a rather more interesting story: John Bale records in his *Index* a considerable number of books which he, or his mentor John Leland, had seen in numerous specified libraries, including Queen's College, Oxford.[46] It does not take long to go through the *Index* to list the Queen's books: our searching produced thirty-seven entries. Not all are equally interesting, but for the present enquiry there is a striking number of authors cited by Ullerston or known from the arguments familiar in Wyclif. All the specified works by all these authors are provided with incipits, showing that the accuracy of Bale's claims to have seen them can be checked. In several cases it may be reasonable to see a similarity with the 'anthology' of relevant material still extant in Oxford, Merton College, MS 68 (see the description below)—works, many of them quite short, arguing on variable sides the 'hot topics' of the day.

Had Ullerston worked at his determination whilst resident, even if only temporarily, in Queen's, he could well have argued that his mixed response to the basic issue of the legitimacy of translation fairly reflected the views of men holding opinions which ranged from firm Wycliffism (as William Taylor or Peter Payne, both principals of St Edmund Hall, which was in many ways dependent upon Queen's) to immovable orthodoxy (as William Woodford).[47] Pushed to position himself more precisely, would Ullerston have aligned himself with Trevisa or with Peter Pateshall (an Augustinian friar and also possible author of two political poems that Bale claimed to have seen in the library at Queen's)?[48] Or does the evidence of the present defence of translation point to an intellectual independence that would find Arundel's rigidity a narrower and more lamentable

---

Fowler, *John Trevisa* (Aldershot 1993); the *Dialogue* is further discussed below in the section 'The Views on Translation in Late Middle English Texts'.

[45] See P. Kidd, *A Descriptive Catalogue of the Medieval Manuscripts of The Queen's College, Oxford* (Oxford 2016), and *MWBO*, 269–74.

[46] The interest of Bale's information concerning Queen's books is outlined by Thomson, *University and College Libraries of Oxford*, 1235, together with comments on other evidence pointing in the same direction, 1233–41.

[47] See A. B. Emden, *An Oxford Hall in Medieval Times* (Oxford 1927), esp. 125–61.

[48] See also A. Hudson, 'Peter Pateshull: one-time friar and poet?', in *Interstices: Studies in Middle English and Anglo-Latin Texts in Honour of A. G. Rigg*, ed. R. F. Green & L. R. Mooney (Toronto 2004), 167–83.

response? Though it is tempting to believe that having worked his way through to a view of language and translation that significantly anticipates modern understanding of these topics, he was prepared to allow for translation of scripture without restriction, a closer analysis suggests a more realistic conclusion. Translation, Ullerston argues, should be by learned bishops—but these he does not believe to exist in his day (44.88); inspection by the clergy is imperative and their judgement is unassailable (112.2102–6); whether translated material should be allowed to circulate, and to whom, is for the church to determine (112.2107–10). Butler and Palmer would understand the implications of these last points—translation is a power tool, just as is the availability of texts. Ullerston is certainly closer to modern perceptions, but not without many reservations. He is not that far from the Arundel of the Constitutions. Arundel might have drawn the limits more narrowly, and he certainly took more care to retain the most crucial strings to himself, but in the last resort even Ullerston, perhaps more realistic and certainly with a more open mind, approves the last restriction. As other parts of his career must admit, obedience to the archbishop's Constitutions seems to have taken precedence: '. . . I do not intend to argue anything contrary to our holy mother the catholic and Roman Church, and if the Church should instruct me otherwise, or if my understanding is deficient in any article of faith or morals I will certainly and instantly obey' (26.458–62).

[AH]

III. THE PARTICIPANTS

Since many observations made so far rely on what is known about the authors of the three Latin treatises, it is fitting to offer a more detailed account of their biographies. Richard Ullerston is first noticed in the historical record at his ordination to the priesthood in 1384. At that time he must have been reading arts at Oxford, since he was Master of Arts and a newly instituted fellow of Queen's in the accounts of that college for 1391–2. His name derives from Ulverston in Furness, now in Cumbria though then in Lancashire, and he described himself as *ducatus vestri Lancastrie natus homo*, 'a native of your duchy of Lancaster', in the dedicatory letter to Henry Prince of Wales which prefaces his *De officio militari*.[49] Though not

---

[49] The best account of Ullerston is that of Margaret Harvey, 'English Views on the Reforms to be Undertaken in the General Council, 1400–18', DPhil thesis (University of Oxford 1963), 1–58; see also Emden, *BRUO* 1928–9. On his ordination see Register of Bishop Robert de Stretton (Coventry and Lichfield), abstracted by R. A. Wilson,

subject to the bishop of Carlisle, he may well have benefited as a near neighbour from the preference for natives of the diocese laid down in the college statutes, and is likely to have lived with compatriots at Oxford, or even as one of the poor boys whom the college was bound to put through the arts course. In accordance with the statutes, he was already Master of Arts in 1391, and a scholar of theology; there is no specific evidence of the date of his inception as a doctor, but it must have occurred before the doctoral determination from which his *Defensorium dotationis ecclesiae* was drawn, and therefore in or before 1401. He was one of the doctors before whom an unnamed bachelor of theology made his *replicatio*, probably in the academic year 1402–1403.[50]

Ullerston's name recurs in the accounts as a fellow of Queen's consistently between 1391 and 1403. He had joined one of the liveliest secular colleges in the turbulent Oxford of the last quarter of the fourteenth century. Among the sojourners living from time to time in the college were Robert Alington, a notable logician who was chancellor of the university in 1393–5, and John Trevisa, the translator of Higden's *Polychronicon* and other popular Latin texts; both of them had either lived in college with or had been partisans of John Wyclif and Nicholas Hereford, the controversial masters whose ideas had been condemned at the Blackfriars Council of 1382.[51] By the 1390s Alington, like Hereford and other radical masters of 1382, had dissociated himself from the dangerous opinions of his earlier days, and had argued in the schools in favour of the veneration of images; but he had maintained his critical view of the friars, and as chancellor must have had a hand in the petition to remove the university from the jurisdiction of William Courtenay, the archbishop of Canterbury whose firm action had led to the condemnation of Wyclif and Hereford.[52] Another occasional visitor may have been Philip Repingdon, canon and from 1394 abbot of St Mary in the Meadows at Leicester, who had probably resided at Queen's in the academic year 1386–7; he too had been associated with Alington and Hereford before the

William Salt Archaeological Soc. new ser. 8 (1905), 393. His fellowship is first recorded in QCA, Long Rolls (1391–2). His *De officio militari* is in Cambridge, Trinity College, MS B. 15. 23, fols. 16v–22r.

[50] Oxford, Corpus Christi College, MS 280, fol. 141v; for the date of the bachelor's *lectio biblica* see fol. 138r.

[51] For the known writings of the scholars mentioned see Sharpe under their names; their known careers are outlined in *BRUO*; only editions and critical studies particularly relevant to the present debate are here given in full. For Trevisa see Fowler, *Life and Times*, and for his translation of Higden see R. Waldron, *John Trevisa's Translation of the Polychronicon of Ranulph Higden Book VI*, Middle English Texts 35 (Heidelberg 2004).

[52] Jeremy Catto, 'Wyclif and Wycliffism at Oxford', 232.

Blackfriars Council, but had submitted and distanced himself from the radical masters, perhaps in step with John of Gaunt, the active patron of his house. It was presumably Gaunt himself, with or without the advice of Repingdon, who chose the college as the residence of his son Henry Beaufort from 1390 onwards, while he completed the arts course and embarked on the study of theology, though whether he resided continuously is not clear. Beaufort would briefly be chancellor in 1397–8 and would renew his college association as bishop of Lincoln in the academic year 1402–1403.[53] During these years the college continued to recruit notable logicians such as John Scharpe, elected in the same year as Ullerston, and Roger Whelpdale, who would successively be provost (1403–1404 and 1404–19).[54]

Ullerston himself did not add to the contributions to logic made by Alington, Scharpe and Whelpdale. In 1401, however, after his inception as doctor of theology, he determined as a regent master on two controversial topics. One of them in literary redaction is the subject of the present edition; the other examined the justification of church endowments and was circulated as his *Defensorium dotationis ecclesiae*. The latter topic was already a subject of public controversy; the former, whether an English version of the Bible could be justified, had on the evidence of Ullerston's introductory words been disputed during the past academic year, presumably 1400–1401. The resulting determinations in literary form were given similar colophons, and were both dated to 1401, though the *Defensorium* was based on Hilary Term lectures, whereas the determination which the tract on biblical translation embodies was more likely to have taken place towards the end of the academic year, since it refers to doctors who have devoted *totum tempus lecture* to the topic (2.8).[55] Were they intended as elements of a unitary programme on Ullerston's part? Superficially, their import is contradictory: the determination on translation supported the Wycliffite masters' insistence on having the scriptures in English, while the *Defensorium* defended the endowment of the church in accord with their Wycliffite opponents. A careful reading of both texts, however, brings out a less straightforward stance on each question. As pointed out earlier, Ullerston, as his final summary makes clear (112.2102–6), wanted the hierarchy to oversee the translation of the scriptures, and believed that a careful vernacular version would fortify orthodox teaching against the impact of heretical tracts. Nor did he unequivocally endorse the endowment of the church, but sought a

---

[53] QCA, Long Rolls 1386–7 (Repingdon); *BRUO* 139–42; G. L. Harriss, *Cardinal Beaufort* (Oxford 1988), 2, 12.

[54] *BRUO* 1680 and 2031–2.

[55] BL MS Lansdowne 409, fol. 39r.

middle way between the views of Uhtred of Boldon and of Wyclif, both of whom he cited with respect, to relate endowments to the evangelical task of the clergy. He had already argued, he reminded his audience, that the clergy were obliged to manual labour.[56] In both determinations Ullerston seems to have promoted the ideal of a reformed and disciplined clergy with the resources to preach the orthodox faith in a form accessible to the laity. His stance was compatible with the orthodox but critical views of his older colleague Robert Alington, as put forward in his defence of the cult of images, and perhaps represented the attitude of a fellowship which remembered the involvement of more than one of its members in the project to translate the scriptures.

Ullerston continued in fellowship until 1403, and then resided in college as a sojourner, perhaps until 1416, though not continuously; gaps in the record of his residence may correspond to service as the principal of an Oxford hall, such as Black Hall in School Street which was customarily associated with Queen's. In these years the college seems to have enjoyed the favour of the house of Lancaster: as mentioned already, Henry Beaufort spent some time there, and Richard Courtenay, by 1402 evidently already close to Henry of Monmouth, the future Henry V, was a sojourner in 1402–1403 as well as during his first period of office as chancellor of the university.[57] Roger Coryngham, who had been a fellow from 1379 to 1399, became Henry IV's confessor in 1406, and helped to smooth relations between the university and government in the difficult years thereafter. Robert Hallum, a well known Oxford canonist who became chancellor of Oxford in succession to Repingdon in 1403, was entertained at Queen's, and was the patron of Dr John Luke, another sojourner, whom he took to the Council of Pisa in 1409. Ullerston too was close to Coryngham, Hallum and Courtenay; though most of Hallum's associates were canonists, Luke and Ullerston, as theologians, were the exception. Ullerston's first benefice, the vicarage of Silkstone in Yorkshire, to which he was collated in 1402, may have been the result of these associations, and though his attempt to secure a prebend at York was due to his own efforts, his indult of 1404, which permitted him to avoid residence while he either studied at a university, or was employed

---

[56] ibid. fols. 48r, 55v, 39v.

[57] For the involvement of Queen's men in the events leading up to the Council of Pisa and on to the Council of Constance, see especially the three books by M. Harvey, *Solutions to the Schism: a Study of Some English Attitudes 1378–1409* (St Ottilien 1983); *England, Rome and the Papacy 1417–1464: the Study of a Relationship* (Manchester 1993); and *The English in Rome 1362–1420: Portrait of an Expatriate Community* (Cambridge 1999).

by a prelate or in the Roman curia, hints at hopes of promotion out of Oxford.[58] In the event he remained in the university, acting as Courtenay's commissary in 1407, but using his pen in the service of his patrons. He had already presented his *Defensorium* to Thomas Arundel, to whom it must have provided welcome ammunition in the defence of church endowments; and shortly afterwards, perhaps during Courtenay's residence at Queen's in 1402–1403, he had, as he put it, yielded to his young friend's repeated requests to supply Henry of Monmouth with advice on his conduct as a military commander. In *De officio militari*, while commending the utmost *strenuositas* in the field, he advocated the necessity of military discipline in the exercise of justice, citing the example of Judas Maccabeus and the stern precepts of Deuteronomy within a framework of reference to Aristotle and Augustine.[59] These authorities had already been cited in the different context of his tract on translation, but understandably, given the variety of topics, there is little further in common between the two works.

For the next few years Ullerston seems to have been occupied in university business; he acted as commissary for Courtenay, now chancellor, in October 1407. At the same time he was emerging as a spokesman for the English church as Arundel finally resolved to confront the Roman pope, Gregory XII, in a determined effort to end the schism. It was evidently at Hallum's instance that he composed a set of *Petitiones pro ecclesiae militantis reformatione* on the reform of abuses in the English church, written in 1408 for discussion at the Council of Pisa, and presented to Henry IV at the instance of Roger Coryngham.[60] The guiding principle of Ullerston's petitions was the authority of bishops in their dioceses, which had been diminished by the exercise of the pope's plenary power in favour of individuals, by exemption, appropriation or dispensation. He took up the theme of clerical abuses touched on in his determination on the English Bible, the unrestrained pride of the clergy, 'their envy, their laziness, their greed, their simony and other abominations', to which an empowered and reforming episcopate could provide a remedy. These aspirations clearly had the approval of Henry IV and presumably of Arundel,

---

[58] *BRUO* 1929; see Harvey, 'English views', 3–4, citing his correspondence with William Swan at the Curia, now Bodl. MS Arch. Seld. B.23, fol. 3v.

[59] Cambridge, Trinity College, MS B. 15. 23, fols. 16v–22r. Henry of Monmouth as king would exemplify in the field the firm discipline of Moses in Deuteronomy.

[60] These details appear in the accompanying introductory letter in Oxford, Magdalen College, MS lat. 89, fol. 31r–v, which is not printed with the substance of the text in H. von der Hardt, *Magnum oecumenicum Constantiense concilium*, 6 vols (Frankfurt 1697–1700), I. 1126–70.

the patron of Hallum, and if the adoption of this programme by the English delegates at Pisa bore no immediate fruit, the items of it were largely incorporated in the concordat negotiated by Martin V with the government of Henry V in 1418, and generally, if not fully, observed in the practice of the fifteenth-century *ecclesia anglicana*. This marked the high point of Ullerston's engagement with the government of the church. He does not seem to have attended the Council of Pisa with Hallum and John Luke.[61] His remaining years at Oxford were devoted to expounding texts recited in public worship: one of them, an exposition of the Creed, is no longer extant, but according to Bale, who saw a commentary on it by John Stanbury OC, it was written in 1410.[62] He seems to have lectured on the Psalter, expounding the commentary of Peter of Herentals, and to have followed it up with a commentary on the ferial canticles, which he delivered *ex cathedra* in 1415; the practice of lecturing *secundum alium* was common enough in late medieval universities.[63] A copy seen by Bale contained a dedicatory letter to another member of Hallum's circle, Henry Chichele, then archbishop of Canterbury. As Kraebel has pointed out, Ullerston evidently revised his text after 1415. A year later he was collated to the prebend of Axford and a canonry at Salisbury, doubtless at Hallum's behest, and thereafter evidently resided in Salisbury until his death in 1423. Only one literary work survives from that period of Ullerston's life, a sermon on the life of St Osmund preached in the chapter house on 4 May 1416, as a contribution to a canonization cause vigorously promoted by the Salisbury chapter; what appears to be his autograph text, with corrections, is bound into one of the chapter Act Books.[64] At Salisbury, as at Oxford, he put his pen to work at the behest of colleagues and patrons.

We have much less certain information about Ullerston's critic, William Butler. That he was a Franciscan friar and a regent master of Oxford in 1401 is asserted in the colophon to his determination; its text, which addresses the masters of the university and makes a pun on his name, is clearly his *principium* on inception as a doctor of theology; and his apparent reference to Ullerston's determination indicates with reasonable certainty that he was responding to an estab-

---

[61] The sermon supposedly preached by him there (*BRUO* 1929) was probably preached by Mr Richard Derham; see Harvey, 'English views', 56.

[62] Bale, *Catalogus*, I. 611–12.

[63] See A. B. Kraebel, 'The manuscript tradition of Richard Ullerston's *Expositio canticorum scripturae*', *Medieval Journal* 3 (2013), 49–82, esp. 58–60.

[64] A. R. Malden (ed.), *The Canonization of St Osmund*, Wiltshire Rec. Soc. (1901), 236–42. See Harvey, 'English views', 295–6.

lished master's contribution to an active debate on translation of the scriptures (cf. 84.1594–5). He is therefore likely to have been slightly junior to Ullerston, though if he followed the friars' usual progress to the doctorate, he was probably about forty when he incepted. Nothing is known of his origin or activities before 1401, apart from an apparent reference to his lectures on the Sentences in Bale's attribution to him of a tract on indulgences, beginning *articulus pro finali cessacione lecture sententiarum*.[65] Almost all the information available on his later career is derived from the letters of his embittered opponent, John de la Zouche OFM, to the English proctor in the Roman curia, William Swan.[66] As a doctor of theology he was on the path to high office in the English Franciscan province, but at a time of unprecedented disturbance. In 1402, in a wave of popular disaffection with the Lancastrian regime, Franciscans in Leicester and elsewhere openly preached the cause of the deceased Richard II and suffered the penalty for treason accordingly. Their minister provincial since about 1400, John de la Zouche, was described as a nobleman and was presumably related to William Lord Zouche, a supporter of the House of Lancaster.[67] He did his best to control his recalcitrant confrères; but according to the well informed continuator of the *Eulogium Historiarum*, his imperious manner of ruling the province alienated them, and his attempt to enforce the strict observance of the rule drove the powerful London convent and several others into outright defiance of his authority. From May 1405, if not before, his hold on the province was precarious, and dependent on the support of the minister general, Antonio de Pereto, which was withdrawn in the summer of 1407.[68] By then William Butler had emerged as a leader of the opposition to Zouche, who later alleged that on 18 December 1406 Butler had asked to leave the Order and become a monk at Abingdon Abbey.[69] This tendentious but circumstantial

[65] K. W. Humphreys, *The Friars' Libraries*, CBMLC 1 (1990), 296, from Bale's notebook, Bodl. MS Selden supra 64, fol. 215r.

[66] On the relations between Zouche and Butler see D. W. Whitfield, 'Conflicts of personality and principle: the political and religious crisis in the English Franciscan Province, 1400–1409', *Franciscan Studies* 17 (1957), 321–62. The entry on Butler in Leland, 684, no. 480, is based on a lost version of the *Catalogus illustrium Franciscanorum* and may be reliable (see above, p. xxi).

[67] *The St Albans Chronicle: the Chronica Maiora of Thomas Walsingham*, ed. J. Taylor, W. R. Childs & L. Watkiss (Oxford 2003–11), 570; Whitfield, 'Conflicts of personality', 322 n. 1.

[68] *Eulogium Historiarum*, ed. F. S. Haydon, RS 9, 3 vols (1858–63), 3. 390–94; Whitfield, 'Conflicts of personality', 339.

[69] Zouche's articles of complaint sent to Angelus de Senis, Gregory VII's vicar-general of the Franciscans, 12 March 1409, in Willam Swan's letter book, Bodl. MS Arch. Seld. B.23, fols. 55v–56v; ed. Whitfield, 'Conflicts of personality', 349–58.

statement probably distorts a real encounter between the two friars, and shows that Butler represented the conventual idea, prevalent in northern Europe, that the Order's evangelical mission took precedence over strict adherence to the Rule. In any case the minister general personally visited England in 1407 and concluded that Zouche should resign; Zouche's resignation in August was compensated by his promotion to the see of Llandaff shortly afterwards. Butler was elected to the office of minister provincial, though his affronted predecessor pursued a claim against him, as his letters to Swan in the spring of 1409 reveal: he accused Butler and his accomplices to pursuing 'graces' in the Roman curia, contrary to the Franciscan Rule. By then Zouche had manœuvred himself into lonely adherence to Gregory XII, whereas the convocation of July 1408, with Henry IV's full support and with the backing of Pereto and the Franciscan chapter general, had put their weight behind the rebel cardinals. Butler himself had determined on the schism in the school of St Paul's, advocating the cause of the cardinals.[70] Like Ullerston, he must have been in the confidence of the English government and episcopate as they prepared to withdraw from the obedience of Gregory XII. In the circumstances it is not surprising that Butler was able to enjoy the full six years of his office, 1407–13, in spite of Bishop Zouche's protest.

Zouche had accused Butler, in his tendentious and not very credible complaint, of heretical views on the eucharist, and of not celebrating mass for many years on the excuse of infirmity. He was probably right, however, that Butler did not put a strict interpretation on the vow of poverty and was not averse to seeking papal (or conciliar) exemptions, since Butler was apparently at the Council of Constance after leaving office and making trouble, possibly, for his successor.[71] These activities would have put him at odds not only with Ullerston's strictures against exemptions from ordinary episcopal authority, but with the prevailing climate of opinion in the English church which would soon be given legal force in the concordat of 1418, and with Butler's own evocation of harmonious order in the ecclesiastical hierarchy, eloquently expressed in the sixth argument of his determination of 1401. Beyond that nothing further is recorded of him,

---

[70] Zouche's articles of complaint in Whitfield, 'Conflicts of personality', 357. For the location of the Franciscan house at St Paul's see the maps detailed in n. 96.

[71] He was enjoined to cease these activities and return home, presumably after a complaint about him, by a writ of the Privy Seal, 9 June 1416, ed. E. Deprez, *Etudes de Diplomatique Anglaise* (Paris 1908), 29–30. As John XXIII had reappointed him to the office of minister provincial on 17 May 1414, without effect, he may well have been seeking to reoccupy his former position; see *Bullarium Franciscanum*, ed. J. J. Sbaraglia & K. Eubel, 7 vols (Rome 1759–1904), 7. 479, no. 1325.

except Leland's perhaps reliable report that he died at the Reading convent.[72]

There is more information about the third participant in the argument, Thomas Palmer OP, but no clear indication of the circumstances or the date of his intervention.[73] He was evidently older than Ullerston and Butler, having been ordained acolyte in 1371 and deacon in 1376 in the Winchester diocese. In 1378 he was assigned by the Dominican General Chapter to read the Sentences at Cambridge, and presumably graduated there as doctor of theology; in spite of the assertions of numerous scholars, there is no reason to believe that he ever graduated at Oxford or determined in the Oxford schools.[74] He preached before Richard II at Southampton, probably as a doctor of theology, in June 1384, and in other places in 1389, 1390 and 1393.[75] Palmer's court connections must have helped his promotion in the order. The master general Raymond of Capua appointed him as visitor in the two provincial districts of London and the marches on 1 April 1393, and confirmed his election as prior provincial on the following 22 November.[76] But Raymond of Capua, like the Franciscan minister general Antonio de Pereto a decade later, soon had occasion to question the rule of his English provincial. During the next two years he received a number of complaints of Palmer's high-handed conduct: the prior provincial, it was alleged, had been hasty in his judgements and oppressive in meting out punishment, and had treated the customs of the Order with contempt and his superiors with disrespect. The *rigiditas* of his governance had driven a number of friars out of the Order altogether, and one of them, so he was told, to suicide. The master general asked William Bacthorp, the prior of the Lynn convent, to investigate and report.[77] Bacthorp must have found some substance to the allegations, as Palmer was relieved of office on 28 June 1396. Even then he continued to act as provincial

---

[72] Leland, 684, no. 480; Bale had seen Butler's tract on indulgences at Reading.

[73] See Linde, 'Arguing with Lollards'; *BRUO* 1421–2; and A. B. Emden, *A Survey of Dominicans in England: Based on the Ordination Lists in Episcopal Registers (1268 to 1538)* (Rome 1967), 418.

[74] *Acta capitulorum generalium ordinis Praedicatorum* (*Monumenta ordinis Fratrum Praedicatorum historica*), ed. B. M. Reichert, 9 vols (Rome 1898–1904), 2. 447. Deanesly believed he determined at Oxford because she identified his opponent as Peter Payne, and was followed by Emden, who omitted him from the Cambridge Register (*BRUC*). Emden further assumed that Palmer determined on the schism at Oxford (*BRUO* 1421), but Leland's notice of this item mentions no university (*Joannis Lelandi antiquarii De rebus Britannicis collectanea*, ed. T. Hearne, 2nd edn, 6 vols (London 1774), 4. 49; Leland, 690, no. 488).　　　[75] For the details see *BRUO* 1422.

[76] Raymond of Capua, *Registrum litterarum fratris Raymundi de Vineis Capuani magistri ordinis 1380–1399*, ed. T. Kaeppeli (Rome 1937), 175; Linde, 'Arguing with Lollards', 236.

[77] Raymond of Capua, *Registrum*, 181–2 (30 November 1395).

until at least April 1397.[78] He must have had some support from his brethren, as the London Blackfriars elected him prior in the same year, a place which he held until 1407.[79]

The loosening of central control which followed upon the schism may have encouraged Palmer's casual attitude to his superiors in the Order, but his favour at Richard II's court and with the leaders of the English church probably afforded him some protection.[80] He may have been involved in proceedings against Lollards, it seems, as early as 1393, when, presumably as one of the theologians assisting in the prosecution of Walter Brut at Hereford, his name was recorded in the official record as respondent to an unknown Lollard who had impugned Nicholas Hereford's reversion to orthodoxy.[81] The Lollard's letter and the text of the response make it clear that the author of the latter text was Hereford himself; consequently the attribution to Palmer cannot be correct, but perhaps indicates his presence during the trial. A further effort in defence of orthodoxy was made in 1398 (see p. xlii for the dating), when he determined in the schools of St Paul's in favour of the cult of images.[82] His argument, which made much of the function of images as a lay equivalent to the books appropriate to clerical use, was directed at *adversarii* who, he noted incidentally, wanted the whole Bible to be translated into the vernacular for reading and study.[83] A determination by Palmer on the schism, seen by Leland in the library of Westminster abbey, has not survived, but seems to have been one of a series of opinions by theologians; the others were written by John Colton, archbishop of Armagh, Nicholas Fakenham OFM, Nicholas Rishton and Palmer's fellow Dominican John Acton, who was a supporter of the rival pope Benedict XIII. Only Fakenham's, an Oxford determination of 1395, is extant, and the miscellaneous nature of the collection can provide no indication of the date or place of Palmer's tract.[84] These two

[78] ibid. 185, 189–90.

[79] Linde, 'Arguing with Lollards', 237–8; Jens Röhrkasten, *The Mendicant Houses of Medieval London, 1221–1539* (Münster 2004), 183.

[80] He was left ten marks by Archbishop William Courtenay in 1396: Courtenay's will, ed. L. Duncan, *Archaeologia Cantiana* 23 (1898), 58–67, at 65.

[81] *Registrum Johannis Trefnant Episcopi Herefordensis*, ed. W. W. Capes, Canterbury and York Soc. 20 (1916), 396–401. On the attribution to Palmer see A. Hudson, 'The problem of scribes: the trial records of William Swinderby and Walter Brut', *Nottingham Medieval Studies* 49 (2005), 80–104, at 92–3.

[82] Assisi, Biblioteca Comunale MS 192, fols. 133r–146r, with a colophon specifying the date and place. The cathedral employed a lector, notably William Woodford OFM, earlier in the 1390s, whom Palmer may have replaced; alternatively, he could have determined there during convocation, like William Butler in 1408.

[83] Assisi, Biblioteca Comunale MS 192, fol. 134r.

[84] Three bifolia of contemporary comments on one of these tracts are extant in London,

tracts must have been useful contributions to questions currently under debate, and from his base at the London Blackfriars he would continue to play a part in the maintenance of orthodoxy; he preached before Henry IV in April 1403, and participated in the heresy trials of Sir John Oldcastle in 1413 and John Claydon in 1415.[85] Palmer's contribution to the argument on the translation of scripture would not be out of place among his efforts to vindicate orthodox belief.

[JC]

IV. AUTHORSHIP, DATES AND CIRCUMSTANCES

As mentioned earlier, Richard Ullerston's authorship of the determination in the Vienna manuscript rests primarily upon the unambiguous colophon in the Caius fragment: *Explicit tractatus Magistri Ricardi Vllerston d[octoris in theologia] de tran[slacione] sacre scripture in vulgare editus ab eodem Oxon' a[nno] domini 1401.* This information is confirmed by the use of the same passage of Augustine's *De coniugiis adulterinis*, as quoted in the *Glossa ordinaria* on 1 Corinthians 6:12, *omnia mihi licent*, both in the determination and in Ullerston's *Defensorium dotationis*; this latter work has an equally unambiguous colophon asserting Ullerston's authorship, and dating it to the same year, 1401.[86] There can be very little doubt, therefore, that Ullerston was the author of the determination. Though the reading of the last figure of the date in the colophon in the Caius fragment has been doubted, and an alternative date, 1407, has been proposed,[87] the conclusion that it reads 1401 is confirmed by the relation of Ullerston's determination to that of William Butler, the colophon of which reads *Explicit determinacio fratris et magistri Willelmi Butler ordinis minorum, regentis Oxonie. Anno domini MCCCC primo.* That this text is a *principium*, that is a determination which inaugurates the degree of doctor of theology and the beginning of the candidate's regency in the schools, and that Butler is the author, is shown by the customary punning on the candidate's name, *pro cognomine habeat nomen pincerne*, towards the end of the text (146.578). Though the beginning of Butler's text is lost, he made at least one reference to an opponent. He referred

---

Westminster Abbey, MS 34/2, perhaps an item in one of Richard II's consultations on the schism. See M. Harvey, *Solutions to the Schism* (St Ottilien 1983), 69.

[85] *FZ*, 442–3; *The Register of Henry Chichele, Archbishop of Canterbury*, ed. E. F. Jacob, 4 vols, Canterbury and York Soc. 42, 45–7 (1937–47), 4. 136; *BRUO* 1422.

[86] BL MS Lansdowne 409, fol. 43v.

[87] Kelly, *The Middle English Bible*, 53–4; see p. xxiv, note 23 for further discussion.

to the *assertor opinionis contrarie* (140.449–50), who conceded that
the laity should be spared knowledge *de relacionibus originalibus, de
attributis, uel de accidentibus eukaristie*; this seems to refer directly
to Ullerston's invocation of some of Wyclif's ideas, 'in diuinis de
attributis et ydeis, de relacione nature humane ad uerbum, de accidentibus sine subiecto' ('divine attributes and divine ideas, the relation of human nature to the [incarnate] word, accidents without
a subject'), as notions which should not be explained to everybody
(84.1594–5). If we had the beginning of Butler's text we might have
found a more explicit identification of an opponent; but even as
it is, there is one further indication that he had Ullerston's determination in mind. Bale gave the incipit of Butler's determination
from the manuscript he saw at Queen's: *Vtrum sacre scripture canon
pro vulgari. Hic asserit Bedam transtulisse psalterium atque episcopum
quendam Eboracensem alias scripturas.* In the extant part of Butler's
text there is no mention of Bede or of any bishop of York. But
Bale, casting an eye over the original opening paragraphs, could
have telescoped a citation from Ullerston of Bede translating the
Bible, Richard Rolle translating the Psalter, and an archbishop of
York authorizing a translation of the Creed and other texts, all of
which occur together in Ullerston's first main argument (34–6.598–
660).[88] The confusion may be Bale's or possibly Butler's, but nothing in the extant part of Butler's determination corresponds to this
description; it would be explicable, however, if Butler had made a
reference to Ullerston's determination at the beginning of his own
text. It seems clear that Butler used the occasion of his *principium* to answer the case which Ullerston had argued earlier in the
same academic year. Both texts, therefore, can be securely dated
to 1401.

At first sight the attribution of the determination in the Trinity
manuscript to Thomas Palmer looks less certain than either of the
others; a hand different from that of the text, though contemporary
with it, has written *Palmer de translacione* over the first leaf of the
text. But here too there is a coincidence of authorities with another
tract which on the basis of its colophon can confidently be attributed
to Palmer and dated to 1398, namely his tract *De veneratione imaginum* in Assisi, Biblioteca Comunale, MS 192, fols. 133v–146r, which
concludes, 'explicit tractatus fratris et magistri Thome Palmer qui de-
terminavit in scolis sancti Pauli Londonie anno domini 1398'. In this
tract Palmer referred to 'Carnocensis' on the Psalms for a description
of the tetragrammaton on the Jewish high priest's headdress; though

[88] Bale, *Index*, 119.

the author is currently unidentified, the same passage is quoted in slightly different words in the determination on translation.[89] Two different authors can hardly have cited this passage independently. It is more difficult to pin down the date of Palmer's argument on translation. As pointed out earlier, Deanesly assumed that he was answering the Lollard master Peter Payne in an Oxford determination, some time between Butler's in 1401 and the prohibition of the Wycliffite scriptures in 1407.[90] Nothing in the text indicates that Payne was Palmer's opponent, nor is it certain whether Palmer was aware of what either Ullerston or Butler had argued.[91] More recently Cornelia Linde has proposed that the determination originated as an Oxford *quaestio disputata*, belonging to Palmer's putative period of regency at Oxford, that is at some date between 1378 and 1393.[92] There are, however, several reasons to question this solution. First of all, the practice of publishing or circulating *quaestiones disputatae*, which had been common at the beginning of the fourteenth century, had long ceased, whereas the determination, as a literary production not necessarily deriving from a disputation, was an established genre from about 1370 onwards.[93] Secondly, as pointed out earlier, there is no reliable reason to think that Palmer was an Oxford master; the only solid evidence of his university is his assignment by his order to Cambridge in 1378, whereas Oxford was the focus of debate between Wycliffites and their opponents. Thirdly, the question of scriptural translation does not appear as an item in theological controversies at any point in the 1380s or early 1390s, although William Woodford, arguing in the Oxford schools against Wyclif's idea of the Bible in 1389 or 1390, could easily have brought it up.[94] Fourthly, compared with the determinations of both Ullerston and Butler, Palmer's text does not evince much development of the arguments. It may be the case that Palmer's final response to the original arguments adduced only biblical texts to refute the Lollards on their own ground, as Linde suggests.[95] However, the determination, even if the first and second sections were derived from a real educational exercise, appears to be addressed to a less theologically advanced audience than the other two.

---

[89] Assisi, Biblioteca Comunale, MS 192, fol. 140v; Cambridge, Trinity College, MS B. 15. 11, fol. 43va. On the identity of 'Carnocensis' see below, 'Authorities Cited in the Texts', p. lix, note 135. [90] Deanesly, 293.

[91] See, however, below, p. lxxxiii, on the overlap between Palmer's arguments and those of Ullerston and Butler. [92] Linde, 'Arguing with Lollards', 235–54.

[93] See pp. xlvii–l below.

[94] See Woodford's second *determinatio*, Bodl. MS Bodley 703, fols. 76rb–86vb.

[95] Linde, 'Arguing with Lollards', 248.

Though an earlier date cannot finally be disproved, it seems more likely that Palmer determined on scriptural translation in the wake of the Oxford debates of 1401. Admittedly, there is no discernible reference to any other participant in the debates, and no mention of events or circumstances which might indicate the date of its composition or verbal delivery, though, as pointed out earlier, Palmer twice mentioned Lollards in general terms. If he had personally participated in the Oxford debates, a more precise reference to opponents might be expected; though he adopted a roughly scholastic form, as he had in his tract on the veneration of images, his work is a literary construct and probably confronts a merely putative antagonist. The obvious place for it, if it originated as a scholastic exercise, would have been at the schools of St Paul's or at his own priory, the London Blackfriars, where his remarks on the administration of the eucharist would have commanded the attention of an audience of parish priests or friars.[96] As mentioned earlier, Palmer had already, in St Paul's schools in 1398, referred to adversaries who wanted a vernacular Bible, and it cannot be ruled out that he was taking part in an independent London debate; but if he had been writing after 1401, it is not likely that he would have been unaware of an extended public argument on the question at Oxford.[97] The simplest hypothesis would place the tract after that argument, directed to hearers and readers with a more down-to-earth perspective, to whom the English adaptation of Ullerston's tract might have also been addressed.

In any case the determinations of Ullerston and Butler show that the question of biblical translation was widely debated at Oxford in the academic year 1400–1401, together with the issue of church endowments; and as pointed out earlier, the propriety of an English translation does not seem specifically to have been discussed, at least in Oxford, during the previous two decades of vigorous argument over Wycliffite teaching. The question therefore arises, why did this issue become so controversial in 1401? A scholarly English translation of the Bible had been projected, apparently under Wyclif's auspices, and had been carried out over several years in the 1370s and 1380s by more than one scholar associated with Wyclif.[98] It is not clear how widely this translation was disseminated in the 1380s and 1390s,

[96] For the location of the Dominican house see the maps 8 and 9 in *St Paul's: the Cathedral Church of London (602–2004)* (New Haven, CT, 2004); ch. 38 (pp. 413–29) by Nigel Ramsay has a useful account of the history of libraries associated with the cathedral, but not all of it is relevant to the medieval Dominican house.

[97] Assisi, Biblioteca Comunale, MS 192, fol. 134r.

[98] On the inception and achievement of the translation see A. Hudson, 'The origin and textual tradition of the Wycliffite Bible', in *ESWB*, 133–61.

though at least one copy had reached the library of Thomas of Wood-stock, duke of Gloucester, before 1397.[99] The existence of the transla-tion was known to the chronicler Henry Knighton in the early 1390s, but his information probably came from his fellow canon of St Mary in the Fields at Leicester, Philip Repingdon, who had been asso-ciated with Hereford and other followers of Wyclif in 1382.[100] This translation must always have been suspect, as it was to Knighton, because of its association with John Wyclif; on the other hand, it had not specifically been prohibited. The decretal *Cum ex iniuncto* (1199; 106.1972–6, Friedberg, 2. 784–7), which forbade unauthorized persons from expounding the scriptures, did not mention translation. Where inquisitors of the thirteenth and fourteenth centuries came upon vernacular versions in the possession of Cathar or Waldensian heretics, they seem to have treated the texts as evidence of unlawful preaching of the scriptures, but they did nothing to prohibit biblical translation in itself, of which, by 1380, there were abundant examples in most European languages.[101]

Whatever the state of knowledge of the translation generally in 1401, it was undoubtedly known among the fellows and sojourners of Queen's. One possible reason, though it cannot be certainly demon-strated, that the subject of biblical translation was ventilated in the schools in that year is that the debate was initiated by Philip Repingdon, now abbot of his house at Leicester, who had been elected chancellor on 5 May 1400. His election, as implied in an unusually explicit statement issued by the university, was to give the masters traction in the new Lancastrian regime, in which, as shown earlier, Leicester abbey was a favoured foundation and Repingdon a *clericus specialissimus* of the new king Henry IV.[102] At the same time, it was indicated, the university desired to put an end to its internal irregularities by electing a *vir potens et Deum timens, amans veritatem et detestans avariciam*, that is, a strong and well-connected reformer.

By the turn of the fifteenth century, the former Wycliffite master had matured into a respected churchman, who had been evidently close to the great patron of his house, John of Gaunt. Both Re-pingdon's Wycliffite sympathies and his submission to church au-thority in 1382 mirror the changing attitude of Gaunt to the radical Oxford masters; Repingdon's election as abbot in 1394 is likely to have had the blessing of the patron. After 1399, when Gaunt's son

[99] See Dove, *FEB*, 246–7.

[100] *Knighton's Chronicle 1337–1396*, ed. G. H. Martin (Oxford 1995), 242–4.

[101] J. I. Catto, 'The Wycliffite Bible: the historical context', in *ESWB*, 11–26, at 23–5.

[102] *Statuta antiqua universitatis Oxoniensis*, ed. S. Gibson (Oxford 1931), 189–90.

Henry Bolingbroke seized the throne, Repingdon became the king's confessor as well as *clericus specialissimus*, and in 1404 was promoted bishop of Lincoln. He was, however, still in touch with at least some of his old associates: at Queen's in 1386–7, he was once more Robert Alington's colleague; and he had maintained relations with at least one of the former 'Lollard knights', Sir Thomas Latimer, of whose widow's will in 1402 he was an overseer, together with the Lollard Robert Hook.[103] He also preserved from his radical days a strong interest in the evangelization of the laity, to which he contributed a short tract in English, although the Latin sermon-cycle which was once attributed to him has now been shown to have been the work of the prior of St Bartholomew's, Smithfield, John Eyton. He must have been the master Philip, *quondam abbatem de Leycestria*, who compiled a short explanation of the ten commandments in English which has survived in a single manuscript. As bishop, he did his best to promote his pastoral mission by recruiting learned preachers to his diocese. If he took the opportunity as chancellor to advance the cause of an English Bible, his action would have been perfectly consistent with his enduring values.[104]

Richard Ullerston succeeded as a fellow of Queen's to the lively tradition of Hereford, Trevisa and Alington. It is inconceivable that he was not fully cognizant of the existing translation of the scriptures to which some of his predecessors had devoted so much effort; his knowledge of it would have been refreshed by Chancellor Repingdon himself, whom the fellows of Queen's entertained to wine and fruit at some point in the academic year 1400–1401.[105] But nowhere in his determination did he refer to the translation; the focus of his case was the desirability of a new English version, supervised by the bishops. This bold initiative did not in the event bear fruit, perhaps in part because of the opposition in principle which arose in the course of the debate, which Butler's and Palmer's determinations illustrate. Ullerston's text must have been circulated by the author, as the colophon's phrase, *editus ab eodem*, makes clear; but it was seized upon by Lollards who transmitted it to the Hussites in Prague and adapted it in an English version. Yet, as pointed out earlier, Ullerston himself remained close to influential figures of the church establishment, including Robert Hallum, Richard Courtenay

---

[103] K. B. McFarlane, *Lancastrian Kings and Lollard Knights* (Oxford 1972), 214.

[104] On Repingdon's career see *BRUO* 1565–7. On the sermon-cycle, see R. Sharpe, 'John Eyton alias Repyngdon and the *Sermones super evangelia dominicalia* attributed to Philip Repyngdon', *Medium Ævum* 83 (2014), 254–65. His exposition of the Decalogue is in BL MS Cotton Vespasian A. XXIII, fols. 107r–115r.

[105] QCA, Long Rolls, 1400–1401.

and perhaps Arundel himself, to whom he had addressed his defence of church endowments. In 1408 he was encouraged to submit his *Petitiones pro ecclesiae militantis reformatione* to the English delegation to the Council of Pisa. By then the archbishop had issued his Constitutions, which prohibited the reading of vernacular scriptures written in or after the lifetime of Wyclif, an unmistakable reference to the existing version. In one respect only was there a possible faint trace of the impact of Ullerston's advocacy, in the hint that a future translation might be approved by the hierarchy.[106] If an authorized translation had been undertaken, its text could not have been very different from that of the *Wycliffite Bible*. In its absence, the existing translation was very widely read throughout the fifteenth century.

[JC]

V. THE FORM OF THE DETERMINATION

The texts of Ullerston, Butler and Palmer on the translation of scripture fall into a broad category of theological literature, derived from university exercises, which was usually termed the *determinatio*. Originally the *determinatio* was the part of a *quaestio disputata* or a *quodlibet* in which, after the opponent and the respondent had presented arguments, the presiding master determined the question and then answered the arguments which he had rejected. In the heyday of the theological schools, from the middle of the thirteenth century to the middle of the fourteenth, most of the leading theologians of Paris and Oxford had issued literary redactions of questions they had determined as part of their teaching duties; but after 1350, this convenient vehicle for the transmission of advanced theological ideas to other professional theologians was generally abandoned. The masters of the sacred page gradually transferred their attention away from the abstract philosophical questions which had occupied them for over a century, and which had been expressed in an arcane vocabulary barely penetrable by outsiders, to a much broader range of religious, moral and ecclesiological issues which could be discussed with reference to past and present human experience. These issues, which were of course discussed, often with passion, outside the schools and by laity as well as clergy, were of their nature controversial; and the literature which they generated accordingly took whatever form was

---

[106] Wilkins, 3. 317, constitution vii: 'si res exegerit, per concilium provinciale ipsa translatio fuerit approbata: qui contra fecerit ut fautor haeresis et erroris similiter punietur'.

most likely to persuade its intended readers. The leading part in the
numerous religious debates of the late fourteenth and early fifteenth
centuries was, however, still taken by university theologians, whose
original contributions were often made in the schools. Many of these
lectures or exercises were then written up and expanded, usually with
an array of authorities cited with book and chapter, and circulated to
a somewhat wider, though still restricted readership. Both Pierre
d'Ailly in 1381 and Jean Gerson in 1390, for instance, inaugurated
their many controversial contributions to the literature of the Great
Schism with a question in the Paris schools, which they then expanded and published.[107]

In England, the controversy over the status and activities of the
friars which Richard Fitzralph had provoked in 1356 was pursued
both in and out of the schools in a variety of literary genres, including questions. Wyclif, though he certainly debated questions in the
Oxford schools in his theology course, did not circulate either his
philosophical or his controversial writings in question form, prefer-
ring to expound texts and to develop arguments in a looser and more
rhetorical framework. His contemporary, William Woodford OFM,
on the other hand, divided most of his extremely long commentary of 1373–4 on the first five chapters of Matthew into questions,
which in its literary form retained the structure of *quaestiones* in the
schools, though in a looser and more conversational form with numerous references to everyday phenomena and to his own experience.
Woodford's later work of exposition, the *Quaestiones 72 de sacramento
altaris*, was originally given as lectures in the schools at St Paul's
cathedral in 1383 or 1384 and then circulated; it retained the shell of
the academic *quaestio*, but developed its arguments more rhetorically
by posing a series of points, or *veritates*, without answering arguments
ad oppositum. The work was essentially a straightforward explanation
of the eucharist, and only a rejoinder to Wyclif's opinions as a secondary objective. This procedure was repeated in his *Determinationes*

---

[107] Pierre d'Ailly, *Utrum indoctus in iure diuino posset iuste praeesse in ecclesiae regno*,
ed. L. E. Dupin, *Johannis Gersonii Opera omnia*, 5 vols (Antwerp 1706), 1. 646–62; Jean
Gerson (the work is anonymous), *Utrum Parisiensis uniuersitas ad prosequendum unionem
ecclesiae ad semper et pro semper*, ed. P. Glorieux, *Jean Gerson, œuvres complètes*, 10 vols in
11 (Tournai 1960–73), 6. 1–21. On the *determinatio* as a scholastic exercise see B. C. Bazàn,
G. Fransen, D. Jacquart & J. W. Wippel, *Les Questions disputées et les questions quodlibé-
tiques dans les facultés de théologie, de droit et de médecine*, Typologie des sources du moyen
âge occidental, Fasc. 44–5 (Turnhout 1985), 120–22. For a recent summary of academic
quaestiones and disputations see O. Weijers, *A Scholar's Paradise* (Turnhout 2015), 95–137;
and on the development of scholastic genres in Oxford see W. J. Courtenay, *Schools and
Scholars in Fourteenth-Century England* (Princeton, NJ, 1987), 251–5, 359–65, and Catto,
'Wyclif and Wycliffism', 178–90.

quattuor, a more direct response to some of Wyclif's controversial views on the religious orders and on scripture which originated as Oxford lectures in 1389 and 1390.[108]

Ullerston's colleagues at Queen's, Robert Alington and John Sharpe, each determined on items of Wyclif's controversial opinions in a similar loose form within the conventional structure, as did an older master, Nicholas Radcliffe OSB; Radcliffe set out his views on the schism and on the cult of images in more traditionally structured questions, though for his longer works of controversy he preferred to use the form of a dialogue.[109] By 1401, then, the *determinatio* was an established literary form, used typically by theologians, who had already incepted as doctors, to put controversial issues before a Latinate readership who may or may not have been trained theologians themselves. Its forceful and versatile form of argument provided preachers with points which could be transferred to sermons before a lay audience, and was therefore particularly useful in controversy over the role of the friars, in the wake of Richard Fitzralph's onslaught on them, and over the doctrines of John Wyclif.

All three participants in the controversy about translation made their contributions in the form of academic exercises. Though what survives of them in each case is a revised written redaction, they may have all originated in verbal performances in the schools, not necessarily in Oxford. University exercises in Oxford both before and after 1400, recording the process but not the final determination, are extant in several notebooks.[110] The texts published here, however, belong to a different genre: though probably based on lectures, they were then written up for circulation in the established form of a magistral *determinatio*. Ullerston's text (about 1,600 lines) is much too long to correspond to a single performance in the schools; he referred at the beginning to previous conclusions which he had established, presumably in earlier lectures, and then made his points at

---

[108] Woodford, *Quaestiones 72*, Bodl. MS Bodley 703, fols. 102r–183v; *Determinationes quattuor*, fols. 69r–101v.

[109] Robert Alington, *Determinatio de adoratione imaginum*, Oxford, Merton College, MS 68, fols. 32r–40r; John Scharpe, *De orationibus sanctorum*, Oxford, Merton College, MS 175, fols. 257r–269v; Nicholas Radcliffe, *Utrum pro scandalo schismatice prauitatis sedando dominus papa Bonefacius una cum antipapa cedere teneatur*, BL MS Royal 6 D. x, fols. 277v–283r; *Utrum sit licitum christiano imagines adorare*, fols. 274r–277v. His dialogues are in the same manuscript, fols. 2r–143r and 144r–228v. For full listing of copies of manuscripts, mostly unprinted, with texts by these authors, see Sharpe, with references there.

[110] Cf. Worcester Cathedral, MS F.65 (from the 1360s); Cambridge, St John's College, MS 103 (1390s); Oxford, Corpus Christi College, MS 280 (AD 1402); Bodl. MS Bodley 692 (AD 1448–9).

length, with numerous citations of authorities. The work we have is
a literary version, derived perhaps from several lectures, of a virtual
university act, in response to a real debate the quality of which he
apparently did not rate very highly. Palmer's determination follows
roughly the same format more briefly, posing a second set of arguments against his case besides the usual initial points. He allowed
himself a digression on the circumstances in which priests should
or should not refuse the eucharist to communicants, which further
distances the written text from a disputation in the schools, and suggests that the work originated in lectures to clergy. The incomplete
treatise of William Butler comes closest to a scholastic exercise, since
it addresses an audience of senior masters; but it is too long to be a
mere transcript of the doctoral *principium* from which it must have
derived. All these texts in their extant form, therefore, are determinations on a controversial topic designed to persuade a wider public
than a body of university masters and students.

Ullerston began by referring to a controversy in the schools which
had been running during the current academic year, and after summarizing four points made by one of the protagonists, set out twenty-
six more to bolster the argument against scriptural translation, in
conformity with the traditional structure of the determination. Arguments *ad oppositum* were omitted, and the determination proper
followed, in which terms were defined, and the case of the first doctor
was vigorously refuted with reference both to biblical and patristic
authority, and to existing translations. Ullerston's method, common
in the schools, was to accept the general principle embodied in the
major premise, but to deny the particular application stated in the
minor. His disclaimer that his views were subject to the authority
of the church, and his surprisingly tentative conclusion in favour of
translation as probable only, came in this central section and not,
as would be more usual, at the end of his tract. Its moderation was
rather overborne by the tone of what followed. In a rather rhetorical
passage, an attempt was made to distinguish the underlying reasons
for the case against translation; and then the thirty arguments were
refuted in turn and at length, again by citing biblical and later authorities and by invoking human experience, with some not very relevant
excursus, and some strictures on the current moral state of the clergy.
This was followed by a peroration, and the argument was summarized
in nine points at the end. Ullerston seems to have wanted to raise the
tone of a debate which he regarded as having been, on both sides,
rather superficial. He achieved his object by measured consideration
of what the Fathers and some scholastic authors had written, but
in the process he adopted the techniques of rhetoric, employing the

rhetorical question, introduced by *queso*, in several responses. This implies that the circulated text was addressed to a broad educated readership, and targeted particularly, perhaps, at active clergy with pastoral responsibilities, who might be persuaded of the usefulness of a careful vernacular version of scripture. These readers would respond to his criticisms of the moral standards of the beneficed clergy, a topic which had been trenchantly addressed by moralists of the previous generation like Thomas Brinton, and which would be taken up in his own *Petitiones*, a reforming statement pressed by Hallum at the Council of Pisa.

Ullerston's argument in the schools in 1401 was, it seems, challenged shortly afterwards by William Butler. As pointed out earlier, his determination includes a punning reference to his surname, which indicates that the academic lecture in which it originated was his *principium* or inaugural lecture as a doctor of theology.[111] As has been shown, he was answering an opponent, evidently Ullerston, in the same year, 1401, losing no time in both attempting to refute the opposite case in the Oxford schools, and then circulating the text in literary form. Butler did not arrange his case in the form of an academic *quaestio*. In accordance with the conventional structure of the *principium*, he presented a rhetorical exposition of his argument under six headings, without points made for and against, in contrast to both Ullerston and Palmer. Wyclif's *principium*, the most recent Oxford example which has survived, followed much the same pattern though less argumentatively.[112] Butler grounded his argument in the standard authorities with detailed references, even if, perhaps through faulty transmission, they are often inaccurate. He presented his authorities with considerable art; his arguments were sometimes convoluted but nearly always spirited, and on occasion enlivened by a sense of the absurd, such as his comparison of the laity to toes, with a playful appeal to 'your reverences' to adjudicate (142–3.510–13). The brio is appropriate to a university audience on a festive occasion. Though Butler must have revised and circulated his text to further a serious theological case, its light-hearted asides retain the character of its ceremonial origin.

The structure of Palmer's determination has been usefully analysed by Cornelia Linde.[113] It can be divided into six parts: first, eighteen

---

[111] On the custom of punning on the author's name in *principia* see D. Trapp, 'Augustinian theology of the 14th century', *Augustiniana* 6 (1956), 146–274, at 269–70, and B. Smalley, 'Wyclif's *Postilla* on the Old Testament and his *Principium*', *Oxford Studies presented to Daniel Callus*, Oxford Historical Society, new ser. 16 (1964), 253–96, at 268–9.

[112] Smalley, 'Wyclif's *Postilla*', 288–96.

[113] Linde, 'Arguing with Lollards', 240–46; see especially 241. Linde's references give

points in favour of scriptural translation (152–6.1–92); second, eighteen points against (156–65.94–247), which do not correspond to the first set of points; third, thirteen *veritates* against translation (165–76.250–435); fourth, arguments against some of the *veritates*, and against some of the eighteen points in the second section (176–9.436–99); fifth, replies to some points in the fourth section (180–82.500–55); sixth, a systematic response to the eighteen points in the first section (182–8.556–670). Palmer's text, though shorter than Ullerston's, is more elaborate in structure. The first section of arguments *quod sic*, and the sixth, Palmer's responses, are the essential features of a published determination and are also present in Ullerston's text. The third section too, Palmer's substantial case, is comparable with the central section of Ullerston's argument. But Palmer, unlike Ullerston, included a second section of arguments *quod non* (156–65.94–247) which are independent of the arguments in the first section; and he inserted a second set of arguments *quod sic* (180–82.500–55), with rejoinders to some of them, in the fourth and fifth sections; they include his brief excursus (178–82.486–548) on the administration of the eucharist. The determination taken as a whole appears much less polished than Ullerston's, with many arguments which amount to little more than the tendentious citation of a passage of scripture, and only sporadic engagement between them. The eighteen points for and against with which he began might well have originated in arguments thought up independently by an opponent and respondent; the other four sections, including the points *ad oppositum* in section four against his substantial case, look more like objections he had thought of himself. Though we cannot be certain whether the text as it appears in the unique manuscript descends from an unfinished draft, or whether it was circulated as it now stands, it is probably a literary form of a lecture delivered not in the Oxford schools, like the prototypes of Ullerston's and Butler's texts, but in the school of St Paul's or that of the London Blackfriars.

[JC]

VI. AUTHORITIES CITED IN THE TEXTS

All three debaters cite a considerable range of earlier commentators on various aspects of biblical language. Their choice of cited texts may give some indication of their approach to the problems and

---

the page numbers of Deanesly's edition; here, line numbers of the present edition show the division between sections more precisely.

highlight their own academic backgrounds. They are worth further investigation.[114]

Ullerston's argument on translation rests on the fundamental discussion of signs and language, specifically in relation to the Bible, in the second book of *De doctrina christiana*, the treatise in which Augustine sought to remould classical culture on the foundation of the scriptures. Though he cited the text only sparingly, Ullerston had clearly absorbed its full argument, especially on the relation of words in the mind to words in the mouth or on the page. His use of this well-known text is not surprising. It was buttressed by reference to several of Augustine's other works, particularly *De trinitate* on the Divine Word and on the relation of knowledge and love, and to his letters, sermons and *Soliloquies*. Augustine's ideas on translation had been developed in the light of Jerome's new Latin version, and partly through correspondence with the older master, some of which was cited by Ullerston; but where their opinions diverged, Ullerston tended to prefer the often better informed opinion of Jerome, notably on the circumstances of the Greek translation of the Old Testament. He carefully expounded a sermon of Augustine's on the propriety of putting the Creed in writing, but otherwise his several citations of Augustine were on peripheral points. His other authority, Jerome, conveyed his experience of the problems of translation in his various prefaces to parts of the Bible, which were duly noted. Ullerston had a good enough acquaintanceship with Jerome's letters to point out that about twenty-eight of them were addressed to women on erudite topics, some of which he cited in support of his argument; he was not to know that one of his citations was from a letter whose real author, it seems, was the heretic Pelagius (74.1362–7). He broke new ground in deploying these unimpeachable authorities on the topics of signs, language and translation, to buttress a case which was founded primarily on his own observation and experience.

The question of language and translation had of course occurred to other, more recent writers, notably the thirteenth-century Franciscan Roger Bacon, whose preoccupation, in the wake of Robert Grosseteste's translations from the Greek, was the necessity for scholars to learn Greek and Hebrew if they wanted to understand either the Bible or ancient philosophy. Bacon had therefore put emphasis on the difficulty of translation into languages which lacked terms equivalent to the subtleties of Greek. His argument, as summarized in his letter (with treatise appended) to Pope Clement IV, was useful for the

---

[114] For details of the sources here discussed see notes to translations and the relevant entries in the indexes below; see also *ODCC* for further information on the authors.

opponents of biblical translation into the vernacular, and Ullerston duly deployed it in his case *ad oppositum* and then answered it in his own reply.[115] Though he dissented from Bacon's view on translation, he quoted the earlier master extensively and approvingly on the education of youth. The book was evidently in the library of the Oxford Franciscans, though no copy is recorded in college libraries until John Leland, in 1535, took note of it in Merton.[116] Ullerston cited a sermon from Robert Grosseteste's well known collection, and, in vaguer terms, Grosseteste's commentary on the *Hierarchia ecclesiastica* of the pseudo-Dionysius. Both the sermons, which had circulated widely, and the commentary were easily accessible in Oxford; Merton's was a copy of the latter.[117] More unusually, he quoted the *Corrogationes Promethei* of Alexander Nequam (64.1186), canon and later abbot of Cirencester, on Greek characters in the name of Jesus. This manual of difficult terms in the Bible, written about 1200, had a wide circulation; there was a copy at Merton, though it may not have reached the college by Ullerston's time.[118] The attention paid to all three authors is a sign of the renewed interest in Oxford in the scholarly achievements of the age immediately before philosophical speculation drove other considerations out of the schools; Ullerston's reading of the *Didascalicon* of Hugh of St Victor on Jerome, and the Sentences or *Summa aurea* of the early thirteenth-century Paris master William of Auxerre, where he found an arresting image of Augustine on gradual enlightenment, perhaps confirm this interest. Both works were accessible in Oxford; a copy of William's Sentences was at New College by 1400.[119]

Both Ullerston and Palmer cite Huguccio's *Magnae deriuationes.*[120]

---

[115] Ullerston cited Bacon's *Epistola ad Clementem*, which has been printed in several parts as *Opus maius*, ed. J. H. Bridges, 3 vols (Oxford 1897–1900); *Opus minus*, ed. J. S. Brewer, *Fratris Rogeri Bacon Opera quaedam hactenus inedita*, RS 15 (1859), 313–89; *Opus tertium*, ibid. 3–310; cf. Sharpe, 581. Recently a number of new studies and editions of Bacon's writings have appeared, though they are not focused on his views on language; see particularly A. Power, *Roger Bacon and the Defence of Christendom* (Cambridge 2013), and the two editions by T. Maloney, *Compendium of the Study of Theology* (Leiden 1988) and *Compendium of the Study of Philosophy*, Auctores Britannici medii aevi 32 (Oxford 2018).

[116] Thomson, *University and College Libraries of Oxford*, 2. 1019.

[117] S. Harrison Thomson, *The Writings of Robert Grosseteste* (Cambridge 1940), 160–82; Oxford, Merton College, MS 86, bequeathed in 1329.

[118] Oxford, Merton College, MS 254. See R. W. Hunt, *The Schools and the Cloister: the Life and Writings of Alexander Nequam, 1157–1217* (Oxford 1984), 25, 119–20, 131–3; Sharpe, 52.

[119] Thomson, *University and College Libraries of Oxford*, 2. 1130.

[120] See 16.259, 46.857 and 166.278,166.281, and the source notes to these in the translation.

It is not clear whether the early twelfth-century Pisan author of a canon-law handbook, the *Summa de decretis*, is the same person as the author of the *Deriuationes* or merely shares the same name—if only one person is in question, he was very productive.[121] How much either Ullerston or Palmer knew about either text or author is unclear, but their quotations are mostly accurate, and a more exhaustive search is likely to turn up further cases of their unstated indebtedness. How widely known the *Deriuationes* was in England by *c.* 1400 is not clear.[122]

Not surprisingly, Ullerston had to hand the corpus of canon law, in which he found Clement V's decree *De magistris*, encouraging the study of oriental languages, as well as an extensive passage reported to be the work of Origen, distinguishing, in a way useful to Ullerston's argument, between the laity as such and unworthy persons. This passage, however, was not Origen's; it circulated as the third letter attributed to Clement of Rome, but was really taken from the pseudo-Isidorian decretals, a concoction of the mid-ninth century.[123] He had in addition the *Glossa ordinaria* (20.333), where he found a genuine quotation from Augustine's *De coniugiis adulterinis*, and the standard Bible commentary of the Paris Franciscan Nicholas Lyra, universally used for reference since the 1330s, with its useful information on the rites of the early church. Lyra had used, not always with acknowledgment, the *Catena aurea* of Thomas Aquinas with its translated passages from the Greek fathers, including 'Theophilus', whom Ullerston portentously quoted without, it is clear, knowing who this author was (98.1840). Lyra himself may have had no better idea. Modern scholarship has shown that the name hides the identity of Theophylact of Ochrid, an eleventh-century Byzantine exegete.[124]

---

[121] The suggestion of W. P. Muller, *The Life, Works, and Thought of a Twelfth-Centgury Jurist* (1994) is that they are likely to have been different men, dating the *Deriuationes* to the decade around 1161 (p. 47) and therefore unlikely to have been by the jurist.

[122] J. M. W. Willoughby, *The Libraries of Collegiate Churches*, CBMLC 15, 2 vols (2013), 1035 s.n. Hugutio Pisanus, lists examples and indicates (pp. lxxi, lxxiv) that this reference work was familiar in the libraries of parish and collegiate churches. The copy of *Deriuationes* that is now Queen's College MS 321 did not reach the college until the seventeenth century (see Kidd, *Descriptive Catalogue*, 181–4).

[123] The letter is edited in P. Hinschius, *Decretales pseudoisidorianae et capitula Angilramni* (Leipzig 1863), 52–60, at 59 for the passage cited by Ullerston.

[124] Theophylact of Ochrid, *Commentariae in Marcum*, cited by Lyra from Thomas Aquinas, *Catena aurea*, ed. A. Guarienti, 2 vols (Turin 1953), 1. 464, in the lost Latin version made for Aquinas; this passage is in *PG* 123. 535–6. On the translation, see C. G. Conticello, 'Théophylacte de Bulgarie, source de Thomas d'Aquin (*Catena aurea in Ioannem*)', in *Philomathestatos. Studies in Greek and Byzantine Texts Presented to Jacques Noret for his Sixty-Fifth Birthday*, ed. B. Janssens, B. Roosen & P. van Deun, Orientalia Lovaniensia Analecta 137 (Louvain 2004), 63–75, esp. 65–6.

However egregious the pitfalls of attribution into which Ullerston fell in his pursuit of prestigiously ancient authorities, his quest for them is evidence of his sense of historical development and the varying weight of ancient and modern authority.

Ullerston's other citations are merely ancillary. Aristotle's *Ethics*, *Politics* and *Rhetoric* in the translations of William of Moerbeke, fundamental to any university education, furnished him with the general principles of the arts and the use of words; the *Antiquitates* of Josephus with the circumstances of the Greek version of the Old Testament; Gregory's homilies with a story of a self-taught layman. The homilies attributed universally in this period to John Chrysostom, though evidently written by a cleric of Arian sympathies in the Balkans in the mid-fifth century, contributed notes on Jewish practice with implications, in one instance, for Christian conduct.[125] The work on the ecclesiastical hierarchy ascribed to Dionysius the Areopagite, which was probably written between 485 and 515 by a Greek or oriental author, provided information on contemporary practice on guarding sacred objects in churches. Ullerston's quotations from Seneca are a little more complex: one, on not being too literal, is ascribed to a tract *De breuitate uitae* (22.392), but is found in his *Dialogus ad Serenum de tranquillitate animae*. His second quotation is purported to be from Seneca's letter to St Paul, on keeping up appearances: it is in one of Seneca's letters to Lucilius (92.1711). If Ullerston had been using a text similar to that in Oxford, Merton College, MS 297, these misattributions could be explained as confusion between two sets of adjacent texts.[126]

There are a few citations from more contemporary authors. Aquinas was cited, unsurprisingly, on intelligible beings, and Richard Fitzralph's *Summa de questionibus Armenorum* (22.379, 76.1421) on the efficacy and legitimacy of translated texts. Fitzralph's *Summa*, compiled at Avignon about 1342, circulated independently of the works of Fitzralph favoured by Lollard writers;[127] it was in the library of the Oxford Greyfriars, but before it became popular in the wake of the Council of Florence (1438–9), it was best known

---

[125] On the authorship of these homilies, generally referred to as the *Opus imperfectum* of Chrysostom, see J. van Banning, *Opus imperfectum in Matthaeum*, 1: *Praefatio*, CCSL 87B (1988).

[126] In the Merton manuscript, written about 1350 and left to Merton in 1385, the first text is Jerome's supposed prologue to the letters of Seneca and St Paul (fol. 1r–v), followed by Seneca's genuine letters (fols. 1v–68r). Seneca's dialogue *ad Serenum de tranquillitate animae* (fols. 163r–171v), followed by his dialogue *ad Paulinum de breuitate uitae* (fols. 172r–185r), are items 12 and 13 in this manuscript.

[127] When a full study detailing quotations of and references to Fitzalph is compiled, the circulation may prove more complicated than this implies.

in eastern Europe, where it was mined for arguments against the Orthodox church. Ullerston probably knew it in the copy belonging to his German colleague at Queen's, John Scharpe, who brought it from Germany and eventually returned with it.[128] Giles of Rome's *Liber contra exemptos* on the supposed excesses of the Templars is slightly more unusual, but it circulated under the authorship of Parisiensis as cited by Ullerston and as ascribed in Oxford, Merton College, MS 50. Richard Rolle's Latin commentary on the Psalter provided a sharp critique of people who try to found virtue on an untruth. Ullerston would refer to it again in 1415, in his *Expositio canticorum scripturae*; the earliest extant manuscript, Bodl. MS Bodley 861, was written in 1409–11.[129] This citation is therefore evidence of his rather precocious access to Rolle's commentary.[130] He took the *exemplum* of the Amazons from thirteenth-century light fiction, Guido delle Colonne's *Historia destructionis Troiae* (76.1405), and his information on Bede's and Alfred's translations from William of Malmesbury, *Gesta regum Anglorum* and the more recent *Polychronicon* of Ranulf Higden, which had been translated into English (though he cited the Latin) by Ullerston's colleague at Queen's College, John Trevisa. The citations taken together show him to have had access to a wide-ranging library of texts, which on the whole he quoted accurately.

If Ullerston usually quoted his authorities *verbatim*, with careful references, both William Butler and Thomas Palmer preferred to paraphrase. Butler's references, perhaps because of the imperfect text in the unique manuscript, are often incomplete or inaccurate. He did not respond to Ullerston's arguments on the nature of language, and therefore did not propose any alternative reading of Augustine's analysis of physical and verbal signs in *De doctrina christiana*; his only indirect reference to that book was his mention of the rules of Tyconius on the interpretation of scripture (134.359). Instead he found an abundance of material on the difficulty of understanding the Bible in Augustine's correspondence and on the corruption of variant texts in his *Retractationes* (116.5); on the preference of hearing scripture over reading it in Augustine's commentary on the Psalms; and more

[128] K. Walsh, *A Fourteenth-Century Scholar and Primate: Richard FitzRalph at Oxford, Avignon and Armagh* (Oxford 1981), 160–81 and 469–73. Scharpe's copy is now Berlin, Staatsbibliothek zu Berlin, Preussischer Kulturbesitz, MS Magdeburg Domgymnasium 47.

[129] See A. B. Kraebel, 'The use of Richard Rolle's *Latin Psalter* in Richard Ullerston's *Expositio canticorum scripturae*', *Medium Ævum* 81 (2012), 139–44.

[130] On the manuscripts of the commentary see H. E. Allen, *Writings Ascribed to Richard Rolle* (London 1927), 22–34, 165–9.

extensively on the obscurities and ambiguities of the written word in general in his *Dialectica* (122.118). Butler's sustained analogy of the angelic and ecclesiastical hierarchies (an idea derived from pseudo-Dionysius) was argued with reference to Augustine's discussion of the orders of angels in his commentary on Genesis; and he found in one of Augustine's homilies on the miracle at Cana in John's Gospel the pretext to refer to his own name (146.577). With the possible exception of his reading of Augustine's *Dialectica*, Butler's use of Augustine is merely rhetorical, as was appropriate in the academic exercise of the *principium*. As he declined to engage in debate on translation, he had no reason to refer to Jerome's reflections on the topic; he merely found in Jerome's correspondence, as in Augustine's, texts on the difficulties of understanding scripture. Gregory's *Moralia in Job* provided an example of analogical expression in his exposition of the Church as the mystical body of Christ (134.357). Besides the homilies misattributed to Chrysostom, which Ullerston had used, he referred both to his genuine homilies (132.289) and to Origen's homilies on Leviticus in the translation of Rufinus, where an explanation of priestly vestments in the Old Testament marked the distinction between clergy and laity.

Butler had access to both civil and canon law texts (140.462), together with a letter of Innocent II (140.454) which circulated in the letter collections of Bernard of Clairvaux (140.455). He cited the *Ductor neutrorum* of the twelfth-century Jewish philosopher Moses Maimonides under the title *De duce dubiorum* on Hebrew priests' restriction of knowledge of the scriptures (140.438), and William of Auxerre on their covering the vessels in the tabernacle (136.378).[131] For other arguments he had recourse to doctors of his own order: to the *Summa* of Alexander of Hales (120.99), compiled in Paris in the 1230s, on the corruption of the human intellect by original sin, reinforced by the opinion of the late thirteenth-century Franciscan Peter John Olivi in his commentary on Genesis (122.110).[132] Nicholas of Lyra was cited only once (138.411 and cf 140.447).

---

[131] William Woodford had cited the same work of Maimonides under the title *De duce dubiorum*, which was presumably its title in the Oxford Greyfriars copy. It had been translated into Latin at Paris about 1240. Some consideration of the references to the text is given in D. C. Klepper, *The Insight of Unbelievers: Nicholas of Lyra and Christian Reading of Jewish Text in the Later Middle Ages* (Philadelphia, PA, 2007).

[132] The *Summa* of Alexander was a standard resource in the Oxford theology faculty; Olivi, a radical Franciscan, was a more suspect author, who had been cited by Woodford only as *quidam postillator*. His work on Genesis is likely to have been in the Greyfriars library; there are no surviving copies now known in British libraries; useful and relatively recent bibliography is in *Pierre de Jean Olivi (1248–1298)*, ed. A. Boureau & S. Piron (Paris 1999).

Whereas Butler had access to the well-stocked library of the Oxford Greyfriars, Thomas Palmer presumably used the resources of the London Dominican convent.[133] Though he engaged with the question of language and translation, he did not refer either to Augustine's *De doctrina christiana* or to Roger Bacon; and he made only one general reference to Jerome (170.340, cf 184.596). His arguments on this question derived entirely from his own observation of the English language. His assertion that those parts of scripture which imparted knowledge necessary for salvation should be available in the vernacular, but that other parts, too difficult for lay understanding, should be left to learned clergy, rested on a limited number of scriptural texts. He expounded them with the help of a remarkably old-fashioned selection of commentators: Gregory's commentary on the gospels (172.386) and his *Moralia in Job* (164.220); the *Opus imperfectum* attributed to Chrysostom (180.524); Bede on the Apocalypse (170.345); the ninth-century monastic writer Berengaud (174.395); the early thirteenth-century Paris Dominican commentator on scripture, Hugh of Saint-Cher (156.96, 158.135, 174.388, 174.406); and the later thirteenth-century Dominican Nicholas Gorran on the epistles (166.256) and the Apocalypse (160.150, 164.232, 172.355).[134] Palmer referred to an unidentified *Carnocensis* apparently on the Psalm *Confitemini* (156.108).[135] Other citations are merely ancillary: Augustine's *Opus LXXXIII quaestionum* (178.496, 180.534) and his work on the Sermon on the Mount (180.502); William of Auvergne's *De fide et legibus* (184.604); and, as mentioned already, the *Magnae deriuationes* of Huguccio on Latin rhetorical terms, cited as the *Catholicon* (166.278).[136] A seemingly mysterious reference to a sermon *De natali Domini* of Isidore of Seville (168.295), mentioning the Sybilline

---

[133] The library was probably well stocked; the prior provincial, Richard Winkley, had catalogued it in 1339, from which source Bale noted a few books (*Index*, 513).

[134] Berengaud's work on the seven visions was a standard item in Apocalypse commentaries; Hugh of Saint-Cher's commentary on the whole Bible and Nicholas Gorran's on parts of the New Testament were favoured authorities for Dominican writers, and were generally available in Oxford and elsewhere; see the various papers in *Hugues de Saint-Cher (d.1263)*, ed. L.-J. Bataillon, G. Dahan & P.-M. Gy OP (Turnhout 2004).

[135] *Carnocensis* could refer to the younger Ivo of Chartres, not the canonist, who was a master of Paris active *c.* 1160, but this citation does not seem to appear in his commentary on the Psalms (Paris, Bibliothèque Ste-Geneviève, MS 1560, fols. 58ra–139vb), either on the psalms *Confitemini* (Pss 91, 104, 105, 106, 110, 117, 135, 137) or anywhere else. The title could apply as well to Gilbert of Poitiers, the chancellor of Chartres, but the passage cited is not to be found in his commentary on any of the psalms *Confitemini* (Bodl. MS Laud Misc. 459). It is similar to, but not identical with, the words on the tetragrammaton in Peter Lombard's comment on Psalm 61:10 (*PL* 191. 568). Palmer cited the same passage in slightly different terms in his work *De ueneratione imaginum* (Assisi, Biblioteca Comunale, MS 192, fol. 140v).   [136] See pp. liv–lv.

verses, is explicable if he had been using a version similar to the text in a Vatican manuscript. [137] This frame of reference, so markedly different from Ullerston's, diminishes the likelihood that Palmer was directly familiar with the work of the Oxford masters.

[AH and JC]

VII. THE PARTICIPANTS' VIEWS ON LANGUAGE AND TRANSLATION

The authors of the three Latin treatises discuss language and aspects of linguistic theory while making their case for or against biblical translation. The same threads of thought and biblical quotations occur in all three works reflecting their closeness in time and, in the case of Ullerston and Butler, a similarity of situation and audience. As will be demonstrated below, the authors focus on different aspects of the linguistic argument, presumably pursuing their individual interests. All three display a tendency to give considerable attention to some topics and mention others only briefly, apparently anticipating an audience that could fill in the gaps from familiarity with the debate or general knowledge, though the complex history of all texts, their imperfect preservation in single copies, and uncertainty about their original form preclude full confidence in judging their coverage and organization of material. Some of the main arguments are summarized below to illustrate the range and learning of the discussion of the linguistic aspects of translation.

A. Language and Thought

The relationship between language and thought is the most crucial part of Richard Ullerston's linguistic argument in favour of translation, and he addresses it at the beginning of his determination. The questions he is considering include the following: can meaning be separated from the linguistic form and be re-expressed in another language? If meaning is independent of language, how is it represented in the human mind? Ullerston's answers to these questions rely primarily on earlier discussions by Augustine and Aristotle. Citing Augustine, *De trinitate*, he points out that 'there exists a double

---

[137] Palmer was presumably using a manuscript similar to BAV MS Reginensis lat. 125, where a sermon *De natali domini* is attributed to Isidore of Seville (actually from his *De officiis ecclesiasticis*, I 25), and followed, after some other sermons on the same topic, by *versus Sibyllae de judicio extremo*. The text of the verses is in Augustine, *De ciuitate dei*, XVIII 23 (*PL* 41. 579).

meaning of speech, internal and external, for there is the mouth of the heart, and the mouth of the body' (18.292–3).[138] Ullerston explains that Augustine places words and propositions into two different categories: those that are in some idiom or language and those that are in no language (18.294–5). To illustrate this he cites the following statement by Augustine: 'Whoever can understand a word, not only before it is sounded, but also before we hold in our mind the images of its sounds? For no part of it is in any language, that is, those which are called national languages, among which ours is Latin.'[139] According to Augustine, Ullerston continues, when we speak, we speak from the knowledge stored in our memory and this may generate 'a word entirely of the same character as this remembered knowledge' (18.302–3). This internal word, that we say in our heart, is an idea, formed from the thing we know and is 'neither in Greek nor in Latin, nor in any other language' (18.305–6).[140] Ullerston further explains that, according to Augustine, words of all languages that we hear, as well as music, are also thought silently and contemplated by the mind through mental images. As to the external words, Augustine writes: 'But when we need to convey an idea to other people, then some sign is given to represent it. And generally we produce a sound, or sometimes a silent sign, the one given to the ears, the other to the eyes, so that the word we have in mind can be transmitted to the bodily senses by physical signs' (18.316–17).[141]

---

[138] Bk XV c. 10: 'Some thoughts, then, are speeches of the heart, and that a mouth is also there is shown by the Lord when He says: "What goes into the mouth doth not defile a man, but what comes out of the mouth, that defiles a man". In one sentence he has included the two different mouths of man, the one of the body, the other of the heart'; trans. S. McKenna, *The Trinity* (Washington, DC, 1963), 475.

[139] Bk XV c. 10: 'Whoever, then, can understand the word, not only before it sounds, but even before the images of its sound are contemplated in thought—such a word belongs to no language, that is, to none of the so-called national languages, of which ours is the Latin'; ibid. 473.

[140] See n. 139 and the following, Bk XV c. 12: 'The human mind, therefore, knows all these things which it has acquired through itself, through the senses of its body, and through the testimonies of others, and keeps them in the treasure-house of its memory; and from them a true word is begotten when we say what we know, but the word that is anterior to every sound and to every thought of sound. For then the word is most like the thing that is known, and from which its image is also begotten, since the sight of thought arises from the sight of knowledge. This is the word that belongs to no language, the true word about a true thing, having nothing from itself, but everything from that knowledge from which it is born'; ibid. 483.

[141] Bk XV c. 10: 'For when we speak the truth, that is, speak of what we know, then the word which is born from the knowledge itself which we retain in the memory must be altogether of the same kind as that knowledge from which it is born. For the thought formed from that thing which we know is the word which we speak in our heart, and it is neither Greek, nor Latin, nor of any other language, but when we have to bring it to

The view that concepts can be represented in the mind without language and are a reflection of things that exist in the external world was widely accepted by medieval scholars and goes back to Aristotle. To Aristotle the relationship between words and things is indirect and mediated by concepts stored in the human mind. Whereas the relationship between things and concepts is mimetic—concepts are 'representations or likenesses' of perceived things, the secondary relationship between concepts and words is conventional and the linguistic sign is therefore arbitrary.[142] According to Aristotle, the world is 'the same for the whole of mankind' and its mental representation is also the same for all, whereas words are not the same because historically different communities developed different conventions.[143]

The nature of the relationship between language and thought remains controversial in modern linguistics. Two influential positions can be described as firstly, the hypothesis of linguistic relativity and, secondly, the hypothesis of the language of thought. According to the linguistic relativity hypothesis, also known as the Sapir–Whorf hypothesis, language embodies different conceptual classifications of the world characteristic of different cultures and shapes the perceptions of its speakers.[144] Thoughts are determined by categories available in language and this concerns both words as lexicalized con-

---

the knowledge of those to whom we are speaking, then some sign is assumed by which it may be made known. And generally this is a sound, but at times also a nod; the former is shown to the ears, the latter to the eyes, in order that that word which we bear in our mind may also become known by bodily signs to the senses of the body', ibid. 476.

[142] Aristotle, *De interpretatione*, c. 1: 'Words spoken are symbols or signs of affections or impressions of the soul; written words are the signs of words spoken. As writing, so also is speech not the same for all races of men. But the mental affections themselves, of which these words are primarily signs, are the same for the whole of mankind, as are also the objects of which those affections are representations or likenesses, images, copies'; *Aristotle, Categories. On Interpretation. Prior Analytics*, ed. and trans. H. P. Cooke & H. Tredennick (Cambridge, MA, 2014), 115. See also R. Harris & T. J. Taylor, *Landmarks in Linguistic Thought: the Western Tradition from Socrates to Saussure* (London 1989), 20–34 ('Aristotle on Metaphor').

[143] ibid. c. 2 (p. 117): 'We have already said that a noun signifies this or that by convention. No sound is by nature a noun: it becomes one, becoming a symbol. Inarticulate noises mean something—for instance, those made by brute beasts. But no noises of that kind are nouns.'

[144] The view that language constrains thought and the only conceptual distinctions that one can make are those encoded in one's language is associated with the names of the American linguists Edward Sapir (1884–1939) and Benjamin Whorf (1897–1941). For a philosophical justification of the language of thought hypothesis see J. A. Fodor, *The Language of Thought* (Hassocks 1975). See introductory discussions of the relationship of language and thought in P. Elbourne, *Meaning: a Slim Guide to Semantics* (Oxford 2011), 140–55; 'Meaning, thought and reality', in J. I. Saeed, *Semantics*, 4th edn (Chichester 2016), 23–50. See also D. Gentner & Susan Goldin-Meadow, *Language in Mind: Advances*

cepts and grammatical structures, such as number, aspect and tense, that all impose restrictions on possible ways of thinking. According to a much cited statement of Edward Sapir, 'No two languages are ever sufficiently similar to be considered as representing the same social reality. The worlds in which different societies live are distinct worlds, not merely the same world with different labels attached.'[145]

A strong version of the Sapir–Whorf hypothesis, known as linguistic determinism, is not currently a widely held view and a strict identification of thought and language is rejected by most linguists and cognitive scientists. Accepting that language can influence thought in a limited way and that words available in a language can, for example, have an effect on memory, association and categorization, scholars point to the existence of cognitive processes outside language,[146] and the fact that, as linguistic analysis demonstrates, meaning is richer than language.[147] To many, such evidence suggests that thought is independent of the linguistic form, and that humans have the same cognitive architecture and mental processes even though they may speak different languages.[148]

Ullerston clearly distinguishes between language and thought, and uses their separateness to assert that adequate translation is possible. If linguistic form is external to meaning, it has to be expendable. Since the perception of the world is the same for all humans and concepts have a mental representation independent of any historical language, it is only the difference in linguistic conventions that can hinder satisfactory translation from one language into another. Ullerston describes translation as a process in which a translator 'transfers the material he is teaching into the auditor's mind' (24.430–31) and suggests that the words of Wisdom 7:27, describing eternal wisdom as 'imparted' or 'translated' 'among all peoples into holy souls' (*per naciones transfert se in animas sanctas*) (24.438–9), should be understood in a similar way. Ullerston does not trivialize this process

---

in the *Study of Language and Thought* (Cambridge, MA, 2003), and R. Jackendoff, *Patterns in the Mind: Language and Human Nature* (New York, NY, 1994).

[145] E. Sapir, 'The status of linguistics as a science', *Language* 5 (1929), 207–14, at 209.

[146] Such evidence is discussed in all publications listed in n. 144 above.

[147] Language commonly underspecifies meaning that has to be enriched by hearers from linguistic and situational context, see A. Cruse, *Meaning in Language: an Introduction to Semantics and Pragmatics*, 3rd edn (Oxford 2011), 359–445.

[148] The language of thought is conceptualized as innate, universal among thinking beings and physically realized in the brain. It is considered to be a system that is language-like in the sense that it is probably symbolic and uses some kind of propositional representation, but it is more abstract and does not have the surface syntax of a natural language like English. See 'Language of thought' in S. Chapman & C. Routledge, *Key Ideas in Linguistics and the Philosophy of Language* (Edinburgh 2012), 110–12.

and acknowledges difficulties involved by drawing attention to interpretative aspects of translation. He describes translators as 'those who
adjust or fit together one tongue with another or expound one by
the other' (16.267–8). He further argues that 'by translation we must
understand interpretation, or the exposition of the meaning of one
language in another; a translator must be an interpreter' (16.269–70).
Though translation shares this interpretative nature with commentary and criticism of texts, or a 'divinely inspired' ability 'to expound,
to reveal, to explain or unlock the meaning hidden in the words'
(16.272–3), Ullerston asserts that it does not require any 'special gift'
but only 'a knowledge of languages acquired by application and hard
work' (16.284–5).

Ullerston points out that the reason why translation has to be
interpretative is the lack of a one-to-one match between vocabu-
laries and grammars of different languages. He acknowledges that
widely used academic and biblical translations into Latin can be seen
as imperfect because some Greek, Hebrew and Syriac words of the
originals could not have been translated as a result of the lack of
equivalents in Latin (20.360–64). Such words had to be either 'expressed in circumlocution' or borrowed, either in their original form
or 'rendered in a Latin format or declension' (22.365–6). There are
also words that 'any wise translator would leave untranslated'—those
expressing emotions rather than concepts, such as 'Racha' and 'Osanna' (62.1153).[149] To put this in modern terms, languages organize
and articulate reality differently because linguistic signs are arbitrary,
not only in their form, but also in what they stand for. There is no
universal inventory of concepts represented by linguistic signs in all
languages—that would have made translation easy as a simple act
of substitution of words in one language with words from another
language. Languages, however, divide semantic space and organize
the world into concepts differently, and therefore word-for-word
translation is impossible. The proponents of linguistic determinism
would go further and say that if a linguistic sign is not available for
a particular concept, such a concept could be difficult or impossible
not only to express, but also to comprehend.

Recognizing that literal, word-for-word or 'stencil' translation
is counterproductive, Ullerston argues that adequate rendering is
nevertheless possible, and the sense of the original can be preserved in
another language by using more sophisticated techniques. Outlining

---

[149] In *De doctrina christiana*, II 11, Augustine remarks that interjections 'which signify
the motion of the spirit rather than any part of a rational concept' cannot be translated; trans. D. W. Robertson, *Saint Augustine, On Christian Doctrine* (Indianapolis, IN,
1958), 43–4.

different uses of the term 'translation', Ullerston points out that it can be defined as 'the change which happens to an exemplar in one language, when the meaning is written down in another' (26.453–4), and this is how Jerome translated scripture from Hebrew into Latin. The lack of exact correspondences in vocabulary is not a problem and does not mean that concepts themselves are not available or cannot be expressed. They can be represented through borrowed words and circumlocutions which are 'a good, lawful and praise-worthy thing' so long as they preserve 'the same meaning in both languages' (22.368). According to Ullerston, 'the apostles and evangelists translated meaning for meaning, not just word for word, and took no note of irrelevant considerations' (22.369–71).[150] He also cites Richard Fitzralph, asserting that it is possible to reproduce the sense of someone's speech in different words or in a different language: 'when you quote someone who utters a sentence, repeating what he has said but not in the same words, only similar, you are not telling a lie, since you do not set out to repeat his own words, but the sense of what he said. Otherwise, if you were to hear someone speaking in Greek, and you repeated what he said in Latin, asserting that he said it, you would be telling a lie' (22.379–83).[151] The same is further supported by a quotation from Seneca: 'it is a great, a high, a nearly divine virtue to be calm. The Greeks call this stable state of mind *euthymian* . . . I call it tranquillity; for it is not necessary to translate word for word in slavish imitation. The word to be sought for the thing intended should convey the force of the Greek expression rather than its charm' (22.393–8).[152] What Ullerston is arguing is that translation is lawful because the meaning of the original is not tied to a particular language and can be re-expressed in a different language. This can be achieved through a variety of linguistic strategies that are all acceptable as long as the meaning remains unaltered. It is interesting to note that Ullerston never gives any examples of his own translations—nor of anyone else's. Neither do Butler and Palmer, even though arguments on both sides could have been reinforced if they had done.

B. *Richard Ullerston's Debate with Roger Bacon*

Ullerston's disagreement with Roger Bacon concerns the nature of differences between languages and the implications of such

[150] *Liber de optimo genere interpretandi* (*ep.* 57): 'Alii syllabas aucupentur et litteras, tu quaere sententias'; ed. G. J. M. Bartelink (Leiden 1980), 14.

[151] Richard Fitzralph, *Summa in questionibus Armenorum*, IX 2 (Rome 1512, fol. 56vb).

[152] Seneca, *Dialogi* IX, *Ad Serenum*, 2.3.

differences for translation. As pointed out earlier, Bacon emphasized the problems of translations that in his view cannot replace the original texts. He condemned most existing translations, and argued that it would have been better if Aristotle had not been translated at all.[153] In addition to noting numerous errors in translations resulting from insufficient understanding of texts and limited knowledge of the original languages, he criticized translation more generally from a position approaching that of linguistic relativism. According to Bacon, 'an excellent piece of work in one language cannot be transferred into another as regards the peculiar quality that it possessed in the former'.[154] Ullerston cites Bacon's example of a logician trying to render logic in his mother tongue (6.83–5) as an illustration of the difficulties a translator must face, but whereas Ullerston's main concern is the paucity of technical vocabulary in the target language, Bacon describes the translator as also 'lacking in thoughts', invoking the difficulty of conceiving of ideas in the absence of relevant vocabulary: 'For let any one with an excellent knowledge of some science like logic or any other subject at all strive to turn this into his mother tongue, he will see that he is lacking not only in thoughts, but words, so that no one will be able to understand the science so translated as regards its potency. Therefore no Latin will be able to understand as he should the wisdom of the sacred Scripture and of philosophy, unless he understands the languages from which they were translated.'[155]

Ullerston cites Bacon's claim that one language cannot be faithfully translated into another 'because of the different characteristics of speech in different languages' (6.80–81) and agrees that such differences exist. Thus Greek has an article and Latin does not, whereas English has 'several articles' and 'the Greeks often combine their adverbs with their adjectives, but not speakers of Latin' (58.1057–8). Ullerston does not, however, agree with Bacon's generalizations and observes, that 'it is impossible to conclude on that ground that one language cannot be translated into another' (58.1059–60). The experience proves the opposite and in spite of their differences in grammar, both Greek and English have been successfully translated into Latin. Ullerston points out that translation is done routinely as an exercise, and a teacher in a grammar school may say 'translate

---

[153] 'For so great is the perverseness, crudity, and terrible difficulty in the translated works of Aristotle that no one can understand them, but each one contradicts another, and false statements are found again and again, as is clear from a comparison of the different translators and of the texts of the different languages'; R. B. Burke, *The Opus majus of Roger Bacon. A Translation*, 2 vols (Philadelphia, PA, 1928), I. 77.

[154] ibid. I. 75.

[155] ibid. I. 76.

that into Latin for me' which in his view is better than saying 'make (or compose) the correct Latin usage for me' (58.1065–7). Translation does not have to involve the creation of new meaning, rather a different encoding of the original meaning.

Though Ullerston accepts Bacon's view that the lack of appropriate vocabulary creates problems for translation, as pointed out already, he does not consider such problems to be unsurmountable. Bacon was suspicious of lexical borrowing and saw changes in pronunciation, spelling, grammar and meaning, that inevitably accompany assimilation of a new word into a language, as a form of corruption that hinders the understanding of texts.[156] Ullerston, on the contrary, argues that borrowing is a common and necessary practice. Borrowed words are often adapted to English through apocope of inflectional endings; in this way 'the name of Christ or the Blessed Virgin, or other saints, or countless other names' are altered and used by preachers in English (60.1128–30). Once assimilated, borrowed words, including the terminology of logic, cause no problems of understanding: 'So now, when we talk in the vernacular of *Consequences*, or *Obligations*, or *Insolubles*, etc., varying some Latin terms, we are understood without difficulty' (62.1133–6). Responding to an interpretation by his opponents of St Paul's statement in 1 Timothy 6:20 as prohibiting the introduction of new words,[157] Ullerston argues that the 'Apostle does not forbid any neologisms at all . . . but profane new words' (94.1779–80), and points out that new words were needed to express new concepts such as 'Christianus' (94.1784–5).

Bacon's negative comments on translation may reflect his concern with the corrupt state of the Vulgate, particularly the Paris text.[158] Bacon recommends the study of unadulterated ancient codices that

---

[156] 'Secondly, we must consider the fact that translators did not have the words in Latin for translating scientific works, because they were not first composed in the Latin tongue. For this reason they employed very many words from other languages. Just as these words are not understood by those ignorant of those languages, so are they neither pronounced correctly nor are they written as they should be' (ibid. 1. 76). Bacon further observes that in borrowed words 'error is frequent on the part of the Latins in their pronunciation, writing, and meaning' (ibid. 1. 97) and comments on the effects of this: 'For it is no small impropriety to make mistakes in words; because as a consequence a man errs in his statements, then in his arguments, and at length in what he reckons as conclusions. For Aristotle says, "Those who are ignorant of the meaning of words often reason falsely"' (ibid. 1. 97).

[157] 'O Timothee, depositum custodi, devitans profanas vocum novitates, et oppositiones falsi nominis scientiae, quam quidam promittentes, circa fidem exciderunt' (1 Tim. 6:20–21).

[158] 'But there are many contradictions in the edition of Paris. Therefore this edition needs a thorough correction by means of ancient texts'; Bacon, *Opus majus*, trans. Burke, 1. 78.

may preserve a text free from alteration and error, a suggestion later repeated by the author of the *General Prologue* to the *Wycliffite Bible*.[159] On the authority of Augustine, Bacon writes: 'For Augustine says against Faustus, "If there is disagreement in the Latin codices, we must have recourse to the ancient ones and to several of them". For the ancient ones, as he thinks, are to be preferred to the late ones, and the larger number to the fewer. But all the ancient Bibles, which lie everywhere in monasteries, and which up to the present time have not been glossed nor touched, have the true translation, which the holy Roman Church received in the beginning, and ordered spread abroad throughout all the churches.'[160] Bacon was, however, highly sceptical of the efforts of contemporary critics of the text of the Vulgate. In a brief discussion of the *correctoria* he points to frequent disagreement between correctors, confusion and 'dreadful length' of the *correctoria* that contain 'along with many truths incomparably more false statements'.[161] Following Augustine, he argues that 'if a doubt still remains in the ancient Bibles, we must have recourse to the Hebrew and Greek languages'.[162]

Bacon gives numerous examples of errors in the text of the Vulgate.[163] His particular focus is on errors that resulted from translators'

[159] See the comments in the *General Prologue* on the study of multiple old bibles and distrust of new copies at ll. 2803 and 2850 (Dove, *EAEB*, 80, 82).

[160] Bacon, *Opus majus*, trans. Burke, i. 88.

[161] ibid. i. 89. On the *correctoria* see the incomplete survey by H. Denifle, 'Die Handschriften der Bibel-Correctorium des 13. Jahrhunderts', *Archiv für Literatur- und Kirchengeschichte des Mittelalters* 4 (1888), 263–311, 471–601; and the work of Gilbert Dahan, especially his *L'Exégèse chrétienne de la Bible en Occident médiéval* (Paris 1999), 161–238, and his paper 'La méthode critique dans l'étude de la Bible', in *La méthode critique au Moyen Age*, ed. M. Chazan & G. Dahan (Turnhout 2006), 103–28; perhaps the most useful introduction to the *correctoria* can be found in his paper 'La connaissance de l'hébreu dans les correctoires de la Bible du xiiie siècle', *Revue théologique de Louvain* 23 (1992), 178–90, esp. 178–85. For the possible use of *correctoria* by the *WB* revisers see *ESWB*, 120–26.

[162] Bacon, *Opus majus*, trans. Burke, i. 88.

[163] 'Study of Tongues', ibid. i. 75–115, particularly 87–93. Since Ullerston was clearly familiar with Bacon's discussion of errors in the Vulgate, it is worth considering whether it may have also influenced the translators of the *Wycliffite Bible* and the author of the *General Prologue* to the Bible. Most examples of errors given by Bacon in c. 5 of 'Study of Tongues' (ibid. i. 89–93) are not corrected in either the Earlier or Later versions of the Wycliffite translation. The only exceptions are: the reading *fortem/fontem* at Psalm 41:3 where, according to Forshall and Madden's edition (1850), seven LV manuscripts correct an error in EV (discussed in Dove, *FEB*, 182–3, and H. Hargreaves, 'The Latin text of Purvey's Psalter', *Medium Ævum* 24 (1955), 73–90, at 87–9); the reading 'thirty' corrected to 'twenty' in a group of LV manuscripts at Genesis 37:28; and the reading '*ad tempus orelad tempus horae*' at 1 Thessalonians 2:17 translated as 'for a tyme, bi mouth and in biholding' in EV, but corrected to 'at the tyme of an hour, in biholdynge' in LV. It should be noted that all Bacon's examples in c. 5, apart from 1 Thessalonians 2:17, are

and scribes' insufficient knowledge of original languages, though he comments on other matters as well, including the fact that 'many prologues are placed in the text superfluously', a statement that may have influenced the translators of the *Wycliffite Bible* who in the Later Version abandoned many prologues included in the Earlier Version.[164] Ullerston cites some examples offered by Bacon, namely the use of the letters 'IHC' in writing the name Jesus that results from a misinterpretation of its Greek spelling (64.1184–91).[165] Ullerston acknowledges the presence of errors in the Vulgate and comments that 'in this respect we do not measure up to our predecessors' standards', but nevertheless rejects Bacon's view that 'the texts which were once well translated are now defective', including the whole of the Bible and natural science (6.100–103). Ullerston comments 'But when he [Roger Bacon] goes further and states that true understanding is lost in translation, I deny that it follows, for we have just as much real understanding of the subject, for we understand it through words, as do those who know far better how to write them than to explain them' (64.1196–8).

C. *The Status of Vernaculars*

Ullerston demonstrates a wide awareness of the translations of scripture into different languages, mentioning those into French, German, Flemish, Spanish, Russian, and Armenian.[166] Discussing vernacular translations, he notes that one objection against them is that all existing translations were made into 'literary', 'grammatical' or 'structured' forms of various languages: 'we do not read that the saints and apostles wrote or translated into any but structured languages, and so they did not translate into demotic Greek, if by unstructured languages we understand the vernacular' (78.1473–6).

---

from the Old Testament, and Forshall and Madden (1950) do not record any glosses at these points. An exception is again Psalm 41:3 where a gloss attributed to Nicholas Lyra in Bodl. MS Bodley 554 explains that 'fontem' is a scribal error; see M. P. Kuczynski, *A Glossed Wycliffite Psalter: Oxford, Bodleian Library MS Bodley 554*, 2 vols, EETS 352, 353 (2019), 2. 98–9.

[164] 'For many prologues are placed in the text superfluously, since they are not prologues of the text giving an explanation of the translation of the books to which they are prefixed; but they are either letters sent to friends, like the letter of Jerome to Paul, which in the caption of the Bible is reckoned a prologue and is commonly so called, and yet it is contained in the book of Jerome's epistles; or they are prologues to commentaries on originals not to the text, like the one prefixed to the book of Ecclesiastes. For without doubt it is the prologue of the original itself and this is clear from its purport. And the same is true of many others which are not in ancient Bibles'; *Opus majus*, trans. Burke, I. 89.   [165] ibid. I. 108.

[166] Ullerston's awareness of earlier translations is further illustrated in section VIII below.

Ullerston repeatedly uses the term *gramaticata* to describe languages and seems to give it two meanings: 'cultivated', 'educated' and 'possessing a literary tradition' on the one hand, and 'structured' or 'rule-governed' on the other. He defends vernaculars by arguing that they can be 'grammatical' in both senses, both cultivated and structured. He firstly points out that sacred texts in the vernaculars existed in antiquity. Referring to the testimony of Nicholas Lyra, he argues that in the early church blessings and consecrations were in the vernacular (30.541–7). He also points out that the apostles, who were not formally educated and did not know the liberal arts, wrote in demotic Greek (80.1480–89). To him 'grammatical' (in the first sense, that is possessing a literary tradition) languages are not just Hebrew, Greek and Latin, but also Arabic and Chaldean because they have mathematics and sciences expounded in them, and English because Bede translated the liberal arts 'so that nobody would think the English people to be barbarians' (60.1102–5).[167] Ullerston gives numerous examples to prove the existence of a lengthy literary tradition in English encompassing theological and academic works.[168] He mentions the story about St Oswald's translating for bishop Aidan as told by Bede in *Historia Ecclesiastica* III 2 (32.587–91), as well as claims about Bede's own translations: 'You must be aware that our own Englishman, the Venerable Bede, inspired by the spirit of God, translated the Bible into the demotic English of his time (*in uulgare Anglicum sui temporis*), of which translation some copies remain in numerous English monasteries, as those who have seen it could testify' (34.598–902).[169] Citing Higden's *Polychronicon*, he argues that King Alfred was also an author of several translations and 'had Werfreth, bishop of Worcester, translate the books of Gregory's *Dialogues* into the Saxon language' (34.613–17). Ullerston mentions that he himself owns 'a tract in which the subject matter treated by the author of *De sphaera* is discussed, as well as the subject matter of the *Meteorics*, in very old

---

[167] A very similar statement that 'the venerable Bede translated the whole of scripture into English, so that his language would not be deemed barbarian' is found in Palmer's account of arguments in favour of the translation of the Bible (152.26–8).

[168] Ullerston's examples come from Higden and William of Malmesbury, see p. 34 n. 38. For further discussion see E. Solopova, 'From Bede to Wyclif: the knowledge of Old English within the context of Late Middle English biblical translation and beyond', *Review of English Studies* (2019), Advance Access Doi: 10.1093/res/hgz134.

[169] William Butler seems to be responding to a similar argument in his determination when briefly and without giving any background (clearly expecting the audience to know), he claims that the authorization of a translation by an important figure from the past does not mean that it should be recommended in the present: 'If it were established that some doctor among those approved or canonized [by the Church] had translated holy scripture for a particular people to read, or had admonished them to read it, we should not infer that it would still be desirable now' (124.164–7).

English which by now is incomprehensible to nearly everybody, and written by Bede or some other ancient father' (60.1106–10). This Old English text is most probably either Ælfric's *De temporibus anni* or Byrhtferth's *Enchiridion*.[170] Ullerston also mentions Richard Rolle's translation of the Psalter (38.695–7) and argues that a similar literary tradition in liberal arts and biblical texts exists in French (60.1110–14), and that if this can be done in French, it can be done in other vernaculars.

Having dealt extensively with the issue of literary traditions that enable vernaculars to be 'grammatical' or 'cultivated', rather than 'barbarous', Ullerston turns to the question of structure, arguing against the view that vernaculars have no grammar (80.1496–7). He believes that 'Grammar consists in the habit of speaking, pronouncing and writing a particular language correctly; grammar as a general property (*genus*) is not identical to the grammar of any particular tongue. So it varies in its particular manifestations (*species*), as is evident among the Greeks and Latins, and it is probable that any stable language has its own particular grammar; even if that grammar is not passed on in writing' (80.1497–1503). Ullerston seems to suggest that grammar encompasses certain universal properties that languages share, and that grammars of individual languages are the species of a common grammar. He also points out that speakers of vernaculars can distinguish between well-formed and ill-formed utterances and that this is evidence of the underlying grammar: 'Correct and incorrect usage can be detected in their own way in English as in French, and so the language has a corresponding grammar' (80.1508–10). Ullerston thus proposes a very modern principle of the rule-governed nature of language and of grammar as a shared characteristic of all languages, whose individual manifestations may vary but within certain constraints.

An interest in defining grammar in relation to its concrete realizations and concern with the unity rather than diversity of languages is generally characteristic of medieval scholars whose linguistic environment was much more varied than that of the scholars of classical antiquity.[171] Ullerston's immediate source for such ideas may have been Roger Bacon who was also interested in the universal properties

---

[170] *De temporibus anni* is the more likely as the more widely circulated text: it survives in eight copies, whereas *Enchiridion* in only one (also preserved are short exerpts from *Enchiridion* in two manuscripts, one of which was probably copied from the only surviving near complete text, Bodl. MS Ashmole 328). See Ælfric, *De temporibus anni*, ed. H. Henel, EETS 213 (1942); Byrhtferth, *Enchiridion*, ed. P. Baker & M. Lapidge, EETS SS 15 (1995).

[171] P. A. M. Seuren, *Western Linguistics: an Historical Introduction* (Oxford 1998), 29.

of human language. Bacon believed that the grammar of all languages was the same in substance, with divergences being merely accidental, resulting from the conventional nature of language.[172] This is evident in his comparison of Latin, Greek and Hebrew grammars and efforts to find analogies between them.[173] At different points in his Greek grammar Bacon undertakes a comparison of Latin and Greek, drawing attention to similarities in the structure of the two languages; similar comparisons can be also found in 'Study of Tongues' in the *Opus maius*.[174]

Bacon's and Ullerston's interest in linguistic universals is not unique. The school most closely associated with the idea of universal grammar is known as Modism.[175] The Modists were a group of scholars who studied and taught at the University of Paris and elsewhere in northern Europe in the second half of the thirteenth century and the first half of the fourteenth century. Modism was an attempt to establish a relationship between the structures of the real world, mental categories and grammatical categories of language. The term used for these categories was 'modes'. The 'modes of being' were thought to be mirrored in the 'modes of thought' and in turn in the 'modes of signifying' existing in language. For Thomas of Erfurt, who wrote *Grammatica speculativa* probably in the first decade of the fourteenth century, there is a connection between grammatical structure, logical structure of thought and the organization of the world.[176] The external world is understood by the human mind and grammar acts as a framework within which this understanding is systematized and represented. Language is therefore not just a matter

---

[172] 'Cupiens igitur exponere grammaticam grecam ad vtilitatem latinorum necesse est illam comparari ad grammaticam latinam, tum quia latine loquor vt in pluribus, sicut necesse est, cum liguam grecam nescit vulgus loqui, tum quia grammatica vna et eadem est secundum substaciam in omnibus linguis, licet accidentaliter varietur, tum quia grammatica latina quodam modo speciali a greca tracta est, testante Prisciano, et sicut auctores grammatice docent euidenter'; ed. E. Nolan & S. A. Hirsch, *The Greek Grammar of Roger Bacon and a Fragment of his Hebrew Grammar* (Cambridge 1902), 27.

[173] See S. A. Hirsch, 'Roger Bacon and philology', in *Roger Bacon: Essays*, ed. A. G. Little (Oxford 1914), 101–51.

[174] According to Bacon, 'Latin grammar was formed from Greek and Hebrew' (*Opus majus*, trans. Burke, I. 97).

[175] According to V. Law, *The History of Linguistics in Europe from Plato to 1600* (Cambridge 2003), 177, 'they were the first to enunciate, explicitly and consciously, the principles of universal grammar'. See G. L. Bursill-Hall, *Speculative Grammars of the Middle Ages: the Doctrine of* Partes orationis *of the Modistae* (The Hague 1971); I. Rosier-Catach, *La Grammaire spéculative des modistes* (Lille 1983).

[176] R. Harris & T. J. Taylor, *Landmarks in Linguistic Thought: the Western Tradition from Socrates to Saussure* (London 1989), 75–85; G. L. Bursill-Hall (ed. and trans.), *Thomas of Erfurt: Grammatica Speculativa*, The Classics of Linguistics 1 (London 1972).

of human agreement, but systematically reflects reality.[177] As a result, languages have universal properties that outweigh their accidental differences.

Ullerston's view that the vernaculars are as grammatical as biblical languages may have developed in response to the thirteenth- and fourteenth-century discussions of linguistic universals. These discussions were part of a long tradition of linguistic thought that anticipated a trend of modern linguistics to see the basic design of all languages as universal and forming part of a biologically endowed human linguistic facility.

D. Written and Spoken Language

A discussion of language occupies a less prominent place in William Butler's determination than in Richard Ullerston's, but it is nevertheless given a role. Butler's focus is the lack of explicitness in language, particularly in its written form. As part of his argument against biblical translation Butler cites Augustine's letter to Paulinus where Augustine observes that a passage from the Epistle to the Colossians[178] is ambiguous because its less-than-explicit meaning has to be supplemented from context: 'You have said that this passage is mysterious to you; nor do I understand it clearly, and I wish that you were here to ask me in person, for in the sense which these words seem to me to have, they rely on a facial expression and tone of voice, which cannot be conveyed in writing, to clarify their meaning to some extent, and so the text is difficult to understand because, I think, it is not correctly enunciated' (116–18.29–34).[179] Butler sees this as a flaw of the written medium as a whole, rather than an imperfection of a particular text. Extra-linguistic information, such

[177] The Aristotelian view that language is conventional was not acceptable to all, and speculative grammarians (Modists) are particularly known for their attempts to demonstrate the non-arbitrary nature of grammatical categories. Such attempts were criticized by William of Ockham, who argued in *Summa logicae* for the lack of one-to-one correspondence between linguistic categories and those of mental language. According to Ockham, universality belongs to thought and not to language, since thought is articulated in words that do not belong to any language (Law, *History of Linguistics*, 178–9).

[178] Col. 2:18–19: 'Nemo vos seducat, volens in humilitate, et religione angelorum, quae non vidit ambulans, frustra inflatus sensu carnis suae, et non tenens caput, ex quo totum corpus per nexus, et conjunctiones subministratum, et constructum crescit in augmentum Dei'.

[179] *Ep.* 149: 'You said that the words in the Letter to the Colossians, *Let no one mislead you by wanting to feign humility* (Col. 2:18) and the rest that follow are extremely obscure to you . . .'; trans. R. Teske, *The Works of Saint Augustine. A Translation for the 21st Century, 2/2: Letters 100–155 (Epistulae)* (Hyde Park, NY, 2003), 371; available in the Electronic Edition, 4th release (Charlottesville, VA, 2014).

as a 'facial expression', is unavailable and some features present in the spoken chain, such as many aspects of prosody, cannot be expressed. In Butler's view the written medium is also incapable of providing the necessary clues to differentiate words ascribed to wise and foolish, and to virtuous and vicious persons in Ecclesiastes, whereas it is possible to 'distinguish the different voices' when reading the text aloud with appropriate intonation and pauses (118.44–7).[180]

Butler argues that therefore 'hearing is a better, safer and more convenient procedure than reading' (120.72–3) and recommends that 'ordinary people should be advised not to aspire to read holy scripture, but to follow the counsel of James and be "swift to hear", rather than rashly presume to read it' (118.51–4).[181] Butler's distrust of written texts is given further authority with a quotation he attributes to Chrysostom: 'Chrysostom teaches us . . . that the pure in heart need no help from texts; they should offer a pure life, so that the grace of the Holy Spirit acts like a book in our souls' (130.273–6).[182] Butler argues that according to 'Chrysostom', 'God did not speak to Noah, or to Abraham and his sons or to Job or Moses, by means of writing, but directly in himself, finding them of pure mind; and by contrast, explaining why he gave the Law to Moses in written form, he distinctly says that the people of the Hebrews had fallen into a pit of wickedness, and he therefore ordained that they should receive it in writing and on tablets' (130.276–81).[183] Butler further explains, on the authority of St Paul, that there is a difference in

---

[180] The problem of distinguishing different voices also concerns the Song of Songs. In the manuscripts of the Vulgate this was achieved through the use of rubrics identifying speakers, but these were often missing or difficult to see because they were frequently in the same ink as the main text. The rubrics are used consistently, and tend to be prominent and in red in the manuscripts of the Earlier Version of the *Wycliffite Bible*, but this practice was abandoned in the Later Version in favour of gender-specific translations of Latin terms such as 'spousesse' and 'frendesse', presumably in order to avoid commitment to the interpretation of the text associated with rubrics (see M. Dove, 'Love *ad litteram*: the Lollard translations of the Song of Songs', *Reformation* 9 (2004), 1–23; Hudson and Solopova, 'The Latin text', in *ESWB*, 107–32, at 113). It is not impossible that the consistency of the Earlier Version results from attempts to make the written presentation more explicit, inspired by discussions of the written medium such as the ones preserved in the works edited here. The strengths and weaknesses of the written medium were clearly an issue of great interest to all three authors.   [181] James 1:19.

[182] Homily 1: 'It were indeed meet for us not at all to require the aid of the written Word, but to exhibit a life so pure, that the Grace of the Spirit should be instead of books to our souls, and that as these are inscribed with ink, even so should our hearts be with the Spirit'; trans. G. Prevost, *The Homilies of S. John Chrysostom on the Gospel of St. Matthew* (Oxford 1852), 1.

[183] 'Since unto Noah, and unto Abraham, and unto his offspring, and unto Job, and unto Moses too, he discoursed not by writings, but Himself by Himself, finding their mind pure. But after the whole people of the Hebrews had fallen into the very pit of wickedness,

the transmission of the Old Law and the New Law: whereas the Old Law was given on tablets, the New Law was communicated verbally to apostles (132.292–305).[184] Butler concludes that this way of communication is 'the safest possible, and the most appropriate to the age of grace' (134.328–30).

Written as opposed to oral communication and transmission are discussed by Ullerston and Palmer as well. The importance of this issue is evident both in its centrality to Butler's argument and in Ullerston's propensity to comment on it frequently and even repetitively. Relating Bede's story about Oswald translating for Bishop Aidan, Ullerston writes: 'But I ask you, what harm could have been done if the translation of King Oswald had been written down in English?' (32.591–2). Discussing a priest unable to preach and advised instead to translate Sunday gospel pericopes for his congregation, Ullerston comments: 'We deduce from this that anyone may lawfully preach the plain text of the gospel in the vernacular, and what a man can lawfully preach he can lawfully put down in writing' (36.635–7). Shortly afterwards he mentions this issue again: 'Doubtless, if it were lawful to preach the gospel, it would be equally lawful to write it down' (38.687–8). He invokes the authority of saints as he comments on this topic once more: 'If someone who heard one of the saints preaching through an interpreter were later to write down the interpreter's words, do you really think the saint would wish to say, "Stop, you are doing a stupid thing, write no more of this in the vernacular"? He would much more likely have rejoiced to see such desire to commit the law of God to memory' (42.774–8).

Ullerston discusses the written transmission of scripture even more fully further on, using examples later reused by Butler, but giving them a different interpretation. He cites an argument of an unnamed opponent that in the sermon on the Creed Augustine says that 'it is not lawful to write down the Creed, and men should not write it down in any circumstances even though they know it' (48–50.900–901).[185] Ullerston denies that this should be understood as

---

then and thereafter was a written word, and tables, and the admonition which is given by these'; ibid.

[184] 2 Corinthians 3:7.

[185] Sermon 398, cc. 1–2: 'Receive, sons and daughters, the rule of faith, which is called the symbol. And when you have received it, write it on your hearts, and say it to yourselves every day; before you go to sleep, before you go out in the morning, fortify yourselves with your symbol. Nobody writes a symbol for it to be read, but for purposes of recall; to prevent forgetfulness from deleting what carefulness has handed over to you, let your memories be your books'; trans. E. Hill, *Works of Saint Augustine*, 3/10: *Sermons (341–400) on Various Subjects*, 445. Hill comments on this passage in a footnote as follows: '*Symbolum* was a common word for a sign, or a token, or a ticket, and that is the meaning he is playing

a prohibition of recording biblical translations and points out that
Augustine himself wrote down the Creed, and the same was done
by Athanasius and many others. Like Butler, Ullerston observes that
the commandments of the Old Law were written down on 'tablets
of stone before they were given to the people' (52.953–4), but to him
this is neither a condemnation of the written medium nor a prohibition of giving scripture to the laity in writing. His interpretation is
different: the New Law, as a law of love, was firstly 'written by love
in the hearts' (52.958) of Christians, and only afterwards physically
recorded. Similarly to Butler, Ullerston observes that Christ taught
by word of mouth and the primitive church 'waited a considerable
time' before the New Testament was given to them 'in physical written form' (52.969–71), but his interpretation of this is again entirely
different from Butler's: 'So the law was written in the hearts of the
disciples long before it was committed to material writing, and Jesus
Christ, the wisdom of God the Father, did this for a very good reason,
namely to signify that he desired their faith . . . to be written in the
hearts of men indelibly through love, and not transitorily through
fear' (52.971–6, cf. 130–32.273–305).

Some of Palmer's arguments also seem to be part of the same
debate about the merits of writing—he responds to claims of its
inferiority, as well as to the view that the Bible does not authorize
the transmission of the doctrine in written form. Palmer does not
share Butler's perception of written language as an inferior medium
set aside for those who are not sufficiently 'pure in heart' to deserve
a better form of communication; his primary concern is not with
writing as such, but with the laity's ability to understand the whole of
scripture if given direct access to it. Palmer points out that 'the angel
admonished John in Apocalypse, chapter 10, "What you see, write
in a book"', but he is quick to qualify that not all parts of scripture
should be revealed to all: 'there are things, which should be written
down for some, but not revealed to others' (170.347–50). Palmer also
argues that according to the 'gloss' (*Glossa ordinaria*), the statement
'those things which the seven thunderclaps uttered, write them not'
in Revelation, chapter 10 is not an outright prohibition of writing,
but an instruction to keep the doctrine 'open to the friends of God
and closed to his enemies' (172.364). In an account of the arguments
in favour of translation, Palmer lists and leaves uncontested some
benefits of writing, such as its role as the only means of communi-

---

on here. The creed was seen as the sign of faith, a kind of password, I suppose, to the
mysteries, as well as a sort of ticket to heaven. Catechumens were forbidden to write the
creed down' (p. 455).

cating scripture to those who are deaf or dumb (184.607–9), and its usefulness as an aid to memory (152.10–15). This last is singled out as particularly important, as a way of ensuring that scripture, containing knowledge essential for salvation, will not fall into oblivion.

One of Butler's illustrations of the problems caused by writing is Augustine's discussion of two kinds of ambiguity, one in the spoken word and the other in the written (124.141–2). Butler believes that multiple meanings of the word *acies*, which Augustine examines as his first example of ambiguity, can cause confusion in both written texts and in speech: 'So if someone either hears, or reads, the word *acies*, he does not know whether it refers to a line of soldiers, a line [or edge] of a sword, or a line of sight' (124.142–4). Butler reproduces Augustine's account of multiple meanings of *acies*, but omits his qualification that the word is ambiguous only if used without context: 'anyone who reads it, may be uncertain, unless it is cleared up by a sentence'.[186]

Augustine's second example of ambiguity concerns only written texts: the word *leporem* as accusative singular of *lepus*, 'a hare', has a short [o] and is therefore distinguished in pronunciation from *leporem* with a long [ō], accusative singular of *lepor*, 'charm' (124.144–5). Since the vowel length is not indicated in written Latin, the two are homonymous in spelling but not in speech. Butler reproduces Augustine's example, but again omits his remark about the clarifying role of context. According to Augustine, one is cast into doubt as to the meaning of *leporem* only if 'there is no sentence in which it is placed'.[187] Butler ignores this qualification and uses the example to assert yet again the inferiority of writing, commenting that 'difficulties accumulate in the written text' (124.145–6).

Butler's arguments contradict not only the modern view that written language is generally more explicit than spoken language— spoken language tolerates opacity better because of its greater reliance on extra-linguistic information—but also somewhat surprisingly go against the spirit of Augustine's positive evaluation of ambiguity. For Augustine, ambiguity is not a flaw but an essential feature of the language of scripture: its particular richness and complexity assist

[186] Augustine, *De dialectica*, IX: 'Nam et si quis audierit "acies" et si quis legerit, potest incertum habere, nisi per sententiam clarescat, utrum acies militum an ferri an oculorum dicta vel scripta sit'; ed. and trans. B. D. Jackson & I. Pinborg, *Augustine, De dialectica* (Dordrecht 1975), accessed from Library of Latin texts, Series A (Turnhout 2010), 16.

[187] Augustine, *De dialectica*, IX: 'At vero si quis inveniat scriptum verbi causa "lepore" nec appareat qua sententia positum sit, profecto dubitabit, utrum paene ultima huius verbi syllaba producenda sit ab eo quod est "lepos" an ab eo quod est "lepus" corripienda—quam scilicet non pateretur ambaginem, si accusativum huius nominis casum voce loquentis acciperet'; ibid.

exploration and fuller understanding of biblical meaning.[188] Butler accepts that 'holy scripture is full of obscurities and ambiguities, and . . . of holy poetical concepts' (124.149–50), but nevertheless condemns ambiguity and lack of explicitness in ascribing them primarily to the written medium.

Butler, Palmer and Ullerston were not the only late medieval English thinkers interested in the strengths and weaknesses of written and spoken language. Such interest seems to have focused on numerous passages from the Bible that could be understood as condemning not only the literal interpretation of texts, but also the written medium, and affirming the spoken word.[189] The author of the *General Prologue* to the *Wycliffite Bible* uses St Paul's statement in 2 Corinthians 3:6 that 'þe lettre sleeþ'[190] in a traditional way, as a warning against taking only the literal sense into account. *Piers Plowman*, however, seems to display a distrust of written documents, dramatically evident in an episode with a pardon sent by Truth, but also in a satirical passage describing a deed of endowment drawn up by False in preparation for Meed's first marriage that granted the couple the deadly sins and an eternal dwelling place in hell.[191] In another episode a document shown to the narrator by Spes, even though containing commandments that saved 'of men and of wommen many score thousandes' and written with a gilt pen on a piece of rock, is nevertheless unsealed and has no validity without Christ's death on the Cross.[192] This may be a reflection of the distrust of script and the perception of the vernacular as primarily a spoken language that, as demonstrated with very rich material by M. T. Clanchy, accompanied the rise of literacy and the establishment of writing as a culturally dominant medium in the late middle ages.[193] This can, however, also be understood as a contribution to the debate,

---

[188] 'But Augustine gave a profound philosophical and religious dimension to the doctrines of the Hellenistic grammarians and dialecticians. . . . This new dimension entailed a crucial difference of emphasis in his view of ambiguity: ambiguous words are no longer a problem to be cleared up nor merely a figurative ornament so much as a resource for learning about the Creator and the created world'; J. Chamberlin, *Medieval Arts Doctrines on Ambiguity and Their Places in Langland's Poetics* (Montreal 2000), 24–44, at 31.

[189] For example, 'He has made us competent as ministers of a new covenant—not of the letter but of the Spirit; for the letter kills, but the Spirit gives life' (RSV, 2 Cor. 3:6); 'The words I have spoken to you—they are full of the Spirit and life' (RSV, John 6:63).

[190] Dove, *EAEB*, 63, l. 2196.

[191] A. V. C. Schmidt (ed.), *Piers Plowman: a Parallel-Text Edition of the A, B, C and Z Versions*, rev. edn, 3 vols (Kalamazoo, MI, 2011), 1. 62–6 (B2.72–107).

[192] ibid. 1. 636–8 (B17.1–47).

[193] M. T. Clanchy, *From Memory to Written Record: England 1066–1307*, 3rd edn (Chichester 2013), esp. 262–8 ('The Spoken Versus the Written Word'), 256–62 ('Symbolic Objects and Documents'), 309–18 ('The Symbolism of Seals and Crosses').

discussed earlier in this chapter, about the nature of meaning and its place of residence, whether in the mind, or in language, or in some material forms.

As pointed out by Anne Hudson and other scholars, Wyclif had little to say about the importance of the vernacular until the final years of his life.[194] In several works he argued that 'the teaching of Christ was not affected by language and that therefore the most familiar should be used' and this idea was taken up in several Lollard texts.[195] As demonstrated by Ian Christopher Levy, Wyclif's views on the relationship between language and thought were similar to the ones expressed by Ullerston. Wyclif compared human language to a garment in which God's law is clothed, and perceived languages as extrinsic, interchangeable and provisional, positioned at a distance 'from the meaning and law of the Lord'.[196] Wyclif did not have any special regard for English and saw human language and biblical codex, or the written medium, as a 'useful, but ultimately dispensable, set of artificial signs which point to the Eternal Truth'.[197] This is probably a reason for the somewhat surprising fact that, as Levy remarks, Wyclif 'only sporadically took up the question of biblical translation'.[198]

E. *Liabilities of English and Multiplicity of Scriptural Meaning*

Palmer writes more extensively than the other authors specifically about English, rather than vernaculars in general. Similarly to an unnamed opponent Ullerston argues against, Palmer believes that not all languages are 'controlled by the rules and forms of grammar' (166.270–71). He claims that scripture cannot be translated into such languages without error because its text is dependent on grammatical and rhetorical conventions and 'can only be rescued from inconsistency and untruth by recourse to figures of speech and grammatical rules' (166.265–7). The true meaning of scripture therefore cannot be preserved in a language that does not have the necessary rules and conventions. Palmer argues that English is such a language, but his way of demonstrating this differs from the arguments addressed and refuted by Ullerston.

[194] A. Hudson, 'Lollardy: the English heresy?', *LB*, 141–63, at 144–5 and references there.   [195] ibid. 152–3.

[196] I. C. Levy, 'The place of holy scripture in John Wyclif's theology', *ESWB*, 27–48, at 44. See also D. Lavinsky, "*De Pellibus Bestiarum*': scripture, realism, and material form', in his *The Material Text in Wycliffite Biblical Scholarship: Inscription and Sacred Truth* (Martlesham 2017), 23–66, on Wyclif's realism and his understanding of scripture, as *liber vitae*, a 'supralinguistic' transcendental foundation of Christian belief and practice.

[197] Levy, 'Place of Holy Scripture', 44.   [198] ibid.

One of Palmer's points is that the large number of monosyllables in English precludes the use of certain grammatical and rhetorical devices. With reference to the '*Catholicon de tropis*',[199] Palmer discusses the doctrine of permitted poetic licence or intentional use of linguistic deviations for artistic purposes. What is an error of pronunciation or grammar in ordinary usage (*barbarismus* or *solecismus*) can be acceptable in embellished speech as tropes, namely *metaplasmus* or *scema*. Similarly, metrical values of syllables in poetry may differ from their prosodic values in everyday language, thus justifying a 'wrong use of a syllable' for metrical reasons:

> . . . *barbarismus* is a fault, which consists in joining up letters and introducing one or more syllables or their accents, a fault to which vernacular speakers are particularly prone; but the *Catholicon* says about tropes, that *metaplasmus* [the alteration of a word by addition, subtraction or transposition] excuses *barbarismus*, which is a fault of speech; *scema* excuses *solecismus* [grammatical mistake], which is a fault of prose; and metre excuses the wrong use of a syllable (166.275–81).

Palmer argues that most devices described in the '*Catholicon*', involving 'adding or taking away letters or syllables', require polysyllabic words, whereas the majority of English words are monosyllabic, such as *ston, bon, non, don, gon, man, that, math, rat* (168.285–6). His assertion that English lacks polysyllables would perhaps be true for some forms of early Middle English, where mono- and disyllabic words indeed dominated as a result of the loss of Old English inflections due to phonetic reduction. It is, however, hardly justified in the late fourteenth and early fifteenth centuries when borrowings from Romance languages resulted in prosodically highly varied vocabulary, as evidenced, for example, in the works of Chaucer. Palmer was clearly thinking only of words of Anglo-Saxon derivation that constitute all his examples,[200] and perhaps had difficulty in conceiving of borrowed words as English.

Negative attitudes to vernacular terms, that were generally shorter

---

[199] Huguccio, *Magnae deriuationes*, ed. E. Cecchini, 2 vols (Florence 2004), 2. 768, s.n. *Meta*; 2. IIII, s.n. *Soloe*.

[200] The only word in Palmer's list that is not easy to identify is 'math'. It is most likely either modern 'moth' (Old English *moððe*) or 'mathe' (Old English maða/maðu, 'a maggot, a grub'). Both words are attested in Middle English and are probably etymological doublets that influenced each other, see MED and OED. Palmer's choice of terms is suggestive: whereas his Latin examples tend to be learned words, his English examples include words for animals seen as pests, such as 'moth/mathe' and 'rat'. This is probably yet another rhetorical device aimed at denigrating English, similar to comparing it to 'the grunts of pigs or the roaring of lions' (168.305–6).

than words of French and Latin derivation, reflect their perception as inferior to Romance borrowings, many of which belonged to abstract, stylistically elevated and learned vocabulary. Stephen Ullmann explains that in some languages, including modern English and French, there is a 'double scale' of synonyms: native words as opposed to learned Graeco-Latin formations.[201] Ullmann observes that the 'differences between the two scales are very consistent: the learned term is usually "colder", more formal, and more precise than the native', and this is true even when the two derive historically from the same root.[202] Palmer's comments are an early example of linguistic attitudes inspired by stylistic differences in English between vernacular and borrowed words, and correspondingly between texts that contain them.[203]

Another liability of English, according to Palmer, is that its phonological system is different from Latin and therefore some of its sounds cannot be adequately represented by letters of the Latin alphabet (168.303–13). One of Palmer's examples, that of the English dental fricative rendered in spelling by thorn, indeed demonstrates this, but his other example, that of yogh, confuses spelling and pronunciation. A semivowel represented by yogh, as in 'ӡonge', also existed in Latin and was rendered there just as inconsistently as in English with the letter 'i' that was also used to represent a vowel. Palmer is highly dismissive of the sounds of English on aesthetic grounds, comparing them to 'the grunts of pigs or the roaring of lions' (168.305–6) and idealizing Latin as a model of linguistic perfection.

---

[201] Stephen Ullman, 'Descriptive semantics and linguistic typology', *Word* 9 (1953), 225–40, at 233.

[202] Ullman points out that there are also examples of 'more complex arrangements involving a threefold scale: native-French-Graeco-Latin: *rise-mount-ascend*, *time-age-epoch*; here the French words occupy an intermediate position, being less formal than the learned terms but more formal than the native ones' ('Descriptive semantics', 233).

[203] Commenting on this passage from Palmer, Cornelia Linde cites research on Chaucer's artistic exploitation in *The Canterbury Tales* of stylistic differences resulting from the presence or absence of Latinate terms, see Linde, 'Arguing with Lollards', 235–54, at 244. According to M. Silk, I. Gildenhard & R. Barrow, *The Classical Tradition: Art, Literature, Thought* (Chichester 2014), 147, the large proportion of monosyllabic words in the first few lines introducing the Miller in the *General Prologue* is a literary strategy that emphasizes the 'boorish' character of the Miller. The monosyllabic words, however, were not always viewed negatively. The author of the *Cloud of Unknowing* asserts the usefulness of monosyllabic words, such as 'god' or 'love', as prayer words, arguing that the shorter they are, the better they accord with the 'work of the spirit' that is hindered by rational conceptualization normally present in the use of language. See a discussion of teaching on affective prayer in the *Cloud of Unknowing* in D. McCann, 'Words of fire and fruit: the psychology of prayer words in the *Cloud of Unknowing*', *Medium Ævum* 84 (2015), 213–30, at 222–6.

Yet a further problem with English, from Palmer's point of view, is the poverty of its scholarly vocabulary, an issue also discussed by Ullerston, as demonstrated above. English does not have words corresponding to commonly used Latin terms—Palmer gives Aristotelian categories, such as *substantia, quantitas, qualitas* and *relatio* as examples (170.317–20). Palmer expresses scepticism as to whether they can be adequately represented in English, observing that although English is 'richer than others in monosyllables, these terms can barely be rendered by a circumlocution' (170.321–2).

Palmer seems to believe that meaning is independent of language and even argues that some meaning cannot be outwardly expressed: 'Some portion of holy scripture can only be expressed in the mind, not outwardly in writing or in speech. We know this is true because the exultation of the mind can be so intense that it cannot be outwardly manifested' (176.427–8). Palmer admits that this point does not apply directly to the case under discussion, but is nevertheless highly sceptical about the possibility of adequate translation. He argues that even when two languages are both governed by grammatical rules, as is the case with Latin and Greek, the meaning cannot be fully transferred from one to the other. His example is the Sybil's prophecy, a verse text appended, in his description, to a sermon *De natali* that he attributes to Isidore of Seville (168.295).[204] The poem is an acrostic where initial letters of the verses spell out words, a feature that cannot be retained in translation.

Palmer advances his most powerful argument, pointing out that if the Bible were to be translated it would have to be translated either 'word for word' or 'sense for sense', but neither can be done adequately. The problem with translating 'word for word', from his point of view, is the lack of terms in English corresponding to Latin terms, and the impossibility of using rhetorical devices described in the '*Catholicon*' . Consequently if the Bible were to be translated, it 'would have to be rendered in circumlocutions' (170.325–7), but this is also impossible. Translation 'sense for sense' cannot be achieved because the biblical text has multiple meanings, including literal, moral, allegorical, and anagogical. Palmer accepts that one could argue that only the literal sense should be translated, but objects to this that 'there are various literal senses, according to different interpretations, and so the argument stands' (170.333–5). This point, that in order to be translated a text needs to be understood, but interpretations can differ even at the most basic literal level, is a powerful one indeed. Palmer does not claim that the same meaning cannot be expressed

---

[204] See above, 'Authorities Cited in the Texts', pp. lix–lx.

in different languages, a view vigorously opposed by Ullerston; his point is much more compelling—the complexity and multiplicity of meaning within the biblical text is not an imperfection or a one-off problem, and cannot be easily avoided. He sees the difficulty of isolating the meaning or meanings that need to be rendered in the target language as pervasive and, similarly to Augustine, fundamental to biblical language.

F. *Conclusions*

As pointed out earlier, a number of overlaps in the arguments of the three authors suggest that their contributions are related, whereas a cursory treatment of some topics, particularly evident in the shorter works of Palmer and Butler, presumes an audience familiar with the debate about biblical language. Thus the issue of writing the scripture down is introduced at the beginning of Palmer's determination, and later on the Bible is cited in support of the legitimacy of writing, but the nature of the problem is never fully explained. The same can be said about Palmer's brief observation that 'the venerable Bede translated the whole of scripture into English, so that his language would not be deemed barbarian' (152.26–8). This short comment does not give any details of Bede's translations and does not explain in what sense they may have rescued English from being barbarian. The remark would therefore be difficult to understand for anyone unfamiliar with other discussions of this topic. A reliance on the audience's knowledge of the terminology and logic of linguistic arguments in favour and against biblical translation makes all three works difficult for a modern reader.

Ullerston offers by far the most advanced analysis, displaying erudition in a wide range of topics in linguistic theory and philosophy of language. In contrast to the other two authors, much of what he writes would be entirely acceptable to a modern linguist, even if today it would be differently expressed. Ullerston's relatively short piece does not equal the scope or learning of the works of Roger Bacon, the most wide-ranging and prolific earlier English writer on language and logic, and his knowledge of languages does not match Bacon's knowledge. But Ullerston's independent and critical assessment of Bacon's views is nevertheless very impressive. His defence of translation and its techniques, such as lexical borrowing and the creation of new words, is perceptive and agrees better with modern linguistic theory than Bacon's highly idiosyncratic position.

Ullerston's achievement is particularly obvious when compared to Butler's discussion of linguistic issues that is much less scholarly

and focused largely on a single topic, the written medium. As in other respects, Palmer's contribution is the most puzzling. It uneasily combines ingenious examples, such as the untranslatable acrostic in the Sybil's prophecy, and important observations, such as the scale of problems facing translators due to the multiplicity of potential interpretations of the biblical text, with profoundly naive, though not unusual opinions, such as a suggestion that the phonological system of Latin is superior to those of other languages. Unlike Ullerston, Palmer never claims personal familiarity with earlier forms of English (see 34.598–602, 60.1106–10). It is difficult to avoid a conclusion that Palmer's determination is somewhat later than the other two, and that not being a scholar of the same calibre as Ullerston, he benefited from more learned and creative earlier discussions. Evidence of polarization of views visible in Palmer's comparison of English, repeatedly and respectfully referred to by Ullerston as 'our own English tongue', to 'the grunts of pigs or the roaring of lions' (168.305–6) agrees with Anne Hudson's observations on the hardening of opinions that led to the perception of any advocacy of translation as Lollard.[205] Though of different value, all three texts are important witnesses to the development of linguistic thought in late medieval England and demonstrate the prominence of scholarly discussions of language and translation in what is often seen as a primarily political debate.

[ES]

VIII. THE PARTICIPANTS' KNOWLEDGE OF EARLIER TRANSLATIONS INTO VERNACULARS

As pointed out previously, besides his natural concern as an apologist of biblical translation with the established *linguae grammaticatae*, the classical codified literary languages, Ullerston displays a notable interest in both current and ancient vernaculars. Some of his knowledge came from his reading: he found in the Clementines the decree of the Council of Vienne which enjoined university teaching of 'Chaldaean', that is Aramaic, and Arabic for converting the heathen (32.578–83), and in Higden's *Polychronicon* he found Bede's references to St Aidan preaching in Irish (*scotico*) with King Oswald's translation into English (32.587–91). Ullerston was aware that English had changed almost beyond recognition: as mentioned earlier, he had by him a work in Old English which was 'by now incomprehensible to almost everybody' (60.1108–9). More remarkably, Ullerston exploited his own social contacts to expand his awareness of other vernaculars.

[205] Hudson, 'The debate on Bible translation', 1–18.

This included an implicit perception of language families: the derivation of French from Latin was of course obvious to every literate person, and Ullerston noted, with reference to Bacon, the spread of the Romance vernaculars 'from Apulia and Calabria to the far reaches of Spain, and to the English Channel as well' (60.1115–16). He had learnt from 'a venerable German', who may well have been his colleague at Queen's, John Scharpe of the diocese of Münster, of Jacob van Maerlant's Flemish version of the Bible, and of 'Teutonic' versions too (32.592–5).[206] Another occasion, very possibly the visit of the Byzantine emperor Manuel II to London in December 1400 and January 1401, brought Ullerston into contact with an Armenian priest who had shown him a Psalter written in the Armenian language and alphabet (32.559–60); Ullerston noted that both the script and the sound of the language differed sharply from written and spoken Greek. Perhaps it was on the same occasion that he learnt of 'the Russians who have [the Bible and the liturgy] translated into the Wendish or Slavonic language' (*Ruteni qui Wandalico sive Slavico habent*, 30.555), from reliable travellers among them; but his use of the terms *Ruteni* for Russians and *Wandalico* for their language is more unusual. These were terms employed in German Latin sources, and it is likely that his venerable German had communicated them to him.[207] As *Wandali* was used of the Wends, or western Slavs of Lusatia, Ullerston and his source must have been aware of the relationship of their language to that of the Russians. Perhaps the same source had given him his information on missionaries in Livonia relying on translation into a local language (24.436). Ullerston's perception of the development of language among so many different vernaculars is one of his more notable contributions to the debate on translation. Earlier translations are also briefly mentioned by Palmer, who asserts that the Bible can already be read in Hebrew, Greek, Latin, Aramaic, and French (152.22–3). Below we outline some of the main events in the medieval history of the translation of the Bible into the vernaculars discussed by the participants—line references to such discussions are provided after the heading of each section. The difficulties of discernment between strict translation, paraphrase and versification should be born in mind, as also between efforts which covered only a single biblical book (or even briefer extract) and the complete whole.

---

[206] For images and discussion see *De Rijmbijbel van Jacob van Maerlant*, ed. R. E. O. Ekkart (Gravenhage 1985). For Scharpe, see above, pp. xxxiii, lvii.

[207] *Ruteni* was frequently used in German chronicles for the Kievan Russians, for instance in the *Annales Augustani, s.a.* 1089; ed. G. H. Pertz, MGH *Scriptores* 3 (1839), 133. For *Wandali* as a by-form of *Wenden* see H. Oesterley, *Historisch-Geographisches Wörterbuch des Deutschen Mittelalters* (Gotha 1883), *s.n. Wenden*.

Equally challenging is the anonymity of most translations and the obscurity of intended audience.[208]

A. *Germany and the Low Countries* (32.583, 32.593, 112.2083, 196.83, 196.92)

The first extensive prose translations into Dutch and German seem to have originated within the context of the Waldensian movement. Translations were also made for the Beghards and the Beguines, a movement popular from the last quarter of the twelfth century in both Germany and the Netherlands.[209] According to W. B. Lockwood, the New Testament and at least parts of the Old Testament existed in German in the thirteenth century, and it is not impossible that the whole Bible was translated before the end of the century.[210]

Jacob van Maerlant published *Rijmbijbel*, a free Middle Dutch verse paraphrase of the biblical narrative based primarily on Peter Comestor's *Historia scholastica*, in 1271, and between 1359 and 1390 *Bijbel van 1360* (*Hernse Bijbel*), a translation of almost the entire Bible from the Vulgate with the inclusion of some material from the *Historia scholastica* and other sources, was produced. It was the work of a Carthusian monk from the charterhouse at Herne near Brussels who has been identified as Petrus Naghel working for Jan Taye, a Brussels nobleman.[211]

In 1384 a very popular translation of the NT and Psalms into Dutch was made by Johann Scutken (d. 1423). It was accompanied by a translation of passages from OT used in liturgical readings and incorporated patristic commentary. In 1477 Naghel's translation of OT, without the glosses and corrected against the text of the Vulgate, was printed in Delft. Two years later a fairly literal translation of the complete Bible into Niederrheinish dialect was printed in Cologne and became widely disseminated in the Low Countries.[212]

A complete translation of NT into High German, the Augsburg Bible, became available in 1350 and a translation of OT survives in the Wenzel Bible that contains no NT material and dates from between 1389 and 1400. Other translations of psalms and select Old and New

---

[208] Deanesly stresses these problems in her account of medieval translations of the Bible in Europe, especially acute when only reference to the text was available, not a translation itself, 18–130.

[209] W. B. Lockwood, 'Vernacular scriptures in Germany and the Low Countries before 1500', in *CHB2*, 415–36, at 427–8.   [210] ibid. 427.

[211] P. W. M. Wackers, 'Authority in Middle Dutch', in *Translation and Authority— Authorities in Translation*, ed. P. De Leemans & M. Goyens (Turnhout 2016), 17–38, at 18–23.

[212] F. van Liere, *An Introduction to the Medieval Bible* (Cambridge 2014), 199.

Testament books in both High and Low German also survive from the fourteenth century, most dating from its second half. Particularly popular, preserved in over thirty medieval manuscripts, was the translation of the Psalter by Henry of Mügeln, which included a commentary derived from the *Postilla* of Nicholas of Lyra. In 1369 the emperor, Charles IV, issued an edict prohibiting German translations of religious books, and in 1375 a papal rescript was issued against vernacular scriptures in Germany, but these measures seem to have had no significant or long-term effect. Andrew Colin Gow observes that 'Other than in England, actual bans on making or owning translations of the Bible into the vernacular were generally local and temporary, or even equivocal: the decree of the archbishop of Metz of 1199 against "Waldensians" and their Bibles was confirmed by Innocent III but without expressly prohibiting Bible translations . . .'.[213]

The first printed German Bible, the Mentel Bible of 1466, based on a now lost manuscript, is believed to represent a translation made at the beginning of the fourteenth century. This Bible was extremely popular, and eleven new editions, with a considerably updated translation, were produced before 1500. It was superseded by Luther's version.

B. *France* (14.228, 32.583, 58.1060, 60.1110, 60.1113, 80.1508, 82.1522, 112.2083, 152.22, 196.83)

The earliest extensive prose French translations were interlinear glosses in the Psalter, attested in several manuscripts, including the Eadwine Psalter made at Christ Church, Canterbury, *c.* 1150–60.[214] More idiomatic translations of the Psalter were made in the thirteenth century. As C. A. Robson remarks, 'in France, the cause of biblical translation, like that of Aristotelianism a generation later, was rapidly won after initial ecclesiastical suspicion and even opposition',[215] and the way lay open for a complete vernacular translation that was achieved by the middle of the thirteenth century.

Bible du XIIIe siècle is a compilation assembled, probably in Paris, from earlier partial translations produced *c.* 1220–60. It was circulated not only in France, but also in England: one and possibly more

---

[213] A. C. Gow, 'The Bible in Germanic', in *NCHB2*, 189–216, at 198.

[214] For a recent overview, specifically examining the knowledge of French translations in England, see D. Russell, 'The European background: þe Bible and oþere bookis of deuociun and of exposicioun' in French', in *ESWB*, 49–65.

[215] C. A. Robson, 'Vernacular scriptures in France', in *CHB2*, 436–52, at 441.

of the surviving manuscripts is of English origin.[216] As Robson observes, 'French-speaking families on both sides of the Channel had a great and growing familiarity with Scripture in their mother tongue during the century before Wyclif'.[217] A very literal Anglo-Norman translation was also made; its most complete surviving manuscript, containing the whole Bible as far as Hebrews 13:17, was made for John de Welles who died in 1361 (Paris, Bibliothèque nationale de France, MS français 1).[218]

The *Bible historiale* was an expanded translation of Comestor's *Historia scholastica* by Guyart des Moulins, a canon of St Peter's church at Aire-sur-Lys between 1291 and 1295. Comestor's commentary was combined with translations from the Vulgate, particularly in NT. Starting with the early years of the fourteenth century, copyists began to incorporate into this portions of *Bible du XIIIe siècle*, eventually resulting in what is known as *Bible historiale complétée*. *Bible historiale complétée* was available in both France and England, and the kings of France encouraged and supported the orthodox translation and copying of the Bible broadly from the thirteenth to the fifteenth century.[219] Charles V and his brother, duc de Berry, had multiple copies of the vernacular Bible in their libraries. Due to its large size and extensive use of illumination, however, the ownership of the complete Bible, normally circulated in two folio volumes, was restricted to the wealthy. Robson observes that 'scriptural knowledge was never censored, merely rationed by the purse', though he also points out that at least one 'unpretentious' copy of NT from *Bible du XIIIe siècle* with simple penwork initials survives from fourteenth-century England (London, British Library, MS Royal 20 B. v).[220] *Bible historiale complétée* was eventually printed and had several editions between 1487 and 1545.

C. *Italy* (76.1425, 80.1479, 80.1480, 80.1488)

The earliest Italian translations of the Gospels and Psalter are believed to have been made in the mid-thirteenth century, though the first surviving manuscripts are datable to the turn of the fourteenth. The first copies of the complete or near-complete Bible, incorporating earlier translations, also date from the fourteenth century.[221] Until the middle of the fourteenth century the translations circulated

[216] Russell, 'European background', 54; C. R. Sneddon, 'The Bible in French', in *NCHB2*, 251–67, at 257.   [217] Robson, 'Vernacular scriptures', 448.
[218] Russell, 'European background', 56–7.
[219] Sneddon, 'The Bible in French', 266.   [220] Robson, 'Vernacular scriptures', 451.
[221] K. Foster, 'Vernacular scriptures in Italy', in *CHB2*, 452–65, at 452–4.

almost exclusively in Tuscany.[222] A large number of the surviving manuscripts were copied in Florence, most by the friars, particularly the Dominicans, but many also by laymen, members of the city's wealthy merchant class. This widespread copying of biblical books by laymen, often on paper, is a distinctive characteristic of the Italian tradition. Two editions of the complete Bible were published in 1471 in Venice; the first of these, a translation by the Camaldolese monk Nicolò Malerbi, partly a reworking of earlier versions, was very popular and often reprinted.

D. *Spain* (32.584)

Spanish translations survive in fourteen manuscripts of which only three are complete.[223] Only one goes back to the thirteenth century, whereas the rest were produced in the late fourteenth and the first half of the fifteenth centuries. Many Spanish translations, including most translations of OT, were made from masoretic Hebrew rather than Latin by Jews, and some were made for Jews.

General estoria produced in 1270, is partly a literal translation of the Vulgate commissioned by King Alfonso X and partly a paraphrase integrated with commentary, resulting in universal history and an encyclopaedia of universal knowledge. Other compilations also survive from the late fourteenth and early fifteenth centuries containing new and earlier translations made for the higher nobility. Gemma Avenoza observes that 'in general, kings and great lords promoted the vernacular translations', though there were also prohibitions against the vernacular Bible and the burnings of bibles in both Catalonia and Castile.[224] Such measures were aimed at heretical groups and, in the late fifteenth century, primarily at the Jews. The Inquisition attempted to remove the vernacular scriptures from the Jews to prevent them secretly practising their religion when Catholic monarchs intensified their efforts to unify the kingdom under one crown and one religion, forcing Jews and Muslims into obligatory conversion or exile.[225] The disappearance of the centres of study and the destruction of Hebrew bibles made it necessary for the Jews to rely on vernacular translations. Avenoza also notes evidence for a wide circulation of vernacular translations and attributes the scarcity of extant copies to Inquisitorial pressure.[226]

---

[222] L. Leonardi, 'The Bible in Italian', in *NCHB2*, 268–87, at 273–6.

[223] M. Morreale, 'Vernacular scriptures in Spain', in *CHB2*, 465–91, at 466.

[224] G. Avenoza, 'The Bible in Spanish and Catalan', in *NCHB2*, 288–306, at 289.

[225] Avenoza, 'The Bible in Spanish', 289–90.

[226] ibid. 290.

E. *Armenia* (30.557–8, 32.559–60, 32.569, 112.2084)

The first written translation of the Bible into Armenian was made around 406 AD from Greek and Syriac originals following the creation of the Armenian alphabet modelled on the Greek alphabet by Mesrop Mashtots.[227] These translations were revised and completed in the 430s after the Council of Ephesus (431). Biblical manuscripts in Armenian date from 887 onwards and show that both earlier and revised versions of the translation were in circulation and underwent a considerable degree of contamination. The translation was widely copied: according to S. Peter Cowe, 'the current statistics for the revised version are quite imposing, registering inter alia over 3,000 gospelbooks, 450 psalters and about 200 full Bibles'.[228] In the first printed Armenian Bible (1666) the text was harmonized with the Vulgate and supplemented with some new translations from Latin.

F. *Slavonic-Speaking Countries* (30.555, 32.568, 112.2083)

Missionaries and scholars, the brothers Cyril (d. 869) and Methodius (d. 885), have been traditionally credited with translating the Bible for the first time into a southern Slavonic dialect, though their translation may have been partial, comprising a selection of texts from the Old and New Testaments. The earliest Slavonic biblical manuscripts, presumably linguistically close to the original translations, date from the tenth and eleventh centuries. These copies are written in two alphabets, both based on the Greek alphabet: Glagolitic, believed to have been invented by Cyril, and a somewhat later Cyrillic alphabet, developed in Bulgaria at the end of the tenth or early in the eleventh century.[229] More manuscripts, increasingly reflecting regional developments in Slavonic languages and continuing work on translations, survive from the twelfth to the fifteenth centuries. The earliest extant complete translation of the Bible into Old Slavonic was produced in Novgorod in 1499 under the patronage of Archbishop Gennadius of Novgorod. It was a compilation made from earlier translations supplemented with some new translations.

One of the routes by which the knowledge of the Old Slavonic biblical tradition was disseminated in the West, and may have reached England, were the activities of Croatian and Bohemian scholars. Henry R. Cooper, Jr points out that, following earlier disapproval, Pope Innocent IV authorized in the late 1240s and early 1250s the

---

[227] S. P. Cowe, 'The Bible in Armenian', in *NCHB2*, 143–61.   [228] ibid. 159.

[229] Useful references may be found in H. Miklas (ed.), *Glagolitica: Zum Ursprung der slavischen Schriftkultur*(Vienna 2000), 207–26

use of Slavonic in the liturgy in Croatia where the Glagolitic alphabet was traditionally employed.[230] Cooper further observes that
in 1347 the emperor Charles IV invited some eighty Croatian Bene-
dictines to come to Prague to assist in establishing a Glagolitic-script,
Slavonic-language, Roman-rite community at the Prague Emmaus
Monastery.[231] Cooper notes that the Croatians may have been present
in Prague until 1415 or shortly thereafter, and that the monastery
where liturgy in Slavonic was practised continued to exist until 1611.
Cooper also points out that Methodius is commemorated as a translator of the Bible into Slavonic in the preface to the King James
Bible, and that the Old Slavonic biblical tradition and literacy were
known to Jan Hus and influenced his reform of Czech orthography,
as well as possibly his insistence on the vernacular for preaching and
scripture.[232]

Ullerston may have also known of the Bohemian efforts to make
scripture available in the vernacular. The earliest translations of biblical texts into Czech date from the beginning of the fourteenth
century.[233] The first attempt to translate the complete Bible from the
Vulgate into Czech was undertaken in the 1350s and 1360s, probably
with the support of ecclesiastical and secular authorities, and with
the involvement of several religious and academic centres in Prague.
The only manuscript of this translation to survive to modern times,
the Dresden or Leskovecká Bible, was destroyed during the Second
World War and is known only from photographs. Numerous further Vulgate-based translations and their redactions were produced
in Bohemia in the fifteenth century.

G. *Radical Prohibition in England*

Some secular and ecclesiastical opposition to vernacular translations
of the Bible and attempts to censor and restrict their production,
circulation and use existed in most European countries,[234] but as
pointed out above, such attempts had a local and temporary nature,
and England stands out in having a much more radical prohibition
that lasted over a century. Several factors seem to have contributed to
this situation: the time when the translations were made in England
following the Peasants' Revolt and the social and economic upheaval
caused by the Black Death; the association of the translations with
John Wyclif and his followers, and clerical opposition to Wyclif's

---

[230] H. R. Cooper, Jr, 'The Bible in Slavonic', in *NCHB2*, 179–97.

[231] ibid. 192, 194.   [232] ibid. 183, 195–6; see also n. 27.

[233] J. Sichálek, 'The European background: Czech translations', in *ESWB*, 66–84.

[234] On prohibition of Bible reading, see Deanesly, 18–88.

reformist ideas; and perhaps also the elite aristocratic background of two successive archbishops of Canterbury (William Courtenay and Thomas Arundel) that may have fostered authoritarianism and the lack of sympathy with the 'lewid' and 'simple'.[235] As the political situation in England was about to deteriorate, Ullerston argued against the dominant view of the role of the scripture in the spiritual life of the laity by observing that the study of the Bible is common among the Jews (88.1667–8) and is considered to be a duty of all, and not just the clergy.[236] Ullerston defends vernacularity and the need for the laity to understand the language of the scripture and worship by pointing to a rich tradition of biblical translation, vernacular liturgy and commentary over an impressively wide temporal and geographical span.

[ES and JC]

IX. VIEWS ON TRANSLATION IN LATE MIDDLE ENGLISH TEXTS

As translations and adaptations from other languages, many Middle English texts include comments on the methods and problems of translation, and it is instructive to compare opinions and arguments they preserve with those expressed in the Latin works edited here.[237] Several Middle English treatises dealing with translation survive, including the *Cambridge Tracts*, works of diverse origins published by Mary Dove, but most commonly comments on translation appear in prologues or introductory sections of verse and prose texts.[238] The most extensive discussions, including the *Cambridge Tracts*, undoubtedly occur within the context of controversial biblical translation, with the *General Prologue* to the *Wycliffite Bible* containing by far the most learned, sophisticated and detailed analysis of all

---

[235] 'The General Prologue to the Wycliffite Bible', in *EAEB*, ll. 2794, 1895.

[236] Butler seems to be replying to this argument by claiming the opposite on the authority of Nicholas of Lyra: 'among the Jews some prominent people knew the law and the prophets, and others of lower standing, that is the laity, know only what was necessary for salvation' (138.411–14).

[237] Different types of translated texts and approaches to translation are discussed in essays in *The Oxford History of Literary Translation in English*, 1: *To 1550*, ed. R. Ellis (Oxford 2008); a range of theoretical discussions is published in Wogan-Browne.

[238] The so-called *Cambridge Tracts* are an eclectic collection, and the term merely indicates the single manuscript (Cambridge, University Library, MS Ii. 6. 26) in which they survive; see Dove, *EAEB*, xxxiii–xlix, and ensuing editions and notes. In her introduction Dove suggests that the texts were deliberately assembled into a collection advocating the translation of the Bible in English (p. xxxiii), though they are not all Lollard in origin and the history of most is unclear.

medieval English works. The three Latin treatises, edited here, differ, due to their academic nature, from most Middle English discussions in their scope, as well as in their learning and the range of issues treated, and this is particularly true of Ullerston's determination. Ullerston's treatise is the only work to ask philosophical questions about translation, enquiring whether the meaning of the original can be preserved in another language and what makes this possible. These questions are not raised explicitly in Middle English texts, including *GP*, and their discussion is omitted in *First seiþ Bois*. Middle English authors tend to assume that viability of translation is proven by experience—as will be shown below, similarly to Ullerston, they commonly refer to earlier translations of scripture into different languages. Middle English contributions generally have a practical, rather than theoretical orientation—since many comments are found in prefaces, they reflect the opinions of practising translators, offering, unlike Ullerston, Butler and Palmer, their own work to be judged by the reader. In spite of the lack of extensive theoretical discussions, various assumptions about the nature of translation and language are made and widely relied on. In fact almost the full range of issues examined in the three Latin treatises, including the relationship between meaning and linguistic form, language change, polysemy, figurative language, the status of the vernaculars, and the advantages and disadvantages of the written and spoken media, are touched upon in Middle English discussions.

The author of *GP* clearly separates meaning and linguistic form when he argues that his translation should be judged by 'wise men' who 'knowen wel boþe þe langagis and knowen wel þe sentense of hooli scripture'.[239] The same is evident in his claim that the translation of the Bible can be not only 'open' ('clear'), but 'openere' ('clearer') in English than in Latin.[240] This claim is not only in opposition to Palmer's scepticism about the potential of English, but is much more radical than any made by Ullerston in defence of translations—though fully aware that the Vulgate is itself a translation, Ullerston tentatively admits that vernacular versions could be its equals, but does not consider the possibility that they could be its rivals. The author of *GP* has, on the contrary, great confidence in the truthfulness of the new and existing, rather than ancient or hypothetical, English version, and his and his collaborators' ability to identify and preserve meaning-bearing elements and not to sacrifice knowingly even 'þe leeste treuþe, ȝhe þe leeste lettre or titil of

---

[239] Dove, *EAEB*, 82, ll. 2863–4.
[240] ibid. 82, ll. 2862–8.

hooli writ þat beriþ substance or charge'.[241] He boldly invites critics to judge the English Bible and check the validity of his claims, though he seems to think of the work on translation as a process of collaborative enhancement, inviting critics to join in this undertaking and correct any errors.[242] Commenting on the existence of multiple translations in Greek and Latin, he asserts, in a line of argument unparalleled in the Latin treatises edited here, that the variety of translations is beneficial, because the diversity of interpretation compensates for the lack of certain knowledge. On the authority of Grosseteste he claims that it was God's will that many translations, made by different men, should be in the possession of the church for 'where oon seid derkli oon or mo seiden openli'.[243]

Both *GP* and the *Prologue to Isaiah and the Prophets* in *WB* acknowledge that the biblical text is at places 'dark' and frequently relies on 'figuratif speche'.[244] The author of *GP* includes an extensive discussion of polysemy that is significantly longer than one would expect in a text of this overall scope. An explication of figurative speech, the four senses of scripture and Ticonius's rules of interpretation occupy almost entirely chapters 12 and 14, and a large part of chapter 13. Both *GP* and the *Prologue to Isaiah* assert that literal sense is fundamental to understanding scripture and must be the basis for all other senses.[245] Much of the material from chapter 12 of *GP* on figurative language and the rules of interpretation recurs in the prologue to Matthew in the *Glossed Gospels* in Bodl. MS Laud Misc. 235, attesting to the importance of this topic both theologically and for the theory and practice of translation.[246] Though Middle English texts do not explicitly discuss the issue raised by Palmer—the difficulty of expressing multiple possible meanings of a text in translation (see p. lxxxii above)—the attention given to polysemy suggests the translators' awareness of this problem.

This is further evident in the insistence of the author of *GP*, with reference to Augustine's *De doctrina christiana*, that the richness of meaning and ambiguity are fundamental properties of the biblical language that act as a cognitive and hermeneutic device facilitating rather than impeding theological study.[247] Similarly to Augustine,

---

[241] ibid. 83, ll. 2892–4.

[242] ibid. 81, ll. 2843–9.

[243] ibid. 84, ll. 2929–31.

[244] ibid. 63–74, chs 12–13; 87–8, ll. 57–68.

[245] ibid. 74, ll. 2591–9; 87, ll. 40–46.

[246] Hudson, *Doctors in English*, cxlv; Dove, *EAEB*, 174–9.

[247] See Dove, *EAEB*, 65, ll. 2242–55, and particularly the following: 'And in hap þe autour of scripture seiþ þilke sentence in þe same wordis whiche we wole vndurstonde,

and unlike Butler (see pp. lxxvii–lxxviii above), the author sees complexity and richness of language as a gift, a divine investment in humanity's ability to develop and exercise their interpretative skills and critically understand their environment. As for translation, towards the end of chapter 15, discussing the rendering of 'equyuok' or polysemous words, the author asserts, again on the authority of Augustine, that the correct way to translate them is according to the 'sense or vndurstondyng of þe autour'.[248] This appeal to historical and linguistic context offers a possible solution to the problem of multiple 'literal senses, according to different interpretations' pointed out by Palmer (170.337–8 and p. lxxxii above): according to the author of *GP*, a translator should study the meaning of the text 'boþe bifore and aftir', that is a wider context of an ambiguous word or passage, and ensure that the rendering of polysemous words accords with the text's 'sentence'.

Ullerston acknowledges the presence of errors in the Vulgate and, as pointed out earlier, cites some of Roger Bacon's examples of misinterpretation, such as the abbreviated Latin spelling of the name Jesus, but nevertheless defends the Vulgate against Bacon's claim that the texts 'which were once well translated are now defective' (6.100–101 and p. lxix).[249] He also defends Jerome's translation against unfavourable comparison with the Latin translation of the Septuagint, preferred by Augustine, by pointing out that the Vulgate is the version endorsed by the Church, an argument apparently of decisive importance for Ullerston: 'if Augustine were alive now, when the Church privileges Jerome's translation over all others, he would choose it in accordance with the Church' (48.896–7).[250] The author of *GP* goes much further in his criticism of the Vulgate and is closer to Bacon in this respect, pointing out that all Latin bibles he had seen in his life were 'false' and needed correction.[251] As with Bacon, such confidence has to result from experience, most probably gained from research into the Vulgate text referred to in the description of the stages of the translators' work in *GP*.[252] The translators' claim

---

and certis þe Spirit of God, þat wrouȝte þese þingis bi þe auctour of scripture, bifor-seȝ wiþout doute þat þilke sentence shoulde come to þe redere or to þe herere, ȝhe þe Hooli Goost purueide þat þilke sentence, for it is grounded on treuþe, shulde come to þe redere or to þe herere, for whi what myȝte be purueide of God largeliere and plenteousliere in Goddis spechis þan þat þe same wordis be vndurstonden in many maneris, which maneris or wordis of God þat ben not of lesse autorite maken to be preued'.

[248] ibid. 84, ll. 2947–61.

[249] This defence is retained and further elaborated in *First seiþ Bois*; see below, pp. cv–cvi, on the possible reasons for this.

[250] Ullerston appeals to the authority of the Church as a way of resolving the debate elsewhere as well, see p. xxxi.

[251] Dove, *EAEB*, 81–2, ll. 2849–52.   [252] Dove, *EAEB*, 80, ll. 2802–11.

that they compared many Latin bibles in order to produce a corrected original is supported by a recent study of the two versions of
the translation and their relationship to the Latin text.[253] The work
on comparing Latin bibles and editing the source text apparently
took place not only at the initial stages of translation, but continued
throughout the project extending into revision. With the authority of
a practitioner, the author of *GP* gives a detailed account of the problems with the Vulgate text, including the disagreements between the
Latin and Hebrew versions, pointed out by Jerome, Lyra and other
commentators.[254] His solution is to supply glosses in the margins
clarifying the meaning of the Hebrew text, and he explains that he
did this most frequently in the Psalter where such disagreements are
particularly common.[255]

The merits of a 'word for word' as against 'sense for sense' approach is a practical and theoretical issue most frequently mentioned
in Middle English discussions, and there seems to have been a broad
consensus against strictly literal translation, rejected, as demonstrated above, by Ullerston and Palmer as well.[256] Jerome, an authority most widely cited in discussions of translation, unreservedly
advocated a 'sense for sense' approach for secular texts, arguing that
literal translation obscures meaning, but made an exception for the
Bible where he recommended a more literal treatment as a safeguard
against any alteration of the original thought and intention.[257] According to Jerome, the meaning of sacred texts transcends human
understanding, whereas their words and their order are a mystery that
needs to be preserved. The author of *GP* seems to advocate a middle
way between the 'word for word' and 'sense for sense' approaches,
asserting that the best way to translate is 'aftir þe sentense and not
oneli aftir þe wordis'.[258] Wishing to stay close to the source text, he
nevertheless privileges meaning over fidelity to the 'letter', observing

[253] See Hudson & Solopova, 'The Latin text', 120–26; see also Solopova, 'From Bede to Wyclif'.

[254] Dove, *EAEB*, 82, ll. 2853–60. These issues are also a common topic of commentary that appears in the margins of some Later Version manuscripts; see a discussion in 'The context of B 554', in Kuczynski, *Glossed Wycliffite Psalter*, xliv–lii.

[255] Dove, *EAEB*, 82, ll. 2856–60. For the use of commentaries by Nicholas Lyra in the Wycliffite Bible Psalter in Bodl. MS Bodley 554, see Kuczynski, *Glossed Wycliffite Psalter*.

[256] For a discussion of 'word for word' approach in Middle English translations, see R. Waldron, 'John Trevisa and the use of English', in *Proceedings of the British Academy* 74 (1988), 171–202; see also A. Schwarz, 'The meaning of *fidus interpres* in medieval translation', *JTS* 45 (1944), 73–8.

[257] I. Hilberg (ed.), *Ad Pammachium de optime genere interpretandi*, Corpus Scriptorum Ecclesiasticorum Latinorum 54 (Vienna/Leipzig 1910; repr. New York/London 1970), 508.

[258] Dove, *EAEB*, 81, ll. 2813–15.

that 'þe wordis owen to serue to þe entent and sentence, and elles þe wordis ben superflu or false'.[259] *Cambridge Tract I* similarly recommends translation 'sense for sense' and declares that translation 'word for word' is 'wel derk and perilos [in] vnderstondynge in alle langages', because languages differ in complex ways and a simple substitution of words in one with words from another will not produce a desirable result.[260]

A somewhat different position is taken by Richard Rolle, who sets himself an aim of using a literal approach as far as possible for pragmatic reasons, so that his work could serve as an aid in understanding Latin. In the prologue to the *English Psalter Commentary* he writes that he seeks no 'strange' English, but 'lyghtest and comonest and swilk that is mast lyke til the Latyn', so that those without the knowledge of Latin could understand many Latin words through the medium of English ('swa that thai that knawes noght Latyn by the Ynglis may com til mony Latyn wordis'). Despite asserting that he follows the 'letter' as much as he can ('In the translacioun I folow the lettere als mykyll as I may'), similarly to other translators he ultimately privileges sense: 'and thare I fynd na propire Ynglis, I folow the wit of the worde'.[261]

In the *Epistola* that together with the *Dialogue between a Lord and a Clerk* accompanies the *Polychronicon* in several manuscripts, Trevisa similarly expresses a wish to stay close to the original, but accepts that literal translation throughout is impossible.[262] He explains that to make a rendering 'cleer and pleyn' he will translate occasionally word for word, 'actyue vor actyue' and 'passiue vor passyue', keeping the original word order, that is preserving lexical, grammatical, and syntactic characteristics of the original, but occasionally will change all this.[263] He also points out that he left personal and place names unaltered and glossed some words—'yn som place Y mot sette a

---

[259] ibid. 81, ll. 2816–17.

[260] 'euery langage haþ summ apirtee [idiom] þat acordiþ not al wiþ anoþer langage worde for worde but sentence for sentence', ibid. 94, ll. 181–2.

[261] H. R. Bramley (ed.), *The Psalter or Psalms of David, and Certain Canticles, with a Tr. and Exposition by R. Rolle* (Oxford 1884), 4–5; Wogan-Browne, 246. See also Waldron, 'John Trevisa and the use of English', 186–7.

[262] The *Epistola* and *Dialogue* are found in five of the fourteen extant manuscripts of Trevisa's translation of the *Polychronicon* and were printed by Caxton in his edition of the *Polychronicon* in 1482; see R. Waldron, 'Trevisa's original prefaces on translation: a critical edition', in *Medieval English Studies Presented to George Kane*, ed. E. D. Kennedy, R. Waldron & J. S. Wittig (Wolfeboro, NH, 1988), 285–99. On Trevisa's views on translation see Wogan-Browne, 130–31; F. Somerset, 'The 'Publyschyng' of 'Informacion': John Trevisa, Sir Thomas Berkeley, and their project of 'Englysch Translacion'', in *Clerical Discourse and Lay Audience in Late Medieval England* (Cambridge 1998), 62–100, at 62–9.

[263] Waldron, 'Trevisa's original prefaces', 294.

reson vor a word to telle what hyt meneþ'—a practice reminiscent of intertextual glosses in *WB*.[264] Trevisa asserts that in spite of all such changes the meaning remained unaltered: 'Bote vor al such chaungyng, þe menyng schal stonde and noȝt be ychanged'.[265]

The prologue to *Pseudo-Augustinian Soliloquies* (*c.* 1390–1420), a translation of a French version of Latin meditations that originated in the thirteenth century, is another example of a practically-oriented discussion of the problems of translation.[266] The author observes that when translating from one language into another, some words have to be changed and sometimes words have to be added.[267] To illustrate the decisions he had to make he explains that he translated French 'vous' and 'vostre' with English 'ye' and 'youres' when referring to God and notes that some would object against this practice on the grounds that these forms are plural. He defends his use of plural, however, by pointing out that a biblical verse 'faciamus hominem ad ymaginem et similitudinem nostram' (Gen. 1:26) uses a plural pronoun, *nostram*, referring to God which is appropriate for three persons of the Trinity. In the spirit of Jerome's criticism of those who 'trifle with syllables and letters', cited by Ullerston (22.373), the author concludes that God pays attention to men's 'entent' rather than words, and that it does not matter whether a devout man or woman say 'the' or 'yee'—'for both is good and plesyth welle God'.[268]

Yet another short discussion of the practical aspects of translation occurs in the second prologue to Book I of *The Mirror of our Lady* (*c.* 1420–50).[269] Its author acknowledges that it is difficult to translate a lengthy text from Latin into English because many Latin words have no English equivalents, an issue commented on by Ullerston and Palmer. Similarly to the author of *GP*, he writes that he tried to keep both the words and the 'sentence' of the source text 'as farre as oure language wyll well assente', but when this was impossible, he privileged meaning.[270] The author of *The Mirror* also comments on polysemous words and, without giving examples, points out that they can have different meanings within the same clause. Other difficulties for a translator are deviations in the usage of individual texts from the recommendations of grammarians, and considerable linguistic

---

[264] On intertextual glosses see Solopova, *MWBO*, 19–21; M. P. Kuczynski, 'Glossing and glosses', in *ESWB*, 346–67; on Trevisa's possible involvement in the translation of the *Wycliffite Bible* see most recently A. Hudson, 'The origin and textual tradition of the Wycliffite Bible', in *ESWB*, 133–61, at 153–6.

[265] Waldron, 'Trevisa's original prefaces', 294.   [266] Wogan-Browne, 224–9.

[267] ibid. 225.   [268] ibid. 226.

[269] ibid. 258–65.   [270] ibid. 260–61.

variability in England where the language of one part of the country can be difficult to understand in another.

Similarly to Ullerston, Middle English advocates of biblical translation repeatedly point out that it relies on an ancient tradition. The author of *GP* comments that, according to *De doctrina christiana*, biblical translators from Hebrew into Greek can be numbered, but translators from Greek into Latin were so numerous that their number is beyond human knowledge.[271] The author mentions English translations of the Bible by Bede, King Alfred's translation of the beginning of the Psalter, and the translations used by the French, Bohemians, and Bretons.[272] The author of *Cambridge Tract I* points out that Christ's teaching was translated from Hebrew into Latin and Greek, and for the same reason translations into English should also be made for those who cannot understand Latin.[273] The author also observes that Jerome translated most of the Bible, and that the original recipients of this translation were women, Paula and Eustochium, and that other women were the recipients of Jerome's other writings—an observation also made by Ullerston (72.1339–41 and p. liii above).[274] The author further remarks that Augustine also wrote for laity and women—'to lordis and ladis and to holy wymmen', and Ambrose and Gregory did the same.[275] In the *Dialogue between a Lord and a Clerk* Trevisa mentions, in addition to translations by Jerome and the Septuagint, biblical translations by Aquila, Symmachus, Theodotion and Origen, as well as the vernacular translations into French. Within the English tradition he refers to King Alfred's translations of laws and the Psalter, Werferth's translation of Gregory's Dialogues, Cædmon's biblical poetry, Bede's translation of John's Gospel, and the Anglo-Norman text of the Apocalypse written on the walls and roof of the chapel of St Mary at Berkeley castle in Gloucestershire where he was chaplain.[276] Similarly to Ullerston, several Middle English texts appeal to the endorsement of translation by royalty and biblical figures. In addition to a number of references to King Alfred pointed out above, *Cambridge Tract I* invokes the legend about the authorization of the Septuagint by Ptolemy Philadelphus[277] and points out that St Bartholomew translated Matthew's Gospel into the language of the Indians, a legend based on the

---

[271] Dove, *EAEB*, 83, ll. 2920–24.   [272] ibid. 81, ll. 2932–41.

[273] ibid. 92, ll. 125–32.

[274] The same point is made by the author of *Opus arduum*, in Brno, Masaryk University Library, MS Mk 28, fols. 136v–137r; A. Hudson, 'Lollardy: the English heresy?', in *LB*, 141–63, at 152 n. 41.   [275] Dove, *EAEB*, 96–7, ll. 277–88.

[276] Waldron, 'Trevisa's original prefaces', 292.

[277] Dove, *EAEB*, 96, ll. 249–55; 204.

Legenda aurea.[278] Several works, including the *Cambridge Tracts I* and *VII*, and *Pater Noster II*, argue that Christ and his apostles taught people in their own language.[279]

Middle English authors occasionally comment on the audience for translations, whom they usually perceive, similarly to the authors of the three Latin treatises, as the laity and less educated clergy with insufficient knowledge of Latin. Perhaps the most original discussion that breaks away from the narrowly utilitarian view of translations as a substitute for Latin, and attempts to explain why they can be of interest to a well-educated audience, occurs in Trevisa's *Dialogue*. Trevisa's Lord refutes the Clerk's assertion that translations into English are unnecessary because Latin is used internationally and is therefore understood widely, whereas English is understood only locally. The Lord comments on the usefulness of translations for preaching and, most importantly, points out that the *Polychronicon* contains much Latin that cannot be understood even by those who can read it, without study and 'lokyng of oþer bokes'. This elevates translation to a form of commentary on the original that facilitates its study by a Latinate reader. Addressing the question of the medium, discussed by Ullerston, Butler and Palmer, Trevisa's Lord argues that it would be better if translations were written down, rather than 'yseyd and noȝt ywryte', to ensure their preservation. In response to the Clerk's observation that a translation can contain errors, he replies that imperfect translations can be improved, and this is the reason why Origen made two, and Jerome three, translations of the Psalter.[280] This comment seems to anticipate the making of two versions of the Bible by Oxford translators, possibly including Trevisa, and evokes the remarks of the author of *GP* on revision and correction as an essential part of his and his colleagues' work.

Caxton comments on the art of translation in many of his prologues and describes it as 'a noble and a meritorious dede',[281] deserving 'a singuler lawde and thank',[282] because it gives access to information previously unavailable in English, such as the wise sayings of philosophers or works of moral instruction. One of his main concerns is the choice of an appropriate language and style that he links to the question of audience. In the preface to *Eneydos* (c. 1490) he describes himself as being criticized by 'some gentylmen' for

---

[278] ibid. 93, ll. 144–6; 203.

[279] ibid. 96, ll. 272–7; 118–19, ll. 26–31; 162, ll. 52–4; cf. Acts 2:6–17 and the glosses to this in Oxford, New College, MS 67.

[280] Waldron, 'Trevisa's original prefaces', 292–3.

[281] Epilogue to *Cordial*, ll. 48–9; N. F. Blake, *Caxton's Own Prose* (London 1973), 71.

[282] Epilogue to *Dicts or Sayings*, ll. 19–20; Blake, *Caxton's Own Prose*, 73.

using in his translations 'over-curyous termes whiche coude not be understande of comyn peple' and being advised to use 'olde and homely termes'.[283] Caxton accepts that common terms are easier to understand, but points out that he is writing for a learned audience of clerks and gentlemen, thus envisaging, similarly to Trevisa, an educated reader for his translation.[284] He describes himself as choosing a middle way between elaboration and simplicity, and translating 'into our Englysshe not over-rude ne curyous, but in suche termes as shall be understanden by Goddys grace accordynge to my copye'.[285]

Middle English authors occasionally comment on the status of vernaculars advocating their equality with 'biblical' languages, though a common argument is that language simply does not matter, being external to meaning—an approach that avoids the issue of 'grammaticality' of the vernaculars aptly discussed by Ullerston. *Cambridge Tract I* asserts that God understands all his children independently of how they speak, just as a mother understands a child who pronounces words incorrectly,[286] and according to *Pater Noster II*, whereas it is important that people know prayers and the gospel, it does not matter how these are communicated to them, in Latin, English, French or Dutch.[287] According to *Cambridge Tract VII*, 'þe trouþe of God stondiþ not in oo langage more þan in anoþer',[288] and in the opinion of the author of *GP* there is no fundamental difference of status between English and Latin because Latin was 'a comyne langage' of the people when the Bible was translated into it, and when biblical commentaries were written by Augustine and other scholars.[289] Negative comments about English are rare but occasionally also occur. Thus the author of *Pseudo-Augustinian Soliloquies* described English as 'boystous',[290] defined as 'rude', 'harsh', 'artless' and 'simple' in *MED*, and Chaucer in the

[283] Blake, *Caxton's Own Prose*, 79, ll. 26–31. 'Curious'—'subtle, sophisticated; abstruse, recondite' (*MED*).

[284] In the prologue to *Doctrinal of Sapience*, however, Caxton writes that the work is necessary 'for symple prestes that understonde not the scriptures' and that 'it is made for symple peple and put into Englissh'; Blake, *Caxton's Own Prose*, 77, ll. 1–4

[285] ibid. 80, ll. 72–5. Caxton makes a similar point in several of his prologues, including the *Prologue to Of Old Age* where he writes that the book is intended for 'lordes, gentilmen and marchauntes' and not 'for every rude and symple man' (Blake, *Caxton's Own Prose*, 121, ll. 67–72).

[286] Dove, *EAEB*, 98, ll. 349–52; see also 118–19, ll. 30–35.

[287] ibid. 162, ll. 54–9.

[288] ibid. 118, ll. 1–2.

[289] ibid. 83, ll. 2914–19.

[290] Wogan-Browne, 225.

Complaint of Venus remarks that rhyme is so 'scarce' in English that it is difficult for a poet to render 'worde be worde' a complex French original.[291]

Chaucer offers, however, a spirited defence of the vernaculars in the preface to *A Treatise on the Astrolabe*, that seems to echo both the preface to Rolle's *English Psalter* and *GP*, perhaps suggesting knowledge of both these texts. Chaucer asserts that the same information can be adequately expressed in different languages by pointing out that he is providing the same 'trewe conclusions' for his reader in English, as are available for Greeks in Greek, for Arabs in Arabic, for a Jew in Hebrew and for Romans in Latin.[292] In the spirit of Ullerston's defence of translation of sciences against Bacon's criticism (pp. lxvi–lxvii above), he argues that astronomy was translated into Latin from 'othere dyverse langages', and that in all these languages, in spite of their differences, it was successfully taught and understood. Chaucer defines his task as showing his son, in what, like Richard Rolle, he describes as his 'lighte English', the full range and complexity of the meaning of the original: 'not oonly as trewe but as many and as subtile conclusiouns, as ben shewid in Latyn in eny commune tretys of the Astrelabie'.[293] This wording curiously parallels a similar statement of purpose in *GP* to 'make þe sentence as trewe and open in Englisch as it is in Latin, or more trewe and more open þan it is in Latyn'.[294] Finally, in an assertion that elevates English, Chaucer asks God to save the king whom he defines as the 'lord of this langage', described in the notes to the *Riverside Chaucer* as the first known occurrence of the notion of the 'King's English'.[295]

An overlap of material between Middle English works and treatises edited here attests to a widespread interest in the theory and practice of translation, and audiences' familiarity with ideas discussed in the university context and arguments used in such debates. Unlike the texts edited here, not all Middle English treatments are polemical, even among those close in date to the Latin works, and some focus entirely on scholarly, technical and artistic aspects of vernacular versions. As attested by Trevisa's *Dialogue*, however, translation appeared controversial to many, and not just of religious, but probably of all texts. Increasing politicization of the question of the legitimacy of translation and the importance of the issues of authorization and access to translated works, that overshadow academic concerns, can

---

[291] *Riverside Chaucer*, 649, l. 81.
[292] *A Treatise on the Astrolabe*; *Riverside Chaucer*, 662, ll. 28–33.
[293] ibid. ll. 51–5.
[294] Dove, *EAEB*, 81, ll. 2844–6.
[295] *Riverside Chaucer*, 1095.

be seen in the *Cambridge Tracts*, but is nowhere more evident than in the Middle English adaptation of Ullerston's determination discussed below.

[ES]

X. *FIRST SEIÞ BOIS*. A MIDDLE ENGLISH ADAPTATION OF RICHARD ULLERSTON'S DETERMINATION

First seiþ Bois is a contemporary Middle English adaptation of parts of Richard Ullerston's determination. Internal evidence reveals that it was written after the death of Richard II in 1400 (200.209–10) and presumably after 1401, the manuscript date of Ullerston's treatise, but before 1414 for Arundel is still archbishop (201.220). As Mary Dove observes, Arundel is said to have approved Queen Anne's Gospels after she submitted them to him (201.226–7) which suggests knowledge of the terms of the Constitutions of 1407.[296] In fact, it seems likely that the author was writing soon after 1407 and in response to Arundel's Constitutions: this would explain the different focus of the discussion of translation in comparison with Ullerston's.

It is unclear who the author was, but he was probably a scholar with a background similar to Ullerston's. He is unlikely to have been anyone close to Ullerston to whom he refers in an impersonal and distant manner as 'a clerk', a reference that appears at the end of the discussion of a priest who could not preach (197.133). *Bois* is much shorter than Ullerston's determination—it is only about one seventh of the latter's length. The structure of the determination was not retained: *Bois* does not present the material in the same sequence as Ullerston, does not have any internal subdivisions characteristic of Ullerston's treatise, and the arguments of the opposite side, though frequently rehearsed, are not given as numbered points or otherwise organized as a list. *Bois* is by no means a straight translation of the Latin original, but an adaptation, involving a considerable reworking and abbreviation, as well as the addition of new material.

Bois is much less learned than its source. The author leaves out most academic content, central to Ullerston's argument, and puts emphasis on the polemical side of the debate. Thus the questions of what makes translation from one language to another possible are entirely left out, and the discussion of an equal potential of languages and their 'grammaticality' is reduced to a minimum. The

---

[296] Dove, *EAEB*, li.

parts of the argument that are retained and developed are those of particular interest to the laity, including the education of the laity and children, lay ability to understand devotional and liturgical texts, and particularly lay access to scripture. The legitimacy of lay access to scripture is argued strongly and supported by references to the Bible, including an example of Ezra reading to the people, and quotations from Deuteronomy 32:7, 1 Peter 3:15 and 4:10, and the Revelation 22:17, the last two not in Ullerston. The same is further supported by an example of the Jews who have the Bible in Hebrew and among whom both lay people and priests are knowledgeable about scripture (199.165–70).

Defending the potential of the vernaculars to cope with the ideas and material found in the Bible, both Latin and English treatises observe that the apostles were not educated in liberal arts and therefore wrote in demotic Greek. But whereas Ullerston cites Acts 4 to prove that the apostles, being 'unlearned', wrote in the language of the people, the author of *Bois* goes further and argues that clerical education is not and should not be the only source of knowledge. He points out that, though 'rude men and fischeris', the apostles 'legeden þe prophecies', and cites in support of this: Acts 1:16, where Peter says that the betrayal of Judas was prophesized by David; Acts 2:16–17, where Peter speaks of Joel's prophecy that God will pour his spirit 'vpon iche flesche'; and Acts 15:16, where James cites Amos 9:11 ('aftur þes þings I schal turne aȝene') on the need of a mission to the gentiles (194.45–6). None of this material is in Ullerston. The author of *Bois* concludes this discussion by observing that the apostles, 'cleped ydiotes be scripture' ('homines essent sine litteris et ydiote' in Ullerston, 80.1484–5), could cite the Old Testament and that lay people in the Old Testament knew the law, even though, according to Genesis 11, after the Tower of Babel they no longer all spoke the same language (194.49–50).

Considerable attention is given not only to lay religious education authorized by the biblical precedent, but also to the question of whether it is legitimate for the laity 'to prophesie'—'to speak by divine inspiration' and 'to expound or interpret holy mysteries by means of divine inspiration'.[297] An interest in this question is evident in the story of Eldad and Medad, derived from a passage where Ullerston defends religious education of the laity and argues that 'we

should not so much fear their superior knowledge, but much more their ignorance' (70.1308–9). The author of *Bois*, however, does not stop at this and advocates the lay right to teach, offering quotations, all of them independent of Ullerston, from 1 Corinthians, 1 Peter, and Joel. Whereas Ullerston cites 1 Cor. 14:13, 'therefore, one who speaks in a tongue should pray that he may interpret', the author of *Bois* cites a more radical 1 Cor. 14:5: 'I wole euery man to speike with tunges; more, forsoþe, to profecie' (195.67–8).[298] Deviating from his source, he also cites 1 Peter 3:15 on everyone's, not just priestly, responsibility to 'minister' and teach God's law (194.31–2), and Joel 2:28 on everyone's duty 'to prophecie': 'I shal schede ou3t of my spirite vpon iche flesche; 3oure sones and 3oure dou3tteris schulen prophecie and 3oure 3onge men schullen se viciouns' (194.42–4). This is an important departure from the position taken by Ullerston of firm rejection of lay and particularly women's right to minister and teach: 'But if the laity usurp the office of the teacher, which is the prerogative of priests alone, they should be restrained by the prelates of the church' (68.1267–8).

The main exception to the tendency of the author of *Bois* to reduce academic content of Ullerston's treatise is the attention given to the defence of the Vulgate against any criticism. Though, as pointed out earlier, such defence is important for Ullerston, this is an area where the adaptation exceeds the source. A possible reason for such an interest in Jerome's translation is again the likelihood that the treatise was written in the aftermath of Arundel's Constitutions and in response to them. The preamble to the seventh article of the Constitutions, restricting new biblical translation, cites Jerome's account of the dangers of translation, and his confession that he often erred.[299] The discussion of Jerome's translation in *Bois* is considerably developed in comparison to its treatment by Ullerston, and given the flavour of a contemporary public and political debate. The author mentions Friar Tille, further discussed below, who gave a sermon before the bishop of London claiming that Jerome erred in his translation. Tille is compared to Elymas, the sorcerer in Acts 13, who went blind after trying to hinder St Paul and his companions' preaching Christianity on Paphos. Not satisfied with Ullerston's explanation that Jerome, though confident that he did not change anything in the 'Hebrew truth' himself, knew that nothing could

[298] 'Volo autem omnes vos loqui linguis: magis autem prophetare' in the Vulgate.

[299] 'Periculosa quoque res est, testante beato Jeronymo, textum sacrae scripturae de uno in aliud idioma transferre, eo quod in ipsis translationibus non de facili idem in omnibus sensus retinetur, prout idem beatus Jeronymus, et si inspiratus fuisset, se in hoc saepius fatetur errasse . . .'; Wilkins, I. 317.

stop the scribes from altering his text, the author of *Bois* cites the
Prologue to Kings directly: 'For Ierom seiþ in þe prolog of Kyngis
"I am not knowyng to myself in any maner me to haue changyd
anyþinge from þe Ebrew trewiþ. Wel I wot," he seide, "sum tyme þat
holy writ was false aftur þe letter"' (200.188–9).[300] The author also
refers to Jerome's letters to Augustine,[301] claiming that, following
this correspondence, Jerome was 'glad and joyeful of his translacioun'
and cites prologues to Pentateuch and Joshua where Jerome defends
his translation (200.195–204).

Mary Dove characterized the author of *Bois* as 'probably a Wycliffite' and this description, though lacking precision, seems justified if
only because of the treatise's likely date.[302] Whereas, as pointed out
earlier, Ullerston must have been writing at a time when advocacy of
the Bible in English was not perceived as inherently unorthodox, the
situation after Arundel's Constitutions was different—the Constitutions explicitly prohibited contemporary translations of the Bible.
Dove observes that in most manuscripts *First seiþ Bois* is combined
with Lollard material, reflecting its perception as a text advocating
the Lollard cause, though rather surprisingly in New York, Pierpont
Morgan Library, MS 648 it accompanies Nicholas Love's *Mirror of
the Blessed Life of Jesus Christ*.[303]

The author's citations are also significant for the question of his
sympathies—*Bois* shares authorities with Wycliffite texts. Though
references to Grosseteste, Fitzralph and Gaytryge derive from Ullerston, they are preserved, whereas many others are omitted, including
all references to Roger Bacon. Grosseteste was frequently cited by
Wyclif, and Anne Hudson has drawn attention to the impressive
length and diversity of such quotations, as well as to references independent of Wyclif in several Lollard compilations.[304] *Summa de*

---

[300] Note the closeness of *Bois* to the *Wycliffite Bible* here, including the use of a construction approximating the Latin 'accusative with infinitive' ('me to haue chaungid eny
thing fro Ebrews trewth'; EV, FM 2. 5). The 'accusative with infinitive' is found in this
line from the Prologue to Kings in both EV and LV, but is generally typical of EV and
mostly abandoned in LV; for the construction see H. Yonekura, *The Language of the
Wycliffite Bible: the Syntactic Differences between the Two Versions* (Tokyo 1985), 395–400.
See also Hudson, 'Origin and textual tradition', 136–9, on the particular literalness of the
EV translation of the prologues, that considerably exceeds that of the biblical text.

[301] Dove, *EAEB*, 217.   [302] ibid. li.

[303] ibid.; see a description of MS 648 below.

[304] Hudson has pointed out that Wyclif read a wider range of Grosseteste's works than
is provable by quotation in any other contemporary writer, perhaps accessing them in
the library of the Oxford Franciscan house. She also observes that Lollard citation of
Grosseteste was widespread and usually signalled, and that by far the most common
references were from his sermons (as in *Bois*) and dicts. The texts in which they are most
prevalent are the *Floretum*, *Rosarium*, and the *Glossed Gospels*. See A. Hudson, 'Wyclif

questionibus Armenorum is the only work of Richard Fitzralph's used by the compilers of the *Glossed Gospels*,[305] whereas the *Lay Folks' Catechism*, attributed in several medieval sources to John Gaytryge, seems to have been circulated in Lollard contexts: in several collections it is combined with Lollard texts and contains modifications reflecting Lollard views.[306]

Also relevant to the question of the author's views is his exceedingly critical mention of Friar Tille. Mary Dove tentatively identifies him as John Dille, provincial of the Dominican friars in England in 1413, but seems unaware of important biographical details provided in Emden's entry for Dille and sources cited there, that make the identification more secure and the reference highly suggestive.[307] Dille is mentioned in 1408 and 1412 as prior of the London convent that played a prominent part in the Wycliffite controversy. The council of 1382 was held at the London Blackfriars, and the prior, William Syward, and two others of the convent were chosen to take part in the proceedings. The examination of Sir John Oldcastle for heresy in 1413 took place there as well, and the convent's intimate connection with the court is evident in the appointment of Dille as the confessor of Henry IV at the end of his reign in 1413. Dille's own position in the debate over Lollardy, that may have provoked the hostility of the author of *Bois*, is evident in his participation in the trials of prominent Lollards, William Taylor in 1423 and Ralph Mungyn in 1428, when he was still resident in the London convent. These events postdate

---

and the Grosseteste legacy at Oxford Greyfriars', in *Robert Grosseteste: His Thought and its Impact*, ed. J. P. Cunningham (Toronto 2012), 201–216, at 202.

[305] Hudson, *Doctors in English*, cix–cx.

[306] The *Lay Folks' Catechism* is a longer English version of a Latin injunction issued by John Thoresby who became archbishop of York in 1353. The exact relationship between the two texts, Latin and English, is uncertain, but Ullerston's determination and *Bois* contain two (though not independent) of several medieval attributions of the *Catechism* to John Gaytryge, usually identified as a Benedictine monk at St Mary's abbey in York. Wishing to improve sacerdotal education of the laity, Thoresby published the injunction in 1357, suggesting the items on which teaching was needed, including the articles of the faith, the commandments, the works of mercy, the cardinal virtues, the sacraments, and the deadly sins, with a brief exposition of each. The *Catechism* was relatively widely circulated and survives in twelve manuscripts containing the full version and six containing extracts. A. Hudson, 'A new look at the Lay Folks' Catechism', *Viator* 16 (1985), 243–58; 'The Lay Folk's Catechism; a postscript', *Viator* 18 (1988), 307–309'; S. Powell, 'The transmission and circulation of the Lay Folk's Catechism', in *Late-Medieval Religious Texts and their Transmission. Essays in Honour of A. I. Doyle*, ed. A. J. Minnis(Woodbridge 1994), 67–84.

[307] Dove, *EAEB*, 217. The friar is rather unhelpfully listed only once as 'Tille, John' in *BRUO* 1876, making the information difficult to find. Multiple variants of his name are given, including Dille, Scillie, Scillius, Till, Tyle, Tylle, but there is no cross-referencing or any indication of why one is privileged.

the composition of *Bois*, but they are indicative of the views Dille must have held earlier in his career. It is worth remembering that, as pointed out above, Palmer was also prior of the London Blackfriars from 1397 to 1407 and participated in the heresy trials of Sir John Oldcastle and of John Claydon in 1415 (see above, p. xli).

An important area of difference between Ullerston's treatise and its Middle English adaptation is the extensive use of references to contemporary events in the latter. Such references concentrate at the end of the treatise—a part least dependent on Ullerston. Contemporary references in *Bois*, without a precedent in Ullerston, include the mentions of an unidentified Wyring in London possessing a 'Bible in Englische of norþen speche' (196.104), Friar Tille, a bill put before parliament 'to anulle' the Bible in English and its failure after John of Gaunt's speech,[308] Richard II's death, Queen Anne and the approval of her Gospels by Thomas Arundel, and Arundel's sermon at her funeral. Ullerston's work, on the contrary, is notoriously devoid of references to the contemporary situation: as pointed out earlier, it is very likely that he knew about the translation of the Bible undertaken with the possible involvement of his colleagues at Queen's, but it is never mentioned; neither are any late fourteenth-century events relevant to the controversy around the translation.

Bois is considerably more polemical and radical in its tone than Ullerston's determination. Following Ullerston, the author cites Fitzralph's assertion that sacraments can be made in any language, but adds a provocative comment: 'But we coueyten not þat, but prey anticrist þat we moten haue oure bileue in Englische' (199.163–5). Dove observes that the notion of praying to Antichrist 'evidently daunted scribes'—'pray' is erased or omitted in several later manuscripts.[309] Dove also comments that 'By "anticrist" the writer surely means the church authorities who are denying the people the Bible in English'.[310] It is worth noting that Antichrist figures prominently in works representing Lollard reaction to Arundel's Constitutions, including *The Lanterne of Liȝt* and *Tractatus de oblacioni iugis sacrificii*.[311] Both interpret the Constitutions as a ploy

---

[308] See a discussion of the historical accuracy of this claim in M. Jurkowski, 'The selective censorship of the Wycliffite Bible', in *ESWB*, 360–81, at 365.

[309] Dove, *EAEB*, 217.

[310] ibid. 217. Antichrist is also identified with the Pope in several of Wyclif's works, including *De potestate papae*, ed. J. Loserth (London 1907), 118/68ff, and *Super Matthei XXIV, Op.min.* 359/25ff.

[311] Edited in L. M. Swinburn, *The Lanterne of Liȝt*, EETS 151 (1988), and Hudson, *WLP*. Swinburn dates the composition of the *The Lanterne of Liȝt* to the period between 1409 and 1415 (pp. vii–xv), and this is confirmed by Hudson, *PR*, 214; Hudson dates the composition of the *Tractatus de oblacioni iugis sacrificii* to 1413–14 (*WLP*, xlix–xlx).

of Antichrist that ensures that Christ's teachings would be distorted or kept hidden from the people. *The Lanterne of Liȝt* presents licences required by preachers as the 'mark of the beast' bestowed by Antichrist. The author interprets the 'mark of the beast' in Rev. 13:17 as a prophecy applicable to his contemporary situation when no one can preach freely: 'þer schal no man preche Goddis word in þoo daies neiþer here it but if he haue a special lettir of liscence þat is clepid þe mark of þis beest anticrist'.[312] He also mentions the worship of Antichrist, an image reminiscent of prayer in *Bois*, citing Rev. 14: 'Seynt Ion seiþ who þat euer worshipiþ þis beest anticrist & takiþ þis forseid mark he schal drink a drauȝt of þe wyn of Goddis wraþþe'.[313]

Antichrist could conceivably be a reference to Arundel himself in his present role as the sponsor of the Constitutions, though Arundel is referred to in more positive terms at the end of the treatise, as the one who praised Queen Anne at her funeral for owning 'on Engliche al þe foure gospeleris wiþ þe docturis vpon hem' (201.225–6). The author ascribes to Arundel in his 'best' sermon the praise of a lay woman studying the gospels, an admission that an English translation of the gospels can be 'goode and trewe', a sharp criticism of the prelates, as well as tentatively a wish to abandon the office of the chancellor and forsake the world. This looks too much like a collection of sentiments desirable to Arundel's opponents to be based on reality, and it is important that the story about the sermon does not appear anywhere else and could therefore be a Lollard fabrication—the communities in which such stories might be confected and disseminated are discussed in a recent paper by Maureen Jurkowski.[314]

A rather militant tone adopted by the author of *Bois*, drastically different from Ullerston's and reminiscent of more radical polemical works from the period, including *The Lanterne of Liȝt*, is evident throughout the treatise. The author refers to his opponents as 'aduersaries of trewiþ' (199.172) and describes, in words attributed to John of Gaunt, a nation that does not have the Bible translated into its language as 'þe refuse of alle men' (215–16). The claim that English is not grammatical is compared to a threat to destroy it and 'kitte oute þe tunges of hem þat can not speke þus curiosly' (199.177–8). At the same time the author shows an interest in examples and stories, presumably because of their potential to make the discussion of translation more accessible to a non-academic audience. These

---

[312] Swinburn, *Lanterne*, 14, ll. 20–21.

[313] ibid. 14–15, ll. 26–7.

[314] 'The selective censorship of the Wycliffite Bible', *ESWB*, 371–88.

include references to King Oswald and bishop Aidan (196.86–8), James Merland (196.92–3), Bede (196.96–8.197.120–21), King Alfred (197.108–11), a priest who could not preach (197.124–30), and William Thoresby (198.140–41). Comparisons and metaphors are frequently used, some retained from Ullerston, others newly introduced. They tend to be simple, somewhat stereotypical or derived from everyday life, such as a comparison of the clergy and laity to fathers and sons (194.26–9), of Christ to a husband and 'parfite prechouris and doctouris' to a wife (194.34–5).

The author generally displays a detailed knowledge of the Bible and an ability to comment on it independently of Ullerston. Ullerston does not mention, to give just a few examples, that the people wept when Ezra read the law of Moses to them, but this detail (Neh. 8:9, 193.24) is included in *Bois*. Telling the story of Eldad and Medad based on Numbers 11 (70.1292–1300), Ullerston does not write about the appointment of seventy elders, chosen to receive a gift of prophecy from God that precedes this episode. The author of *Bois* not only mentions this detail, presumably to make the significance of the story clearer, but includes additional material immediately after the story, namely a reference to the baptism of the Roman centurion Cornelius (195.64) described in Acts 10, and a quotation from Acts 11:17 (195.65–7) concerning the baptism of gentiles, both absent from Ullerston. Also absent from Ullerston, though appearing in Palmer's determination, is a reference in *Bois* to 1 Cor. 14:19, where Paul writes that he would have preferred five words spoken in church with understanding to ten thousand words in an unknown tongue (195.76–7).

The author of *Bois* also introduces various non-biblical details absent in Ullerston, such as the dates for Bede (732 AD) and King Alfred (873 AD) at the end of a discussion of their activities as translators (196.102–3, 197.111–12), presumably in order to place these figures historically for a non-academic reader. The same tendency to offer basic educational information is evident in a discussion of the languages of the evangelists. The author of *Bois* translates a common Latin mnemonic rhyming quatrain as 'Matheu in Iudee, Marke in Ytalie, Luck in þe partyes of Achaie and Iohn in Asie' (199.158–9). This corresponds to a more learned quotation from Fitzralph in Ullerston that describes Matthew writing his gospel in Hebrew, John in Greek, and Mark in Italian (76.1424–6).

Whereas Ullerston mentions only the translation of the Psalter by Richard Rolle, the author of *Bois* alludes to the gloss on the Psalter and other works by Rolle: 'Also a nobil hooly man, Richerde Eremyte, drewe oon Englice þe Sauter with a glose of longe proces,

and lessouns of *Dirige* and many oþer tretis, by wiche many Engliche men han ben gretli edified' (198.136–8). When discussing a 'tract' (*The Lay Folks' Catechism*) by John Gaytryge, Ullerston writes that it contained an account of the articles of faith, the seven deadly sins and the seven works of mercy (36.644–53), whereas the author of *Bois* adds to this that the treatise also contained a discussion of the ten commandments (198.143). Summarizing Ullerston's response to point 23, concerning the possibility that the translation of the Bible in English will give rise to heresies, the author of *Bois* mentions 'Latyn eretikes' and adds a detail, not in Ullerston, that according to Gratian's *Decretum*, there are sixty Latin heresies (199.157).[315]

Occasionally the author of *Bois* ends parts of his discussion with comments that his sources have more material on the topic, such as 'and moche þer of þis mater' (193.13). This tends to occur after quotations from authorities and seems to refer to them rather than to Ullerston's determination, suggesting independent consultation. Occasionally such remarks appear after quotations that are not derived from Ullerston. Thus 'and more processe þere' follows a citation from Acts 1:16 (194.40) and 'and more þer in processe' a citation from Acts 2:16–17, both absent from Ullerston (194.44).

Biblical quotations in *Bois*, including those independent of Ullerston, differ, as the following examples demonstrate, from either version of the *Wycliffite Bible*. Though they tend to follow the Latin text closely, they are less literal than either version of the Wycliffite translation and sometimes, as the quotation from Joel below demonstrates, paraphrase rather than translate:[316]

(*a*) Wisdom 1:4
Vulgate: Quoniam in malevolam animam non introibit sapientia
Bois: wisdom schal not entre into a wicked soule
EV: For in to an euell willi soule shal not gon in wisdam
LV: For whi wisdom schal not entre in to an yuel willid soule

(*b*) Nehemiah 8:3
Vulgate: et aures omnis populi erant erectae ad librum
Bois: and þe eeres of þe puple weren entently ȝouen þerto
EV: and the eris of al the puple weren riyt to the boc
LV: and the eeris of al the puple weren reisid to the book

---

[315] According to Gratian's *Decretum*, *causa* 24, q. 3, c. 39, *Quidam*, there were sixty-eight Latin heresies; Friedberg, 1001–1006 (Dove, *EAEB*, 216).

[316] The influence of *WB* on contemporary English literary and theological works has not been fully researched. For important recent work see S. Morrison, 'The use of the Wycliffite translation in other Middle English Texts', *ESWB*, 406–25; note particularly his extended recognition of borrowing.

(*c*) Deuteronomy 32:7

Vulgate: interroga patrem tuum, et annuntiabit tibi: majores tuos, et dicent tibi

Bois: aske þi fadris and þei schullen schewe to þee, and þin elderis and þei schulen sei to þee

EV: aske thi fader, and he shal telle to thee, thi more and thei shulen seie to thee.

LV: axe thi fadir, and he schal telle to thee, *axe* thi grettere men, and thei schulen seie to thee.

(*d*) Joel 1:3

Vulgate: Super hoc filiis vestris narrate, et filii vestri filiis suis, et filii eorum generationi alterae.

Bois: how many þings he haþ seid vnto oure faderis, þei schul make hem knowen vnto her sones, and þe sones þat scholen be borne of hem schulen rise and schullen teche þes þings to her sonnes

EV: Vpon this thing telle ye to your sones, and your sonys to her sonys, and the sonys of hem to an other generacioun

LV: Of this thing telle ye to your sones, and your sones *telle* to her sones, and the sones of hem *telle* to another generacioun.

First seiþ Bois is a polemical work, arising probably from the Lollard milieu, and aimed at a much wider audience than its source. This is evident already in the author's choice of language, English rather than Latin, and the use of English for biblical quotations, in defiance of the seventh of Arundel's Constitutions that prohibited the production of complete or partial translations of any part of the Bible, 'by means of book, booklet, or treatise'.[317] The open-mindedness of Ullerston's determination, mostly lost in the adaptation, is consistent with a relatively early date of Ullerston's work, *c.* 1400. Anne Hudson has described the largely uncontentious nature of the commentary in the *Glossed Gospels* as an effort that was 'worthy of Oxford Wycliffism in the 1390s', and argued that the compilers 'grasped the importance of a balanced rationality, imparting basic instruction on biblical texts in a dispassionate and almost pedantically correct form'.[318] This fostered the Wycliffite causes, and particularly the Wycliffite insistence upon scripture, but in a manner that was 'academic rather than stridently polemical'.[319] The same can be said about the *Wycliffite Bible*, another production of the 1380s and 1390s, presenting not only an uncontentious and highly scholarly translation, but also marginal

---

[317] Wilkins, I. 317.
[318] Hudson, *PR*, 258.
[319] ibid. 258–9.

commentary devoid of openly polemical material and concerned primarily with textual-critical issues. Such 'balanced rationality' was apparently much more difficult after Arundel's attack on academic freedom, and the author of *Bois*, whose interests and background were probably not that different from Ullerston's, took a different approach. It is worth noting that almost all the evidence that survives of any interest in Ullerston's determination, its study and dissemination, stems from the heterodox Wycliffite and Hussite context, including one and possibly two Bohemian manuscripts (see above, p. xxv) and *First seiþ Bois* attested in seven manuscripts and two early printed copies.[320] John Bale and John Leland also lack awareness of Ullerston's determination, as demonstrated above (p. xxi), which suggests that it was little known in England in its original form.

[ES]

XI. MANUSCRIPTS

In what follows we offer descriptions of all known manuscripts of the three Latin texts, each used in the preparation of the present edition: Richard Ullerston's treatise, items 1 and 2; William Butler's treatise, item 3; and Thomas Palmer's treatise, item 4. The only two surviving complete medieval copies of *First seiþ Bois*, used as witnesses for the edition here, are described as items 5 and 6. The descriptions give details of the textual contents, decoration, physical make-up, binding, and known history of each manuscript.

(1) Vienna, Österreichische Nationalbibliothek, MS 4133

A composite manuscript, dating from the first quarter of the fifteenth century, of 207 leaves in three parts, all in paper, measuring *c.* 306×210 mm, bicolumnar throughout, 42–7 lines per page, on a ruled space of *c.* 220–24×143 mm. It is foliated throughout in modern ink. It is the work of four main scribes writing Secretary: scribe 1 (items 1–3), scribe 2 (item 4), scribe 3, i.e. Paul of Slawikowicz (fol. 194r–v); scribe 4 (item 5). Decoration is restricted to red and blue initials, occasionally with simple penwork, in different styles in each of the three parts. *Secundo folio*: 'quippe qui semper'.

Collation: (fols. 1–120) I–X (12) ‖ (fols. 121–156) XI–XIII (12) ‖ (fols. 157–192)

---

[320] In addition to copies described here, *Bois* survives in the following manuscripts and early printed editions: Cambridge, Corpus Christi College, MS 298; TCC MS B. 1. 26; BL MSS Cotton Vitellius D. VII, Harley 425; London, Lambeth Palace Library, MS 594; *A proper dyaloge betwene a Gentillman and a husbandman* (Antwerp: J. Hoochstraten, 1530) (*STC* 1462.5); *A compendious olde treatyse* (published separately by the same printer in the same year) (*STC* 3021). See short descriptions in Dove, *EAEB*, lii–liv.

XIV–XVI (12) || (fol. 193) XVII (1) a single leaf wrapped around the preceding quire XVI; its stub appears before the start of this quire, fol. 181 || (fol. 194) XVIII (1) a single leaf, presumably supplied to replace the lost end of text 4. It is bound with text 5: a parchment stub that appears before fol. 194 belongs to Slawikowicz's 'diploma' that was used in the binding and is wrapped around fol. 194 and the whole of Ullerston's treatise, fols. 195–207 || (fols. 195–206) XIX (12) || (fol. 207) XX (1) singleton

Quires I–X (fols. 1–120) have catchwords and numbers, I–X, at their ends. A new sequence of numbers starts at quire XI (the beginning of text 3); quires XI–XII are numbered I–II and have catchwords, quire XIII does not have a number or a catchword. Yet another sequence starts at quire XIV (the beginning of text 4) and quires XIV–XVI are numbered 1–3, but do not have catchwords. There are no numbers or catchwords on fols. 195–207 (text 5); quire XIX has a strengthening strip at the centre as is the practice elsewhere in the manuscript.

Ruling: (fols. 1–156) ruled faintly in plummet; (fols. 154–193) ruled in black ink with bounding lines extending the full length and width of page, 59–64 lines per page, ruled space of *c.* 257×167 mm; (fol. 194) no visible ruling, 53 lines on the verso, written space of *c.* 227×154 mm; (fols. 195–207) ruled faintly in plummet with bounding lines extending the full length and width of page, 53–61 lines per page, ruled space *c.* 227×150 mm.

Texts: a composite manuscript of three parts: (1) texts 1–3, (2) text 4, (3) text 5. Items 1–2 occupy quires I–X; item 3 occupies quires XI–XIII; item 4 occupies quires XIV–XVIII; item 5 occupies quires XIX–XX.

1. (fols. 1r–97v) Jerome's Commentary on Jeremiah, six books with a prologue (Stegmüller 3356). Rubrics: 'Incipit prologus sancti Ieronimi presbiteri ad eusebium in explanacionem Iheremie prophete' (fol. 1r), 'Explicit prologus incipit explanacio in Ieremiam prophetam' (fol. 1r). Beginning: 'Post explanationem duodecim prophetarum . . .'. Biblical references in the margins consist of abbreviated titles of books, chapter numbers and indexing letters, a–g, in this text and in texts 2 and 3. Contains extensive notes in the margins in a medieval hand different from the main hands of the manuscript; similar notes occasionally appear in texts 2 and 3 (e.g. fols. 119r, 126v, 149v).

2. (fols. 98r–120v) Hrabanus Maurus, Commentary on Jeremiah, bks XVIII–XX ('Explanatio in lamentationes Jeremiae') (*PL* 111. 1183A–1268D; Stegmüller 7055). Rubric: 'Incipit explanacio in lamentaciones Ieremie prophete liber 1 de primo alphabeto & secundo per Ieronimum' (fol. 98r). Beginning: 'Habes in lamentacionibus ieremie quatuor alphabeta...'. Fol. 121r is blank.

3. (fols. 121v–156v) Jerome, Commentary on Daniel (Stegmüller 3358), starting without a rubric; thirteen chapters and a prologue, beginning: 'Contra prophetam Danielem duodecinum librum scribit Porphirius . . .'.

4. (fols. 157r–194v) Honorius Augustodunensis, Commentary on the Song of Songs (Stegmüller 3573), without a rubric, beginning: 'Donum sapientie cum salomone poscente a vero pacifico postulata consequi . . .'.

The last leaf, fol. 194, is codicologically separate (see *Collation*) and in a different hand. The ruling and the dimensions of the written space on fol. 194 differ from preceding folios and the chapter numbers consistently entered in the

upper margin elsewhere are absent. There is also a lacuna: the text on fol. 193v ends at '. . . quasi enim in fremitu bellorum' (*PL* 172. 490B), whereas the text on fol. 194r starts at '*Non confundetur cum loquetur inimicis . . .*' (*PL* 172. 494A). This lacuna corresponds to the amount of text that would have occupied about one leaf in MS 4133.

The text on fol. 194v occupies about two thirds of the first column, the rest is left blank. At the end on fol. 194v: 'Explicit Orosius [*sic*] super cantica finitus per manus pauli dc Slawikowicz Anno domini M°CCCC°XVIII° feria III in die anne qui pro tunc vices gerebat in Gyczin'. Fol. 194 was probably supplied by Paul of Slawikowicz to replace a missing leaf—according to the colophon, the commentary was finished ('finitus'), rather than copied in its entirety by him. MS 4133 appears to contain only one leaf in his hand, but another commentary on the Song of Songs, by Alain de Lille, copied by Slawikowicz survives in Prague, City Archive (Archiv Prašého hradu), MS A CII.[321]

5. (fols. 195r–207v) Richard Ullerston, determination on the translation of the Bible, beginning: 'Stabilita siquidem translacione Ieronimi tamquam vera . . .'.

Frequently corrected. The main scribe is writing in brown ink and is responsible for some corrections. There may be more than one corrector, but most corrections are in a single contemporary hand, different from that of the main scribe, and using a much darker ink and a finer pen. This corrector is also responsible for alterations to chapter numbers (see section XII below, 'Chapter Numbering') that are often crossed out in dark ink.

Binding: Medieval binding, white leather over wooden boards, heavily repaired. A parchment document ('diploma' of Paul of Slawikowicz) used as outer flyleaves at the beginning and end (see Provenance): the flyleaf at the beginning wraps around 12 further blank laid paper flyleaves; the flyleaf at the end wraps around leaves containing text 5 (Ullerston's determination) and the last leaf (supplied by Slawikowicz) of text 4. Paper pastedowns on both covers with moral verses in Latin are in a medieval hand different from other hands in the manuscript. All quires have parchment (?) strengthening strips at the centres. Fittings of clasps (now missing) have left rust marks at the back of the manuscript that penetrate the 'diploma' and the final leaves of text 5.

Provenance: (*a*) Three independently produced parts. Texts 1–3 share a scribe, features of presentation (quire numbering and catchwords), textual features (the form of biblical references), and ownership (contain added notes in the same hand). Other texts are codicologically separate, and are by different scribes with initials executed by different artists.

(*b*) Colophon by Paul of Slawikowicz dated 1418 on fol. 194v who supplied the missing final leaf of text 4.

(*c*) Parchment document used as flyleaves is a Latin 'diploma' in which Petrus de Tassnowicz (Tišnov), 'canonicus' of the church of the Virgin Mary in 'Wolfframskirchen' and 'rector sive plebanus ecclesie parrochialis sancte Marie

---

[321] For MS A CII see K. Hruza, 'Liber Pauli de Slauikouicz. Der hussitische Codex 4937 der Österreichischen Nationalbibliothek in Wien und sein ursprünglicher Besitzer', in *Handschriften, Historiographie und Recht. Winfried Stelzer zum 60. Geburtstag*, ed. Gustav Pfeifer (Vienna 2002), 128–52, at 133.

[. . . Olomucensis] diocesis', appoints 'Paulus de Slawikowicz', described as 'bacalarius in artibus' of Prague University, 'tabellio' (notary) by the authority of 'Ganfridus de Barra de Monteburgo dei gratia Comes Palatinus'.[322]

Paul of Slawikowicz may have been not only the owner of MS 4133, but a compiler who put the collection together. He was admitted to the examination for the bachelor's degree at the University of Prague in 1395.[323] He was a deputy of the Hussite leadership in the negotiations at the Council of Basel and is described as 'artium liberalium baccalaureus, plebanus S. Aegidii et corrector cleri eiusdem curiae archiepiscopalis Pragensis' in a letter of 1435.[324] He is a known owner of several books in addition to MS 4133, including three manuscripts in the National Library of Austria and seven manuscripts in the National Library of Prague and the City Archive (Archiv Prašého hradu). His manuscripts contain predominantly Hussite and Wycliffite theological and polemical works.[325] There is a record of his donation of books to Charles University.[326] He comes through as a bibliographer and a collector of texts who spent much of his career within the Hussite university milieu. He seems to have been well supplied with texts, including those of English origin, and knowledgeable about works associated with Wyclif. This is particularly evident in an exceptionally full and detailed catalogue of Wyclif's works, the earliest copy of which is preserved in ÖNB MS 3933, which he owned.[327] According to Anne Hudson, the catalogue is a remarkable achievement due to its comprehensiveness, accuracy and scholarly approach, unmatched by other listings of Wyclif's works up to the twentieth century.[328] Another of his manuscripts, ÖNB MS 4509,[329] contains in addition to theological texts, works by Hus, articles against Hus with his responses, a testimonial letter of the university of Oxford concerning Wyclif, dated 1406.[330]

[322] For a further discussion of this document see K. Hruza, 'Liber Pauli de Slauikouicz. Der hussitische Codex 4937 der Österreichischen Nationalbibliothek in Wien und sein ursprünglicher Besitzer', in Handschriften, Historiographie und Recht. Winfried Stelzer zum 60, ed. G. Pfeifer (Vienna 2002), 128–52, at 131–2.

[323] Monumenta historica Universitatis Carolo-Ferdinandeae Pragensis, 2 pts (1830–32), I. 308–309, 'Item eodem die Paulus de Slawikowitz obtinuit consimiliter dispensationem biennii pro Joanne de Stropnicz'.

[324] Hruza, 'Liber Pauli de Slauikouicz', 132.   [325] ibid. 133.

[326] ibid. 131–2.

[327] Denis, I. 1473–6; K. Schwarzenberg, Katalog der kroatischen, polnischen und tschechischen Handschriften der Österreichischen Nationalbibliothek (Vienna 1972), 32; ÖNB-HANNA-Katalog, Handschriften, Nachlässe und Musikhandschriften (http://aleph.onb.ac.at). The catalogue was published by A. Hudson in 'The Hussite catalogue of Wyclif's works', STWW, § III, 1–35. The manuscript is dated by W. R. Thomson, Wyclyf, on palaeographic grounds to c. 1415.

[328] Hudson, 'The Hussite catalogue', 12.

[329] Denis, I. 869–76; Unterkircher, Die datierten Handschriften, 99; Schwarzenberg, Katalog, 205; ÖNB-HANNA-Katalog, Handschriften, Nachlässe und Musikhandschriften (http://aleph.onb.ac.at).

[330] The testimonial was edited by K. Höfler, Concilia Pragensia, 1353–1413 (Prague 1862; repr. Vienna 1972), 53, and by Wilkins, 3. 302. See also M. Van Dussen, From England to Bohemia: Heresy and Communication in the Later Middle Ages (Cambridge 2012), 89–93, 94–5, 96–105.

Similarly to MS 4133, manuscripts that belonged to Paul of Slawikowicz tend to be anthologies, some possessing a degree of thematic consistency;[331] the texts they contain are partly or entirely in his hand.

(d) The medieval binding suggests that all texts were together in the fifteenth century. Inscriptions in a fifteenth-century hand on the upper pastedown and the front cover, however, list texts 1–4, but not text 5, 'Ieronimus in Ieremiam et danielem Orosius super cantica'. The inscriptions may be by Paul of Slawikowicz. Another of his manuscripts, ÖNB MS 4509, has on the front cover his name, now partly covered by a label, written in black ink in a large contemporary cursive script. This is preceded by the title of the first text 'Ieronimus ad nepotianum', probably in the same hand. As in MS 4133, there is no attempt to list the contents fully, which suggests that the absence of Ullerston's treatise from the lists on the cover and pastedown of MS 4133 does not necessarily mean that it was a later addition. Unlike other books owned by Slawikowicz, MS 4133 does not have an ownership inscription at the front. It may, however, originally have existed: the inscription summarizing contents on the upper pastedown is preceded by an erasure.

(e) Prague, Charles University, pressmark 'O 6' (?); not in the *Registrum librorum collegii Reczkonis* or *Registrum librarie nacionis Boemorum*, ed. Z. Silagiová & F. Šmahel, *Catalogi librorum vetustissimi universitatis Pragensis*, CCCM 271 (Turnhout 2015), where different works have pressmarks 'O 6'.[332]

(f) A third copy of Ullerston's treatise may have existed in the second half of the fifteenth century in the library of the College of the Bohemian Nation in Prague: a catalogue compiled before 1461 has an entry 'L26 Item tractatus Magistri Richardi de translacione sacre scripture in wlgare ydiomate'.[333]

(g) Kaspar von Niedbruck, c. 1525–1557, diplomat under Maximilian II and humanist.[334] Borrowed from Charles University in 1556, number 19 in the surviving list of borrowed books.[335]

(h) Earlier shelfmarks/notes: '(?)4. 19' (medieval, front cover, beginning unreadable), 'No 147' (spine), '140 N CLXXXII. ol. 147' (parchment 'diploma' at the front), 'CLXXXII' (upper pastedown, spine), 'M 3875' (lower pastedown; signature of Hugo Blotius, the first official Librarian of the Imperial Library

---

[331] See Anne Hudson's discussion of Wyclif's 'opera omnia' in Bohemia in '*Opera omnia*: collecting Wyclif's works in England and Bohemia', in *Religious Controversy in Europe, 1378–1536: Textual Transmission and Networks of Readership*, ed. M. Van Dussen & P. Soukup (Turnhout 2013), 49–69.

[332] Facsimiles of the catalogues are available in J. Bečka & E. Urbánková, *Katalogy knihoven kolejí Karlovy university* (Prague 1948).

[333] Silagiová & Šmahel, *Catalogi librarum*, 98; Bečka & Urbánková, *Katalogy*, pl. 66, col. 144. See further discussion at p. xxv.

[334] *Allgemeine Deutsche Biographie*, 52 (1906), 621–9; see A. Hudson, 'The survival of Wyclif's works in England and Bohemia', STWW, § XVI, 1–43, at 31–2.

[335] F. M. Bartoš, 'Vzácný dokument z dějin knihovny Karlovy university', *Jihočeský sborník historický* 17 (1948), 31–4; K. Schwarzenberg, 'Bücher der Österreichischen Nationalbibliothek aus dem Prager *Karolinum*', *Biblos* 19 (1970), 97–103, with correction ibid. 20 (1971), 103.

who produced a catalogue of the collection in 1576),[336] '179' (lower pastedown), 'VII. C. 25' (upper pastedown), 'D. V. 1. p. 842' (upper pastedown), '61' (upper pastedown, medieval page number (?)).

(2) Cambridge, Gonville and Caius College, MS 803/807, fragment 36

A single parchment leaf used as a pastedown in a binding, measuring *c.* 172× 125 mm.[337] All the text, including the colophon, is by the same English early fifteenth-century scribe who also made some corrections on the recto. He wrote using a brown ink in a single column on 39 lines on the recto side. Traces of glue around the edges on three sides.

Text: The final part of Richard Ullerston's determination, comprising the second half of the concluding summary and a list of nine propositions. Starts on the recto '. . . tionem notus tamen/tantum in iudea . . .' and ends '. . . rerum naturalium proprietatibus tropis'; continues on the verso '[equiuocis] et sinonomis . . .' and ends '. . . hiis que in Christo Ihesu Amen'.

The text on the recto is clear, but the verso faced the binding and is faint and discoloured. In spite of this and the bleed-through from the recto, enough can be read on the verso to show that the text is the same as in the Vienna manuscript described above. Nine propositions at the end of the determination are numbered in arabic numerals (numbers survive on the verso, and their fragments are visible on the recto).

The text on the verso occupies just under half a page. The rest of the page is left blank, apart from the colophon laid out in two lines after a break: *Explicit tractatus Magistri Ricardi Vllerston d[octoris in theologia] de tran[slacione] sacre scripture in vulgare editus ab eodem Oxon' a[nno] domini 1401.*

Provenance: James (*Gonville*, 3. 46) gives no detail of the source of the fragment, but its status is likely to be an outcome of the large-scale rebinding project undertaken in the library of Gonville and Caius College between 1906 and 1912, when many medieval vellum covers were removed and subsequently lost, whereas pastedowns were retained and are now part of the library's fragments collection.

(3) Oxford, Merton College, MS 68

A parchment manuscript,[338] datable to the 1440s–1450s, of 306 leaves measuring *c.* 355×265 mm, ruled for two columns, 49–59 lines per page, *c.* 255×190 mm.

---

[336] The catalogue was edited by H. Menhardt, *Das älteste Handschriftenverzeichnis der Wiener Hofbibliothek von Hugo Blotius 1576. Kritische Ausgabe der Handschrift Series nova 4451 vom Jahre 1597 mit vier Anhängen*, Österreichische Akademie der Wissenschaften: Denkschriften 76 (Vienna 1957).

[337] For discussion see A. Hudson, 'The debate on Bible translation', 1–18.

[338] A recent detailed description of MS 68 is in Thomson, *Merton*, revised and supplemented by R. Hanna, 'Merton College, MS. 68: production and texts', *Bodleian Library Record* 27 (2014), 129–52. Bibliographic details for texts, omitted here, can be found in these catalogues and article; this account is consequently abbreviated.

Medieval foliation in ink throughout, including leaves containing texts added by scribes 2 and 3 and an added bifolium at the end, probably in the hand responsible for the table of contents; regular 1–301, but original fols. 118–20 are now missing; modern foliation in pencil, i–v+1–301. Seventeenth-century Merton binding, sewn on six bands, formerly chained. Paper flyleaves; leaves from a printed copy of 'Expositio topicorum Aristotelis', s. xvi, at the beginning and end. *Secundo folio*: 'miserat ad'.

Collation: (fols. i–v) two paper flyleaves; quire of four parchment leaves, 4 canc. || (fols. 1–108) I–IX (12) || (fols. 109–117) X (12–13) missing 10–12 || (fols. 118–297) XI–XXV (12) || (fols. 298–299) parchment bifolium || (fols. 300–301) paper flyleaves

Quire and leaf signatures in the first six quires only, a–f (fols. 1–72); signatures elsewhere preserved only partially.

Script: A single main scribe, writing a mixture of Anglicana and Secretary, with contributions from two near-contemporary scribes. These contributions occur only at quire ends (Hanna, 'Merton College, MS. 68'): scribe 2, writing a mixed hand, provided additional indexes to texts 19 (fol. 198r–v) and 23–25 (fol. 298r); scribe 3, writing Secretary and working later than other scribes, copied texts on originally blank leaves at the ends of quires X and XVII, in the second case following indexes added by scribe 2. At the end of quire X he added Eyton's treatise on usury (text 17, fols. 113r–117v), an extract from Ps-Methodius's *Apocalypsis* and the opening of Butler's determination. The last two are now lost, but appear, as additions in a contemporary hand, in the medieval table of contents. At the end of quire XVII scribe 3 copied the now extant part of Butler's determination (text 19, fols. 199r–201v).

Decoration is restrained. A red and blue initial with penwork and one-sided penwork border on fol. 1r. Blue initials with red penwork elsewhere. Texts added by scribe 2 have initials highlighted in red and no other decoration; texts added by scribe 3 have unfilled spaces left for initials and lack rubrication entirely.

Texts: items 1–18 occupy quires I–X; items 19–20 occupy quires XI–XVII; items 21–22 occupy quires XVIII–XIX; items 23–25 occupy quires XX–XXV+a bifolium.

    1. (fols. 1r–2r) 'De adoratione, latria, hyperdulia, et dulia libellus'.

    2. (fols. 2r–6r) Ps-Bonaventura, *Centiloquium*.

    3. (fols. 6r–17v) An alphabetical bestiary, with an alphabetical index of moralizations, fols. 16r–17v.[339]

    4. (fols. 17v–18v) Thomas Sutton, *De vita apostolica*.[340]

    5. (fols. 18v–23v) Walter Hilton, *De adoratione imaginum*.[341] Attributed here to Thomas Palmer: '*Tractus de adoracione ymaginum*', 'Palmer' added above

---

[339] M. W. Bloomfield, *Incipits of Latin Works on the Virtues and Vices, 1100–1500 A.D.* (Cambridge, MA, 1979), no. 2875.

[340] Sharpe, 684.

[341] ibid. 735. On the authorship of this tract see J. M. Russell-Smith, 'Walter Hilton and a tract in defence of the veneration of images', *Dominican Studies* 7 (1954), 180–214.

the line; '*Explicit tractatus de adoracione ymaginum secundum Thomam Palmer fratrem predicatorem et professorem theologie*'.

6. (fols. 23v–29r) Giles of Rome, *De originali peccato*.[342] Attributed here to Palmer: '*Tractatus de originali peccato secundum Palmer ut dicitur*'; '*Explicit Palmer de peccato originali*'.

7. (fols. 29r–31v) John Deverose, *De materia peregrinationis*.[343]

8. (fols. 31v–32r) Petrus Alfonsi, *Dialogus contra Iudaeos*, a brief excerpt only.

9. (fols. 32r–40r) Robert Allington, *Determinatio de adoratione imaginum*.[344]

10. (fol. 40r) Thomas Aquinas, *De iudiciis astrorum*.

11. (fols. 40r–42r) *De observatione sabbati tractatus*.[345]

12. (fols. 42r–64r) Gilbert the Minorite, *Liber de exemplis sacrae scripturae*, with alphabetical word-index, fols. 63r–64r.[346]

13. (fols. 64v–74v) Malachi of Ireland, *De septem venenis*.[347]

14. (fols. 74v–88v) *Stimulus conscientiae*, the Latin prose translation of *The Prick of Conscience*.

15. (fols. 88v–95r) Richard Rolle, *Emendatio vitae*.[348]

16–17. (fols. 95v–112v) An anonymous commentary on the nine readings from the Office of the Dead. Ends about half way down the second column; text originally occupying the remainder of the column, beginning 'Tabula tractatus precedentis . . .', is erased.

18. (fols. 113r–117v) John Eyton, *De usuris*;[349] copied on blank leaves by scribe 3. Spaces left for initials, but not filled in. Ends imperfectly at '. . . secundum parisiensem comparatus usurarius cuiusdam'. After fol. 117 three leaves (fols. 118–120 in medieval numbering) are excised that contained, according to the medieval table of contents,[350] Ps-Methodius, *Apocalipsis* ('Liber Metodii de tempore Antechristi et de die iudicii') and the beginning of Butler's determination.

19. (fols. 118r–192r) John Wykeham, *Quaestiones quas mouet Notyngham*,[351] followed by a table of gospel readings for the year, including temporal, sanctoral, common and commemorations (fols. 192r–198r), and an alphabetical index of keywords, the second added by scribe 2 on fol. 198r–v.

20. (fols. 199r–201v) William Butler's treatise (title in the upper margin of fol. 199r: 'Buttiler contra translacionem anglicanam'), imperfect at the beginning, starting 'intellexisse scripturam sacram et eam false composuisse . . .'. This is a continuation of Butler's determination copied by scribe 3 on originally empty leaves at the end of quire XVII, after he ran out of space on originally empty leaves at the end of quire X, where he copied the now lost beginning of the determination (see Collation). This is the only known copy of this text. Spaces are left for initials but these are not filled in. At the end: 'Explicit determinacio

[342] Bloomfield, *Virtues*, no. 1886; Sharpe, 674.   [343] Sharpe, 235.

[344] ibid. 522.

[345] Bloomfield, *Virtues*, no. 4674.   [346] ibid. nos 5978, 0143.

[347] Sharpe, 369; Bloomfield, *Virtues*, no. 5102.

[348] ed. Rüdiger Spahl, *De emendatione vitae: eine kritische Ausgabe des lateinischen Textes von Richard Rolle* (Göttingen, Bonn, 2009).

[349] Sharpe, 242; Bloomfield, *Virtues*, no. 5719.

[350] See Hanna, 'Merton College, MS. 68', 130–33.   [351] Sharpe, 354.

fratris et magistri Willelmi Buttiler ordinis minorum regentis Oxonie anno Domini m°cccc° primo'.

A note in a medieval hand, probably also responsible for the table of contents (fol. iii^v), at the foot of fol. 199r referring to 'fo. 119', a now lost leaf in quire X that contained the beginning of Butler's determination: 'Quere principium huius tractatus fo. 119 precedente'. According to the medieval table of contents (see below, *Provenance*), Ps-Methodius started on fol. 118, the first of three leaves now missing at the end of quire X, and Butler's determination started on fol. 119, the second of these three leaves. This suggests that up to two leaves of Butler's determination are lost. Butler's determination currently occupies three full leaves in the hand of scribe 3 which suggests that about a third is missing. Presumably all of the missing fol. 120 was occupied by Butler's determination, prompting the scribe to look for empty leaves later in the volume to finish it. It is unclear how much of fol. 119 was occupied by Butler's text.

21. (fols. 202r–221r) Augustinus Trionfi of Ancona, *Quastiones super Magnificat*.[352]

22. (fols. 221r–225v) Thomas of Ireland, *De tribus ordinibus angelicae hierarchiae et ecclesiasticae*.[353]

23. (fols. 226r–254r) John Waldeby, sermons on the *Pater noster*.[354]

24. (fols. 254r–269r) John Waldeby, sermons on the *Ave Maria*.[355]

25. (fols. 269r–291v) John Waldeby, sermons on the Apostles Creed,[356] followed by two alphabetical indexes, the first on fols. 291v–298r, the second added by scribe 2 on fol. 298r, the first leaf of an added bifolium.

The first thirteen texts are the work of university scholars of *c.* 1385–1410, some anti-Lollard, whereas the rest are texts of northern provenance (*Emendatio uitae*, *Stimulus*, and the sermon cycles of John Waldeby).[357] There are some differences of presentation between the two sequences. The university texts follow one another separated only by their rubrics and colophons, and are on quires that are fully signed with quire-letters and leaf numbers.[358] Signatures cease after quire VI. Texts after fol. 63 start at the head of a leaf or at the head of a column with blank lines left at the foot of a preceding column, though the practice changes again at Thomas of Ireland, *De tribus ordinibus* (text 22, fol. 221r), and the remaining works start in the middle of a column. Text 16 comments on the Office of the Dead and the works by Waldeby explicate basic prayers, thus providing a 'handbook for pulpit instruction in Christian basics'. These and many other materials in the book are 'copiously indexed for ready use in the construction of sermons'.[359] Several works are associable with Augustinian

---

[352] Stegmüller 1548.

[353] Sharpe, 661.

[354] Sharpe, 336; Bloomfield, *Virtues*, no. 9123; Stegmüller 5045–6.

[355] Sharpe, 336; Stegmüller 5048. For recent work on Waldeby see A.Yuichi, *A Mendicant Sermon Collection from Composition to Reception* (Turnhout 2015).

[356] Sharpe, 335; Bloomfield, *Virtues*, no. 1010; Stegmüller 5049.

[357] Hanna, 'Merton College, MS. 68', 130, 134.

[358] ibid. 134.

[359] ibid. 137.

friars, including the commentary on the Magnificat by the Italian Augustine of Ancona (the only copy of his work surviving in an English manuscript), also the works by Walter Hilton, Giles of Rome, and John Waldeby.[360]

Provenance: (*a*) Probably produced for Hammond Haydock (d. 1465), fellow of Merton *c.* 1417–32, an owner of several other manuscripts.[361] As pointed out by Hanna, his library reveals his professional interests as a priest and has an emphasis on catechetic materials, exempla and the gospels. As Hanna also observes, the opening sequence of MS 68, containing university and anti-Lollard texts, is unusual for Haydock's library that generally reflects more basic interests in simple Christian instruction within a parish context.[362]

A table of contents was supplied on fol. iii[v], including titles and folio references, in a contemporary hand, probably the one that foliated the manuscript. Ps.-Methodius's *Apocalypsis* and Butler's determination are listed as an addition underneath the main table, probably in a different contemporary hand.

(*b*) Donated to Merton College, among other books, by Haydock; [363]'Liber domus scolarium de Merton' ex", cropped by the binder, fol. i[v].

(*c*) Examined by John Bale at Merton: texts 9, 19, 23–5, and texts attributed to Palmer are in his *Index*.[364]

(*d*) A sheet of paper inside the front board with a table of contents, s. xvii.

(*e*) Earlier shelfmarks: 'N. 6. 2. Art:', s. xvii, cancelled and replaced with modern 'K. 2. 2'. College bookplate.

(4) Cambridge, Trinity College, MS B. 15. 11

A composite parchment manuscript of two parts of *c.* 1430, with 148 leaves (including two unnumbered flyleaves at the beginning and one at the end). Leaves measure *c.* 315×195 mm with a ruled space of *c.* 220×135 mm, two columns of 52 lines per page. There is a medieval foliation on fols. 1–54 (up to the middle of quire 5), modern foliation (55–145) thereafter. The same hand throughout, using a brown ink. The same artist throughout. 5-line initial and two-sided penwork border in red, blue and purple inks at the beginning of item 1; 3- to 4-line blue initials with red penwork at the beginning of texts with the exception of item 3 that starts with a 2-line initial (see below). Blue 2- to 3-line initials with red penwork at the beginning of chapters. Alternating red and blue paraphs throughout. The binding is modern, brown leather over pasteboard. *Secundo folio*: 'post consecracionem'.

Consists of two codicologically discrete parts, sharing a scribe and an artist responsible for flourished initials. The parts were produced separately, as is suggested by leaf signatures in the second part that form an independent sequence starting with 'a'; but they were presumably designed to be bound together, as is suggested by their identical format, size and dimensions of the written space. The first part has the only decorated border in the volume and was presumably

---

[360] ibid. 142.

[361] *BRUO* 894; F. M. Powicke, *The Medieval Books of Merton College* (Oxford 1931), 204–6; Hanna, 'Merton College, MS. 68', 138–9.   [362] ibid. 139.

[363] ibid.   [364] Cited by Thomson, *Merton*, 284–6.

intended to be at its start. This, however, may have been an afterthought: that the second part was originally independent is suggested by the position of a note by the scribe stating his patronage and location, and dating the time of writing to 1430. The note appears at the end of current item 4, but originally this would have been at the end of the first item.

All texts begin at the start of a new leaf or column with a part of the preceding column left blank, and are headed by 4- or 3-line initials. Palmer's determination is an exception: it starts with a 2-line initial immediately following item 2 from the middle of the second column on fol. 42v. This suggests that it was seen by the scribe as related to items 1–2, and therefore an anti-Wycliffite text.

Collation: one paper and one parchment flyleaf, unnumbered || (fols. 1–48) I–IV (12) || (fols. 49–144) V–XII (12) || one parchment flyleaf (numbered 145) and one paper flyleaf; the fragment of a parchment stub before fol. 132 probably extends from the first of these.

There is a complete break between quires I–IV (item 3 ends mid-way in the first column of fol. 47v and fol. 48 is blank on both sides) and V–XII. Quire signatures are only rarely fully preserved, but the first two leaves of quire V (fols. 49 and 50) have a signature 'a' and quire VIII includes 'd.1' (fol. 54, the first leaf of present quire 8), whereas quire IX includes 'e.1' (fol. 86, the first leaf of present quire IX).

Texts: A composite of two parts: (1) texts 1–3, (2) texts 4–8. Items 1–3 occupy quires I–IV; items 4–8 occupy quires V–XII.

1. (fols. 1ra–42rb) *Contra trialogum Wyclyffe* by William Woodford, beginning 'Uenerabili in christo patet . . .', ending '. . . humilis suus seruuitor frater Willielmum Wodeford'. Woodford's most widely disseminated text against the teachings of Wyclif, written at the prompting of Thomas Arundel in 1396.[365]

2. (fols. 42va–b) The preceding text is structured on eighteen statements by Wyclif, and these are cited in full as a separate item on fol. 42va–b.

3. (fols. 42vb–47va) Thomas Palmer's determination with a rubric in a medieval hand, but not by the main scribe: '*Palmer de translacione scripture sacre in linguam barbaricam*'; beginning 'Utrum sacra scriptura in liguam anglicanam uel in aliam barbaricam sit transferenda' and ending '. . . qui est benedictus in secula. Amen. deo gracias'. The title is given again in a table of contents written in the same medieval hand on a flyleaf at the beginning of the manuscript with the final word 'Anglicanam' rather 'barbaricam'. The only known copy of this text.[366]

4. (fols. 49ra–54vb) Simon of Boraston OP, *De unione ecclesiastice veritatis*, beginning 'Fiet vnum ouile et vnus pastor . . .' and ending '. . . errorem meum si in quem incidi reuocare'.[367]

[365] For a listing of the copies see Sharpe, 819–20. The text was printed in *Fasciculus rerum expetendarum ac fugiendarum* ([Cologne] 1535) and reprinted in the collection of the same title, ed. E. Brown (London 1690), i. 191–265. For the circumstances of its production and its outlook on Wyclif's theology see especially J. I. Catto, 'William Woodford OFM (c. 1330–c. 1397)', DPhil thesis (University of Oxford 1969).

[366] Sharpe, 674.

[367] For Simon of Boraston see T. Kaeppeli, *Scriptores Ordinis Praedicatorum medii aevi*,

5. (fols. 55ra–56ra) *Ius regis Anglie in Normandiam et Andegauiam*, beginning 'Sciendujm est quod anno domini m.c.xxxvi . . .' and ending '. . . liberam submitti alicui extranee seruitutui'. An anonymous compilation listed in the medieval table of contents as by Boraston.

6. (fols. 56rb–69rb) *De ordine iudiciario circa crimine corrigenda*, attributed to Simon of Boraston in the list of contents, but not at the head of this item, beginning 'Coripiet me iustus in misericordia . . .' and ending '. . . et nomen cum cognomine compilantis'.[368]

7. (fols. 69rb–71ra) *De mutabilitate mundi*, attributed to Simon of Boraston in the list of contents, but not at the head of this item, beginning 'Cum omnibus mobilibus mobilior sit sapiencia . . .' and ending '. . . tam pro viuis quam pro defunctis frequencius celebrantur'.[369]

8. (fols. 71rb–144vb) Text attributed to Vincent of Beauvais OP, *De instructione puerorum nobilium*, beginning 'Clarissimis ac religiosissimis in christo viris . . .' and ending '. . . mementote nostri cum in uobis uirginitas honorari'.[370] Steiner lists three copies in England, of which the third is the present volume, but does not appear to have used any of these.[371]

Provenance: (*a*) Written in Oxford by Cornelius Oesterwik, perhaps an itinerant scribe, for Dominican John Courteys, a regent master at Oxford University.[372] Colophon on fol. 54vb: '*Explicit tractatus de unitate et ordine ecclesiastice veritatis ffinitus per manus cornelii oesterwiic anno domini M CCCC XXX in vniuersitate oxoniensis ad mandatum ffratris Iohannis Courteys sacre theologie professoris ordinis predicatorum et conuentus exoniensis tunc regentis vniuersitatis predicte*'.

The second part, containing items 4–8 and a concluding note about the origins of the material, has a strongly Dominican emphasis and the materials derive from the thirteenth century. Dominican authorship is also asserted for item 3, whereas items 1–2 are Franciscan writings. These first three items, forming part 1, are of decidedly later origin, reflect in detail on late fourteenth-century causes and are treated by the scribe as parts of a separate, thematically coherent sequence.

(*b*) Table of contents in a fifteenth-century hand,[373] that also supplied a title for Palmer's treatise, is added on the verso of a parchment flyleaf at the beginning, and lists the contents of the manuscript in their present order. The first line, preceding an entry for Woodford's treatise, has been erased. The list of

---

4 vols (Rome 1970–93), no. 557, and for the text, Sharpe, 609, where three other extant copies are listed. The text has not been edited.

[368] Sharpe, 609, lists eight other extant copies.

[369] Sharpe, 609, lists two other extant copies.

[370] As the alternative title implies, the work is a 'mirror for princes', part of the vast, and much circulated, *Speculum maius*. The text was edited under the title *De eruditione regalium filiorum* by A. Steiner (Cambridge, MA, 1938) from three continental copies.

[371] ibid. xxix. For Vincent of Beauvais (*c.* 1194–1264) see Kaeppeli, *Scriptores*, no. 4003. The editor mistakenly gives the present copy as 374 in James's catalogue, but the page references make its identity clear; the other two English copies mentioned are Cambridge, Corpus Christi College, MS 325, and Oxford, Merton College, MS 110.

[372] *BRUO* 1389 and 504.   [373] Printed by James, *Trinity*, i. 474.

contents indicates that the present ordering of the two parts must have been in place soon after they were written.

(c) 'Ihc' on the verso of a parchment flyleaf at the beginning and on fol. 1r (s. xv).

(5) New York, Pierpont Morgan Library, MS M 648

A mid-fifteenth-century parchment manuscript of 146 leaves, measuring c. 285 × 195 mm, bicolumnar (35 lines to a page) with a ruled space of c. 200×130 mm. It is foliated in modern pencil; two unnumbered flyleaves at the beginning+ 145+one unnumbered flyleaf at the end. It is the work of two scribes, the first responsible for fols. 1r–141v, the second for fols. 142r–144r. The binding is of red morocco with gilt decoration; marbled paper pastedowns and flyleaves; English eighteenth century; gilt edges of text-block (eighteenth-century addition?). *Secundo folio*: 'hour Captulum xliiij'.

Collation: (fols. 1–10) I (10) || (fols. 11–138) II–XVII (8) || (fols. 139–141) XVIII (3) || (fols. 142–144) XIX (3). Catchwords at the ends of quires. Patterns of water damage at the beginning of the book and on fols. 142-4, as well as off-prints of text in red on fol. 144v suggest that these leaves were originally located at the front of the book. The same is suggested by marks from an earlier binding found on fol. 141v (previously the final leaf), but absent from fols. 142-4 (previously at the front).

Texts: 1. (fols. 1r–141v) Nicholas Love, *Mirror of the Blessed Life of Jesus Christ*, followed by the *Memorandum* (fol. 141v).[374] Heading at the beginning of the table of contents: '*Her begynneth the table of þe boke þat is cleped þe mirrour of þe blessid lif of Iesu crist*' (fol. 1r).

2. (fols. 142r–143v) *First seith Bois*, starting without a rubric with a small initial with modest penwork decoration, all in the same ink as the text. The text occupies only the top of the left column on fol. 143v, the rest is left blank.

3. (fol. 144r) *Revelationes* of Birgitta of Sweden, IV 7, an extract containing 51 lines of text.[375] Starts without a rubric on a new page; occupies just over half of the left column, the rest of the page is left blank.

Decoration: Full borders, 6- to 7-line decorated initials on gold background, and 16 miniatures at textual divisions in the *Mirror*. The miniatures occupy between a quarter and a half of a page and depict Bonaventure (fol. 2v), the Trinity (fol. 5v), the Annunciation (fol. 10r), the Nativity (fol. 19r), the Presentation (fol. 25r), the Flight into Egypt (fol. 27v), the Temptation (fol. 38r), the Sermon on the Mount (fol. 46r), Plucking the Corn (fol. 54v), the Loaves and Fishes (fol. 57r), the Agony (fol. 92v), the Crucifixion (fol. 102r), the Resurrection (fol. 113r), the Ascension (fol. 123v), Pentecost (fol. 129r), and Corpus Christi

---

[374] M. G. Sargent (ed.), *Nicholas Love The Mirror of the Blessed life of Jesus Christ: A Full Critical Edition* (Exeter 2005), intro 137–8.

[375] C.-G. Undhagen & others (ed.), *Sancta Birgitta. Revelaciones*, Royal Academy of Letters, History and Antiquities (Stockholm, Uppsala, 1956–2002; online at http://www.umilta.net/bk.html), Book IV (ed. H. Aili), ll. 53–70.

(fol. 131r).[376] Gold initials 3- to 4-lines high on blue and pink background with floral sprays at minor textual divisions; gold and blue paraphs with red and blue penwork.

The borders are made of gold, pink and blue bars with acanthus leaves and sprays of flowers, leaves and gold disks. According to Kathleen Scott, the border decoration may be by the artist responsible for the decoration in Edinburgh, National Library of Scotland, Advocates' Library, MS 18.1.7 alsp containing Love's *Mirror*.[377]

Provenance: (*a*) *First seith Bois* is codicologically separate and is by a different scribe than the *Mirror*.

(*b*) An eighteenth- or nineteenth-century hand, apparently describing text on the original binding, wrote: 'N.B. This name was writ on the cover which was much decayd and consisted of two very thick oak boards covered with vellum' (fol. 144v). This inscription seems to refer to another inscription of a similar date to its right: 'Episcop. Thom Arundell Anno Domni 1390'.

(*c*) Given in the seventeenth century by Henry Williams to Hugo Hibbard (inscription on fol. 144v).

(*d*) Given *c.* 1750 by William Saunders MD of Wadham College, Oxford, to Edward Walmsley (inscription on fol. 144v); his sale (London (?) Mar. 1795; perhaps Sotheby's, 16 Mar. 1795, lot 343: Life of Christ) to Captain Perrott Noel of the Worcestershire Militia (inscription on fol. 144v, bookplate on front pastedown with armorial and motto: '*jus suum cuique*'); inherited in 1916 by General Sir Neville Lyttelton (inscription on fol. 144v).

(*e*) Purchased by J. P. Morgan (1867–1943) from Agnew in 1920.

(6) Cambridge, Trinity College, MS B. 14. 50

A fifteenth-century manuscript of two parts, pt I a mixture of parchment and paper (outer and inner bifolia of quires are parchment, the rest is paper), pt II is parchment throughout; paper flyleaves. The manuscript has 73 leaves and measures *c.* 150×115 mm, written in a single column, *c.* 25 lines to a page. It is foliated in modern pencil: i–ii+1–70+unnumbered paper flyleaf. It is the work of two scribes, each responsible for one of the two composite parts. Red initials or spaces left for initials at the start of texts in part II. Trinity College binding, rebacked. *Secundo folio*: 'indicium iudicate'.[378]

---

[376] See further M. G. Sargent, 'The program of illustration in Edinburgh, National Library of Scotland, Advocates' Library MS 18.1.7 and New York, Pierpont Morgan Library MS 648 of Nicholas Love's *Mirror of the Blessed Life of Jesus Christ*', in *Tributes to Kathleen L. Scott. English Medieval Manuscripts: Readers, Makers and Illuminators*, ed. M. Villalobos Hennessy (London 2009), 251–9; and K. Scott, 'The illustration and decoration of manuscripts of Nicholas Love's *Mirror of the Blessed Life of Jesus Christ*', in *Nicholas Love at Waseda*, ed. S. Oguro, R. Beadle & M. G. Sargent (Cambridge 1997), 61–86.

[377] *Later Gothic Manuscripts, 1390–1490*, 2 vols (London 1996), 2. 236, 274, 275.

[378] As well as the description by James, *Trinity*, 1. 456–7, the manuscript is described by F. Somerset, *Four Wycliffite Dialogues*, EETS 333 (2009), xvii–xxiii. Texts are listed by

Collation: (fols. 1–12) I (12) || (fol. 13) II (single leaf) || (fols. 14–25) III (12) || (fols. 26–35) IV (10) || (fols. 36–43) V (8) || (fols. 44–52) VI (8+1) || (fols. 53–61) VII (8+1) || (fols. 62–70) VIII (8+1)

Catchwords survive. Quire signatures 'b', 'a' at the beginning of part I; in part II the first four leaves of the first quire are numbered 1–4, the remaining quires have signatures 'a', 'b', 'd', 'c'. Stubs from leaves added at the ends of quires VI–VIII are visible between fols. 43v–44r, 52v–53r and 63v–64r.

Texts: a composite manuscript of two parts, (1) texts 1–2, (2) texts 3–15. Items 1–2 occupy quires I–III; items 3–15 occupy quires IV–VIII.

1. (fols. 1r–13v) First words of readings from the gospels (in Latin) with book and chapter references for Sundays and saints' days, and suggestions for the topics of sermons (in English) appropriate to them. Some notes have references to the *Rosarium*[379] and cite or resemble English Wycliffite Sermons.[380]

2. (fols. 13v–25v) Latin notes on contrition (fol. 13v), the seven properties of the Cock (fol. 14r), the nine daughters of the devil (fol. 14v), verses on the Eucharist (fol. 14v), articles of faith (fol. 15r), alms (fol. 16r), seven sacraments in English from *The Mirror of Saint Edmund*, ch. 13 (fol. 16v),[381] seven causes why the Sabbath is changed to Sunday (fol. 17r), Sunday prayer (fol. 17v), miscellaneous extracts in Latin and English from Isidore, Grosseteste, Richard Rolle, etc. (fol. 18r), and John Wyclif, *Descriptio fratris*, attributed to 'doctor euangelicus' (fol. 20r).[382]

3. (fols. 26r–30v) *First seiþ Bois*.

4. (fols. 30v–34r) *Sixteen Points on which the Bishops Accuse Lollards*, Wycliffite tract.[383] Rubric: 'þes ben þe poyntis wiche ben putte be bischoppis ordinaris vp on men whiche þei clepen lollardis'.

5. (fols. 34r–35r) *A Tretyse of Ymagis*, Wycliffite tract.[384] Rubric: '[þ]es bene þe eiȝte condicions of mawmentrie þat men vsen abouȝte ymages'.

6. (fols. 35r–55v) *Dialogue between Jon and Richerd*, Wycliffite dialogue against the friars.[385] Rubric: 'Jon and Richerd'; colophon: 'Explicet dialogus fratrum amen amen amen amen'.

7. (fols. 56r–58r) John Wyclif, *De fide sacramenti*.[386] Rubric: 'De fide sacramenti'.

8. Short excerpts from the *Rosarium*:[387]

L. R. Mooney, *The Index of Middle English Prose Handlist 11: Manuscripts in the Library of Trinity College, Cambridge* (Cambridge, 1995), 13–15. See also C. von Nolcken, 'Notes on Lollard citations of John Wyclif's writings', *JTS* 39 (1988), 411–37.

[379] C. von Nolcken, *The Middle English Translation of the Rosarium Theologie* (Heidelberg 1979), 36–7.   [380] *EWS*, 77–8.

[381] Wells Rev. 7. 2299 [83].

[382] Thomson, *Wyclyf*, 433; ed. R. Buddensieg, *John Wiclif's Polemical Works in Latin*, WS, 2 vols (1883), 2. 409.

[383] Wells Rev. 2. 528–29 [54]; *IPMEP* 676; ed. Hudson, *SEWW*, 19–24.

[384] Wells Rev. 2. 530 [73]; *IPMEP* 57.

[385] ed. Somerset, *Four Wycliffite Dialogues*.

[386] ed. S. H. Thomson, 'John Wyclif's 'lost' *De fide sacramentorum*', *JTS* 33 (1932), 359–65.   [387] see von Nolcken, *The Middle English Translation*, 36–7.

(a) (fols. 58r–60r) Rubric: 'Contra temporalia clericorum'; inc.: 'Confessio duplex est s. secularis et spiritualis . . .'

(b) (fols. 60v–62v) Rubric: 'Contra mendicacionem fratrum'; inc.: 'Mendicacio triplex est . . .'

(c) (fols. 62v–64v) Rubric: 'Contra edificaciones fratrum et aliorum'; inc: 'Si fratres et alii dicunt quod mendicant ad fabricandum . . .'

(d) (fols. 64v–65r) Rubric: 'Nota quod homines non deberent elemosinas dare ffratribus cum sint validi'; inc.: 'Nunc patet per omnia ista . . .'

(e) (fol. 65v) Rubric: 'Contra mendicacionem fratrum propter predicacionem verbi dei'; inc.: 'Si fratres vel alii mendicant . . .'

(f) (fols. 66r–67r) Rubric: 'Contra mendicacionem fratrum propter eorum suffragia scilicet oraciones etc.'; inc.: 'Si fratres mendicant uel accipiant . . .'

(h) (fols. 68v–70r) Rubric: 'Contra modernam adoracionem ymaginum'; inc.: 'Ymagines sanctorum non sunt contempnende . . .'. Includes an extract from Wyclif's *De mandatis diuinis*[388] with erased ascription to Wyclif: 'd.e.'.

(fols. 67r–68v) Pseudo-Hildegard, *Insurgent gentes*, prophecy against the friars. Rubric: 'Nota de distinccione ffratrum per prophetiam'; inc.: 'Beata virgo hildegardis turonice [teutonice(?)] nacionis . . .'. Interpolated throughout.[389] Fol. 70v is blank.

Provenance: *(a)* Probably a preacher's notebook with a pronounced Wycliffite interest. Two parts, though in different hands, are united by their quotation of Wyclif and the *Rosarium*.[390]

(b) 'Quo quid antiquius eo melius G. Buggyn', s. xv (fol. 1r). The name appears in James's Trinity catalogue as 'Guggyn' and has been cited as such by many critics, but Neil Ker corrected this. Buggyn is probably to be identified with William Buggyn, a member of Trinity College, Cambridge in the second half of the sixteenth century.[391]

(c) Given to Trinity College by John Whitgift, probably after his death in 1604.[392]

[ES]

---

[388] Thomson, *Wyclyf*, 26).

[389] Somerset, *Four Wycliffite Dialogues*, xxii; K. Kerby-Fulton, M. Hayton & K. Olsen, 'Pseudo-Hildegardian prophecy and antimendicant propaganda in late medieval England: an edition of the most popular insular text of 'Insurgent gentes', in *Prophecy, Apocalypse and the Day of Doom: Proceedings of the 2000 Harlaxton Symposium Harlaxton Symposium*, ed. N. Morgan (Donington 2004), 160–94.

[390] See further A. Hudson, 'Wycliffite prose', in *Middle English Prose: a Critical Guide to Major Authors and Genres*, ed. A. S. G. Edwards (New Brunswick, NJ, 1984), 249–70, at 260.

[391] See the report by R. W. Hunt of Neil Ker's list of manuscripts owned by G. Buggyn, several of which are Wycliffite collections, in *Bodleian Library Quarto Catalogues*, 2: *Laudian Manuscripts*, ed. H. O. Coxe, rev. R. W. Hunt (Oxford 1973), xiii.

[392] Somerset, *Four Wycliffite Dialogues*, xxiii.

XII. CHAPTER NUMBERING IN RICHARD
ULLERSTON'S DETERMINATION

As this introduction and the description of the Vienna manuscript make clear, the single surviving copy of Ullerston's work stands at a considerable remove, geographically and textually, from the author's holograph. For the most part the present editors have accepted the text of the Vienna manuscript, amending only details of its references and a few other readings. But the Vienna text is marked up apparently by its main scribe into chapters, and many chapter headings show traces of alteration or are heavily crossed through. This subdivision is unlikely to be authorial, seems to do little to clarify the structure of Ullerston's argument, and indeed shows a failure to realize that chapter division is not appropriate to a determination. Whether it was introduced by the scribe of the Vienna manuscript or by a copyist further back in the transmission is unclear. An attempt therefore has been made in the edition to suppress the chapter numbering that is most probably scribal, but to retain those number sequences that may be original and are helpful to an understanding of the whole.

Ullerston's text in the Vienna manuscript reflects an attempt to change a structure with thirty-nine sections to a structure with twenty-four. The opening of the text is presented on fol. 195ra with *Articulus principalis* beside the capital at the start. After the introductory paragraph follows the marginal heading *Questio principalis*. Ullerston's introduction admits that the question of biblical translation has been previously treated by two doctors, one arguing the negative case, the other the positive, and the narrator proposes to start with recapitulating the negative points. The sequence of negative views that follows is numbered in red in arabic 1–10 in the margins on the first leaf (fol. 195ra–va). But, whilst the marginal numbering continues with 11–30 (again in red arabics) on fols. 195va–196rb, there are new indications of structure by what is marked as *Capitulum* from fol. 195va on; these are initially numbered in arabic, but from *Capitulum* 7 practice changes to roman numerals, and are heavily corrected, as will be seen in the chart below.

The first irregularity of the *capitulum* subdivisions appears at the very start: the numbering of the *capitula* begins with 2, suggesting that earlier *Articulus principalis* and *Questio principalis* count as the first chapter. The placing of *capitula* in this initial part of the determination seems fairly random, except that it attempts to subdivide the text into even segments: *Capitulum* 2 stands marginally above the start of negative-view 11 on fol. 195va, *Capitulum* 3 above

the start of view 21 on fol. 196ra. When Ullerston's responses to negative points, introduced by *Ad primum, Ad secundum*, and so on, begin on fol. 199rb, the first of these is labelled *Capitulum 10*, and each subsequent numbered argument corresponds to a new *capitulum*, thus making *capitula* subdivisions redundant. These subdivisions stopped when numbered arguments ended after *Ad 30^m et ultimum* (fol. 206ra), resulting in the total of 39 *capitula*.

This earlier system of subdivisions was later corrected to a system of 24 chapters. Corrections resulting from this new system begin at the start of Ullerston's numbered responses (fol. 199rb). Whereas originally, as pointed out above, each argument corresponded to a *capitulum*, the new numbering arranges arguments into groups and continues after they end with the final chapter 24, beginning *Istud tamen* on fol. 207va. The change was achieved by erasing and over-writing in red some Roman numerals and by crossing out other, no longer needed numerals, in black ink. The numerals that were crossed out remain readable, and in cases where correction was made by erasure and overwriting, the earlier numeral is in most cases still possible to make out.

It seems likely that these alterations were made by the main scribe himself. The final chapter number, 24, shows no sign of erasure or alteration. The scribe seems to have changed his mind before or at the time of arriving at the 24th chapter, and worked to ensure that it was preceded by twenty-three chapters by altering chapter divisions in the section containing Ullerston's numbered responses. The red used to alter partially erased numerals seems identical to the red used by the main scribe elsewhere.[393] Under this new system the arguments were grouped as follows:

ch. 10: arguments 1–2
ch. 11: arguments 3–4
ch. 12: argument 5
ch. 13: arguments 6–8
ch. 14: argument 9
ch. 15: arguments 10–12
ch. 16: arguments 13–14
ch. 17: arguments 15–16
ch. 18: arguments 17–18
ch. 19: arguments 19–21

[393] It seems clear that the main scribe was working simultaneously with ordinary and with red ink; there are no clear instances when he left a blank space for a number to be provided later. Red is used by the scribe throughout to underline parts of references to asserted authorities (usually author's name or title of work).

ch. 20: arguments 22–23
ch. 21: argument 24
ch. 22: arguments 25–29
ch. 23: argument 30

As can be seen, the new system seems to be little more than an attempt to arrange the material into relatively even segments. This could not have been done exactly because *capitula* had to respect textual divisions into numbered points, but most *capitula* comprise two numbered responses and the responses that are short, such as 25–29, are grouped together, resulting in sections most of which contain between 500 and 1,000 words.

As mentioned earlier, neither of the two *capitula* structures is accepted in the text since the authority behind both is unclear and neither seems to facilitate the understanding of Ullerston's argument. The following chart presents the evidence fully. The section headings were transcribed exactly, whenever possible; uncertainty due to correction in the manuscript is indicated by question marks. The opening words of the sections are from the edited text.

Folio	Section heading in MS	Opening words
fol. 195ra	*Articulus principalis*	*Stabilita siquidem* (2.1)
	Questio principalis	*Querit enim* (2.18)
fol. 195va	*Cap^m 2^m*	*Item, beatus Ieronimus* (8.106)
fol. 196ra	*C 3^m*	*Item, quod simpliciter* (12.191)
fol. 196rb	*C 4^m Responsio*	*Antequam enim* (16.255)
fol. 196vb	*Cap^m5^m*	*Uidendum est* (18.319)
fol. 197rb	*Sequitur Cap^m 6^m*	*Quinto et ultimo* (24.425)
fol. 197va	*Capitulu(m) vii^m*	*Primum quod mouet* (26.471)
fol. 198rb	*Capitulu(m) viii^m*	*Et si obicias* (32.562)
fol. 198vb	*C ix^m*	*Consequenter ad* (36.661)
fol. 199rb	*Se(quitur) Cap^mx^m*	*Ad primum* (42.750)
fol. 199va	*Ca^m xi^m* crossed out in black	*Ad secundum* (42.787)
fol. 199vb	originally *C xii^m*corr. to *C xi^m*	*Ad 3^m* (44.805)
fol. 199vb	*Sequit(ur) Ca xiii* crossed out in black	*Ad 4^m* (44.821)
fol. 200rb	originally *C xiiij*, corr. to *C xii*	*Ad quintum* (48.899)
fol. 201ra	*xiij* corr. from *xv*?	*Ad 6^m* (54.1002)
fol. 201rb	*Ca^m xvj^m* crossed out in black	*Ad septimum* (56.1027)

fol. 201rb	*Capitulu(m) xvii* crossed out in black	*Ad octauum* (56.1036)
fol. 201rb	originally *Sequit(ur) Capi(tulu)m xviij*, corr. to *xiiij*	*Ad nonum* (56.1049)
fol. 202ra	*xv* corr. from *xix*?	*Ad decimum* (62.1167)
fol. 202rb	*Sequit(ur) Ca xx* crossed out in black	*Ad vndecimum* (64.1199)
fol. 202rb	*Sequit(ur) Cap^m xxj* crossed out in black	*Ad duodecimum* (64.1204)
fol. 202va	originally *Cap^m xxii*, corr. to *xvi*	*Ad tredecimum* (66.1220)
fol. 202va	*xxiii^m* crossed out in black	*Ad 14^m* (66.1235)
fol. 202vb	originally *xxiiij^m*, corr. to *xvii*	*Ad quindecimum* (68.1281)
fol. 203ra	*xxv* crossed out in black	*Ad sedecimum* (72.1329)
fol. 203rb	originally *xxvi*, corr. to *xviij*	*Ad 17^m* (74.1368)
fol. 203va	*xxvij* crossed out in black	*Ad decimum* (74.1392)
fol. 203vb	*xxviij* crossed out in black, *xix^m* add. in red	*Ad 19^m* (78.1441)
fol. 204ra	*Sequi(tur) Capi^m xxix^m* crossed out in black	*Ad vigesimum* (78.1473)
fol. 204rb	*C xxx* crossed out in black	*Ad 21^m* (80.1514)
fol. 204va	originally *xxxj^m*, corr. to *xx*	*Ad 22^m* (82.1534)
fol. 205ra	*xxxij* crossed out in black	*Ad 23^m* (86.1612)
fol. 205ra	originally *Capitulu(m) xxxiij*, corr. to *xxi^m*	*Ad 24m* (86.1630)
fol. 205va	originally *xxxiiij^m*, corr. to *xxii^m*	*Ad uigesimum quintum* (92.1728)
fol. 205vb	*xxxv^m* crossed out in black	*Ad 26^m* (92.1738)
fol. 205vb	*Capi^m xxxvi^m* crossed out in black	*Ad 27^m* (94.1746)
fol. 205vb	*Ca^m xxxvii^m* crossed out in black	*Ad 28^m* (94.1763)
fol. 206ra	*Cap^m xxxviii* crossed out in black	*Ad 29^m* (94.1776)
fol. 206ra	originally *xxxix^m*, corr. to *xxiii^m*	*Ad 30^m* (96.1792)
fol. 207va	*Cap^m xxiiij^m*	*Istud tamen* (108.2015)

[ES and AH]

XIII. NOTE ON EDITORIAL PRACTICE

A. *General*

The edition of the three Latin texts follows the modern habit of reproducing the orthography of the witness, and not classicizing nor standardizing this, nor attempting to regularize a scribe's usage. Since each of the Latin texts here survives as a whole in only a single copy,

the ideal edition of each would attempt to reproduce each without alteration (save where it can reasonably be supposed the scribe on reflection would have corrected his first spelling). It follows from this last point that any departure from a scribe's words, inflections or syntax must be editorially recognized. No abbreviation marks are used in the edition. Scribal usage of i/j/y and of u/v is retained in so far as it is possible to make a judgement on the intention; the disambiguation of -ct- and -tt- is an editorial decision. Punctuation and capitalization throughout is modern, but attempts to reflect the style of the medieval Latin.

Each text contains lengthy quotations from a variety of earlier authorities; in most cases those exist in editions of variable reliability and with divergent aims. It is not the purpose of the present volume to retrace the history of these underlying texts. Indeed, while modern editions typically attempt to reconstruct the earliest accessible version of a text, this is not always helpful for the study of how the texts were used in the later Middle Ages. Citations from the Bible and authorities in texts edited here often diverge in detail or more considerably from the versions available in modern editions. To avoid misrepresenting the authors' knowledge of authorities and textual fluidity characteristic of this period, no attempt has been made to 'correct' the authors' quotations to bring them in line with Migne or modern editions, or to record these numerous divergences. The very few exceptions to this practice are cases where a manuscript reading is likely to be an error on the grounds of both context and palaeography. An example of this is the manuscript reading *solicitudine* in a quotation from Seneca in Ullerston's text (90.1709) emended to *solitudine* to preserve the original contrast between 'company' and 'solitude'. Such cases, as all emendations, are commented on in the critical apparatus.

B. *Numerals*

Despite the discrepant origins, and consequent training of the three scribes involved in the Latin texts edited, the treatment of numerals by these three was for the most part similar. All three normally use arabic and not roman numerals in all positions, whether the expected form would be cardinal or ordinal;[394] in a very few cases the full word is spelled out, but for the most part the symbol alone was provided. It would seem that all three scribes aimed to provide ordinal numerals in a fully inflected system; cardinal numerals were also inflected as

[394] A few cases of Roman numerals are found in Ullerston, for example, 38.679, 42.761, 48.900.

if they had been converted into ordinals by notional addition of an unexpressed noun (thus in a list of objections in Palmer 153–156.1–92 numbers 1–18 appear with a superscript 'o' following the number in every occurrence). Abbreviation marks usually consist in small, superscript letters. It seems clear, however, that none of the scribes put much effort into the task of making usage regular or logical. Indication in a list, as with the same example, is usually with the same superscript letter in every case, but very often less predictable sequences, such as numerical chapter references, have no indication of case at all, and a few incomplete or unusual abbreviations also occur. The editors' objective here is to reflect as far as is possible in modern print the usage of the scribes; hence superscript letters are those found in the relevant manuscript. The absence of a superscript letter implies absence by the scribe; abbreviation marks occasionally used instead of superscript letters, when no letter is distinguishable, are not reproduced. The consequence of this is irregularity of forms, but not, we hope, obscurity of meaning. In a few cases, for the convenience of the reader, we represented numerals in the manuscripts with words in the edition; this was done where a word, rather than a number, is expected in a modern text, for example, when numerals are used adverbially ('firstly', 'secondly', and similar).

C. *References*

The frequent biblical quotations are usually indicated in all three texts by book and chapter numbers; for convenience, these are completed here editorially within the text by placing the verse numbers afterwards in square brackets. In the unusual instances where no biblical reference is provided, the whole is supplied within square brackets.[395] In other quotations (e.g. from Augustine, Roger Bacon and others) the information provided by the exemplar is given where it occurs, but no further clarification is added in the edited text. Full references are supplied in the commentary notes along with any relevant information or clarification. At the end of the volume may be found an index of biblical citations, as well as a general index including authorities cited, and a bibliography of sources, which includes additional discussion of the identification and editorial treatment of quotations from the Bible and authorities.

---

[395] Allusion to biblical wording which is not taken up by a declared reference is usually not editorially supplied; if, however, the argument seems based on uncited biblical material, the detail is given in square brackets.

D. *Editorial Conventions*

Where a correction or confusion in the manuscript is not otherwise glossed in the apparatus criticus, the following symbols are used.

Square brackets are used to supply text which is absent from the manuscript but whose addition is necessary to complete the sense. They are likewise used to complete biblical references in the text where only a biblical book or chapter number was referred to. It was thought helpful to complete references to chapter and verse within the text rather than relying on the apparatus; the brackets make it clear what part of the reference is editorial.

Solidi are used to show scribal insertions in the text: single ones \ / are placed around letters or words which are interlineated; double ones \\ // surround material which is supplied in the margins.

In all three texts manuscript folio numbers are provided, 'r' and 'v' indicating recto and verso, 'a' and 'b' indicating columns. A vertical bar (|) in the text indicates a page turn in the manuscript.

Editorial abbreviations used are *add.* (added), *canc.* (cancelled), *corr.* (corrected), *om.* (omitted).

1. Ullerston

It should be remembered throughout that the scribe of the single complete manuscript was plainly Bohemian: his script and its letter forms, and especially its abbreviations, are notably different from their English equivalents of a similar date; many marks are simply indications of absence but not specification of what is omitted (e.g. *q'* or *tn* with a line over 'n'). The scribe's usage and the general accuracy of his transcription can to some extent be gauged from his quotations, often long, from patristic and other authorities. The main scribe seems to have been attentive, and his occasional mistakes are often readily explicable from repetition of particular words in the context. His copy was carefully scrutinized and corrected, and the footnotes to the text attempt to give an account of the changes made by the corrector (though not his overwriting of some letters when no change seems to have been intended). The corrector could have been the original scribe writing later with a sharper pen, and with closer attention to individual readings; he could, however, have been another scribe of similar date and style. Throughout the text red is used for chapter headings, to highlight names of authorities (but not most other names), and to (re)punctuate the text: how much of this was done immediately after the writing of the material, how much at a later time and from an exemplar other than that used by the main

copyist, is hard to determine. Material in this red ink is not reliably caught by photography; further details of its use can be found above, 'Chapter Numbering in Richard Ullerston's Determination'. Many readings highlighted in red appear to be emphasized by that colour, and not (as a first glance might suppose) marked for deletion.

The text in ÖNB MS 4133 has been collated with the fragment preserved in Gonville and Caius, MS 803/807 frag. 36 (siglum G) with substantive variants recorded in the apparatus. It has not been possible to use *First seiþ Bois* to emend the text in ÖNB MS 4133: even when closely following Ullerston, the translation is not sufficiently literal to serve this purpose.

2. Butler and Palmer

The present edition differs substantially from an earlier edition by Margaret Deanesly in *The Lollard Bible* (1920) due to re-examination of manuscripts and differences in editorial practice. Deanesly classicized the scribes' orthographic habits (p. 401); here, on the contrary, the scribes' usage throughout has been retained. A number of Deanesly's emendations have been accepted and are acknowledged in the critical apparatus.

3. *First seiþ Bois*

The most recent edition of *First seiþ Bois*, based on all surviving manuscripts, is Mary Dove, *The Earliest Advocates of the English Bible* (Exeter 2010), 143–9. We provide a text for comparison with Ullerston's determination based on the only two complete medieval manuscript copies in Cambridge, Trinity College, MS B. 14. 50 and New York, Pierpont Morgan Library, MS M 648. Trinity B. 14. 50 was used as the base text and collated against M 648 (siglum N1). Only substantive variants from M 648 are provided. The spelling of Trinity B. 14. 50 is followed throughout; punctuation, word and sentence division, and capitalization are editorial. Abbreviations are expanded silently. Passages from Ullerston's determination are provided on the facing page whenever sufficiently close to *Bois*.

[AH]

Plate 1

Vienna, Österreichische Nationalbibliothek, MS 4133,
fol. 195r, Richard Ullerston's determination, opening page.

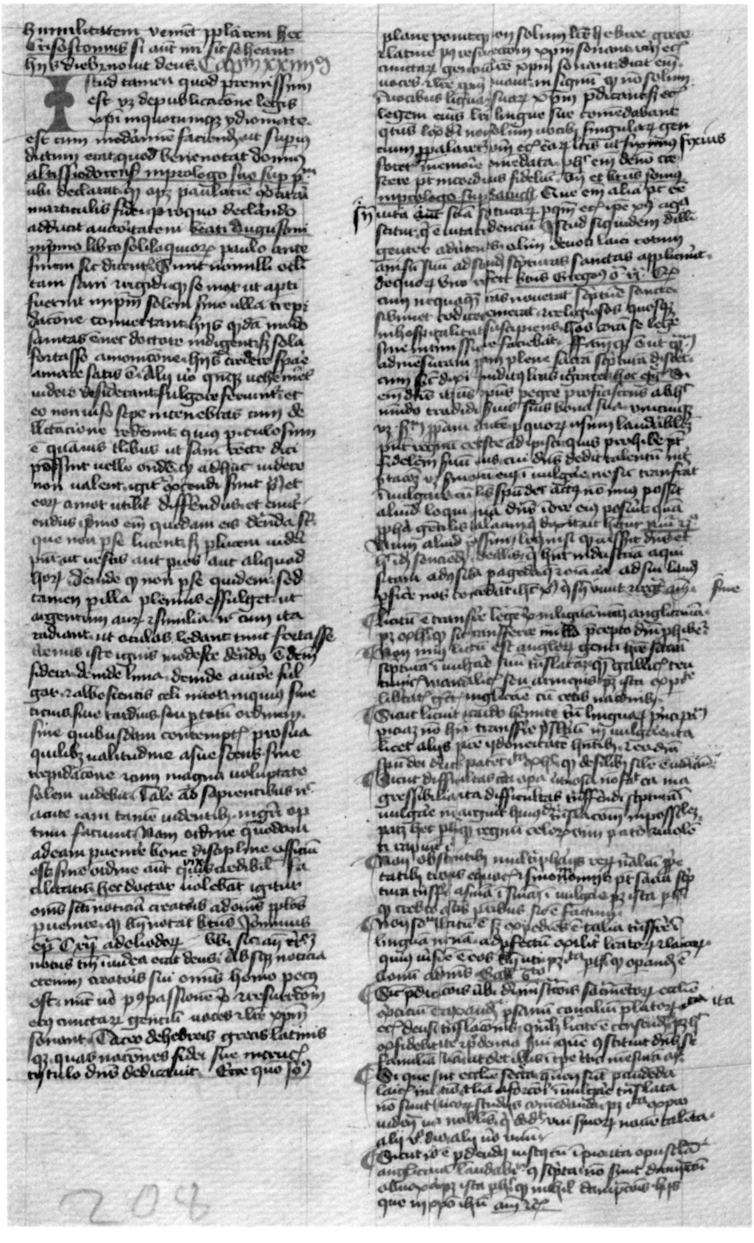

Plate 2

Vienna, Österreichische Nationalbibliothek, MS 4133,
fol. 207v, Richard Ullerston's determination, final page.

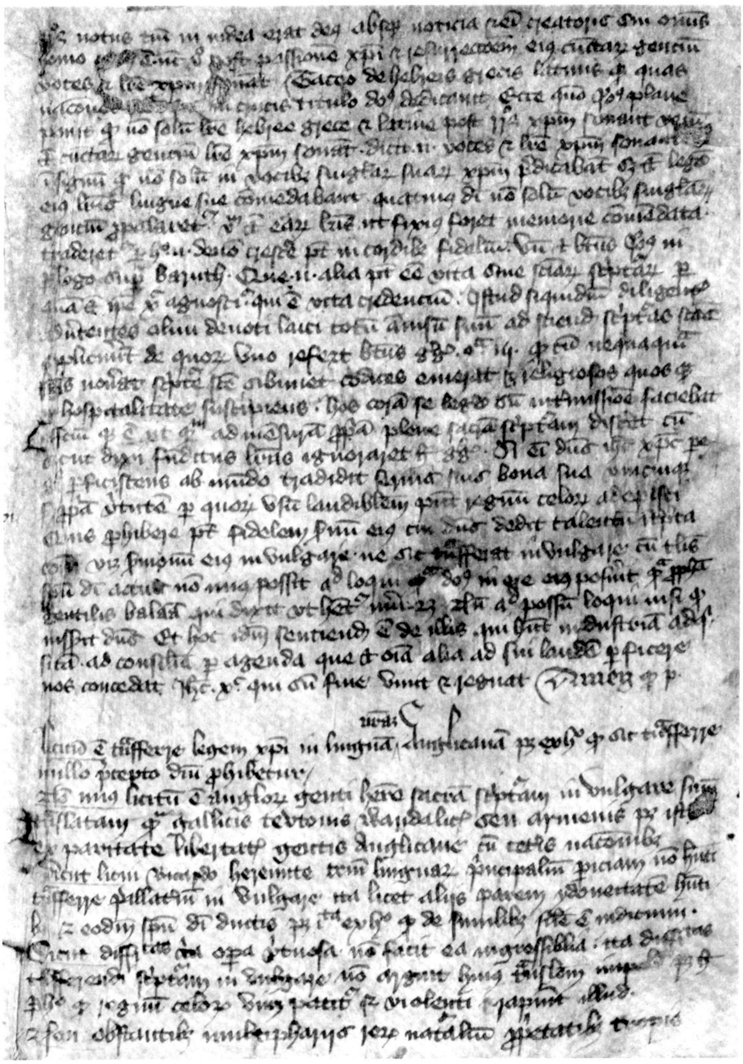

Plate 3
Cambridge, Gonville and Caius College, MS 803/807,
fragment 36, recto, Richard Ullerston's determination.

Plate 4
Cambridge, Gonville and Caius College, MS 803/807,
fragment 36, verso, Richard Ullerston's determination.

Plate 5
Cambridge, Gonville and Caius College, MS 803/807, fragment 36,
verso, ultra-violet image, Richard Ullerston's determination.

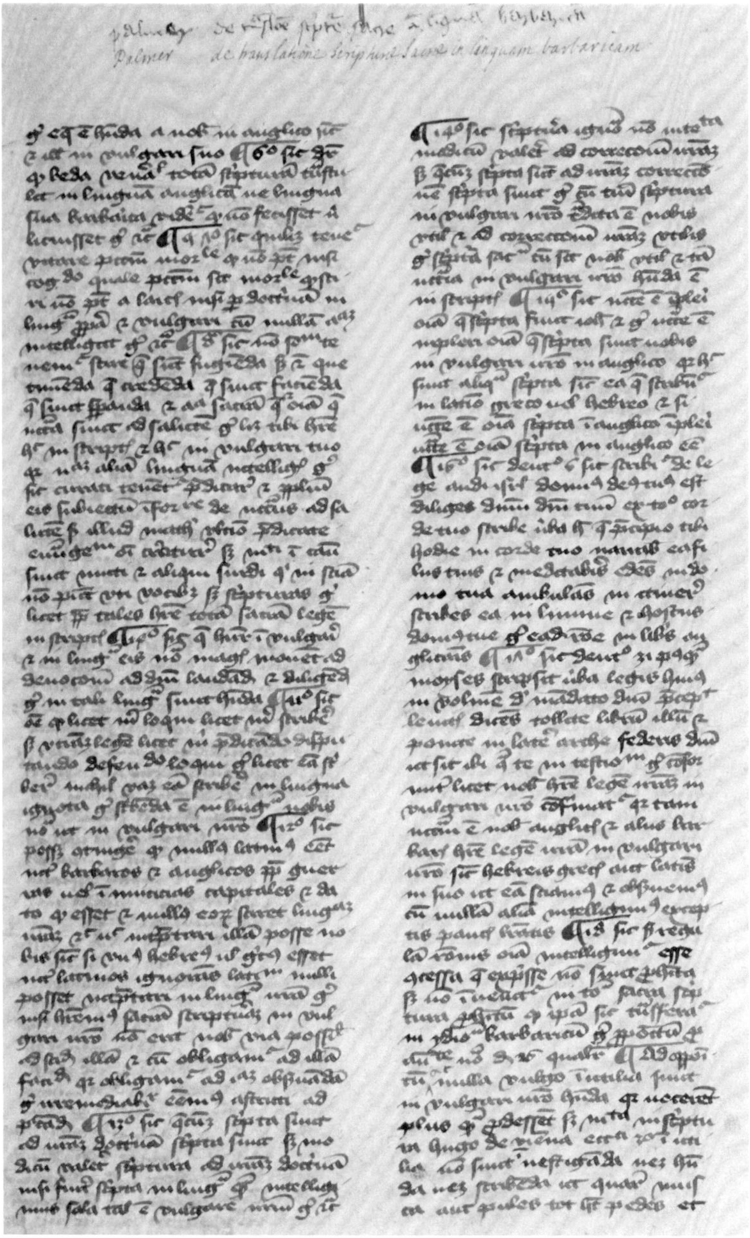

Plate 6
Cambridge, Trinity College, MS B. 15. 11,
fol. 43r, Thomas Palmer's determination.

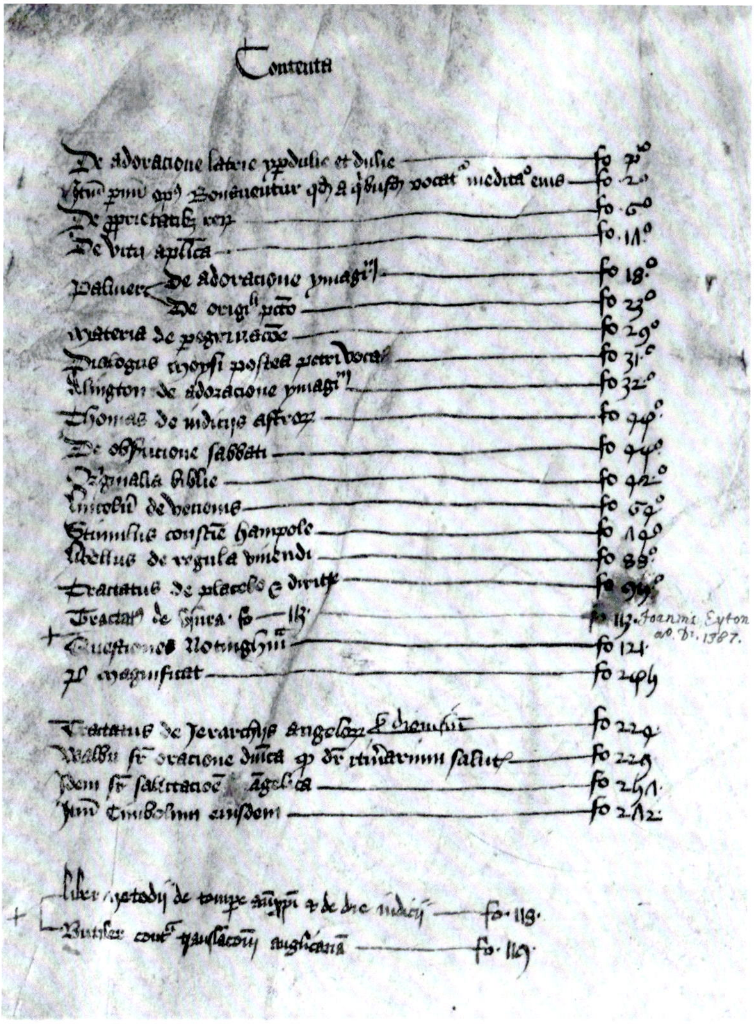

Plate 7
Oxford, Merton College, MS 68, fol. iii^v, added table of contents with William Butler's determination listed as an addition underneath the main table, probably in a different contemporary hand.

Ageyns hem þat seyn þat Goddis lawe shulde not or may not be drawen
in to englishe. See maken þes resons. Ffirst seiþ Bois in his boke de
Disciplina scolarum: þat children shulde be taught i þe bokis of senek
and Beda expouneþ þis seyng children shulden be taught in vertues
ffor þe bokis of senek ben morals. and for þei ben not taught whil in
her ȝongþe. þei conseyuen yuel manys 4 ben vnabel to conceyue þe
sotil sciense of treuþe seyinge þe wise man. Wisdom shal not entre
in to a wickked soule. and moche þ of þe sentence of Bede. 4 also seiþ
in his logik seiþ þe soule of a man is as clene myrro neþer polich
is in swiche is sene liȝtliche þe ymage of man. But for þe puple
hay not konynge in ȝouþe. þei han derke soulis 4 blyndid. so þ þei
prfiten not. but in falsenes. malice 4 oþ vices. and moche þ of þ is
mater. O siþen heþen philosofris wolden þe puple to prfiten in
naturnal sciense: hod myche more shulden cristen men willen þe
puple to prfiten in science of vertues for so wold god. ffor whane
þe lawe was ȝouen to moises i þe mounte of synay. god ȝaf it i
Ebreu for þ al þe puple shuld vnderstoud it 4 bad moises to
rede it vnto hem. to þe tyme þei vnderstode þ it. and sle rede it as
is pleyn in Deteronomie 31º cº. and Esdras also rede it froi
morou to mydday as it is pleyn in his ffirst boke 8º cº. aptily
in þe strete. and þe eeres of þe puple weren entenly ȝoue þ to
and þei vnderstoden it. and þis þei miȝt not haue done but if
it hadde ben redd in þ moder tonge. so þat þe puple heryng felle
i to grete wepynge. 4 in Deut 31º cº it is write. asse þi faders
and þei shullen shewe to ȝee 4 þi elderis. 4 þei shulen sei to ȝee

RICHARD ULLERSTON

De translatione sacre scripture in vulgare

*On the Translation of Holy
Scripture into the Vernacular*

Vienna, Österreichische Nationalbibliothek,
MS 4133, fols. 195ra–207vb

De translatione sacre scripture in vulgare

195ra *Articulus principalis*

Stabilita siquidem translacione Ieronimi tamquam uera in duobus
articulis prelibatis, superest ad tertium procedendum istum: videlicet vtrum, sicut Ieronimo licuit ab Hebreo et Greco in Latinum
transferre sacrum canonem, ita liceat ipsum in alias lingwas minus
principales et famosas transferre. Et quamuis iste articulus in tem- 5
poribus patrum nostrorum nullatenus in dubium uertebatur, modo
uero tam grandis dubitacio oritur super illo, quod duo ualentes doctores huius kathedre[1] quasi in ista materia totum tempus lecture sue
consumebant.[2] Quorum vnus ad articuli partem negatiuam arguebat
per aliquot argumenta, alter uero succedens ad articuli partem affir- 10
matiuam arguebat nescio per quot argumentorum uigenarios. Neuter
tamen apparuit scole quid uoluit vltimate in materia articuli diffinire.
In pertractando igitur hunc articulum, sic procedam. Primo quidem
recitabo quedam argumenta primi doctoris, secundo adiciam plura
de propriis ad partem articuli negatiuam. Et tertio pro modulo meo 15
soluam argumenta que fiunt ad oppositum articuli antedicti, per que
luculenter patebit quid velim sentire circa articulum pretaxatum.

Questio principalis

1. Querit enim primus doctor vtrum scriptura sacra est in omnes
lingwas interpretanda. Que quidem questio aliqualiter coincidit cum
articulo nostro contra quem arguit doctor primo sic: scriptura sacra 20
nemini reuelatur nisi ex speciali gracia, cum interpretacio sit speciale
donum, ergo nullus atemptaret sine speciali gracia hoc facere.

2. Item, si aliqui deberent, precipue deberent esse sacerdotes, et
inter eos illi qui magis obligantur ad noticiam sacre scripture qui sunt
episcopi; sed illi pro hiis diebus sunt insufficientes. Ergo etc. 25

3. Item, uetus testamentum cessauit secundum sensum literalem,
sed interpretacio non est nisi secundum sensum literalem. Ergo etc.

4. Item, Augustinus apeciit translacionem septuaginta in Latinam ligwam propter impericiam Latinorum interpretum; ergo si
sacra scriptura transfereretur in omnes lingwas, multo plures inter- 30
pretes imperiti corrumperent scripturam. Ergo etc.

TITLE: *The title is based on the colophon at the end of the text*   13 *letter*
erased after pertractando *MS*   15 propriis] *corr. from* proprio *MS*   29 sa *canc.*
after impericiam *MS*

---

[1] The meaning 'faculty' is not recorded for *cathedra* in *DML*; the concept of a 'faculty'
in a modern sense was only emerging at this time (see *facultas* in *DML*) and the terminology was probably not yet fixed (see also *scola*—'educational establishment, school,
university' in *DML*—used by Ullerston in next sentence).

Richard Ullerston on the Translation of Holy Scripture into the Vernacular

Principal Matter

Now that Jerome's translation has been established as the true version in the two sections already treated, it remains to go on to the third: that is whether, as it was permissible for Jerome to translate the sacred canon from Hebrew and Greek into Latin, it is equally licit to translate it into minor and less prestigious languages. Now although this question was regarded as not at all doubtful in the time of our ancestors, a great issue has been made of it in our time, since two doughty doctors of this faculty[1] have devoted their whole course of lectures to it.[2] One of them has argued the negative case in a number of points, and the other in turn has put the affirmative position in countless scores of arguments. Neither of them has made clear to the faculty what he wished to conclude on the substance of the question. Therefore in dealing with this question, I will proceed by recapitulating some of the arguments of the first doctor, and then I will add some more of my own which are pertinent to the negative side of the argument. Then thirdly I will resolve in my own way the arguments which can be made on the opposite side, from which it will be quite clear what my own opinion is on this contested question.

Principal Question

1. The first doctor asks whether holy scripture can be translated into all languages. This accords with our own question, on which he first argues thus: the meaning of holy scripture is only revealed by a special grace, and as its interpretation is a special gift, nobody should attempt it without that grace.

2. Again, if any persons should do it, they should above all be priests, among whom those most bound to knowledge of holy scripture are the bishops; but in our time they are not capable of it.

3. Again, the Old Testament no longer binds us in a literal sense, but a translation can only be according to the literal sense.

4. Again, Augustine sought out a Latin translation of the Septuagint because of the [existing] Latin translators' lack of learning; so if holy scripture were to be translated into all languages, many more unlearned translators would corrupt its meaning.

---

[2] Literally 'have been using up the whole time of their teaching on this very subject'.

5. Ista siquidem argumenta ostendit michi quidam amicus de manu prefati doctoris scripta. Sed contra articulum arguitur sic Augustinus in sermone suo de simbolo qui sic incipit 'Tempus est ut simbolum accipiatis', et est sermone 137° secundum vnam cotacionem, secun- 35 dum vero aliam cotacionem est tercia parte sermonum sermone 58°. Sic scribit: 'Hunc', inquit, 'breuem sermonem de vniuerso simbolo uobis debitum reddidi, in quo simbolo quod audiueritis totum in isto sermone nostro breuiter collectum cognoscetis. Nec ut eadem simboli teneatis uerba, vllo modo debetis scribere, sed audiendo per- 40 discere, nec cum didiceritis, scribere, sed me|moria semper tenere at\que/ recolere. Quidquid enim in simbolo audituri estis, in diuinis sacrarum scripturarum literis continetur, sed quod ita collectum et in formam quandam redactum, non licet scribi; comemoracio fit promissionis Dei, ubi per prophetam pronunccians nouum testa- 45 mentum, dixit, "hoc est testamentum quod ordinabo illis post dies illos, dicit Dominus, dabo legem meam in mente eorum, et in corde eorum scribam eam". Huius rei signande causa audiendo simbolum, nec in thabulis, nec in aliqua materia, sed in corde discitur.'³ Hec Augustinus. Ex isto dicto huius sancti doctoris plane habetur quod 50 simbolum nullo modo debet scribi, nec eciam licet scribi; sed quod non licet scribi a fortiori, non licet transferri, et potissime in liguam barbaricam. Ergo oppositum articuli.

6. Item, secundum beatum Augustinum 2° *De doctrina christiana*, capitulo 2°, plerumque a sensu auctoris deuius aberrat inter- 55 pres si non sit doctissimus, sed talem non est facile invenire,⁴ cum illud quod per excellenciam dicitur vni soli conuenit.⁵ Ergo idem quod prius.

7. Item, secundum Origenem et ponitur in *Decretis*, distinctio 43 *In mandatis*, quod inquinatis et in peccatis involutis non oportet 60 aliquid de secrecioribus et remotis diuine sciencie proloqui; et infra eadem distinccione, capitulo *Dispensacio*, pariter sic habetur, 'pariter sic', inquit, 'obseruare debet sacerdos ne indignis et non intelligentibus secreta misteria sua predicacione reserare incipiat. Qui enim ea docet que ab auditoribus non ualent intelligi, non eorum utilita- 65 tem, sed sui ostentacionem facit.' Vnde, in exposicione *beati inmaculati*, dicitur, 'vicium animi est indignis secreta uulgare, quod fit vel loquacitate incauta, dum sine iudicio uolat irreuocabile uerbum; vel

195rb

---

35 -is *in* accipiatis *add. in darker ink MS*   36 98° *in text,* 58° *added in margin MS*
43 literarum *canc. before* scripturarum *MS*   52 licet transferri] debet *canc.,* licet *in margin MS*   59 distinctio 43] di.8 *canc.,* di.43 *in margin MS*

---

³ Augustine, *Sermo in traditione Symboli I* (*sermo de tempore* 212) (*PL* 38. 1060).

⁴ *secrecioribus*: 'not generally known, learned through investigation or revelation' (*DML* sense 9).

5. Now these arguments, written in the hand of this doctor, were shown me by a friend. But Augustine argues on the negative side in his sermon on the creed which begins 'It is time that you receive a creed', number 137 according to one system of enumeration, and sermon 58 in part 3 of the sermons according to another. He says, 'I have put together for you a short sermon on the universal creed, a creed in which you can find in summary everything in my sermon. You should not attend to the precise words of the creed, or on any account write it down, but learn it thoroughly by hearing it, rather than writing it down, when you have learnt to hold it and recollect it permanently in your memory. For whatever you will hear in the creed is written in the words of God in the holy scriptures, and what is put together in scripture and rendered in a particular way must not be written down; the promise of God is committed to memory, as the prophet says, enunciating a new covenant, "this shall be the covenant which I will make for them, says the Lord, after those days, I will put my law in their inward parts, and write it in their hearts". What is signified by the words is learnt in the heart by hearing the creed, not from a tablet or some other material.'[3] So says Augustine, and it plainly follows from the words of the holy doctor that the creed should not and is not allowed to be on any account written down; and *a fortiori* what should not be written should not be translated, especially into a vernacular. This proves the negative case.

6. Again, according to St Augustine in chapter 2 of book 2 of *De doctrina christiana*, a wayward translator will frequently depart from the author's meaning unless he is particularly learned,[4] and it is not easy to find a very learned person, as everyone agrees that only one person can excel.[5]

7. Again, Origen says, as quoted in the *Decreta*, distinction 43 *De mandatis*, it is not appropriate for the impure and those who are beset with sin to discourse on more advanced and abstruse topics; and we find further on in the same distinction, in the chapter entitled *Dispensatio*, the similar point, that 'a priest should take care not to embark on preaching secret mysteries to the unworthy and the uncomprehending. For whoever teaches things which his hearers are incapable of understanding gives them nothing useful, and is showing off.' So, in the exposition of *beati immaculati*, it is pointed out that 'it is a spiritual sin to divulge secret matters to the unworthy, because it is done either out of foolish loquacity when irrevocable words are

[5] Augustine, *De doctrina christiana*, II 13 (*PL* 43. 44).

adulacione, ut ei placeat cui secreta reuelat; uel iactacione sciencie, ut plura sciencie uideatur'. Hec canon.[6] 70

8. Item, secundum Bacon in epistola ad Clementem, qui debet aliquam scienciam vel scripturam transferre, debet illam scire et linguam a qua transfert, et linguam in quam transfertur.[7] Sed quamuis hec duo extrema uideantur multum difficilia, medium uidetur tamquam impossibile; quis vmquam, post apostolos, sciuit totam sacram 75 scripturam? Quo ausu ergo atemptaret quis totam sacram scripturam transferre, et potissime in uulgare?

9. Item, quod non potest fideliter transferri in uulgare, non debet transferri in uulgare. Sed vna lingwa non potest fideliter per aliam exponi, propter diuersitatem proprietatum loquendi in diuersis lin- 80 gwis, ut dicit idem Bacon vbi supra. 'Et hoc', inquit, 'potest quilibet probare, si scienciam quam nouit uelit in liguam maternam conuertere.' 'Certe', inquit, 'logicus non poterit exprimere suam logicam si iurasset per uocabula lingue materne; sed oporteret eum noua fingere, et ideo non intelligeretur nisi a seipso.'[8] Et sic de aliis scienciis: 85 uocabula infinita que ponuntur in textubus theologie et philosophie |

195va de alienis lingwis que non possunt scribi nec proferri nec intelligi nisi per eos qui linguas sciunt. 'Et necesse', inquit, 'fuit hoc fieri propter hoc, quod sciencie fuerunt proposite in lingua propria, et translatores non invenerunt in ligua Latina uocabula sufficiencia.' Huic siquidem 90 sentencie aludit beatus Augustinus 2° *De doctrina christiana*, capitulo 10, ubi ad propositum ita scribit. 'Sunt', inquit, 'certa uerba certarum linguarum que in vsum alterius lingue per interpretacionem transire non possunt: et hoc maxime interieccionibus accidit, que uerba per motum animi significant, pociusque sentencie concepte vllam parti- 95 culam'; et exemplificat de istis uocabulis *Racha* et *Osanna*.[9]

10. Preterea, si ab olim translacio erat fidelis, et modo corrupta, periculosum est secundum illam transferre; sed sic est de translacione quam habemus. Ergo etc. Patet consequencia cum maiore, et pro minore est Bacon, vbi supra, ubi sic: 'illa', inquit, 'que fuerunt bene 100 translata, sunt modo corrupta, propter hoc quod lingwas ignoramus; sicut', inquit, 'patet per totam Bibliam et philosophiam, quia nec scimus scribere, nec legere, nec proferre. Et per consequens perit

---

69 adulacione] *corr. from* adolacione *MS*   87 nec'] *originally* neque, que *canc.*, -c *inserted MS*   proferri] *originally* proferre, *final* -e *corr. to* -i *MS*   95 pociusque] *originally* pocius quam, quam *canc.*, que *add. MS*   100 supra *originally* su^ra

---

[6] *Decretum Gratiani*, pars 1 dist. 43; ed. Friedberg, 1. 155–6.
[7] Roger Bacon, *Opus tertium*, c. 10; ed. J. S. Brewer, *Fr. Rogeri Bacon, opera quaedam hactenus inedita*, 3 vols, RS 15 (1859), 1. 33.
[8] ibid. c. 25; 1. 89–90.

injudiciously uttered; or out of flattery, to please the person to whom they are divulged; or out of vanity in knowing things, to appear to know more'. These are the words of the *Decreta*.[6]

8. Again, according to Bacon in his Letter to Clement, whoever aspires to translate any learned work or written text should understand the subject, and both the language from which it is translated, and the language into which it is rendered.[7] But while the languages admit of many difficulties, the material mediated between them presents a virtual impossibility; for who, after the apostolic age, has known all holy scripture? And who would dare to attempt to translate the whole of it, and especially into the vernacular?

9. Again, what cannot be translated faithfully into the vernacular, should not be translated at all. But one language cannot be accurately rendered into another, because of the different characteristics of speech in different languages, as Bacon points out in the text cited above. 'And anyone can establish this', he says, 'who desires to express his expert knowledge in his native tongue.' 'Clearly', he continues, 'a logician cannot expound logic if he is restricted to the vocabulary of his native language; he must invent new terms, and then he will not be understood by anyone except himself.'[8] The same is true of other subjects: the vast vocabulary in foreign languages used in philosophical and theological texts cannot be written down, or put forward, or understood by anyone who is ignorant of those tongues. 'And they were used', he says, 'for this reason, that ideas were expressed in their original language, because the translators could not find adequate words in Latin.' St Augustine touches on the same point in chapter 10 of the second book of *De doctrina christiana*, where he says 'there are certain words in particular languages which cannot be rendered by translation into another tongue: especially interjections, words which signify an emotion, rather than any distinct conceptual statement'; for instance, *Racha* or *Osanna*.[9]

10. Besides, if at one time there was a faithful translation, but now [the texts] are deficient, it would be dangerous on that account to translate; but that is the case with the translation which we have now. The major premise is obvious, and for the minor we can cite Bacon in the place noted above, where he says that 'texts which at one time had been well translated are now defective, for this reason, that we do not know the languages; as is clear in the case of the whole of the Bible and natural science; because we do not know how to write them, or read them, or expound them. And so true understanding

---

[9] Augustine, *De doctrina christiana*, II 11 (*PL* 34. 42–3).

uerus intellectus; et hec causa', inquit, 'habet locum in corrupcione
textus sacri.'[10]   105

11. Item, beatus Ieronimus, prouocatus a Desiderio episcopo ad
transferendum Penthateucum, fatetur quod est periculosum ualde.[11]
Super quo doctor de Lira: 'quia difficile est et arduum, vnde posset
ibi homo defficere uel errare, et ideo', inquit, 'dicit periculosum; sed
si homo de facili posset errare transferendo in Latinum, a multo   110
forciori in uulgare et barbaricum ydioma?'[12] Sed nullus sue salutis
memor exponeret se errandi periculo. Ergo idem quod prius.

12. Item, secundum doctorem de Lira super 1° ad Romanos 14°,
'Contra caritatem fraternam uidetur esse quod aliquis non dimittat
ad tempus de hiis que potest licite dimittere, ad uitandum scandalum   115
simplicium qui opinantur illa esse illicita, quousque super hoc plenius informentur'.[13] Sed multi simplices reputant esse illicitum quod
sacra scriptura in uulgare transferatur. Ergo etc.

13. Item, prebere occasionem mulieribus docendi ubi docere prohibitum est illicitum. Sed hoc fieret euidenter si scriptura sacra   120
in ligwam uulgi esset translata, tunc enim quelibet uetula docendi
officium vsurparet, quoniam inpromptu haberet scripturam sacram
in lingua materna. Ergo etc. Patet consequencia et pro maiori est
apostolus 1 Cor.14°[:34], 'Mulieres', inquit, 'in ecclesiis taceant, non
enim permittitur eis loqui; sed subditas esse, sicut et lex dicit. Si   125
quid autem uolunt discere, domi uiros suos interrogent; turpe enim
est mulieri in ecclesia loqui.' Et 1ᵃ Thimotheum 2°[:11–14] dicit
Apostolus, 'Mulier in silencio discat cum omni subieccione. Docere
195vb autem mulieri non permitto, neque dominari | in virum, sed esse in
silencio.' Et causam statim subiungit: 'Adam enim primus formatus   130
est, deinde Ewa. Et Adam non est seductus, mulier autem seducta
in preuaricacione fuit.'

14. Item, illud est illicitum quod euidenter tolleret honorem debitum bonis presbiteris. Sed hoc uerisimiliter fieret, si sacer textus
fore\t/ in uulgare translatus, tunc enim quilibet rusticus docere pre- 135
sumeret, et sic duplex honor bonis presbiteris debitus, qui uerbo
laborant et doctrina, ut uult Apostolus 1ᵃ Thimotheum v°[:17], a
probabili tolleretur. Ergo etc.

15. Item, illud est illicitum per quod compago corporis Christi
mistici dissolueretur, doctorum ordo uilesceret, et membra loca sibi   140

119 prebere] preesse illicitum *canc.;* bere *written faintly in margin with insertion sign*
indicating it is to replace esse *in the cancelled reading* preesse   125 gen 3 . e . *in*
margin MS

---

[10] Roger Bacon, *Opus tertium*, c. 25; ed. Brewer, *Rogeri Bacon opera*, I. 92.

[11] Jerome, *Praefatio in Pentateuchum ad Desiderium* (*PL* 28. 147).

[12] Nicholas de Lyra, *Postilla litteralis super totam Bibliam*; pr. Venice 1488, in three parts,
I, fol. [14ra] (*super praefationem in Pentateuchum*).

fails; and this is the reason', he adds, 'for the corruption of the text of scripture.'[10]

11. Again, St Jerome, when asked by Bishop Desiderius to translate the Pentateuch, declared that it was a risky enterprise.[11] On which Dr Lyra comments, 'because [the original] is difficult and hard to grasp, one can fail to understand it and fall into error, and so Jerome calls it dangerous; but if one can easily make mistakes translating it into Latin, how much more easily can one go wrong in rendering it in a vernacular or unlearned language?'[12] And no person mindful of salvation should expound it for fear of error.

12. Again, according to Dr Lyra on Romans, chapter 14, 'It would seem to be against fraternal charity for someone not to give up for the time being those practices which he can legitimately give up, to avoid scandal to simple souls who believe that they are not lawful, until they are more fully informed in the matter'.[13] But many simple souls believe that translating scripture into the vernacular is unlawful.

13. Again, it is not lawful to give women occasion to teach when teaching is forbidden to them. But this would clearly be the case if holy scripture were to be translated into a vulgar tongue, since every old woman would take up the task of expounding it, with the scriptures available in her native language. In support of the major premise are the words of the Apostle in 1 Corinthians 14, 'Let your women keep silence in the churches, for it is not permitted unto them to speak; but they are commanded to be under obedience, as also says the law. And if they will learn anything, let them ask their husbands at home; for it is a shame for women to speak in the church.' And he says in 1 Timothy 2, 'Let the women learn in silence with all subjection. But I suffer not a woman to teach, nor to have authority over the man, but to be in silence.' And then he gives the reason: 'for Adam was first formed, then Eve. And Adam was not deceived, but the woman, having been deceived, came into transgression.'

14. Again, something which clearly deprives good priests of proper respect is not lawful. But this would certainly happen if the sacred text were translated into the vernacular, since every bumpkin would take it on himself to expound it, and thus good priests, who strive both to teach and preach, would very likely be deprived of the double honour due to them, as the Apostle says in 1 Timothy, chapter 5.

15. Again, anything which might dissolve the bond of the mystical body of Christ, or diminish the standing of doctors [of the church], or displace them from their proper position, is not lawful.

[13] Lyra, *Postilla in epistolam ad Romanos* 14:21.

indebita vsurparent. Sed hoc fortasse continerent habita translacione canonis in uulgare; laici enim et simplices tunc docere presumerent, doctoresque contempnerent, et se de archanis fidei intromitterent. Quo habito de facili fides periclitaretur, sequereturque ruina ecclesie satis grauis. Et confirmatur ratio, si enim simplices intelligendo Lati- 145 num ex hoc ut plurimi usurpant sibi docendi officium, quanto magis si Biblia esset in uulgare translata. Istam siquidem presumpcionem temerariam in docendi officium vsurpando deplangit notabiliter bea- tus Ieronimus ad Paulinum, vbi sic: 'Sola scripturarum ars est quam sibi passim omnes vendicant: han\c/ garula anus, hanc delirus senex, 150 hanc zophista uerbosus; hanc vniuersi presumunt, lacerant, docent antequam discant. Alii abducto supercilio, g\r/andia uerba trutinan- tes inter mulierculas de sacris literis philozophantur; alii discunt, proch pudor, a feminis quod uiros doceant. Et ne parum hoc sit, quadam facilitate uerborum ymo audacia edisserunt aliis, quod ipsi 155 non intelligunt; taceo de meis similibus, qui si forte ad scripturas sanctas post seculares literas veniunt, et sermone composito aurem populi mulserint, quidquid dixerint, legem Dei putant. Nec scire dignantur quid prophete aut apostoli senserint, sed ad sensum suum incongrua adaptant testimonia, quasi grande sit, et non viciosissimum 160 dicendi genus, deprauare sentencias et ad uoluntatem suam sensum trahere repugnantem.'[14] Hec Ieronimus.

16. Item, secundum Ieronimum in epistola ad Tesefontem, 'omnis heresis orta est a feminis, sed si mulieres haberent sacrum canonem in uulgari, promciores essent ad hereses excogittandas et diuulgandas'.[15] 165 Ergo ipsum nullatenus habere debent in uulgari.

17. Item, prophanum et detestabile videtur fauere hereticis, eosve fouere, aut eis in alico condescendere, ynde eorum presumpcio extol- leretur sed si sacer canon in uulgare transfereretur; preberetur auda- cia hereticis nostri temporis,[16] qui non solum petunt translacionem 170 sibi fieri in uulgari, sed, ut fertur, transferunt sacrum canonem prout 196ra placet | translatisque utuntur. Ergo etc.

18. Item, pari euidencia qua sacer canon esset transferendus in uulgare, et totum missale, manualeque sacramentorum cum toto seruicio ecclesiastico possent sic transferri; sed hoc sumum incon- 175 veniens; tunc enim uilesceret totus clerus, uilesceret cultus diuinus, uilescerentque omnia ecclesie sacramenta; tunc enim laici reputarent clericos inutiles, quemadmodum modo theologi a residua parte cleri

168 aut] et *canc.*, aut *add. MS*   174 quod (?) nos legendum uolumus (?) *add. in margin; last word represented by* uo *with macron above, and* -us *abbreviation MS*

---

[14] Jerome, *Epistola ad Paulinum presbyterum* (*ep.* 53, 'Frater Ambrosius') (*PL* 22. 544).

[15] Jerome, *Epistola ad Ctesiphontem aduersus Pelagium* (*ep.* 133) (*PL* 22. 1152–3).

[16] Possibly 'their audacity would be on display to the heretics of our time'.

But this might happen if the canon of scripture were translated into the vulgar tongue, for the laity and uneducated people would then presume to expound it; they would lose respect for doctors, and would involve themselves in the arcana of the faith. And then faith would easily be imperilled, and the thorough ruin of the church would ensue. And, further, if uneducated people learn Latin in order to take up the task of exposition, how much more would they do it if the Bible were translated into the vernacular. St Jerome notably deplores their shameless presumption in usurping the duty of the teacher in a letter to Paulinus: 'Everywhere people lay claim to the unique art of exegesis: a garrulous old woman here, a delirious old man there, a wordy sophist somewhere else; they all take it up, mangle it, and expound it before they have learnt anything. Some of them philosophize among young women, frowning as they weigh up long words; others, disgracefully, learn from women expositors what they pass on to men. And as if this were not enough, they glibly and shamelessly explain to others what they do not understand themselves; not to mention the same thing among my own people, who might have come to the sacred scriptures from secular literature, and who might write a sermon and delight the popular ear, thinking that whatever they say is the law of God. They do not deign to find out what the prophets or the apostles meant, but adapt inappropriate texts to their own ideas, as if it were a great thing to do, and not a particularly vicious kind of discourse, to deprave their meaning and wilfully draw a contrary interpretation.'[14] So says Jerome.

16. Again, according to Jerome in a letter to Ctesiphon, 'all heresy starts with women, and if they had the sacred canon in the vernacular, they would be even more ready to think out and spread heresies far and wide'.[15] So they should not by any means have it in the vernacular.

17. Again, to favour heretics, to support them and aid them in anything seems a wicked and detestable thing to do, and their presumption would be greater if the sacred canon were to be translated into the vernacular; audacity (like this) is shown by the heretics of our own time,[16] who not only desire a vernacular translation to be made for them, but, it is said, render the sacred canon just as they wish and use the translations.

18. Again, the whole missal and the manual of the sacraments, together with the entire office of the church could be translated on the same grounds as the Bible; but this would be extremely harmful; for then the clergy would be devalued, and the rites of the church and all its sacraments cheapened; and then the laity would think the clergy redundant, just as theologians are nowadays considered

inutiles iudicantur. Tunc enim prouecti clerici deficerent, scaturiret-
que multitudo heresum infinita. Ergo etc.   180

19. Item, nullum tale est licitum quo posito min\u/eretur deuocio
fidelium, sed multi laici deuote dicunt oraciones suas dominicas, psalterium et alia que in canone Biblie continentur, que, si verterentur
in uulgare, essent multum insipida; teperetque deuocio, nec fieret
aliunde recompensa. Ergo etc.   185

20. Item, quando apostoli et sancti transtulerunt, non leguntur
transtulisse nisi in linguam gramaticatam; vnde et in Grecum uulgarium non transtulerunt, sed solum in gramaticatum. Sed si in uulgare
transfereretur, sacer canon in ydioma non gramaticatum et barbaricum esset translatus. Ergo etc.   190

21. Item, quod simpliciter est invtile, est simpliciter illicitum; sed
talis translacio esset simpliciter inutilis, quia clericis non prodesset,
nec laicis conferret sed a uerisimili ad contemptum doctorum, et
superbiam prouocaret. Ergo etc.

22. Item, secreta mistica, ut uult Dionisius in *Ecclesiastica Ierar-* 195
chia, non sunt pandenda indignis; vnde et scriptum est Heb.12°[:20],
'Bestia', per quam intelligitur populus rudis et carnalis, 'si tetigerit
montem lapidabitur'; sed si scriptura sacra esset uersa in uulgare,
absque excepcione omnibus et singulis panderetur.[17] Igitur etc. Et
cum ista sentencia concordat Crisostomus super M[t], omelia 2[a], ubi 200
reprobat scribas et phariseos ex hoc quod manifestabant misterium
natiuitatis Christi Herodi; 'et facti sunt', inquit Crisostomus, 'non
predicatores operum Dei, sed proditores misteriorum eius, et non
doctores Herodis, sed irritatores malicie eius. Ex quibus', inquit Crisostomus, 'docemur scripturarum oculta non manifestare iniquis, sed 205
fidelibus, sicut precepit Paulus [2 Tim. 2:2]: "Que a me audisti per
multos testes, hec comenda fidelibus qui possunt \et/ alios docere"'.[18]

23. Item, quod plus obesset quam prodesset non est licitum; sed
plus officeret quam prodesset talis translacio, si fieret, sicut uidetur
iamdudum ab experiencia in gente nostra; vbi numerosa heresum 210
multitudo per libros Anglicanos in populum est dispersa, a quibus
semel infectum uulgus, irreuocabile perseuerat.

24. Item, concessis huiusmodi translacionibus in uulgare, approba-
196rb bili omnes ordines | omnesque religiones ecclesie sancte Dei despec-
tui haberentur, tunc enim predicatores mendicantes minus necessarii 215

179–80 scaturiretque] scaturirent que, -n- *canc. MS*   184 deuocio] *repeated for*
clarity in margin MS   189 ydioma] ydoma *canc.*, ydioma *MS*   191 quod]
originally quoque, -que *canc.*, -d *add. MS*   196 *final letter of* indignis *corr. from*
another letter   206 *letter erased at the end of* audisti *MS*   210 *first* -i- *in*
experiencia *corr. from another letter MS*

---

[17] Pseudo-Dionysius Areopagita, *De ierarchia ecclesiastica*, tr. Robert Grosseteste; ed.
P. Chevallier, *Dionysiaca*, 2 vols (Paris 1937–49), I. 1401.

useless by other clergy. Proficient clergy would cease to exist, and a vast number of heresies would swarm forth.

19. Again, nothing is lawful which if done would lessen the devotion of the faithful, but many pious lay people say their Sunday prayers, the psalms and other parts of the sacred canon, which in translation would be very feeble; so their devotion would cool, and would not be revived by any means.

20. Again, when the apostle and saints translated the Bible, we do not read that they translated it into any except a literary language; so they did not render it in demotic Greek, but only in the literary form of the language. But translated into the vernacular, the sacred canon would be in an ungrammatical and barbarous tongue.

21. Again, what is plainly useless is plainly unlawful; but the translation of the Bible is plainly useless, because it would not benefit the clergy, and would give the laity only an approximate version despised by the learned, and would encourage pride.

22. Again, secret mysteries, as Dionysius says in his *Ecclesiastica hierarchia*, should not be opened up to the unworthy; as we read in Hebrews, chapter 12, 'if so much as a beast', by which is meant the rough and carnal populace, 'touch the mountain, it shall be stoned'; but holy scripture in translation would be available to all and singular, without exception.[17] Chrysostom agrees, in his second homily on Matthew, where the scribes and Pharisees are condemned for revealing to Herod the mystery of Christ's nativity; 'and they became', says Chrysostom, 'not so much preachers of the works of God, as betrayers of his mysteries, and not the teachers of Herod, but the stokers of his malice. By this', he continues, 'we learn not to reveal mysteries to the wicked, but to the faithful, as Paul commands: "and the things that you have heard of me among many witnesses, the same commit to faithful men who shall be able to teach others also"'.[18]

23. Again, things which hinder more than they help are unlawful; but a translation, if it were made, would hinder more than it helped, as experience has shown for some time now among our own people; as a great number of heresies have been spread among them through books in English, and having once infected them, irreversibly persist.

24. Again, if translations into the vernacular were permitted, it is probable that all the religious orders of the holy church of God would lose their prestige, as friar preachers would appear less necessary

---

[18] Pseudo-Chrysostom, *Opus imperfectum super Matthaeum*, hom. 2 (*PG* 56. 640).

uiderentur cum quilibet laicus esset impromptu predicator; pos-
sessionatisque eorum regule in linguam uulgarium explanate, eis
in faciem obicerentur; et demum scolasticis multa argumenta fierent tam in speculatiua quam morali ratione talium translacionum
fabricata.   220

25. Preterea, quod est medium vniens Christianorum impedimen-
tum est illicitum, sed talis translacio sic esset, quod sic probatur faceret enim linguam Latinam uilescere, et per consequens demum adeo
sopiri; quod quelibet gens, suo ydiomate per singula contenta, Latinum ydyoma finaliter refutaret. Et confirmatur ratio per hoc quod 225
Latini, quia uidetur eis Latinum suum sufficere, Grecum quod est
ydioma excellencius recusarunt; sic enim gramatici nostri temporis
linguam Gallicam, qua priores gramatici construere solebant, ex toto
tamquam sibi invtilem deseruerunt, sicque multi optant quod fieret
in placitis nostris Gallicanis.[19]   230

26. Item, non est licitum fieri quod prelati uellent pariter condempnare, sed verisimile est quod prelati quamcumque talem translacionem condempnarent. Ergo etc.

27. Item, illicitum est promulgari quod multitudo periciorum clericorum illicitum iudicaret, sed approbabili numerositas legistarum 235
vna cum tota religiosorum concione, ac vniuersis filiis huius seculi
iudicaret quamlibet talem translacionem esse illicitam; a uerisimili
\cum/ multi \et/ magni inter eos iamdudum super ista materia mur-
murarunt, prout uisum est, tam in publico quam ad partem.

28. Item, illicitum est aliquod tale promulgatum esse nisi prius 240
fuerit approbatum; sed non inuenitur qui talia approbarent, ergo talis
translacio inutilis est censenda.

29. Item, illicitum est inducere prophanas uocum nouitates,
quoniam et has apostolus, 1 Thimotheum vltimo [6:36ff], precipit
deuitare; sed hoc verisimiliter fieret in translacionibus in uul- 245
gare, oporteret enim tunc fingere multa noua propter linguarum
peniuriam que nonnullis legentibus satis aliena uiderentur.

30. Item, admissa tali translacione in uulgare sequeretur quod
ewangelium indifferenter populis omnibus promvlgaretur, consequens ut uidetur falsum iuxta illud Mt.13°[:11]: 'vobis datum est 250
nosse misterium regni celorum, illis autem non est datum'; vbi secundum doctorem de Lira, Christus intendit quod secretum ecclesie
militantis uulgaribus turbis eciam incredulis phariseis, non est concessum intelligere. Ergo etc.[20]

---

222 faceret] fret *canc.,* faceret *add. MS*   241 *two or three letters erased after* qui
MS   245 verisimiliter *over erasure; erased text in the margin*

when a layman can easily preach himself; and if the rules of the monastic orders were set out in the popular tongue, they would be used to confront [the regular clergy]; and doctors in the schools would be faced with endless arguments on speculative and moral questions concocted on the basis of the translated texts.

25. Besides, anything which impedes the medium which unifies Christians is unlawful, but this translation would do just that, because it would cause the Latin language to decay, and to slumber; for each people, having everything in their own tongue, would in the end discourage the use of Latin. For Latin speakers, who thought their own language was adequate, refused to use Greek, a more expressive tongue; as modern grammar school teachers have almost all given up as redundant the French language which their predecessors commonly construed, and many people hope that will happen with our pleadings in French.[19]

26. Again it is not lawful to do what prelates desire to forbid, and they would certainly forbid any form of translation.

27. Again, it is not lawful to promote anything which the majority of the more learned clergy consider to be unlawful, and in all probability the greater number of lawyers and the whole body of the religious orders, and all contemporary opinion considers this translation illicit; and the better part of them seem to have complained for some time now about it circulating, either publicly or privately.

28. Again, it is unlawful to make public something which has not already been approved; but we do not find that this translation has been approved, and so it should be considered redundant.

29. Again, it is unlawful to introduce profane new language, since the apostle in the last chapter of 1 Timothy urges us to avoid it as well; but this would undoubtedly happen in translations into the vernacular, which because of the poverty of the language would entail a host of new expressions unfamiliar to many readers.

30. Again, the gospel translated into the vernacular would be available to everybody without distinction, and would thus contravene the words of Matthew, chapter 13: 'it is given unto you to know the mysteries of the kingdom of heaven, but to them it is not given'; on which Dr Lyra comments that Christ intended the mysteries of the church militant should not be divulged to the common people or to the unbelieving Pharisees.[20]

[19] On French in legal proceedings see P. Brand, 'The languages of the law in later medieval England', in *Multilingualism in Later Medieval Britain*, ed. D. A. Trotter (Cambridge 2000), 63–76.
[20] Lyra, *Postilla in Matthaeum* 13:11.

Responsio

Antequam enim ad questionem respondeatur aut ad eius materiam 255
descendatur, uidendum est *quid nominis* huius quod dico *transferri* et
196va *interpretari, trans|lator* et *interpres.* Vnde sciendum est quod *transferre*
componitur de *trans* quod est *ultra,* et *ferre* quod est *portare,* vnde
transferre 'id est *ultra ferre,* uel de vno loco ad alium ferre'.[21] Et
per istum modum 4[ti] Regum xvij°[:6] dicitur: 'Cepit rex Assirio- 260
rum Samariam, et transtulit in Assirios, posuitque eos in Ala et in
Abor iuxta fluuium Cozam, in ciuitatibus Medorum'; et infra eodem
capitulo sic habetur [v.23], 'translatusque Israel est de terra sua in
Assiriorum usque ad diem hanc'. Sed de tali translacione non loquimur pro presenti: alio modo transferre methaforice seu transumptiue 265
sumitur, pro coaptacione vnius lingue siue ydiomatis loco alterius.
Et ex hinc dicuntur translatores qui vnam ligwam alteri coaptant
seu proporcionant, aut vnam per aliam exponunt.[22] Et sic loquendo
de transferre accipitur pro interpretari, quod \est/ vnam lingwam
per aliam exponere, et translator pro interprete sumitur. Vnde et 270
translatores dicuntur interpretes et econtra, quamuis lacius 'interpres'
et 'interpretari' sumantur. Sumitur enim interpretari aliquando pro
exponere, reuelare, explanare seu reserare sensum in uerbis latentem.
Et isto modo loquitur Apostolus, I Cor.14°[:2ff], comparans donum
liguarum ad aliud donum quod est interpretacio sermonum, dicens, 275
'qui linguis loquitur, oret ut interpretetur'. Et ideo signanter dicit
Ioseph, Gen.40[:8] 'Numquid Dei est interpretacio?' Interpres itaque pro expositore sumitur ad conformem sensum, vnde Genesis ubi
supra dicitur [40:23], 'succedentibus prosperis prepositus pincerna-
rum, oblitus est interpretis sui'. Ad istum itaque sensum, interpretari, 280
et interpretacio sumuntur Danielis 2° capitulo. Et planum est quod
interpretacio isto modo sumpta est donum Dei gratuitum, et carisma
diuinitus impertitum. Verumtamen sicut aliquis potest habere noticiam linguarum, absque dono speciali celitus superinfuso, ex industria et labore, quemadmodum creditur Origenem, Ieronimum et 285
multos alios habuisse, ita eciam interpretacionem sermonum, que a
dono supernaturali distingwitur. Sicut patet de modernis multisque
aliis precedentibus, qui ex labore et studio ad scripturarum noticiam
peruenerunt, easque aliis exposuerunt.

257 transla|lator *MS*   284 speciali] *possibly* spirituali, *the abbreviation for 'spiri-*
tuali' and 'speciali' can be identical in this script   289 Augustinus *in margin MS*

---

[21] Uguccione da Pisa, *Deriuationes*; ed. E. Cecchini, 2 vols (Florence 2004), 2. 430; a
close but only briefly verbatim quotation.

Response

Now, before we respond to the question and get to grips with its subject, we must consider the meaning of the words *transferre* and *interpretari*, *translator* and *interpres*. The first thing to notice is that *transferre* is composed of *trans*, which means *over*, and *ferre*, which means *to carry*. So *transferre* 'means *to carry over*, or move from one place to another'.[21] For instance in 4 Kings 17 we read: 'The king of Assyria took Samaria, and carried [Israel] away into Assyria, and placed them in Halah and in Habor by the river of Gozan, and in the cities of the Medes'; and further on, 'so was Israel carried away out of their own land to Assyria unto this day'. But we are not talking of this kind of translation at the moment: translation can also be understood metaphorically, or by transference, to mean adaptation of one language or one idiom to another. Translators, therefore, are those who adjust or fit together one tongue with another or expound one by the other.[22] So by translation we must understand interpretation, or the exposition of the meaning of one language in another; a translator must be an interpreter. However broadly the terms 'interpreter' and 'to interpret' are defined, translators are interpreters and vice versa. To interpret means to expound, to reveal, to explain or unlock the meaning hidden in the words. This is the sense in which the Apostle speaks in 1 Corinthians 14, comparing the gift of tongues with the other gift of interpretation: 'wherefore let him that speaks in an unknown tongue pray that he may interpret'. Joseph says the same thing figuratively in Genesis 40: 'Do not interpretations belong to God?' So an interpreter can be defined as an expounder of the real meaning [of a text]; in the words of Genesis in the same place, 'the chief butler, when his fortunes were restored, forgot the interpreter'. This is the sense in which to interpret, and interpretation, is meant in Daniel, chapter 2. Clearly in this sense interpretation means the free gift of God, a charism which God has imparted. But someone, without a special gift communicated from on high, can have a knowledge of languages acquired by application and hard work, as in the case of Origen, Jerome and many others, and similarly an ability to interpret words, which is something different from the spiritual gift. This is the case in our time, and the case of many others who came before us, who by work and study came to have knowledge of the scriptures, which they explained to other people.

[22] ibid. 2. 991.

Insuper est notandum secundum beatum Augustinum 14 *De tri-* 290
nitate, capitulis 22, 23, 24, 25, 26, 27, quod est dare locucionem
duplicem, interiorem videlicet et exteriorem; duplex os cordis videlicet et corporis. Sed quoad locucionem interiorem ponit, quid sunt
uerba et preposiciones in duplici differentia, videlicet que nullius sunt
ydiomatis et eciam que sunt alicuius ydiomatis siue lingue. De primo 295
exemplificat sub hiis uerbis: 'Quisquis', inquit, 'potest intelligere verbum, non solum antequam sonet, verum eciam antequam sonorum
eius ymagines cogittacione voluantur? Hoc est enim quod ad nullam
partem pertinet linguarum earum, scilicet que lingwe appellantur
gencium, quarum nostra Latina est.' Et statim de eius formacione 300
196vb loquitur dicens, | 'Necesse enim est cum verum loquimur, id est quod
scimus loquimur ex ipsa sciencia quam memoria tenemus, nascatur
verbum quod eiusmodi sit omnino, cuiusmodi est illa sciencia de qua
nascitur; formata quippe cogittacio ab ea re quam scimus, verbum
est quod in corde dicimus, quod nec Grecum est nec Latinum, nec 305
lingue alicuius alterius'. De aliis uero uerbis et preposicionibus men-
talibus que aliquarum sunt linguarum, ita iterum scribit: 'Omnium
namque sonancium uerba linguarum eciam in silencio cogittantur, et
carmina percurruntur animo tacente ore corporis. Non solum nume-
rum silbarum, verum et modi cantilenarum, cum sint corporales, et 310
ad eum qui uocatur auditus sensum corporis pertinentes, per incor-
poreas quasdam ymagines suas presto sunt cogittantibus, et tacite
cuncta ista uoluentibus.' Sed quoad uerba et locucionem exteriorem,
ita scribit: 'Cum id opus est in eorum quibus loquimur proferre
noticiam, aliquod signum quo singnificetur assumitur. Et plerumque 315
sonus aliquando et mutus, ille auribus, ille oculis, exhibetur, ut per
singna corporalia eciam iam corporis sensibus verbum quod mente
gerimus innotescat.'²³
Uidendum est ulterius quid sit 'licitum'. Scio quidem quod sic
posset distingwi de 'licito', quoniam aliquid potest esse simpliciter 320
bonum et simpliciter licitum, et in nullo casu nec aliquo modo illicitum, sicut dilligere Deum; aliquid vero posset esse simpliciter illicitum et nullo modo bonum, sicut odire Deum. Aliquid etiam potest
esse simpliciter bonum et licitum, sed in casu illicitum, sicut cele-
brare missam existenti enim in mortali esset illicitum; item aliquid 325
potest esse simpliciter malum et illicitum, sed in casu licitum, sicut
interficere innocentem est simpliciter illicitum, in casu tamen quod
Deus precipiat alicui, sicut precepit Abrahe immolare filium suum,

296 verbum et proposicio 2ª dicta *in margin MS*   297 verum] vᵐ *canc.,* verum
add. in margin for clarity MS   299 appllantur *MS*   301 verum] vnum *MS*
316 mutus] *originally* mitus, -i- *canc.,* -u- *add. MS*   319 licitum uerum dictum
(in margin, in black underlined in red; the second word could be michi *or* ueri*);* Licitum
quantuplex *(on a separate line in margin in red) MS*   325 Illicitum multiplex *in
margin in red MS*

We might note besides that according to St Augustine, in book 14 of *De Trinitate*, chapters 22 to 27, there exists a double meaning of speech, internal and external, for there is the mouth of the heart, and the mouth of the body. He says, as to the internal sense, that words and sentences can either be in no language, or in a particular idiom or language. He gives an example of the first case: 'Whoever can understand a word, not only before it is sounded, but also before we hold in our mind the images of its sounds? For no part of it is in any language, that is, those which are called national languages, among which ours is Latin.' And about its formation he goes on to say, 'For when of necessity we say what is true, that is, when we speak what we know from the knowledge we hold stored in our memory, a word entirely of the same character as this remembered knowledge may emerge; for the idea formed by what we know is the word which we say in the heart: a word which is neither in Greek nor in Latin, nor in any other language'. And of other words and mental propositions which are in particular languages, he adds: 'For the words of all languages which are enunciated verbally are also thought silently, and the mind runs over verses while the mouth of the body is mute. And not only the number of syllables, but musical phrases, being corporeal, and pertaining to the sense of hearing, are in the mind, which silently contemplates them all through apposite mental images.' But as to words and their external expression, he writes, 'But when we need to convey an idea to other people, then some sign is given to represent it. And generally we produce a sound, or sometimes a silent sign, the one given to the ears, the other to the eyes, so that the word we have in mind can be transmitted to the bodily senses by physical signs.'[23]

Next, we must define what is meant by 'lawful'. I am aware that we can make a distinction between different meanings of 'lawful', since something can be straightforwardly good and straightforwardly lawful, and in no case and no way unlawful, such as loving God; and something can be simply unlawful and in no way good, such as hating God. Again, something can be good and lawful in itself, but unlawful in a particular case, like celebrating mass in a state of mortal sin; and something can be bad and unlawful in itself, but lawful in a particular case, so that killing the innocent is simply unlawful, but can be lawful in such a case when God has commanded it, as he commanded Abraham lawfully to sacrifice his son. Again, something

---

[23] Augustine, *De trinitate*, XV 10–11 (*PL* 42. 1071–2).

esse\t/ licitum. Et iterum aliquid est licitum per indifferentiam, sicut
laico seculari licitum est venari, licitumque sibi a uenacione abstinere. 330
Sed quantum pertinet ad propositum pro presenti, sciendum quod
secundum quod uult beatus Augustinus ad Polentinum, et ponitur in
glossa communi super illo I Cor.6[:12], 'Omnia michi licent', licitum
est omne illud quod nullo precepto Domini prohibetur, ex quo facile
est uidere quid sit licitum, quid etiam illicitum.[24] Vnde ex isto plane 335
sequitur quod nichil de se et simpliciter est illicitum, nisi culpa seu
culpabile. Quomodo autem quedam de se sunt licita, que tamen ex
prohibicione humana redduntur illicita, propter periculum quod ex
inde poterit euenire, aut propter maius bonum a probabili securiturum,
non est presentis speculacionis; hoc etenim est iuris positiui, loquor 340
siquidem pro presenti de illo, quod de se est illicitum, quia malum,
aut de illo quod est illicitum quia a Deo prohibitum. Quamuis de
197ra sua natura intrinseca non sit malum, | quemadmodum erat de come-
stione carnium suillarum multorumque aliorum que prohibita erant
in veteri testamento, que \tamen/ modo in lege perfecte liberatis sunt 345
satis licita, nisi fortassis hiis qui ex uoto temporali aut perpetuo aut
aliis causis rationabilibus ad oppositum sunt astricti.

Vltimo est sciendum quod sicut in aliis rerum generibus, ita eciam
in translacionibus fidelibus, est dare magnam latitudinem, ita quod
aliqua perfeccior, aliqua imperfeccior merito dici debeat; et tamen, 350
cum hec omnes vere licite et laudabiles debent a fidelibus estimari,
patet istud de translacionibus ab Hebreo in Grecum, a Greco in
Latinum, et ab Hebreo in Latinum. Qualis erat nostri Ieronimi, que,
secundum Hugonem in suo *Didascolicon*, 'merito ceteris antefertur,
nam et uerborum', inquit, 'tenacior, et prospicuitate sentencie cla- 355
rior'.[25] Ymo ut uult Ieronimus in multis locis, Latini in suis translacionibus recursum habere debent ad volumina Hebreorum; quia
uero ante tempora Augustini omnes translatores Latini ab Greco in
Latinum transtulerunt, recurrendum esse, dicit, uelud ad regulam
ad translacionem Grece lingue. Inperfeccionem autem aliqualem in 360
translacione nostra ex hoc accipere possumus, quod multa uocabula
tam Greca, quam Hebrea, quam eciam de lingua Sira in biblia nostra
iam habemus, que uel translata non sunt, cuius modi sunt ista:
alleluia, osanna, Ecclesiastes, mammona, Cephas, huiusmodi aut aliter

---

333 licitum quid sit *in margin in red MS*   334 ex] et *canc.*, ex *add. MS*   337 h
canc. before de *MS*   cum *canc.*, tamen *add. MS*   340 iuris *add. in darker ink on a
blank MS*   343 intrinseca] *corr. from* intrinsica *MS*   351 h[c] *add. MS*   vero
canc., vere *add. MS*   360 translacionem] translacione *MS*

---

[24] *GO* I Cor 6:12 (vol. 4, p. 315), citing Augustine, *Ad Pollentinum de coniugiis adulterinis*
(*PL* 40. 480).

can be lawful by being morally neutral; it is lawful, for instance, for a layman to hunt and lawful for him not to hunt. But as far as the present point is concerned, we may note what St Augustine says in his letter to Pollentinus, which is quoted in the ordinary gloss on 1 Corinthians 6, 'all things are lawful unto me', that anything is lawful which is not forbidden by divine precept; which makes it easy to see what is and even more what is not lawful.[24] It plainly follows from this that nothing is of its nature unlawful that is not a sin, and blameworthy. It is not part of the question considered here that there are some things, in themselves lawful, which are made illegal by human prohibition, to avoid the danger that they might incur, or to promote the greater good which is likely to ensue; for that is a matter of positive law, whereas I am talking here of things that are unlawful of themselves, because they are evil, and of things which are unlawful because they are prohibited by God. Although not by nature unlawful, eating pork and many other things used to be forbidden in the Old Testament; they are now allowed to those who have been totally set free in the law, except for those bound by a temporary or permanent vow to abstain from them.

Finally, it may be noted that just as for things in general, so in the case of faithful translations, the rule is to allow a considerable degree of latitude, so that one thing can properly seem more satisfactory and another less so; and thus, as the faithful may consider all these true things licit and praiseworthy, the same applies to translations from Hebrew into Greek, from Greek into Latin, and from Hebrew into Latin. This is the case with our own Jerome's [translations], which, according to Hugh in his *Didascalicon*, are to be preferred over all others, being, as he says, 'more precise in his use of words, and clearer and more perspicacious as to the meaning'.[25] Indeed, as Jerome frequently remarks, Latin translators should have recourse to the books of the Hebrews; and because before the time of Augustine all Latin translators translated into Latin from the Greek, such recourse must be had, he says, as a rule when translating the Greek language. So we can accept a degree of imperfection in our translation, in that we have in our Bible several Greek, Hebrew and indeed Syriac words which have either not been translated, for instance, *alleluia*, *osanna*, *Ecclesiastes*, *mammona*, *Cephas*, or rendered in a Latin format or

---

[25] Hugh of St Victor, *Didascalicon*, IV 5; ed. C. H. Buttmer (Washington, DC, 1939), 76.

propter peniuriam lingue nostre in formam et declinacionem Lati- 365
nam reducuntur, \ut/ *apocalipsis, cenophigia*; aut certe per circumlocucionem. Est tamen bona licita et laudabilis, dummodo seruetur
eadem sentencia in vna lingua que in alia—et hoc in prima questione
ex testimonio Ieronimi fuit superius declaratum—et quomodo apostoli et ewangeliste non solum de uerbo ad uerbum, sed de sentencia 370
in sentenciam transtulerunt, de impertinentibus non curantes. Vnde
Ieronimus in libello suo, *De optimo genere interpretandi*, 'Alii', inquit,
'silbas aucupentur et litteras; tu quere sentencias'.²⁶ Et tangens illud
Mt.[27:9], 'acceperunt triginta argenteos', 'accusent', inquit, 'apostolum falsitatis . . . pro Zacharia quippe Ieremiam posuit. Sed absit hoc 375
de pedisequo Christi dicere, cui cure fuit non uerba et silbas aucu-
pari, sed sentencias dogmatum ponere.' Vnde non aliud intendunt
scribentes nisi sentencias ponere, sed quod bene declarat dominus
Ardmachanus, libro 9°, capitulo 2°: 'cum refers', inquit, 'de aliquo
qui sentenciam aliquam protulit, quod ipse sic dixit repetens sen- 380
sum quem dixit, non tamen singula uerba eadem, sed forte similia,
non dicis mendacium, quando non intendis dicere quod ipse dixit
uerba que repetis, sed sensum eorum. Alias enim, si quemquem ante
audisses loquentem in Greco, et tu eius dictum repeteres in Latino,
dicens ipsum sic dixisse, diceres mendacium, et sic esset magna pars 385
197rb sacre | scripture in Latina lingua, scilicet quod Dominus dixit ad
Adam, dixit Dominus ad serpentem, dixit Dominus ad Abraham,
dixit Abraham ad Dominum, dixit Moises ad Dominum, dixit Pharo
ad Moisen, et sic de similibus innumerabilibus in scriptura, quoniam
constat eos hec in lingua Latina non fuisse locutos.'²⁷ Hec dominus 390
Ardmachanus.

Concordanter ad hanc sentenciam scribit Seneca in *De breuitate
uite*: 'Magnum', inquit, 'et summum est Deoque vicinum non con-
cuti. Hanc stabilem animi sedem Greci eciam [*euthymian* vocant], de
qua Democriti uolumen egregium est; ego tranquillitatem uoco; nec 395
enim imitari et transferre uerba ad illorum uerba est necesse. Res
ipsa de qua agitur, aliquo signanda nomine est, quod appellacionis
Grece vim debet habere, non graciam.'²⁸ Quod autem sentencias seu
sensum aduertere debeamus, et non uerborum proprietatem, luculenter declarat beatus Augustinus, 11° *Confessionum*, ubi loquens de 400

368 *originally* sentencia in eadem lingua in vna; in eadem *canc., transposition signs
indicate that* in vna *should be placed before* lingua   385 magna] maxima *canc.,* magna
add. MS   393 uite] *possibly followed by a gap for number MS*   394 *euthymian*
vocant] *om. without gap in the text MS*

²⁶ Jerome, *Epistola ad Pammachium de optimo genere interpretandi* (*ep.* 57) (*PL* 22. 572–
3), considerably abbreviated.

declension because of a lack in our language, like *apocalipsis*, *cenophigia*; or which have been expressed in a circumlocution. And this is a good, lawful and praiseworthy thing, so long as it preserves the same meaning in both languages—as has been established in the first question above, on the authority of Jerome—since the apostles and evangelists translated meaning for meaning, not just word for word, and took no note of irrelevant considerations. So Jerome says in his short book, *De optimo genere interpretandi*, 'let others trifle with syllables and letters; you must focus on the sense'.[26] Commenting on the passage in Matthew, 'and they took the thirty pieces of silver', he said, 'they accuse the apostle of lying, because he writes Jeremiah instead of Zechariah. Far be it from us to say this of Christ's servant who was intent on setting out the sense of doctrine, not nitpicking syllables and words.' So the writers [of scripture] do not intend to do anything but express their ideas, as the lord Armachanus has well said in book 9, chapter 2 [of his *Summa in questionibus Armenorum*]: 'when you quote someone who utters a sentence, repeating what he has said but not in the same words, only similar, you are not telling a lie, since you do not set out to repeat his own words, but the sense of what he said. Otherwise, if you were to hear someone speaking in Greek, and you repeated what he said in Latin, asserting that he said it, you would be telling a lie, and so a great part of the holy scripture in Latin, for instance that the Lord said to Adam, the Lord said to the serpent, the Lord said to Abraham, Abraham said to the Lord, Moses said to the Lord, Pharaoh said to Moses, and endless other passages in scripture would be lies, since they were certainly not said in Latin.'[27] So says Armachanus.

And Seneca writes in the same sense in *De brevitate vitae*: 'it is a great, a high, a nearly divine virtue to be calm. The Greeks call this stable state of mind *euthymian*, on which there is a fine book by Democritus; I call it tranquillity; for it is not necessary to translate word for word in slavish imitation. The word to be sought for the thing intended should convey the force of the Greek expression rather than its charm.'[28] St Augustine says very well in the second book of the *Confessions* that we should follow the meaning and the sense, and not the particular aspects of the words, where he

[27] Richard Fitzralph ('Armachanus'), *Summa in questionibus Armenorum*, IX 2 (Rome 1512), fol. 56vb.
[28] Seneca, *Dialogi* 'De tranquillitate animi', 9.2.3 (ed. L. D. Reynolds, *L. Annaei Senecae dialogorum duodecim* (Oxford 1977)).

improprietate loquendi circa materiam temporis, ita ait: 'quod autem nunc liquet et claret, nec futura sunt nec preterita, nec proprie dicitur tempora sunt tria, preteritum, presens et futurum. Sed fortasse proprie diceretur tempora sunt tria, presens de preteritis, presens de presentibus, presens de futuris; sunt enim hec in anima tria que- 405 dam et alibi ea non uideo. Presens de preteritis memoria; presens de presentibus contuitus; presens de futuris expectacio. Si hec permittuntur dicere, uideo, fateor quia tria sunt. Dicatur eciam tempora sunt tria, preteritum, presens et futurum; sicut abutitur consuetudo, ita dicatur'; et sequitur notabiliter ad propositum: 'ecce non curo, nec 410 resisto, nec reprehendo, dum tamen intelligatur quod dicitur, neque [quod] futurum est esse iam neque id quod preteritum est. Pauca sunt enim que proprie loquimur, plura non proprie. Sed agnoscitur quid velimus.'[29] Hec Augustinus.

Ecce quod beatus Augustinus non multum curat de proprietate 415 uerborum, dummodo sentencia teneatur. Ymmo sicut ips\e/met dixit in *De doctrina christiana*, libro 2°, capitulo 12, 'non solum uerba singula, sed eciam locuciones sepe transferuntur, que omnino in Latine lingue vsum, si quis consuetudinem veterum qui Latine locuti sunt tenere uoluit, transire non possunt'. Dicit tamen paulo post in eodem 420 capitulo, 'vtrum autem', inquit, '*inter homines* aut *inter hominibus* dicatur, ad rerum non pertinet cognitorem'; et infra, 'enim vtrum ignoscere producta tercia sillaba, an correpta dicatur, non multum curat qui peccatis suis Deum ut ignoscat petit'.[30]

Quinto et ultimo est sciendum, quod penes uerba 'locucionum 425 linguam aut ydioma' triphacie acceptata contingit translacionem fieri; dictum est enim supra quod est locucio mentalis, que est alicuius ydiomatis, et est proposicio composita ex intencionibus vocum. Si ergo aliquis interpres uel translator per vnum ydioma instruit auditorem de alio ydiomate, transfert illud de quo ipsum instruit in | 430
197va eius intellectum; et per istum modum omnes gramatice instructores per uulgare, notum pueris, transferunt gramaticam, seu lingwam gramaticatam, in animas adiscencium. Et per istum modum contingit transferre lingwam in intelligenciam alterius, eciam si sit mutus; ut enim per istum modum predicatores, predicantes per interpretes, 435 transferunt, sicut accidit in Liuonia et multis aliis locis, et regionibus variarum nacionum. Et sic sine repugnancia potest intelligi quod dicitur Sapiencie 7°[:27] de sapiencia increata, ubi dicitur quod 'per naciones transfert se in animas sanctas', et sic 'transferre' comuniter dicitur 'interpretari'. Consimilem modum loquendi in parte habet 440

[29] Augustine, *Confessiones*, XI 20 (*PL* 32. 819).
[30] Augustine, *De doctrina christiana*, II 12 (*PL* 34. 44).

discusses the wrong way of talking about the subject of time: 'for it is perfectly evident that there are neither future things nor past things, and strictly speaking we should not posit three kinds of time, past, present and future. It would perhaps be more accurate to say that the three kinds of time are the present of the past, the present of the present, and the present of the future, for the three things are in the mind, and I see them nowhere else. The present of the past is memory; the present of the present is consciousness; and the present of the future is expectation. If I may put it this way, I can see, and concede, that there are three of these things. So we might as well call the three kinds of time past, present and future; so as not to contravene what we are used to, let us refer to them in that way'; and then the conclusion clearly follows: 'please note: I do not mind, I put up no resistance, I do not criticize, so long as what is said is understood, that neither the future nor the past exist now. For there are only a few things that we can say precisely, many more that we cannot. Let us just understand what we mean.'[29] So says Augustine.

Note that St Augustine cares little about the qualities of words so long as the meaning remains. Indeed, as he says in the second book of *De doctrina christiana*, chapter 12, 'not only particular words, but whole phrases are often translated which are entirely foreign to Latin idiom if one intends to follow the usage of ancient Latin speakers', and a little later in the same chapter he says, 'whether one says *inter homines* or *inter hominibus* is completely irrelevant to knowing things', and he goes on, 'whether one should forgive the long or short third syllable is of no importance to those who seek God's forgiveness of their sins'.[30]

Fifth and last, we should be clear that it is the case that translation can normally be defined in three ways in relation to the words 'language or idiom of locutions'; I have already said what is a locution in the mind and what is a locution in a particular language, which is an expression composed of meaningful sounds. So if a translator or interpreter teaches one language to an auditor who speaks another language, he transfers the material he is teaching into the auditor's mind; this is the way in which grammar teachers convey grammar, or a structured language, in the vernacular familiar to boys, into the minds of their pupils. And this is the way they manage to instil the language into another person's—even a dumb person's—mind; and the way that preachers, preaching through an interpreter, convey information, as in Livonia and numerous other places, and in lands where there is a variety of peoples. So we can undoubtedly understand in this sense the words of the Book of Wisdom, chapter 7, on eternal wisdom 'which is imparted among all peoples into holy souls', where 'imparted' is commonly understood as 'translated'. St Thomas speaks

sanctus Thomas, prima parte *Summe*, questio cvii, articulo primo in pede, ubi sic: 'Intellectum', inquit, 'et intelligibile est triplex; primo quidem habitualiter uel secundum memoriam, ut Augustinus dicit; secundo quod in actu consideratum uel conceptum; tercio ut ad aliud relatum. Manifestum est autem, quod a primo gradu in secundum transfertur intelligibile, per imperium uoluntatis, vnde in diffinicione habitus dicitur "quo quis utitur cum uoluerit". Similiter autem de secundo gradu transfertur in tertium per uoluntatem.'³¹ Hec sanctus Thomas.

Alio modo dicitur esse translacio: quando lingua sic interpretata propter lapsum memorie redigitur in scripturam, et istud aput auctores indifferenter translacio se\u/ interpretacio solet dici. Tercio modo dicitur translacio fieri: quando ad mutacionem vnius exemplaris in vno ydiomate, scribitur eadem sentencia in alio ydiomate, et per istum modum dicitur Ieronimum transtulisse sacram scripturam ab Hebreo in Latinum.

Hiis taliter premissis teneo partem questionis affirmatiuam tamquam michi probabilem, nichil temere asserendo; nec aliter intendo in hac materia seu quauis alia quam sancta mater ecclesia katolica et Romana sentire, quod si contingat ecclesiam aliter me docere, aut quod minus bene sapio in quocumque articulo fidem aut mores, concernente profecto sibi obediam indilate. Sed quoniam, ut dicit Salomon, qui cito credit leuis est corde, recitabo aliqua motiua que me mouent in hac parte ad partem affirmatiuam sustinendam, et signanter dico motiua quia reuera quantum estimo non possunt fieri ualide demonstraciones ad vnam partem seu ad aliam. Sed grosse et figuraliter oportet hic procedere, secundum quod racio materie moralis exigit, ut uult Aristotiles primo *Ethicorum*, consequenterque ponam que credo, aut saltem coniecturo, esse motiua aliorum qui fauent parti questionis negatiue.³²

Primum quod mouet quod ab inicio creature quantum de sacra scriptura fuerat siue in uoce seu in scripto, dicta tum fuerat in uulgari qualis erat prophecia Enoch, qui erat septimus ab Adam, de qua meminit Iudas in epistola sua [vv.14–15]. Et singnanter | dico in uulgari, quoniam usque ad construccionem turris Babel post diluuium, erat eadem lingwa clericis et uulgaribus; dicit enim scriptura, Genesis xj°[:6], 'Ecce vnus populus est et vnum labium omnibus, etc.' Etenim ne dum licitum fuit, verum eciam necessarium, sacram scripturam

445

450

455

460

465

470

197vb

475

472 tum] tamen *canc.,* tum *add. MS*   478 verum] vnum *canc.,* verum *add. MS*

---

³¹ Aquinas, *Summa theologiae* i.107.1; ed. Fratres Predicatores (Leonine edition), 1– (Rome 1882–), 5. 499, citing Augustine *De trinitate,* XIV 6–7 (*PL* 42. 1041–4).
³² Aristotle, *Ethica,* i.1, trans. Robert Grosseteste (*AL* 26/3. 376=Bekker 1394b).

in a similar way in the first part of the *Summa*, question 107, towards the end of article 1, 'an intelligible object [is present to] the intellect in three ways; the first is, habitually, or in the memory, as Augustine says; secondly, as actually considered or conceived; thirdly, as related to something else. Now it is clear that the intelligible object passes from the first to the second stage by the command of the will, and hence in the definition of habit it is said "which anyone uses when he wills". So likewise the intelligible object passes from the second to the third stage by the will.'[31] So says St Thomas.

Translation may be seen in a second way: when a translated text is written down to avoid being forgotten, it is regarded by its authors as either translation or interpretation, indifferently. And it can be defined in a third way: as the change which happens to an exemplar in one language, when the meaning is written down in another, as when Jerome is said to have translated holy scripture from Hebrew into Latin.

On these grounds I agree with the affirmative side of the argument as probable, and not something I would rashly assert; and I do not intend to argue anything contrary to our holy mother the catholic and Roman Church, and if the Church should instruct me otherwise, or if my understanding is deficient in any article of faith or morals, I will certainly and instantly obey. But since, as Solomon says, he who believes at once is light at heart, I will go through the reasons which have inclined me to the affirmative side of the argument, and I wish to emphasize that so far as I can see there are no absolute proofs of one side or the other. We must proceed imprecisely and by analogy, which is appropriate in moral questions, as Aristotle puts it in the first book of the Ethics, and then I will set out what I believe, or at least surmise, are the reasons of others who incline to the negative side of the question.[32]

The first reason is that holy scripture from the beginning had been created either in the spoken or the written word, and was spoken in the vernacular like the prophecy of Enoch, the seventh after Adam, as Jude reminds us in his epistle. And I deliberately say in the vernacular, because up to the time of the building of the Tower of Babel, which was after the Flood, there was only the one language for clerks and for common people; as the Bible says in the 11th chapter of Genesis, 'Behold, the people is one and they have all one language'. Indeed it was not yet lawful for scripture to be translated into the

esse traditam in uulgari. Postea uero, succedente tempore, transito
mari Rubro, cecinit Moises et filii Israelis carmen hoc Domino, et 480
dixerunt, 'Cantemus Domino' [Exod. 15:1], et a uerisimili hoc ceci-
nerunt Domino in uulgari, quod si dicas quod in Hebreo clericali,
hoc non probas nisi forte vtrumque erat intelligibile a populo. Sed
qualitercumque sit de isto, habemus in innumeris locis Penthateuci
quod Dominus dixit, 'hoc dices filiis Israelis', et quod locutus est 485
Moises ad vniuersum cetum filiorum Israelis: et signanter, Devte-
ronimus 31°[:30], 'locutus est ergo Moises audiente vniuerso cetu
filiorum Israelis uerba carminis huius, et ad finem usque comple-
uit'. Et cum quodam modo proponebatur eis per modum omelie, est
verisimile quod hoc dixerat in uulgari; simile uidetur de amonicio- 490
nibus omnium prophetarum, quod illas proclamauerant in uulgari.
Et quis audeat dicere, quod non licuisset deuotis uiris et sciolis illa
sic uulgariter proposita eciam conscribere in uulgari? Et confirmatur hec persuasio per illud Esdre ij°, capitulo 8° [Neh. 8:1–3, 7–8],
vbi sic habetur, 'congregatus est omnis populus quasi vir vnus ad 495
platheam que est ante portam aquarum, et dixerunt Esdre scribe
ut afferret librum legis Moisi, quam preceperat Dominus Israelis.
Attulit ergo Esdras sacerdos legem coram multitudine uirorum et
mulierum, cunctisque qui poterant intelligere, in die primo mensis
septimi. Et legit in eo aperte in plathea que erat ante portam aquarum 500
a mane usque ad medium diem, et in conspectu uirorum et mulierum et sapientum, et aures omnis populi erant errecte ad librum.'
Et sequitur, 'Leuite silencium faciebant ad audiendam legem, populus autem stabat in gradu suo. Et legerunt in libro Dei distincte,
et aperte ad intelligendum, et intellexerunt cum legeretur.' Ex isto 505
passu ad propositum notari potest, quod Esdras legit legem coram
omni populo, uirisque et mulieribus, et quod aures omnis populi
erant errecte ad librum, et quod intellexerunt cum legeretur; quod
non est uerisimile nisi legisset in uulgari—non enim omnes erant
litterati; et si dicatur quod non intellexerunt nisi isti certi dati, eo 510
quod populus non intellexit quod alicui appareret ex eo quod sequitur, quod leuite erant vniuersa interpretantes populo, sed dato illo
adhuc redit questio prius, si enim leuite erant interpretes, sequitur
quod transtulerunt et interpretati sunt Hebreum litteratum in uulgare. Aliter enim populus non intellexisset, cuius oppositum dicit 515
textus, si enim interpretabantur legem, hoc est exposuerunt, sequitur adhuc ut prius, quod litteram legis exposuerant in uulgari, quam
postea declarabant. Sed quis, queso, prohibuisse uoluisset populum

---

484 innumeris *repeated for clarity in margin* MS   499 qui *add. in margin with*
insertion mark MS   504 *letter erased at the end of* gradu   511 ex eo quod]
originally ex eo quoque, -que *canc.,* -d *add.* MS

vernacular, since it was not yet necessary. But later, as time passed, at the crossing of the Red Sea, Moses and the children of Israel sang this song to the Lord, 'Let us sing unto the Lord', and they must most probably have sung it in the vernacular, for if you argue that it was sung in learned Hebrew, you meet the difficulty that it must have been intelligible to the people. In any case we have innumerable examples in the Pentateuch when the Lord said, 'you shall say this to the children of Israel', which Moses repeated to the children of Israel gathered together: in particular Deuteronomy 31, 'and Moses spake in the ears of all the congregation of Israel the words of this song, until they were ended'. And as he must have addressed them more or less in the way of a homily, it is clear that he spoke to them in the vernacular; and the same must be true of the admonitions of the prophets, that they declaimed them in the vulgar tongue. And who would be so foolish as to say that it was unlawful for the pious laity and learners to write down in the vernacular those things so put to them in the spoken vernacular? This point is confirmed in chapter 8 of the second book of Ezra, where we read, 'and all the people gathered themselves together as one man into the street that was before the water gate, and they spake unto Ezra the scribe to bring the book of the law of Moses, which the Lord had commanded to Israel. And Ezra the priest brought the law before the congregation both of men and women, and all that could hear with understanding, upon the first day of the seventh month. And he read therein in the street that was before the water gate from the morning until midday, before the men and the women, and those who could, and the ears of all the people were attentive unto the book of the law.' And it goes on, 'The Levites stilled all the people, to hear the law, and the people stood in their place. So they read in the book of the law of God distinctly, and gave the sense, and caused them to understand the reading.' We may note, arguing from this passage, that Ezra read the law before all the people, men and women together, and the ears of the people were attentive to the book, and that they understood what they heard; which is inconceivable unless it was read in the vernacular, for they were not all educated; and to the argument that only some of them understood, since it appears that most of them did not, as we then read that the Levites were interpreting it all for the people, [we reply that] given that, the question still remains, if the Levites were interpreting, would they not still be translating or interpreting literary Hebrew in demotic Hebrew? Otherwise the people would not have understood, which is contrary to what the text says, for if they interpreted the law, that is to say expounded it, it follows as before, that they translated the letter of the law in the vernacular, and then explained it. Who, I ask you, would have wanted

198ra tam deuotum si expetiuisset | habuisse litteram textus in uulgari, aut eius declaracionem, aut utrumque? Reuera, ut apparet, nullus qui 520 habuisset zelum legis Dei. Quid, queso, quando Christus et eius apostoli predicabant in variis lingwis popularibus? Nonne fuisset magna iniquitas si litterati uiri eorum predicaciones in uulgari ydiomate sub litteris designassent? Profecto, ut reor, si culpa, felix culpa fuisset, qua quis posset esse de sorte beati viri, racione memoralis exemplaris 525 legem Domini meditans die ac nocte. Per tale etenim exemplar, ne dum elleuatur ad Deum hominis affectus, verum eciam et illuminatur et eius intellectus.

Et ideo dicit Apostolus 1ᵐ Cor.14°[:15]: 'Orabo spiritu, orabo et mente', id est affectu et intellectu, et probat consequenter quod hoc 530 est multo melius quam solum habere deuocionem in uerbis, ipsa non intelligendo quod ostendit. Consequenter ita dicet ceterum, 'Si benedixeris, quis supplet locum ydiote quomodo dicet Amen super tuam benediccionem, quoniam quid dicas nescit?' Quam litteram exponens doctor de Lira ita scribit, 'Si populus', inquit, 'intelligat oracionem 535 sacerdotis, melius reducitur in Deum et deuocius respondet Amen'. Ideo dicit, 'Ceterum si benedixeris scilicet tu, sacerdos uel episcopus, spiritu, id est absque hoc quod populus intelligat. "Quis suplet locum ydiote": quasi diceret quid proficit populus simplex, et non intelligens quasi diceret nichil aut modicum, quia nescit se conformare tibi, qui 540 es minister ecclesie, respondendo, Amen.' Propter hoc inquit, 'in primitiua ecclesia benedicciones, et cetera omnia fiebant in uulgari, sed postquam multiplicatus fuit populus et consueuit se conformare ministris ecclesie, utpote stando quando dicitur ewangelium deposito capucio, adorando eukaristiam et consimilibus, fiunt in Latino, 545 et sufficit quod clerus respondeat pro toto populo, expedicius enim fit hoc modo quam in uulgari'.³³ Hec doctor de Lira. Ecce quod in primitiua ecclesia non reputabant inconueniens aut illicitum quod sacra scriptura esset tradita, conscripta et lecta pariter in uulgari; et quamuis clerus reputauit pro meliori quod redigeretur in Latinum, 550 non legitur tamen ipsos pro illicito reputasse, et sic apostoli pro licito et utili predicabant. Et hinc est quod multe gencium naciones laudabilem satis ut creditur, habent in suis ligwis totam sacram paginam cum doctoribus, vna cum seruicio ecclesiastico; cuiusmodi sunt Ruteni, qui Wandalico siue Slauico habent omnia hec translata, sic 555 etenim dixerant michi viri fide digni qui fuerant inter illos. Pariformiter eciam se habet quoad gentem Armenorum, qui consimiliter in Armenico suo habent omnia hec conscripta, sicut retulit michi

---

527 Deum] dominum *canc.*, deum *add. MS*   532 dicet] *possibly* dicent
552 reputabant *canc. before* predicabant *MS*

to obstruct so devout a people if they wished to have the literal text in the vulgar tongue, or its explanation, or both? Nobody, it seems, who had zeal for the law of God. Who, I ask you, when Christ and his apostles preached in various vernaculars? Would it have been a great evil if literate men had written down their sermons in the vulgar tongue? Indeed, if it were a fault, it would have been a happy fault, through which a man could enjoy the lot of a saint, meditating day and night the law of God, with the help of a text to jog his memory. For a text of that kind, even if it did not cause a man's will to rise toward God, would certainly enlighten his mind.

This is what the Apostle says in 1 Corinthians 14: 'I will pray with the spirit, and I will pray with the understanding also', that is, with the will and with the mind, and it follows as a consequence that this is much better than to have devotion only in words, without understanding what it means. So he will go on to say, 'Else when you shall bless with the spirit, how shall he that occupies the place of the unlearned say Amen at your giving of thanks, seeing he understands not what you say?' Dr Lyra writes explaining this text, 'If the people understand the prayer of the priest, they are more easily brought back to God and reply, Amen, with more devotion'. He goes on, 'Otherwise, if you, the priest or the bishop, bless with the spirit, it will be beyond what the people understand. "He that occupies the place of the unlearned": that is, what does it profit the simple layman, if he understands little or nothing of what is said, and does not know to respond to you, the church's minister, by saying, Amen.' For that reason, he says, 'in the primitive church blessings, etc. were always given in the vernacular, but later, when the people were more numerous and had got used to responding to the ministers of the church, by, for instance, standing with head uncovered when the Gospel is read, adoring the eucharist and other customs, they were made in Latin, and it was enough that the clergy should respond on behalf of the people as a whole, because it was more convenient that way than in the vernacular'.[33] So says Dr Lyra. Note that it was not considered bad or unlawful practice in the primitive church for holy scripture to be handed on, written down or read in the vernacular too; and although the clergy thought it better if it were rendered in Latin, it was not considered unlawful, and so the apostles usefully and lawfully preached. And for this reason many nations [think it] laudable enough to have the whole of the Bible with the doctors' glosses, together with the rites of the Church in their own tongue; for instance the Russians, who have all these texts translated into the Wendish or Slavonic language, as trustworthy persons who have travelled among them have told me. The same is the case with the people of Armenia, who have them all written in Armenian, as a

---

[33] Lyra, *Postilla in epistolam primam ad Corinthios* 14:15.

quidam sacerdos de partibus Armenorum, qui eciam ostendit michi
Psalterium in Armenico, que profecto lingwa quoad figuras littera- 560
rum et quoad sonum est a Greco disparatissima.[34] Sequitur. |

198rb   Et si obicias michi quod \hec/ prefata que conscribuntur in signis
gramaticatis et non uulgaribus conscribuntur, de hoc postea uidebitur. Sed sufficit michi pro ueritate articuli si que prefata sunt licita,
quod sacra pagina posset licite transferri in lingwas minus principales 565
et famosas quam sint lingue principales, Hebreum videlicet, Grecum
et Latinum. Si dicas quod eciam ista sunt illicita, mox contra tuam
presumpcionem insurgit contra te tota ecclesia Rutenorum, pariter et
omnis ecclesia Armenorum, qui usque hodie pedibus Romane ecclesie fatentur se subiectos esse, nec in hac parte hactenus legitur eos 570
ab ecclesia culpatos fuisse. Qualis igitur culpa foret quodve periculum, quod nacio Arabum seu Caldeorum ad fidem Christi conuersa
foret hoc pacto, quod sacer textus in eorum linguas translatus esset.
Et si dicas quod nullum utique, eo quod hee lingue gramaticate
sunt, in quarum quibusdam elegantissime descriptum est quadri- 575
uium mathematice, cum multis aliis scienciis, ergo inquam doctor
ille male distinxit, qui dixit quod omnes lingue preter Hebream,
Grecam et Latinam sunt barbare: presertim cum precipiat Papa in
Clementinis, [tit.] *De magistris*, [inc.] *Inter solitudines*, quod sint in
vniversitatibus Parisiensi, Oxoniensi, Bononiensi et Salamancie viri 580
catholici, sufficientem habentes Hebraice, Grece, Arabice et Caldaice
linguarum noticiam, libros de lingwis illis in Latinum fideliter trans-
ferentes.[35] Quid, queso, placet tibi dicere de Galicis, Teutonicis et
Hispanis, qui omnes in suo uulgari habent et habuerant Bibliam,
a tempore cuius memoria non existit? Numquid hos omnes in hac 585
parte dampnabis? Caue autem ne teipsum dampnes!

   Reffert enim Venerabilis Beda, libro 1°, capitulo 2°, quod sanctus
Osualdus, rex Northumbrorum, peciit a gente Scotorum virum sanctum, Aidanum episcopum, ad instruendam gentem quam regebat
uir: 'miro', inquit, 'spectaculo episcopo Scotico predicante, rex ipse 590
interpretaretur Anglice'.[36] Sed quid mali, queso, contigisset si interpretacio sancti Osualdi litteris Anglicis comendata fuisset? Audiui
nempe a quodam venerabili viro Allemanno, quomodo quidam Fla-
myngus, Iacobus de Marland appellatus, transtulit totam Bibliam
in suum Flandricum; super quo a suis emulis impetitus, curiam 595
Romanam peciit, ubi facta proposicione precepit papa librum examini
tradi, quod et factum est. Demum autem comperta est translacio tam

---

[34] Ullerston might have met an Armenian priest when Leo VI, titular king of Armenia, visited England in 1386; alternatively, and perhaps more likely, it was during the visit of the Byzantine emperor, Manuel II, in December 1400 and January 1401.

[35] *Clementinae*, tit. *De magistris*; ed. Friedberg, 2. 1179.

priest from Armenia has related to me; he also showed me a Psalter in Armenian, a language completely different from Greek both in its script and in the way it sounds.[34]

And if you object against me that all these texts are written in structured languages and not in vernaculars, I will get on to that later. It is enough for the present purpose that they are lawful, and so the sacred page may lawfully be translated into minor and less prestigious languages than the principal tongues, namely Hebrew, Greek and Latin. Were you to say that even so they are still unlawful, the whole Russian church will soon rise up against your presumption, and the Armenian church too; churches which up to the present time regard themselves as subject to the Roman church, and I have not read that the Church has reproved them for it. So what is a matter of blame, indeed of dire peril, is that the Arab or Chaldean nation was not converted to the Christian faith because the sacred text was not translated into their language. And if you reply that all the same none of these is a structured language, in some of which the *quadrivium* is very elegantly set out mathematically, with many other sciences, then I retort that this doctor has made a bad distinction when he said that all languages except Hebrew, Greek and Latin are barbarous: especially as the Pope has laid down in the Clementines, titulus *De magistris*, beginning *Inter solitudines*, that there should be catholic men in the universities of Paris, Oxford, Bologna and Salamanca, who have enough knowledge of Hebrew, Greek, Arabic and Aramaic to translate from these languages faithfully into Latin.[35] And what, I ask you, do you say about the French, the Germans and the Spaniards, who all have the Bible in the vulgar tongue, and have had for time out of mind? You are presumably not going to condemn them all? Be careful not to condemn yourself!

For the Venerable Bede mentions in the second chapter of book 1 that St Oswald, king of the Northumbrians, sought a holy man from among the Irish, Bishop Aidan, to teach the people the great man ruled over: 'the king himself, in an extraordinary scene, used to translate into English what the bishop preached in Irish'.[36] But I ask you, what harm could have been done if the translation of King Oswald had been written down in English? Indeed I have heard from a venerable German that a Fleming, called Jacob van Maerlant, translated the whole Bible into his native Flemish; when he was attacked by his jealous colleagues, he appealed to the Roman curia, where the Pope, having heard his case, ordered the book to be examined. On inspection it was found to be so faithful a translation that he was

---

[36] Bede, *Historia ecclesiastica gentis Anglorum*, III 3 (*PL* 95. 119–21).

fidelis, quod dimissus erat libere in confusionem emulorum.[37] Nonne credis quod Anglicus noster Beda Venerabilis, spiritu Dei ductus, |
198va transtulit Bibliam in uulgare Anglicum sui temporis, cuius transla- 600 cionis, ut testantur qui uiderant, relinquntur in multis monasteriis Anglie nonnulla originalia. Vnde \et/ Cestrensis, libro 5, capitulo 24, 'Ewangelium', inquit, 'Iohannis lingua Anglica interpretatus est'. Vnde et ipse habeo vnum libellum de exposicione ewangeliorum quam plurium per anni circulum in vetustissimo Anglico, quod uix 605 aliquis hominum iam viuencium sufficeret intelligere propter mixtio- nem liguarum alienarum cum nostro Anglico. Subsequenter scribit enim Cestrensis, libro 6°, in principio, de rege Aluredo, fundatore vniuersitatis Oxoniensis per hunc modum: 'legitur', inquit, 'quod ille Aluredus composuit libros, transmutans eos in propriam lingwam, 610 scilicet librum Orosii, et *Pastorale* Gregorii, *Gesta Anglorum* Bede, Boecium *De consolacione*, et librum proprium quem propria lingua *Ench\e/ridion* vocant. Fecit quoque Werefrethum, Wigornie episco- pum, transferre libros *Dialogorum* Gregorii in Saxonicam linguam, et in priori opere', sic scribit, 'optimas leges in lingwam Anglicam 615 conuertit, tandem Psalterium transferre aggressus, uix parte prima explicata viuendi finem fecit'.[38] Hec Cestrensis.

Quid eciam astrues de Ricardo, dicto heremita, uirorum deuotis- simo, qui totum Psalterium transtulit in uulgare? Num ipsum peccati argues in hac parte? Dies quippe me defficiet si omnium uirorum 620 illustrium titulos enunnciare voluero, qui sacram scripturam in uul- garia ydiomata transtulerunt. A\u/sculta, queso, et audi quid dicat dominus Lincolniensis in quodam sermone qui sic incipit *Scriptum est de leuitis*: 'Si', inquit, 'aliquis dicat quod nescit predicare, proprium remedium est quod resignet beneficium suum. Tamen melius reme- 625 dium dicam, potest enim quelibet talis persona uel sacerdos repe- tere in septimana nudum textum ewangelii diei dominice, ut tunc sciat saltem historiam grossam subditis suis refferre. Et hoc dico, si Latinum intelligat, sic faciat singulis septimanis anni, et in ueritate bene proficiet, quia eciam sic predicauit Dominus, qui et Iohannes, 630 6°[:63], ait: 'uerba que ego loquor, spiritus et uita sunt". Si uero non

601 relinquntur] relinquit *MS*   602 5] 9° *canc.*, 5 *add. MS*   603 Ewange- lium] enumerabilia *canc.*, ewanᵃ *written in a darker ink in the margin with insertion signs MS*   607 Subsequenter] *originally* consequenter, con- *canc.*, sub- *add. MS*

[37] Jacob van Maerlant, *Rymbybel*; ed. J.-B. David, 3 vols (Brussels 1858–61).

[38] Ranulf Higden, *Polychronicon*, V 24 and VI 1; ed. C. Babington & J. R. Lumby, 9 vols, RS 41 (1865–86), 6. 224, 354–61. Ullerston's list of Alfred's translations is closer to that given by William of Malmesbury, *Gesta regum Anglorum*, whom he does not mention (see R. A. B. Mynors, R. M. Thomson & M. Winterbottom (eds), *Gesta regum Anglorum*, 2 vols (Oxford 1998–9), 1. 193, with commentary, 2. 102–104). Higden mentions only Alfred's translations of laws and psalms, whereas according to William of Malmesbury,

acquitted, to the confusion of his critics.[37] You must be aware that our own Englishman, the Venerable Bede, inspired by the spirit of God, translated the Bible into the demotic English of his time, of which translation some copies remain in numerous English monasteries, as those who have seen it could testify. On this, Ranulf Higden says in book 5, chapter 4, 'The Gospel of St John was rendered into English'. And I have myself a small book expounding several gospel [readings] for the annual cycle written in very old English, which scarcely anyone living can understand after the influx of foreign languages into our own English tongue. And later on Higden writes this at the beginning of book 6 on King Alfred, the founder of the University of Oxford: 'we read that Alfred compiled books, translating into his own tongue the book of Orosius, the *Pastorale* of Gregory, Bede's *History of the English People*, Boethius *On Consolation*, and a book of his own which is called *Enchiridion* in the original. He also had Werferth, bishop of Worcester, translate the books of Gregory's *Dialogues* into the Saxon language, and in the first work', he continues, 'he turned very good laws into English, and though he started on the Psalter, he only just completed the first part of his exposition before he died'.[38] So says Higden.

And what do you make of Richard, called the hermit, one of the most devout of men, who translated the whole Psalter into the vernacular? You are surely not arguing that he sinned in doing this? Life is too short to list all the distinguished men who have translated holy scripture into vernacular languages. But take note, I ask you, and hear what the lord Robert Grosseteste says in a sermon which begins *Scriptum est de Leuitis*: 'If', he says, 'someone says he does not know how to preach, the proper course is for him to resign his benefice. But I will give a better remedy, which is for every parson or priest in this situation to go back over the bare text of the Sunday Gospel during the week, and then he will at least know how to pass on the gist of the story to his congregation. And I say, if he understands Latin, he should do this every week of the year, and he will really do some good, for as the Lord preached, in John, chapter 6, "the words that I speak unto you, they are spirit, and they are life". But

---

Alfred translated Gregory's *Pastoral Care*, Bede's *History*, Boethius, *On the Consolation of Philosophy*, and *liber proprius quem patria lingua Enchiridion, id est Manualem librum appellauit* ('a book of his own which he called in his native tongue *Enchiridion*, that is *Hand-book*'). Alfred's *Enchiridion* has not survived and its exact identity is unclear (see S. Keynes & M. Lapidge, *Alfred the Great: Asser's Life of King Alfred and Other Contemporary Sources* (Harmondsworth 1983), 268 n. 208).

intelligit Latinum, saltim potest adire vicinum aliquem intelligen-
tem qui caritatiue ei exponat, et sic ulterius gregem suum doceat;
et \in/ vno anno potest repetere epistolas festorum, et in secundo
uitas sanctorum, et deinde subditis referre.'[39] Ex isto habemus quod   635
aliquis licite potest nudum textum ewangelii predicare in uulgari, sed
illud quod quis predicare potest licite, licet sibi in scriptis redigere,
et per consequens per processum temporis posset quis licite totum
198vb ewangelium | in uulgare transferre, et conformiter de aliis partibus
sacre pagine.   640

Immo forte multi simplices curati melius facerent sermones, si
haberent suos de uerbo in uerbum conscriptos in uulgari iuxta
modum quo dicerent, quam si ex propria industria fabricarent, quod
intimius dilligencius. Que considerans bone memorie dominus Wil-
lelmus Thoresbi,[40] archiepiscopus Eboracensis quartus a presenti,   645
fecit fieri per quendam reuerendum uirum cognomento Ga\i/trik
quendam tractatum conscriptum in uulgari, in quo continentur
articuli fidei, in quo eciam de septem peccatis mortalibus pertracta-
tur, de septem operibus misericordie, quem tractatum per paginas
precepit laicis ad eorum instruccionem, quatenus doctrina salutaris   650
non defficeret eis in hiis que sunt necessaria ad salutem, ac eciam
ad satisfaciendum imparte conscienciis simplicium curatorum, qui
ex officio ad predicandum subditis obligantur.[41] Vnde profecto noui
quendam predicatorem mediocris tamen litterature, cui in deuota
predicacione similem non audiui, de quo michi prout dictum erat   655
ab hiis qui nouerunt, quod quando predicare cepit habuit sermones
suos in uulgari conscriptos de uerbo in uerbum secundum quod
predicaturus erat. Et plane confessi sunt qui eum audierant quod
numquam tantum placuit eis sermo suus sicut quando sermones
suos in rotulis legendo predicauit.   660

Consequenter ad predicta uidendum est, ex quibus motiuis moueri
possit pars aduersa que non assenti\t/ translacioni sacri canonis in
uulgari. Ex quibus autem motiuis de facto moueantur, asserere non
audeo, presertim cum ut dicit scriptura 1 Cor.2°[:11], 'nemo nouit que
sunt hominis, nisi spiritus hominis qui in ipso est?' Potest tamen quis   665
coniecturaliter estimare, vnde sicut non sine causa creditur, moueri
possunt ad suam partem sustinendum a bono spiritu siue ex pio zelo,
ex carne, ex ignorancia puerili, ex condicione bestiali, a mundo ac
eciam \a/ dyabolo.

637 licet *canc. before* potest *MS*   638 per *corr. from* pro (?) *MS*
655–6 erat . . . sermones] *om., supplied in top margin and keyed to text MS*   668 a
mundo *preceded by* omni modo *canc. MS*

[39] Robert Grosseteste, *Sermo, Scriptum est de Leuitis*, in Bodl. MS Bodley 801,
fols. 193r–203r, at 194v.

if he does not understand Latin, he can at least go to a brighter neighbour who will kindly explain it to him, and so in turn he can teach his flock; and in one year he can expound the Epistles for feast days, and in the second year the lives of the saints, and pass it on to his congregation.'[39] We deduce from this that anyone may lawfully preach the plain text of the gospel in the vernacular, and what a man can lawfully preach, he can lawfully put down in writing, and so in the process of time he can translate the whole gospel into the vulgar tongue, and by analogy other parts of the Bible.

Indeed, it may be that many humble clergy would deliver better sermons if they had them written out word for word in the vernacular for recitation, than if they made them up by their own efforts, as being more heartfelt and more industrious. With this in mind William Thoresby of blessed memory,[40] the fourth last archbishop of York before the present incumbent, had a venerable man named Gaitrik compose a tract in the vernacular, which contained the articles of faith, and in which the seven deadly sins and the seven works of mercy were discussed as well, which he ordered to be used page by page for the instruction of the laity, so that at least they would not lack wholesome teaching on the things necessary for salvation, and so that the consciences of humble clergy, whose unavoidable duty was to preach to their congregations, could be somewhat assuaged.[41] I have actually known a preacher of only limited education, whom I have never heard anyone surpass in devout preaching, but who, I was told by those who knew him, had his sermons written out in the vernacular word for word as he would preach them. And those who heard him frankly declared that a sermon of his never pleased them so much as those he read out from a rolled-up script.

So we must now consider why the proponents of the negative side of the question reject the translation of the sacred canon into the vernacular. What their real motives are, I do not care to speculate, especially in the light of the words of 1 Corinthians, chapter 2, 'for what man knows the things of a man, save the spirit of man which is in him?' We can, however, conjecture, and there is reason to believe it, that they are persuaded of their case by honest considerations or by pious zeal; or for carnal reasons, from childish ignorance, or the herd instinct, or for worldly or even diabolical motives.

[40] John (not William) Thoresby, archbishop of York, *d.* 1373; on whom, see *ODNB*.
[41] *The Lay Folks' Catechism*; ed. T. F. Simmons and H. E. Nolloth, EETS 118 (1901). It is usually attributed to John Gaytrynge OSB of St Mary's abbey, York, working for Archbishop Thoresby.

A bono siquidem spiritu siue ex pio zelo moueri possunt per hunc   670
modum, uident enim quam periculosum sit hereses in materia fidei
seminari, nouerunt eciam \quomodo/ dispersi sunt periculosissimi
tractatus per regnum in uulgari, continentes hereses et errores; ad
quos quidem exstirpandos non uident apercius medium, quam predicare quod sacra scriptura non debet tradi popularibus in uulgari.   675
Sed istud motiuum salua pace sic opinancium, quamuis ex pio zelo
procedat, non tamen quantum michi uidetur secundum scienciam
Dei. Isti etenim, quantum uideo, sunt in capitulo eorum de quibus
meminit apostolus, ad Romanos iij°[:8], 'faciamus mala, ut veniant
bona, quorum dampnacio iusta est'. Nec audeo dicere quod taliter   680
199ra sentientes | ad sic senciendum a Spiritu Sancto moueantur, presertim
cum dicat Apostolus, 1 Cor.12°[:3], 'quod nemo loquens in spiritu
Dei dicit anathema Ihesu', id est aliquam separacionem a Ihesu. Sed
que, queso, maior separacio a Ihesu, quam impedicio publicacionis
ewangelii, quod profecto intendunt, qui nollent quod ewangelium   685
in forma, qua Dominus predicauit, esset in uulgari proclamatum?
Quia non dubitto, quoniam si liceret eciam illud sic predicari, quod
liceret eciam illud pariformiter sic conscribi. Nec mouet quod aliqui
constanter et feruentissime predicent, quod ewangelium non debeat
taliter publicari, cum Christus dicat, Iohannis 16°[:2], 'venit hora, ut   690
omnis qui interficit uos, arbitretur obsequium se prestare Deo'. Nec
eciam mouet et si aliquis uellet magna et grauia sustinere pro sentencia sua, que tendit in offendiculum decursus ewangelici, eciam si
usque ad vltimum terribilium uellet persistere in proposito inchoato.
Sed eo deterius eis continget, quod bene notat Ricardus Hampole   695
super isto uersu P[s].118^m[:43], 'ne aufferas de ore meo uerbum
ueritatis vsquequaque', ubi sic scribit, 'nonnulli sunt qui pro Deo
uolunt sustinere uerbum falsitatis, sciencioribus et melioribus credere
nolentes, similes amicis Iob; quia cum Deum deffendere nitebantur,
offenderunt, tales', inquit, 'si occidantur quamuis miracula faciant,   700
sunt tamen, ut uulgus dicit, fetentes martyres'.[42] Hec Ricardus. Et
iterum causa, siue non causa, supratacta non sufficienter mouet; nam
si propterea non permitteretur ewangelium scribi in Anglico, quia
sunt multi tractatus Anglicani continentes hereses et errores, a pari
siue a forciori prohiberent scripturam in Latino, que per totam Chri-   705
stianitatem posset disseminari. Aufferamus igitur quod malum est de
medio nostri, et nequaquam que sunt licita condempnemus.

---

676 sic] *originally* sicut, -ut *canc.* MS   682 quod *repeated in margin* MS
684 quam *with expunction marks; in the margin with insertion sign is an abbreviation for*
quam *or* quantum *MS*   689 debeat] debet *canc.*, debeat *add.* MS   696 118
repeated in margin for clarity MS   702 supratacta] supra *repeated in margin for*
clarity MS

They might indeed be moved by honest motives or pious zeal, if they see how perilous heresies are in the process of disseminating the faith, since they were also aware that very dangerous vernacular pamphlets have been circulating through the realm, containing errors and heresies; and they do not see any better way of rooting them out than to preach that holy scripture should not be made available to the people in the vernacular. With due respect to its proponents, and although it may originate in pious zeal, this reason does not seem to me to accord with what we know of God. These people, so far as I can see, are those the apostle specified in the epistle to the Romans, chapter 3, 'let us do evil, that good may come, whose damnation is just'. I could not say that those who take that point of view are inspired by the Holy Spirit, particularly as the apostle says in 1 Corinthians, chapter 12, 'that no man speaking by the spirit of God calls Jesus accursed', that is, say anything which separates him from Jesus. But what, I ask, could be a greater separation from Jesus than preventing the preaching of the gospel, which those who do not want the gospel preached in the vernacular, in the form in which the Lord preached it, clearly intend? Doubtless, if it were lawful to preach the gospel, it would be equally lawful to write it down. It is not convincing that some people will preach, repeatedly and emphatically, that the gospel should not be opened up in this way, since Christ said in John, chapter 16, 'the time comes, when whosoever kills you, thinks that he does God service'. It is equally unconvincing that a person is willing to undergo harsh punishment for his opinion, if that opinion inclines to hinder the spread of the gospel, even if he insisted on maintaining his mistaken views to the bitter end. It will be the worse for them, as Richard Hampole says on the verse in Psalm 118, 'and take not the word of truth out of my mouth', on which he writes 'there are some people who for God's sake want to maintain an untruth, unwilling to credit better and wiser persons, like Job's comforters; for they cause offence when they try to defend God, the sort of people', he says, 'who, were they to be killed and perform any amount of miracles, are, in popular diction, stinking martyrs'.[42] So says Richard. So the reason, or lack of reason, mentioned above is not convincing; for if, on those grounds, the gospel should not be written in English, because there are a large number of tracts written in English which contain errors and heresies, they should equally or even more firmly prohibit the scriptures in Latin, which is current through all Christendom. So we should put away the notion that the evil lies in our language, and we should certainly not condemn what is lawful.

[42] Richard Rolle, *Commentarius in Psalmos*, 118:43, in Bodl. MS Bodley 861, fol. 40ra.

Ex carne siquidem puto quosdam in hac materia sicut in aliis impulsum pati, puto gratia patrie aut parentele, aut alterius alligancie proprietarie, ut pote quia talis talia asseuerans est aut fuit de ordine 710 meo, de religione mea, de familiaritate mea, seu de collegio meo, ideo sustineo que sustinuit, siue uera, siue falsa. Etsi hec pestis sit summe periculosa in rebus huius mundi, quanto magis ubi agitur de materia morum et fidei, hoc enim quod absit (tracto in sequelam) sequeretur subuersio miseranda fidei Christiane. 715

Alii quippe ad premissa inclinantur ex ignorancia puerili; sicut etenim pueri ex simplicitate affirmant et negant, laudant et uituperant. Quemadmodum a parentibus audierunt, quantumcumque irrationabiliter, sint locuta que sic in medium proferuntur, ita non-
199rb nulli sim|plices modo, ymmo ab inicio quid quid audierint ab hiis 720 quos magnos reputant, cito credunt, vnde et ex ignorancia quodam modo excusantur, sic etenim in temporibus nostris multi simplices sunt et fuerant periculose festinati. Sed in hoc restat solacium, quod dicit sapiens, Prouer.2°[:7], quod Deus 'proteget gradientes simpliciter', quamuis itaque ad tempus eos seduci sinat, finaliter tamen non 725 deseret.

Ex condicione bestiali mouentur illi ad premissa concedenda qui quod est rationis aut consciencie non aduertunt; sed solum clamorem uulgi preconisant, sicut enim grunniente vno porco omnes gruniunt, latrante eciam vno cane ceteri mox sibi colatrant; et clamante vna auca 730 omnes clamitant indefesse. Sic accidit de rudibus nostri temporis, qui pro et contra clamant sicut audiunt alios clamitare. Sed propter clamorem talium non expedit viro solido in aliquo vacillare.

A mundo autem mouentur hii qui uolentes placere satrapis, student circa pinguia beneficia perquirenda; quibus Dominus ve impre- 735 catur, Eze.13°[:18], 've', inquit, 'qui consuunt puluillos sub omni cubito manus, et faciunt ceruicalia sub capite vniuerse etatis ad capiendas animas', aut certe hii qui de quibus statim sequitur in eodem capitulo: 'violabant', inquit, 'me et populum meum propter pugillum ordei et fragmen panis, ut interficerent animas que non 740 moriuntur, et viuificarent animas que non viuunt, mencientes populo meo credenti mendacio.' Tales nempe sunt cum mundo contempnendi, quoniam 'si quis dilligit mundum, non est caritas patris in eo', prima Ioh.2°[:15]. Sed a diabolo comouentur hii, qui ex presumpcione semel atemptata verecundantur a suis inepciis declinare, 745 aut fortassis ex rancore se de aduersariis vindicandi, bona cum malis pariter perimere satagunt. Sed in concilium eorum non veniat anima

---

712 hec *repeated at line break, second canc.* MS   721 ex] pro *canc., ex add.* MS
728 quod] *originally* quoque, -que *canc.,* -d *add.* MS   735–6 ve imprecatur *on
erasure of a shorter text extending into margin* MS   737 cubito] cubita, -a *canc.,* -o
add. MS   745 semel] *overwritten, clarified in margin as* semel MS

The carnal motives which I believe affect some people in this matter as in others are, I think, the ties of regional, or family, or other natural loyalty, in so far as proponents of this point of view belong or used to belong to my group, my religious order, my friends, my college, and so I agree with them, right or wrong. If this scourge is extremely harmful in the affairs of this world, it is much more so in matters of faith and morals, for the deplorable subversion of Christian faith would, alas, be the outcome (as I discuss below).

And others are inclined to this point of view out of childish ignorance; like callow boys, they assert, they deny, they praise, they blame. Just as they put about whatever they have heard their parents say, however unreasonable, so simple souls in our time, as at all times, believe at once what those they look up to tell them, and so, though they might to some extent be pardoned for their ignorance, many simple people at the present time have been, and still are, hustled dangerously [into error]. But in that lies their solace, as the wise man says in the second chapter of Proverbs, [God] 'is a buckler for them that walk uprightly', though he allows them to be deceived for a time, he will not desert them in the end.

People who are driven to this view by the herd instinct take no notice of reason or conscience; they are only aware of public noise, like pigs who all grunt when one grunts, or like dogs who start barking together as soon as they hear one bark; or geese who honk endlessly once the first begins. Rustics nowadays are the same, raising their voices on one side or another when they hear others start up. In the face of all such clamour, it is not right for a steadfast man to waver.

Worldly reasons convince those who wish to pay court to grandees, and intrigue to acquire fat benefices; they are the people whom the Lord denounces in Ezekiel, chapter 13, 'woe to the women that sew pillows to all armholes, and make kerchiefs upon the head of every stature to hunt souls', or for that matter in the passage which follows straight after it: 'they pollute me', he says, 'among my people for handfuls of barley and for pieces of bread, to slay the souls that should not die, and to save the souls alive that should not live, by your lying to my people that hear your lies.' Such people should clearly be despised together with the world, for as John says in his first epistle, chapter 2, 'if any man love the world, the love of the father is not in him'. But the devil moves those who out of pride have once ventured upon some evil and are ashamed to abandon it, or perhaps, in a rage to justify themselves in front of their opponents, go about to destroy the good and the bad indiscriminately. My soul shall not take counsel with

mea. Dicto de motiuis partis aduerse, respondendum est ad argumenta que fiebant ad oppositum questionis, etc.

Ad primum argumentum doctoris, quando sic arguit sacra scrip- 750 tura nemini reuelatur, nisi ex speciali gracia, cum interpretacio sit speciale donum, ergo nullus atemptaret sine speciali gracia sacram scripturam interpretari, hic dicitur quod hoc argumentum peccat tam in materia quam in forma. In materia, quidem sacra enim scriptura de comuni lege reuelatur per predicatores et doctores, ymo 755 aliquando per demones, ubi ex hoc non oportet specialem graciam ponere in reuelante. | Qualis, queso, specialis gracia erat in scribis et phariseis qui sacram scripturam Herodi reuelabant? Certe Crisostomus super Matheum dicit, quod ob hoc erant ueraciter proditores.[43] Rursum, qualis gracia erat in illis demoniis, qui clamantes primo 760 dixerunt 'tu es filius Dei', de quibus, Marc iij°[:12], dicitur quod 'uehementer cominabatur eis ne manifestarent illum'. In forma uero peccat, quia ex duabus particularibus concludit conclusionem vniuersalem: quamuis enim aliqua reuelacio sit ex speciali gracia, sicut patet ex multis locis scripture, non tamen omnis; nec eciam omnis 765 interpretacio est donum, sicut theologi locuntur de donis, sicut patet ex predictis. Et bene placet michi quod doctor querit questionem suam sub hac forma, utrum sacra scriptura est interpretanda in omnes linguas. Planum est quod non erat tam inprouidus quoniam uolebat dicere quod sacra scriptura esset in omnibus lingwis predicanda; et 770 planum est quod hoc licet fieri per interpretem, ubi predicator non habet noticiam utriusque lingwe. Ergo et interpretanda, et vnde quod sic interpretatum non licet scripto eiusdem ydiomatis comendare? Si enim audiens aliquem sanctorum per interpretem predicantem, uerba interpretis consequenter scripsisset, putas ne sanctum illum 775 uoluisse dixisse, 'dimitte, stultam rem facis, ne scribas amplius aliqua talia in uulgari'? Quin ymmo probabiliter multum gauisus fuisset de tanto desiderio legem Dei memorie comendandi. Ymo ut uidetur ex doctoris argumento, si cui specialiter reuelaretur, aut super hoc haberet speciale donum, puta interpretacionem sermonum, talis profecto 780 posset transferre, sicut habenti donum prophecie foret licitum prophetare. Et cum ista sentencia concordat alius: secundus doctor, de quo supra quemadmodum, michi dixit, sed fortassis uoluit iste doctor querere, vtrum de comuni lege currente, deducto quolibet tali dono, liceret sacram scripturam in minus principales linguas transferre; et 785 ad istum sensum uidetur fecisse argumenta sua.

Ad secundum cum assumit, si aliqui deberent sic transferre, essent

199va (margin)

---

756 oportet] *originally* oportet quere, quere *canc. MS*

---

[43] Pseudo-Chrysostom, *Opus imperfectum in Matthaeum*, hom. 2 (*PG* 56. 639).

them. So, after going through the motives of the opposing party, it is time to respond to their arguments for the opposite side.

In response to the doctor's first argument, that holy scripture should not be revealed to anyone except through a special grace, and as its interpretation is a special gift, nobody should try to interpret it unless they possess that special grace, I say that the argument is defective both materially and formally. Materially, because the Bible in ordinary law is expounded by preachers and doctors, and indeed sometimes by demons, to whom we should not ascribe any special grace of exposition. What kind of special grace, I ask, did the scribes and Pharisees possess when they revealed holy scripture to Herod? Indeed, Chrysostom says on Matthew that in doing this they were really betrayers.[43] Again, what special grace had the demons when they first cried out, saying, 'you are the Son of God', on which, as is related in the third chapter of Mark's gospel, 'they were straitly charged that they should not make him known'. It is defective in form as well, because he draws a general conclusion from two particular examples: for although one revelation may come from a special grace, as many biblical texts show, not all of them do; nor indeed is every interpretation a gift, in the sense that theologians speak of gifts, as I have just shown. And I am very pleased that the doctor has posed the question in this form, whether holy scripture should be translated into all languages. It is obvious that he was not so incautious as to mean that holy scripture should be preached in every language; and it is obvious too that one can lawfully preach through an interpreter when a preacher does not know both languages. So can it be interpreted, but not lawfully written down in the second language? If someone who heard one of the saints preaching through an interpreter, were later to write down the interpreter's words, do you really think the saint would wish to say, 'stop, you are doing a stupid thing, write no more of this in the vernacular'? He would much more likely have rejoiced to see such desire to commit the law of God to memory. Indeed it seems from the doctor's argument that if someone had a special revelation, or a special gift, for instance as an interpreter of language, that person could thereby [lawfully] translate in the way that someone with the gift of prophecy could lawfully prophesy. Another person agrees with this opinion: the second doctor, whom I mentioned above, said to me as much, though he perhaps meant to ask whether, according to current law, it was lawful without such a gift to translate holy scripture into minor languages; he seems to have put forward his arguments in this sense.

I respond to the second point, namely that if anyone should

episcopi, qui pro hiis diebus sunt insufficientes, dico quod non sequitur, quamuis enim bene deceret statum episcopalem circa talia gran-
dia solertem esse. Non tamen sequitur et si illi non sufficerent ad   790
talia deducenda per industriam propriam, quod ceteri omnes tamquam insufficientes relinquerentur; sed sufficit quod sint ellecti viri
qui singulariter sufficiant ad talia peragenda. Quando enim missi |
199vb fuerant 72 interpretes Alexandriam, non legitur aliquem eorum fuisse
pontificem; sed probi et ellecti viri fuerant de qualibet tribu sex,   795
que multiplicata per duodecim constituunt 72, sed a maiori parte
fit denominacio quod uocentur septuaginta. Et iterum quamuis civi-
lis sciencia, ut uult Aristoteles, ordinet in ciuitatibus que sciencie
sint addiscende, et ad quantum et qui debeant istam adiscere, et qui
illam non tamen utitur illis, sed eorum artifex apropriatus.[44] Quam-   800
uis enim cancellarius alicuius ecclesie kathedralis tradat alicui scolas
gramaticales ad regendum, non tamen oportet quod ipsemet regat;
sic enim imperator per suos consules seu iuris consultos fecit fieri
Instituta, videlicet Tribuncianum, Theophilum et Dorotheum.

Ad 3[m] quando sic arguit: vetus testamentum cessauit secundum   805
sensum litteralem, et interpretacio non est nisi secundum \sensum/
litteralem, ergo etc., dicitur quod forma non valet, concluditur enim
conclusio vniuersalis ex duobus particularibus. Si tamen intelligat
maiorem vniversaliter, videlicet quod uetus testamentum cessauit
vniuersaliter secundum sensum literalem, patet quod falsum asumi-   810
tur, cum moralia ueteris testamenti adhuc maneant secundum sensum literalem; et preter hoc figuralia et iudicialia, mistice ad ea que
sunt noui testamenti applicata, multum pulcrificant fidem nostram.
Ex quibus clare libet intueri ut uult Apostolus, I Cor.10[:11], quod
'omnia in figura contingebant patribus ueteris testamenti et propter   815
nos scripta sunt, in quos fines seculorum deuenerunt'. Pari euidencia
posset concludere quod uetus testamentum deleretur quia, cum iam
in parte cessauit quoad sensum literalem, ille partes in nulla lingua essent conscribende. Sed que maior insania quam tali sentencie
assentire.   820

Ad 4[m], ubi ex hoc quod Augustinus apeciit translacionem Septuaginta in Latinum propter impericiam Latinorum interpretum,
concludit quod multi plures interpretes imperiti corrumperent scripturam, conceditur conclusio. Ideo, ut predixi, elligantur periti et

---

791 per] *altered from* pro (?) *by erasure* MS   794 legitur] sequitur *canc.,* legitur
add. MS   805–6 secundum sensum] sed secundum *canc.,* secundum sensum *add.*
MS   806 nem *canc. before* non MS   807 litteralem *preceded by* secundum
canc. MS   videlicet *canc.,* valet *add.* MS   810 sed *canc.,* sensum *add.* MS
811–12 sed *canc.,* sensum *add.* MS   815 figura] *originally* figuram, -m *canc.* MS

---

[44] Aristotle, *Ethica* i.i, trans. Robert Grosseteste (*AL* 26/3. 375=Bekker 1394a).

translate the scripture it should be the bishops, who in these days are incompetent for the task, and say that the argument fails to hold, though to be skilled in an enterprise of this magnitude would be a fit accomplishment for the office of a bishop. It does not follow that if they themselves were incompetent to undertake the task by their own efforts, everybody else should be rejected as incompetent as well; all that is necessary is that men should be chosen who are specifically qualified to carry it out. When interpreters were sent to Alexandria, we do not read that any of them was a bishop; six honest men had been chosen from each tribe, and six multiplied by the twelve tribes makes 72, who were given the name, from their approximate size, of 'the seventy'. Again, although, as Aristotle lays down, the civil magistrate will wisely settle which of the arts are to be learnt in cities, and to what level and who should learn which art, he will not teach any art himself, but the appropriate craftsman will.[44] For although the chancellor of a cathedral chapter will appoint someone to rule the grammar schools, it is not right for him to rule them himself; as the emperor appointed consuls and learned jurists to make the Institutes, namely Tribonian, Theophilus and Dorotheus.

To the third argument, that the Old Testament no longer binds us in a literal sense, but that a rendering can only be made in a literal sense, I say that it is invalid in form, since it draws a general conclusion from two specific cases. For if one interprets the major premise as a universal law, that is, that the Old Testament no longer binds us at all in a literal sense, it is clearly false, as the moral precepts of the Old Testament are still binding in the literal sense; and besides this the prefigurative and prognostic senses, in so far as they mystically refer to the New Testament, greatly adorn our faith. This can be clearly seen in the words of the Apostle in 1 Corinthians, chapter 10, 'all these things happened to our fathers of the Old Testament as examples, and they are written for our admonition, upon whom the ends of the world are come'. One could conclude by this kind of reasoning that the Old Testament should be rejected because, as parts of it have ceased to bind us in the literal sense, those parts should not be transcribed in any language. But it would be egregious folly to subscribe to a view such as this.

On the fourth point, in which, on the grounds that Augustine looked to the translation of the Septuagint into Latin because of the inexperience of the Latin translators, he argued that a large number of inexperienced interpreters would corrupt scripture, I agree. But then, as I said above, learned and competent translators should be

sufficientes et tunc in nullo concludit. Sed pro materia argumenti 825
aliquid est dicendum, uidetur enim doctorem tacite inculpare translacionem Ieronimi de impericia ad hoc enim dictum est supra. Quare
autem Augustinus apeciit translacionem Septuaginta in Latinum,
hoc petit argumentum declarari, cuius causam multiplicem possu-
2oora mus assignare. Vnam quidem quam ipsemet assignat | 2° *De doc-* 830
trina Christiana, capitulo 14°, 'Latinis', inquit, 'codicibus emendandis
Greci adhibeantur, in quibus Septuaginta interpretum quantum ad
uetus testamentum attinet, excessit auctoritas; qui iam per omnes
periciores ecclesias tanta presencia Sancti Spiritus interpretati esse
dicuntur ut os vnum tot hominum fuerit. Qui, si ut fertur, mul- 835
tique non indigni fide predicant, singuli cellis eciam singulis separati cum interpretati essent, nichil in alicuius codice inuentum est
quod non eisdem uerbis eodemque uerborum ordine inveniretur in
ceteris, quis huic auctoritati conferre aliquid audeat?'[45] Quasi diceret
'nullus'. Augustinus enim hic non asserit quod sic fuit, sed condi- 840
cionem annectit et ideo dicit 'si ut fertur'; sed Ieronimus expresse
contrarium dicit, sicut patet in prologo super Penthateucum ubi
sic: 'Nescio quis primus auctorum 70 cellulas Allexandrie mendacio
\suo/ extraxit, quibus diuisi eadem scriptitarent'.[46] Et quod opinio
Ieronimi debeat preualere, uidetur per Iosephum *Antiquitatum,* qui 845
de istis septuaginta in libro suo 12° ita scribit: 'Demetrius concilium
fecit in domo prope littus stante, et apta secretis ad cognicionem uel
cogittacionem negociorum, ubi eos perducens prebebat omnia que
opus habebant ad legis interpretacionem. Cumque laboriose tantam
interpretacionem facerent usque ad horam nonam, ad curam corporis 850
uertebantur, mane autem ad eundem locum redibant et ita legis inter-
pretacioni uacabant. Ita transcripta lege et opere interpretacionis ad
effectum per 72ª dies transacto, congregans Demetrius Iudeos omnes
ad locum in quo leges translate fuerant, presentibus interpretibus
legit eas.'[47] \Dicit/ ideo Ieronimus eos in vna basilica congregatos 855
contulisse, 'basilica enim domus regia dicitur, a *basileos,* quod est rex
uel imperator dicta'.[48] Si autem ista causa a beato Augustino asignata
stare non possit, sed quod oportet opinioni Ieronimi condescendere.
    Tunc statim subdit aliam, ita inquiens, 'Si autem contulerint, ut
vna omnium comuni tractatu iudicioque uox fieret, nec si quidem 860

---

830 vt *canc. before* vnam *MS*   836 cellis] test' *canc.,* cellis *add. MS*
848 prebebat] *originally* preberebat, -re- *canc. MS*   852 interpretacionis]
intersitis *at line break,* -sitis *canc.,* -tacionis *add. MS*   859 contulerint] *corr.*
from contulerunt *MS*

---

[45] Augustine, *De doctrina christiana,* II 15 (*PL* 34. 46).
[46] Jerome, *Praefatio in Pentateuchum ad Desiderium* (*PL* 28. 150).

chosen, and then his conclusion no longer follows. Something more should be said, however, about the substance of the question, namely that by implication the doctor, considering what was said above, is accusing Jerome's translation of inadequacy. So an explanation needs to be given why Augustine relied on the Latin translation of the Septuagint, on which a number of suggestions might be made. He specifies one of them in chapter 14 of the second book of *De doctrina christiana*, 'we must use the Greek text to emend the Latin versions, and among them the authority of the Septuagint, so far as the Old Testament is concerned, is pre-eminent; for it is claimed in all the more learned churches that the translators were so inspired by the presence of the Holy Spirit that they all spoke with one voice. If, as people say, and reliable sources confirm it, they were separated during the work of translation in individual cells, but all their versions agreed, using the same words in the same order, then who can improve on authority such as this?'[45] As if to say 'nobody'. Augustine does not assert that this was the case, but qualifies it with the words 'if, as people say'; but Jerome explicitly says the opposite, as appears in his prologue to the Pentateuch: 'I cannot say who first put about the tall story of the cells of the seventy authors of Alexandria, in which they were all writing away separately'.[46] Jerome's opinion should prevail, since it is confirmed by the *Antiquitates* of Josephus; he writes in Book 12 about the Seventy: 'Demetrius held a council in his house near the sea shore, which was suitable for private meetings and the conduct of confidential business, and there showed the people he had brought there all that was necessary for the translation of the Law. They applied themselves to the work of translation until the ninth hour, when they took refreshment, and returned early the next day to get on with the translation. So they translated the law, completing the work in 72 days; and then Demetrius gathered all the Jews to the place where the work was done, and read the translation to them in the presence of the translators.'[47] So Jerome says they were all gathered together in one basilica, 'that is to say, a royal palace, from *basileos*, which means a king or emperor'.[48] So we must reject the reason adduced by St Augustine and defer to the opinion of Jerome.

Augustine goes on to make another point, 'If they were meeting together, and came after discussion to a common view and text,

---

[47] Josephus, *Antiquitates Iudaicorum*, XII 2; sixth-century Latin translation, pr. *Flavii Iosephi Antiquitatum Iudaicarum libri XX* (Basel 1540), 310–11.

[48] Uguccione, *Deriuationes* (ed. Cecchini, 2. 119).

quemquam vnum hominem, qualibet pericia, ad emendandum tot
seniorum doctorumque consensum aspirare oportet aut decet'. Et si
obiciatur quod non in toto secuti sunt ueritatem Hebraicam, quemadmodum Ieronimus bene declarat in quam pluribus librorum pro-
hemiis, consequenter ad hoc respondet Augustinus, 'Quamobrem 865
eciam si aliquid aliter in Hebreis exemplaribus inuenitur, quam isti
posuerunt, credendum esse arbitror diuine dispensacioni, que per eos
2oorb facta | est, ut libri quos gens Iudea ceteris populis uel religione uel
inuidia prodere nolebat, credituris per dominum gentibus ministra
regis Tholomei potestate tanto ante proderentur. Et ita fieri poterit 870
ut sic illi interpretati sunt quemadmodum congruere gentibus ille,
qui eos agebat et qui vnum os fecerat Spiritus Sanctus iudicauit.'
Hec Augustinus. Conformiter posset dici de translacione Ieronimi,
quod in tempore gracie reuelate nobis qui reuelata facie gloriam Dei
contemplamur, singulariter expediebat quod Ieronimus tam peritus 875
linguarum tot peritorum interpretum operas intuens, luculentissime
nobis sacram scripturam in Latinum transferret.

Aliam autem causam tangit *Epistola 22ᵃ ad Ieronimum*, videlicet
propter promptam correccionem librorum Latinorum ubi ad Greca
uolumina de facili recursum habere debemus, ad Hebrea uix aut nun- 880
quam; vnde sic scribit, 'quis quis autem in eo quod ex Hebreo translatum est aliquo insolito permotus fuerit, et falsi crimine intenderet,
uix aut nunquam ad Hebrea peruenitur testimonia, quibus deffen-
datur obiectum'.⁴⁹ Alia causa poterat esse, quia translacio ipsorum
septuaginta, per laudabilem ecclesie consuetudinem que pro le\ge/ 885
habenda est uel saltem legi equiuallet, longe ante tempora Augustini
fuerat confirmata, translacio uero Ieronimi quamuis melior erat; qui
contemporaneus erat Augustino, pro tempore Augustini non tante
fuerat ut uerisimiliter creditur ab ecclesia accepta, habuit igitur beatus Augustinus tunc temporis rationabilem causam translacionem 890
septu\a/ginta aliis translacionibus preferendi. Quoniam ut ipsemet
dicit in libro *De vera religione*, capitulo xv°, 'In istis temporalibus legibus, quamquam de hiis homines iudicent cum eas instituunt, tamen
cum fuerint institute et firmate non licebit iudici de ipsis iudicare, sed
secundum ipsas'.⁵⁰ Modo vero, quia ecclesia prefert translacionem 895
Ieronimi ipsam pre ceteris, preellegit Augustinus si modo uiueret
esset cum ecclesia concorditer ellecturus. Et per hoc patet aliqualis
solucio ad argumenta doctoris reuerendi.

Ad quintum, ubi ex auctoritate Augustini tercia parte sermonum,
sermone lviii°, qua dicit quod non licet simbolum scribi, nec ullo 900

876 interpretum *corr. from* interpretatum *MS*   luculentissime] *originally* lucalen-
tissime, -a- *canc.*, -u- *add. MS*   880 facili] *originally* facile, -e *canc.*, -i *add. MS*
895 Modo vero] M°v° *in text,* modo vero *add. in margin MS*

then it would not be right or proper for a single individual, however learned, to correct the consensus of so many senior and experienced people'. To the objection that they did not completely convey the Hebrew meaning, as Jerome well points out in the prefaces to several books, Augustine replies, 'Even if some other meaning can be found in the Hebrew originals, I think we must give way to the dispensation of God, who used the translators to make known, with the help of the power of King Ptolemy, those books which the Jews, out of scruple or jealousy, did not want to reveal to other nations, and to make them known long in advance to the people who would in future believe in the Lord. So it may be that the Holy Spirit inspired them, and gave them all one voice, to interpret it in a form appropriate to the Gentiles.' So says Augustine. In accordance with this, it could be said about Jerome's translation that it was particularly appropriate that he, so skilled in languages and with access to the work of so many translators, should make a magnificent Latin version of holy scripture for us in the age of revealed grace, as we behold the glory of the uncovered face of God.

Augustine touches on another reason in his *Epistola 22 ad Ieronimum*, namely on the ready correction of Latin books when we should have regular access to Greek texts, but rarely or never to the Hebrew; on which he writes, 'if one is disturbed by something unusual in a text translated from Hebrew, and suspects that the translation is wrong, it is almost never possible to check the evidence of the Hebrew text by which the question could be settled'.[49] Another reason might have been that the translation of the Septuagint was held to be canonical, or nearly canonical, by the laudable custom of the Church, and had been authoritative long before Augustine's time, even though Jerome's translation was better. Jerome was a contemporary of Augustine, but his authority at that time was not wholly accepted by the Church, and Augustine therefore had reasonable cause to prefer the [received] translation of the Septuagint to others. For as he says in chapter 15 of *De vera religione*, 'In the case of temporal laws, although men weigh them up at the point at which they are introduced, judges must not judge them, but judge according to them, once they have been brought in'.[50] But if Augustine were alive now, when the Church privileges Jerome's translation over all others, he would choose it in accordance with the Church. This provides some kind of answer to the reverend doctor's arguments.

In the fifth argument, on Augustine's authority in the third part of his sermons, sermon 58, where he says that it is not lawful to write

---

[49] Augustine, *Epistola ad Ieronimum* (*ep.* 71), c. 2 (*PL* 33. 242).
[50] Augustine, *De uera religione*, c. 31 (*PL* 34. 148).

modo debent homines ipsum scribere eciam cum ipsum sciuerint, concluditur quod nullo modo licet sacram scripturam transferri, et maxime in lingwam barbaricam.[51] Negetur consequencia intellecta bene auctoritate Augustini, concessoque quod omnis ligua que non est Hebrea, Greca uel Latina sit barbara, de quo uidebitur postea. | 905
200va Supponendum est primo quod beatus Augustinus non fuit de capitulo phariseorum qui vnum predicabant et contrarium fecerant in effectu; scripsit enim ipse simbolum, ante uel postquam ipsum predicauerat, per se uel per notarium, sicut patet ex multis sermonibus suis quos de simbolo fecit. Scripsit Anathasius simbolum, scripserunt 910 multi alii simbolum, \ideo/ non possumus verisimiliter credere quod Augustinus uellet sentire quod illicitum foret simbolum scribi. Quid ergo dicemus ad illud quod ipse\met/ dicit, 'nec ut eadem simboli uerba teneatis, ullo modo debetis scribere, sed audiendo perdiscere?' Forte dicis quod intelligit quod non oportet multum curare de ordine 915 uerborum, sed sufficit quod scribatur alio ordine, dummodo sentencia teneatur; sed uide quod istud non potest stare ad mentem Augustini per illud quod sequitur: 'nec cum didiceritis scribere, sed memoria semper tenere atque recollere'. Ex isto uidetur quod nullo modo debet simbolum scribi, saltem in aliquo libro materiali: sed 920 profecto hoc non est verum, ut patet ex practica Augustini, ymmo tocius ecclesie que scripturam simbolorum auctorisat. Quid ergo erat hic Augustinus contrarius sibi ipsi? Non credo. Quomodo ergo intellexit quando dixit nullo modo debetis scribere? Dicis intellexit quod laici nullo modo debent scribere simbolum, si intelligas de laicis illi- 925 teratis; planum est quod Augustinus non erat ita laycus quod volebat hoc hortari laycis illiteratis, quod non scriberent in personis suis, qui erant inhabiles ad scribendum. Nec iterum laicis literatis hoc indixit, quoniam ut plurimum comunes scriptores sunt omnes laici litterati, et sicut facile est uidere Parisius multe femine sunt scriptrices 930 bibliarum. Ergo non potest sic intelligi ut tu dicis.

Sed respondes quod per hoc concluditur quod nullo modo debet scribi in lingua barbarica uel uulgari. Sed quod iste non erat intellectus Augustini, nec quod istud possit stare, ostendo tibi per illud quod sequitur inmediate in pretacta auctoritate Augustini. Sequitur 935 enim sic in prefata auctoritate: 'quidquid enim in simbolo audituri estis, in diuinis sacrarum scripturarum literis continetur. Sed quod ita collectum et in formam quamdam redactum non licet scribi; comemoracio fit promissionis Dei ubi per prophetam pronunccians

912 transire *canc. before* sentire *MS* 926–7 planum . . . illiteratis] *om. in text, supplied in lower margin and keyed to text MS* 930 multe *over erasure in a different ink MS* 938 licet] debet *canc.,* licet *add. MS*

[51] Augustine, *Sermo in traditione Symboli I* (*sermo de tempore* 212) (*PL* 38. 1060).

down the Creed, and men should not write it down in any circumstances even though they know it, it is argued that it is never lawful to
translate the Bible, and especially not into the vulgar tongue.[51] I deny
the conclusion, provided Augustine's authoritative voice is properly
understood—even allowing that all languages except Hebrew, Greek
and Latin are barbarian tongues, which we will discuss later. We
can take for granted that Augustine was not one of the Pharisees
who preached one thing and in practice did the opposite; for he
wrote down a creed himself, either before or after he had preached
on it, either personally or by the hand of a notary, as is shown by
the many sermons he preached on the creed. Athanasius put a creed
into writing, as did many others, and therefore we cannot seriously
believe that Augustine intended to say that writing down the creed
was unlawful. So how should we understand his remark that 'you
must not retain the words of the creed, or write it down, but learn
it properly from the spoken word?' Perhaps you could interpret him
as meaning that it would not be right to take too much notice of
the order of the words, that so long as the meaning was preserved
they could be put in any order; but the sequel shows that this interpretation of Augustine's meaning cannot be sustained: 'don't write
down what you learn, but keep it in your mind and remember it'. It
would seem on this evidence that the creed should not be written
down at all, at least not in any actual book: but this is clearly not
the case, as it contradicts his own practice, and indeed that of the
whole Church, which permits the creed to be written down. So did
Augustine contradict himself, then? I cannot believe it. Then what
did he mean when he said that you should not write it down? You
might understand him as meaning that the laity should not write
down the creed, if you read him as meaning the uneducated laity;
but it is obvious that Augustine was not so naïve that he wanted to
tell uneducated lay people, who were themselves incapable of writing,
that they should not write it down in their own hand. Nor could he
have meant the educated laity, since frequently ordinary scribes are
all educated laity, as in Paris, where you can find many female biblical
scribes. So it cannot be understood in that sense.

You might reply that in that case [scripture] may never be written
in a barbarian or vernacular tongue. I will cite what follows straight
after in Augustine's text to show that this was not what he meant,
and that it is not the case. What follows in the text is this: 'what you
are about to hear in the creed subsists in the heavenly letters of holy
scripture. But what is there distilled and reduced to form may not
be written down; you must remember God's promise when he made
his new covenant, speaking through the prophet, saying, "this is the

nouum testamentum dixit, "hoc est testamentum quod ordinabo   940
illis: post dies illos, dicit Dominus, dabo legem meam, in mente
eorum scribam eam"' [Jer. 31:33]. 'Huius', inquit, 'rei signande causa,
200vb audiendo simbolum nec in tabulis, | nec in aliqua materia, sed in
corde discitur.'⁵² Ecce quod Augustinus non exponit seipsum, ut tu
dicis, quod non debet scribi in uulgari, sed isto fine dicit non debere   945
ipsum scribi in comemoracioni promissionis Dei, ubi Dominus pro-
misit se scripturum legem suam in cordibus hominum. Dicis adhuc
ex ista glosa imponis Augustino ipsum uelle quod nullo modo liceret
scribere simbolum in Latino aut aliquo alio ydiomate. Respondeo
nequaquam, planum est quod Augustinus in prefata auctoritate non   950
plus facit excepcionem de non scribendo in uulgari quam in Latino
vel in Greco, sed sic uoluit intelligere quod non scriberent sicut in
lege ueteri scribebatur. Mandata etenim legis ueteris scripta erant in
tabulis lapideis antequam populo tradebantur, que thabule postmo-
dum per Moisen in minucias sunt confracte, sicut patet Exo.32°[:19].   955
Post modum autem scripta erant in volumine legis attramento. Erat
itaque lex illa lex timoris, non amoris; non autem erat lex scripta
in cordibus eorum per amorem de quibus Psalmista sic cecinit [Ps.
77:36]: 'et dillexerunt eum in ore suo, et lingua sua mentiti sunt ei';
cor autem eorum non erat rectum cum \eo/, nec fideles habiti sunt   960
in testamento eius. Sicut enim pedagogus informat primo puerum
in litteris et sillabis per uirgam et artam disciplinam, vltimate autem
in sensu, sic in lege ueteri populus instruebatur eciam per modum
pueri in sensu \litterali/ gradus infimi; paucissimi uero ad intellectum spiritualem peruenerunt, in cuius figura uelamen positum erat   965
super oculos Moisi, quando ad populum esset egressurus, ut patet
Exo.34°[:33]. Econtra autem erat in nouo testamento, primo enim
sunt instructi in nouitate spiritus, et potissime post missionem Spiritus Sancti qui et ellectos docuit omnem ueritatem. Per tempus itaque notabile stetit ecclesia primitiua antequam aliqua scriptura noui   970
testamenti \saltem/ sensibilis erat tradita. Vnde longe prius erat lex
scripta in cordibus discipulorum, quam erat aliquibus litteris sensibilibus comendata, et hoc non sine causa fecit sapientia Dei patris
Ihesus Christus ad denotandum quod ipse uult fidem suam primo
et principaliter, et maxime, in cordibus hominum scribi per amorem   975
indelibiliter, et non transitorie per timorem. Et isto modo loquitur
Apostolus, 2ᵃ Cor.3°[:2–3]: 'ita', inquiens, 'epistola nostra uos estis,
scripta in cordibus nostris, que scitur et legitur ab omnibus hominibus: manifestati quoniam epistola estis Christi, ministrata a nobis, et

952 vel] et *canc.,* vel *add.* MS

---

⁵² ibid.

covenant which I shall make: after those days, says the Lord, I will put my law in their inward parts, and write it in their hearts"'. Here he gives the reason why: 'by hearing it, without recourse to tablets on any other material form, the creed is learnt in the heart.'[52] Note that here Augustine is not interpreting himself to mean, as you say, that the creed should not be written down in the vernacular, but to say that it should not be written down in commemoration of God's promise, when he promised that the law should be engraved on the hearts of men. You could retort to this that on this reading I am making Augustine say that the creed should not be written down either in Latin or in any other language. I reply that in that text Augustine was clearly not distinguishing writing in the vernacular from writing in Latin or Greek, but was saying that they should not write down [the creed] as the old law was written. The commandments of the old law were written on tablets of stone before they were given to the people, and Moses afterwards broke them into pieces, as we are told in chapter 32 of Exodus. They were afterwards written down in ink in a volume of the law. For that was not a law of love, but a law of fear; not a law written by love in the hearts of those of whom the Psalmist sings: 'they did flatter him with their mouth, and they lied unto him with their tongues'; for their heart was not straight in his sight, and they were not faithful to his covenant. For as a schoolmaster will first teach a boy his letters and syllables by the rod and by hard discipline, but in the end with reason, so in the old law the people were instructed in the literal sense [of scripture] like a boy on the lowest step; very few of them had attained to any spiritual understanding, in token of which Moses put a veil over his eyes when he went out to the people, as appears in chapter 34 of Exodus. It was a different situation in the New Testament, for now they were first taught in the newness of the Spirit, especially after the Holy Spirit was sent to teach all truths to the elect. The primitive church waited a considerable time before the New Testament was given to them, at least in physical written form. So the law was written in the hearts of the disciples long before it was committed to material writing, and Jesus Christ, the wisdom of God the Father, did this for a very good reason, namely to signify that he desired their faith, first of all, principally and to the greatest degree, to be written in the hearts of men indelibly through love, and not transitorily through fear. The Apostle speaks in this sense in 2 Corinthians, chapter 3: 'you are our epistle written in our hearts, known and read of all men: forasmuch as you are manifestly declared to be the epistle of Christ, ministered

scripta non attramento, sed spiritu Dei viui, non in tabulis lapideis, 980
2011a sed | in tabulis cordis carnalibus'. Et signanter dicit Apostolus, non
atramento, quia attramentum de facili deletur, quod autem scribit
spiritu Dei viui, non de facili aboletur, sed iugiter viuit per amorem;
dicit iterum, nec 'in tabulis lapideis', quemadmodum \et/ lex Moisi,
sed 'in tabulis cordis', supple per caritatem. Et hoc carnalibus, id 985
est tractabilibus, ac impulsui diuino facile cedentibus. Uult igitur
beatus Augustinus, quod nedum simbolum, immo tota lex Christiana maxime et pre omnibus sit in cordibus conscribenda: tum quia
omnibus aliis scripturis non existentibus, seu deletis, illa sola scriptura sufficeret ad salutem; tum quia non libro aut scriptura sensibili, 990
sed corde, ut ait Apostolus [Rom. 10:10], 'creditur ad iusticiam';
et tum tercio quia ista sola scriptura in patria remanebit. Et quod
iste erat intellectus Augustinus \patet/ per illud quod consequenter
sequitur in fine sermonis, ubi sic: 'prestabit ille, qui uos uocauit ad
suum regnum et gloriam, ut eius gracia regeneratis uobis in Spiritu 995
Sancto scribatur in cordibus vestris, ut quod creditis dilligatis, et fides
per dilleccionem operetur in uobis; ac sic Domino largitori bonorum omnium placeatis, non seruiliter timendo penam, sed liberaliter
amando iusticiam. Hoc est igitur simbolum quod uobis per scripturas
et sermones ecclesiasticos insynuatum est, sed sub hac breui forma 1000
fidelibus confitendum et proficiendum est.'[53] Hec Augustinus.

Ad 6^m cum sic arguitur secundum beatum Augustinum 2° *De doctrina Christiana*, 'plerumque a sensu auctoris deuius aberrat interpres
si non sit doctissimus', sed talem non est facile invenire, cum id quod
per excellenciam dicitur vni soli conuenit, ergo etc., dicitur negando 1005
consequenciam sic enim contingeret arguere, quod nullus foret rex
uel princeps.[54] Ad hoc enim quod aliquis conuenienter foret rex,
ut uult Aristotiles 5° *Politicorum*, oportet quod principetur uolen-
tibus subditis, oportet iterum quod que est proporcio dignitatis uel
honoris regis ad dignitatem et honorem subditorum, eadem debet 1010
esse proporcio uirtutis principantis ad uirtutem subditorum. Ideo
uirtus regis debet excedere uirtutem omnium uel plurium; ymo ut
ipsemet 7° *Politicorum* dicit, virtutes principantis non contingit esse
optimas, nisi idem principans tantum differat ab eis quibus princi-
patur quantum uir a muliere, aut pater a natis, aut despotes dominus 1015
a seruis; quare, inquit, si transgrediatur uolens aliquibus dominari
non habens hanc differenciam ad illos quam uir habet ad mulierem,

982 scribit] scribitur *MS*   992 tum *on erasure of a longer text MS*
1001 Hec] *originally* hoc, -o- *canc.*, -e- *add. MS*   1014–15 principatur] *originally*
principaliter, -liter *canc.*, -tur *add. MS*   1015–16 a seruis domini *marked for*
reordering to dominus a seruis *MS*

---

[53] ibid.

by us, written not with ink, but with the spirit of the living God, not in tablets of stone, but in fleshy tablets of the heart'. The Apostle significantly says, not with ink, because ink can easily be rubbed out, but with the living spirit of God, which is not easily removed, but lives constantly through love; and he says too, not 'with tablets of stone', like the law of Moses, but 'with the tablets of the heart', that is, with charity. And he says, fleshy, that is, tractable, and welcoming to God's message. So Augustine means that not just the creed, but the whole law of Christ must be written in full and before everything else in our hearts: because if there were no other scriptures or if they had been destroyed, that scripture would be enough by itself for salvation; because, as the Apostle says, it is not with a book or with physical writing, but with the heart that we 'believe unto righteousness'; and because, thirdly, scripture alone will remain in heaven. That this is Augustine's meaning is confirmed by what follows on at the end of the sermon, where he says: 'he will stand forth, who has called you into his kingdom and his glory, so that his grace is inscribed in your hearts when you are reborn in the Holy Spirit, and so that you will believe and adore, and faith will work in you through love; so will you please the Lord, the giver of all good things, not fearing punishment like a slave, but loving justice in freedom. This, then, is the creed which is instilled in you through the scriptures and through the teaching of the Church, and which should be confessed and put forward by the faithful in this short form.'[53] So says Augustine.

To the sixth argument, where it is argued that, as Augustine says in book 2 of *De doctrina christiana*, 'a wayward translator will frequently depart from the author's meaning unless he is particularly learned', and it is not easy to find a very learned person, as everyone agrees that only one person can excel, I deny the inference drawn from this, that no one could be king or prince.[54] To that I say that, as Aristotle argues in the fifth book of the *Politics*, a person can properly rule, provided his subjects desire it, and provided too that the superiority of his honour and rank over those of his subjects should be matched by the superiority of his qualities over theirs. So a king's qualities should surpass those of all, or most, of his subjects; indeed, as Aristotle says in the seventh book of the *Politics*, the virtues of a ruler cannot be outstanding unless he is as superior to his subjects as a husband is to his wife, a father to his children, or a master (or lord) to his servant; and so, he continues, a ruler who transgresses wishing to lord it over people, but lacking that superiority over them that a husband has

---

[54] Augustine, *De doctrina christiana*, II 13 (*PL* 34. 44).

uel pater ad natos, uel dominus ad seruum, non poterit tantum recte agere in posterioribus quantum transgressus est, in principio uolens principaliter non dispositus ad hoc.[55] Hec Philosophus. Planum | est quod esset satis difficile aliquem talem invenire. Conformiter contingeret arguere de papis, episcopis et curatis, ut enim uult Gregorius 1º *Pastoralium*, capitulo 12: 'Tantum debet accionem populi accio transcendere presulis quantum distare solet a grege uita pastoris'.[56] Concludere igitur ex premissis quod nullus esset rex uel princeps, papa, presul seu curatus esset error maximus.

Ad septimum dicitur quod solum concludit, quod inquinatis et inuolutis in peccatis, indignis et non intelligentibus non debent secreta mistica reuelari, et hoc in predicacione seu sermone, sicut patet ex processu distinccionis allegate, videlicet 43 iuxta dictum Mt.7º[:6], 'nolite sanctum dare canibus, neque spargatis margaritas ante porcos, ne forte conculcent eas pedibus et conuersi dirrumpant uos'. Ex isto tamen non bene concluditur quod deuotis fidelibus Deumque timentibus uel non debeat ewangelium predicari, aut in uulgarem lingwam transferri.

Ad octauum quando sic arguitur, secundum Bacon in epistola ad Clementem, qui debet aliquam scienciam uel scripturam transferre, debet illam scire et linguam a qua transfert, et lingwam in quam transfertur.[57] Hoc conceditur loquendo de sciencia competenti et quando dicitur quod hoc uidetur inpossibile, negetur illud; ymo illud quibusdam statibus est per necessarium, sicut patet in Canone, vbi dicitur quod uolens episcopari debet scire totam diuinam scripturam inscrutabiliter. Ymo distinccione 38, capitulo *Omnes pro conclusione*, ponitur quod uolens episcopari debet perfecte scire omnem diuinam scripturam, atque secundum illam 'docere populum sibi comissum', quod si recusauerit, nullatenus debet consecrari.[58] In signum ergo huius dicunt, quod episcopus habet duas eminencias in mitra sua, ad designandum quod debeat habere scienciam eminentem, etc.

Ad nonum cum sic arguitur quod non potest fideliter transferri in uulgare, non debet transferri in uulgare; sed vna lingua non potest fideliter per aliam exponi, propter diuersitatem proprietatum loquendi in diuersis linguis, ut dicit Bacon in epistola ad Clementem.[59] Ergo etc. Conceditur consequencia et negetur antecedens pro minori, data enim minori sequeretur quod lingua Greca nullo modo

201rb　　　　(line 1020)
(line 1025)
(line 1030)
(line 1035)
(line 1040)
(line 1045)
(line 1050)

1019 in posteribus *canc. after* est MS　　　1041 statibus] *originally* statubus, *first* -u- *canc.*, -i- *add.* MS

---

[55] Aristotle, *Politica*, 5.11, trans. William de Moerbeke (*AL* 29/1. 579=Bekker 1314a); *Politica* 7.3, trans. Moerbeke (*AL* 29/2. 524=Bekker 1325b).

[56] Gregory the Great, *De cura pastorali*, I 12 (*PL* 77. 25–6).

[57] Roger Bacon, *Opus tertium*, c. 25; ed. Brewer, *Rogeri Bacon opera*, I. 89–90.

over his wife, a father over his children, or a lord over his servant, can
never recover later by virtuous action as much as he has lost by his
transgression, as he desires to rule but is not qualified for the task.[55]
So says Aristotle. Clearly it would be quite difficult to find such a
person. One can make the same argument about popes, bishops or
parish priests, as Gregory says in book I of his *Pastoralia*, chapter 12:
'The conduct of a ruler should be as superior to that of the people as
a pastor's way of life to that of his flock'.[56] To deduce from this that
nobody could be a king or a prince, a pope, prelate or priest would
be a gross error.

To the seventh argument I reply that the text only shows that
secret mysteries should not be disclosed in sermons and exhortations
to corrupt and unworthy people who are sunk in sin, nor to those
who will not understand them, as is shown in the course of distinction 43 [of the *Decreta*] which is cited, on the words of Matthew,
chapter 7, 'give not that which is holy unto the dogs, neither cast ye
your pearls before swine, lest they trample them under their feet, and
turn again and rend you'. It cannot seriously be argued from this text
that the gospel should not be preached to the pious and God-fearing
faithful, or be translated into the vulgar tongue.

The eighth argument proposes, citing Bacon in the Letter to
Clement to the effect that whoever desires to translate any learned
work or written text should understand the subject, the language
from which it is translated, and the language into which it is
rendered.[57] I agree that competent understanding is necessary, but
not that the requirement makes the task impossible; competent
understanding, indeed, is indispensable in some positions, as is
shown in the Canon, where we read that aspirants to the episcopacy
should know the mysteries of the holy scriptures. Further, in
distinction 38, in the chapter *Omnes pro conclusione*, we read that
aspirants to the episcopacy should know the whole Bible perfectly
and 'teach the flock entrusted to them' accordingly, and if they jib
at that, they should not be consecrated at all.[58] In token of which,
they say, the bishop's mitre has two eminent points, to show he
should have eminent knowledge.

The ninth argument states that what cannot faithfully be translated into the vernacular should not be translated at all; but one
language cannot accurately be rendered into another, because of the
different characteristics of speech in different languages, as Bacon
says in the Letter to Clement.[59] I agree that the conclusion would
follow, but deny the minor premise, given that if it were true, Greek

[58] *Decretum Gratiani*, pars 1 dist. 6; ed. Friedberg, 1. 142.
[59] Roger Bacon, *Opus tertium*, c. 25; ed. Brewer, *Rogeri Bacon opera*, 1. 89.

transferri posset in Latinum. Alia est enim proprietas loquendi in 1055
20rva Greco, et alia in Latino: Greci enim in loquendo vtuntur | articulo,
Latini uero non; Greci eciam componunt frequenter cum suis adiec-
tiuis aduerbia, qualiter non Latini, sicut patet per Lincolniensem
super *Ecclesiastica Ierarchia*.⁶⁰ Absit ergo ex isto concludere quod
vna ligua in aliam non posset propterea transferri. Vtuntur et Gal- 1060
lici articulo, Anglici uero multis articulis, et tamen quod dicimus
in Anglico, possumus exprimere in Latino. Ideoque audiui quando
in scolis gramaticalibus eram, quod quando aliquid prius dicebatur in
Anglico quod postea diceretur in Latino, solebat a magistro dici,
'transfer michi hoc in Latinum', quod melius, ut michi uidetur, 1065
dicitur quam quod diceretur sicut multi dicunt, 'fac seu compone
michi istam Latinitatem'. Et ad probacionem minoris, quando sic
assumit, hoc, inquit, potest quilibet probare si scienciam quam nouit
uelit in linguam maternam conuertere; negetur minor, quamuis data
minore, quod non do, non probatur intentum suum. Intendit enim 1070
ipse sicut patet ex forma sua arguendi quod nulla lingua posset
in aliam transferri, cuius oppositum est expertum. Et patet eciam
per ipsummet ubi supra; dicit enim quod tria sunt consideranda
in cognicione linguarum: primum scilicet ut ipsam linguam sciat
legere et intelligere; secundum est quod homo sit ita peritus quod 1075
sciat linguam transferre; et hoc est difficilius, sed non ita difficile,
inquit, sicut homines existimant. Et tertium est, quod difficilimum
reputat, videlicet secundum linguam intellectam scire loqui; et ad
hoc multi in diuersis lingwis deuenerunt, ac eciam ad linguarum
gramaticas. Et ad declaracionem asumpti, quando sic ulterius pro- 1080
cedit, certe logicus non potest exprimere suam logicam si iurasset
per uocabula lingue materne, sed oporteret eum noua fingere. Istud
si concedatur non directe eneruat propositum principale, quia non
est questio vtrum logica possit transferri in uulgare, sed de sacra
scriptura, et de illis potissime que sunt de neccessitate salutis popu- 1085
larium, quoad fidem et mores, quoad expressam scienciam; presertim cum sacram scripturam oportet plebem secundum maius aut
minus addiscere, non autem scienciam aut sciencias liberales. Ideoque longa lata differencia inter ista. Et iterum totus textus sacre
scripture est de historiis, de legibus, de monitis salutiferis que tota 1090
die uulgato sermone uersantur. Et igitur si daretur quod logica
non posset in linguam maternam transferri, non propterea sequeretur quod sacra scriptura non posset sic transferri propter causas
supratactas.

1061 dms *elucidated in margin as* dicimus *MS* 1067 minoris] minoum 16ⁱᵐ *canc.*,
minoris *add. MS* 1073 consideranda] *an unclear ending is overwritten with* -da, -da
is also add. in margin MS 1093 *false start of* 'non' (?) *canc. before* non

could never be translated into Latin. For Greek has some characteristics and Latin others: for instance, there is an article used in
Greek, but not in Latin; and the Greeks often combine their adverbs
with their adjectives, but not speakers of Latin, as Grosseteste on
the *Ecclesiastica ierarchia* shows.[60] So it is impossible to conclude on
that ground that one language cannot be translated into another.
The French have an article, and the English have several, and in spite
of that, what we say in English can be expressed in Latin. Indeed
I remember that when I was at grammar school, when something
was said in English first for translation into Latin, the master would
say, 'translate that into Latin for me', which is better said that way,
I think, than if he had said, as many do, 'make (or compose) the
correct Latin usage for me'. Bacon asserts in confirmation of the
minor premise that anyone can establish this, who desires to express
his expert knowledge in his native tongue; I deny this because, even
if it were conceded, which I do not, it would not prove the point.
It appears to be asserted from the form of the argument that no
language could be translated into another, when experience proves
the opposite. This can be demonstrated from Bacon's own words in
the same passage, that is, he says that there are three requirements
for somebody learning a language: first, that he should know how to
read and understand the language; second, that he is learned enough
to know how to translate a language (and this is more difficult, but
not as difficult as people imagine); and third, which he thinks the
hardest, that he should be able to speak the language which he has
learnt; and many people have achieved this in different languages,
even in the correct grammar. On the minor premise, when he gets on
to it, it is true that a logician cannot expound logic if he is restricted
to the vocabulary of his native language, and he must invent new
terms. But conceding that does not weaken the principal proposition,
because the question is not whether logic can be translated into the
vulgar tongue, but whether holy scripture can, and in particular those
parts which are necessary to the salvation of the people, whether faith
and morals, or clear knowledge; especially when they should be familiar with the Bible to a greater or less degree, rather than [secular]
sciences or the liberal arts. There is a wide and considerable difference
between the two. Again, the whole text of the Bible is composed of
historical books, books of the law, and sound exhortations which
are rendered in the vulgar tongue every day. So though we might
allow that logic cannot be translated into a native language, it does
not follow from this that holy scripture cannot be translated on the
grounds we have stated.

[60] Robert Grosseteste, *Super Dionysii de ierarchia ecclesiastica*, in Oxford, Lincoln College, MS lat. 101, fols. 95r–131v, unspecified.

201vb   Verumtamen si verum est quod de sancto Beda fertur, | non opor-   1095
tet concedere quod assumit videlicet quod logica non posset transferri
in lingwam maternam. Dicit enim sanctus Thomas super primum
Politicorum, exponens hoc uocabulum *barbarus* per hunc modum:
'quidam dicunt omnem hominem barbarum esse qui lingwam eius
non intelligit. Vnde', inquit, 'Apostolus dicit [1 Cor. 14:11] quod "\si/   1100
nesciero uirtutem uocis, ero ei cui loquor barbarus, et qui loquitur
michi barbarus". Quibusdam autem illos uidetur barbaros dici qui
non habent litteralem locucionem in suo uulgari ydiomate respon-
dentem; vnde', inquit, 'et Beda dicitur in lingwam Anglicam liberales
artes transtulisse, ne Anglici barbari reputarentur.'[61] Hec sanctus   1105
Thomas ibidem. Et in argumentum huius, habeo aput me vnum
tractatum in quo tangitur de materia quam tangit auctor *De spera*, et
de materia que in libris *Metheowrum* in vetustissimo Anglico, modo
pene per omnia inintelligibili, per Bedam seu aliquem antiquorum
patrum editam. In Gallico quidem plane noui quomodo que ad libe-   1110
rales sciencias spectant aliqualiter pertractantur in libro Gallicano qui
dicitur *Thesaurus*, qui est satis notus aput nobiles.[62] Et si dicas quod
in Gallico quidem possunt hec fieri, in aliis autem lingwis uulgaribus
nequaquam, presertim cum dicat Bacon quod est eadem lingua in
substancia, puta Latina, ab Apulia et Calabria usque ad fines Hispa-   1115
nie, eciam usque ad mare Britannicum; uariatur tamen secundum
ydiomata, id est proprietates loquendi qualitercumque autem sit de
isto, planum est quod omnia ista ydiomata sunt uulgaria.[63]

Et ideo forte ne cogaris consequenter concedere istud licere fieri
in ligua Anglica, super qua sola est contencio hiis diebus. Quoad   1120
translacionem sacre pagine in liguam maternam, uis negare illud esse
licitum in aliquo uulgari ydiomate qualicumque; omnes tamen alie
naciones christiane, non solum uerbo sed eciam facto, hoc tibi con-
stantissime denegabunt. Ad illud autem quod addit Bacon, in argumento suo quod oporteret uolentem conuertere logicam in liguam   1125
maternam noua uocabula fingere, conceditur illud, accipiendo fingere pro formare per modum apocopacionis seu terminacionis uulgaris. Sic enim pene omnes predicatores in nostro uulgari Anglico,
nominando nomina Christi, beate Virginis, et aliorum sanctorum
infinitorumque aliorum, appocopant seu alio modo permutant. Et   1130
quando ulterius additur quod talis sic loquens solum intelligeretur a

1095 Verumtamen] *add. by corrector over cancellation of scribe's unclear form MS*
1104 vnde] *confirmed in margin MS*   1110 In Gallico quidem plane noui] *originally*
quidem plane noui in gallico, *with transposition marks over* in gallico *to indicate that it*
should be placed before quidem *MS*   1117 id est] *letter, perhaps* h, *deleted*, . i . *with a*
macron added in margin MS   1120 super] *originally* supra, -ra *canc.,* -er *add. MS*

[61] Aquinas, *In libros Politicorum Aristotelis expositio*, I 22; ed. R. Spiazzi (Turin 1951), 8.

Indeed, if it is true what is said about the Venerable Bede, we should not even concede that logic cannot be rendered in a native language. St Thomas, commenting on the first book of the *Politics*, explains the word *barbarus* in this way: 'some people say that everyone who cannot understand their language is a barbarian. So, as the Apostle says, "if I know not the meaning of the utterance, I shall be unto him that speaks a barbarian, he that speaks shall be a barbarian unto me". But others define barbarians as people who have no written language corresponding to their spoken tongue; and so', he continues, 'Bede is said to have translated the liberal arts into the English language, so that nobody would think the English people to be barbarians.'[61] So says St Thomas. And in confirmation of this, I have by me a tract in which the subject matter treated by the author of *De sphaera* is discussed, as well as the subject matter of the *Meteorics*, in very old English which by now is incomprehensible to nearly everybody, and written by Bede or some other ancient father. Besides, I am fully aware that topics of the liberal arts are discussed to some extent in a work in French called the *Trésor*, which is well known in high society.[62] If you retort that this might be done in French, but not in other vernaculars, particularly as Bacon says that the same language, namely Latin, is spoken from Apulia and Calabria to the far reaches of Spain, and to the English Channel as well; I reply that it is spoken in various dialects, with individual linguistic characteristics, all of which are obviously vernaculars.[63]

But perhaps this will not convince you to concede that [scripture] may lawfully be translated into English, which is the only question nowadays. You try to deny, as to the translation of the sacred page into a native language, that it would be lawful in any vernacular whatever; but all other Christian nations most consistently contradict you, not only verbally but in their practice. As to what Bacon adds, in his point that anyone wishing to put logic into his native tongue would have to invent new terms, I agree, provided that 'invent' is defined as forming the words by apocope, or by adding a vernacular ending. So virtually all preachers in our own English vernacular, when they use the name of Christ or the Blessed Virgin, or other saints, or countless other names, use apocope or alter the name some other way. So when he goes on to say that whoever talks in this way by inventing new terms would be understood by nobody except

---

[62] On the tract in Old English see pp. lxx–lxxi. John of Sacro Bosco's *De sphaera*, ed. L. Thorndike, *The Sphere of Sacrobosco and its Commentators* (Chicago, IL, 1949), 76–117; Aristotle, *Meteorologica*, trans. William de Moerbeke (*AL* 10/1–2. 2). The *Trésor* of Brunetto Latini, ed. F. J. Carmody, *Li livres dou tresor* (Berkeley, CA, 1948) was a popular French text in fourteenth-century England.

[63] Roger Bacon, *Opus tertium*, c. 25; ed. Brewer, *Rogeri Bacon opera*, I. 89.

seipso, dicitur quod hoc non sequitur, intelligeretur enim ab illis qui scirent logicam in priori lingua, sicut iste. Sicut modo, quando in uulgari loquimur de *Consequenciis*, | *Obligacionibus*, et *Insolubilibus*, et huiusmodi, corrumpendo vocabula quedam Latina, de facili intelligeretur vt predixi; non tamen a populo simpliciter rusticano nisi per magnam asuefaccionem. De translacione scienciarum liberalium modo non loquimur, sed ewangelii populo predicandi.

Ad hec autem quod vltimo addit pro euidencia predictorum quod 'uocabula infinita ponuntur in textibus theologie et philosophie de alienis ligwis que non possunt scribi, nec proferri, nec intelligi nisi per eos qui lingwas sciunt, et necesse inquit fuit hoc fieri, propter hoc quod sciencie fuerunt composite in ligua propria, et translatores non invenerunt in lingua Latina uocabula sufficiencia'. Dicitur quod hoc bene arguit quod translaciones longius deriuate sunt inperfecciores, et iterum quod oportet frequenter in talibus multa uocabula a prioribus lingwis mutuari, et istud specialiter habet locum in scienciis liberalibus, de quorum translacione nichil nobis ad presens. Ad illud uero beati Augustini, 2º *De doctrina christiana*, capitulo 10, quod pro confirmacione adducitur quod 'sunt uerba certarum linguarum que in vsum alterius lingue per interpretacionem transire non possunt, que uerba per motum animi significant, pocius quam sentencie concepte vllam particulam', cuiusmodi sunt talia, *racha* et *osanna*. Dicitur quod prudens interpres debet illa relinquere non translata, quemadmodum fecit Ieronimus, translatorum peritissimus.[64] Non tamen propterea se reputat increpandum, qui de se ipso fatetur in *Prologo Galeato*, quod sibi omnino conscius non est mutasse se quidquam de Hebraica veritate, nichil tamen prohibet vnum scribencium transferre aliquod uocabulum quod alius reliquit non translatum.[65] Exemplum habemus de uocabulo *amen* Hebreo, ubi Mr. 12[:43] habetur '*Amen* dico uobis, quia uidua hec paupercula plus omnibus misit', etc., Luc et 21[:2] capitulo translato uocabulo habetur 'vere dico uobis, etc., quia uidua hec pauper plus quam omnes misit'. Sed in hoc notandum est quod beatus Augustinus notat quod iste interiecciones nullam particulam sentencie exprimunt, sed *amen* motum. Ergo et de illis minor restat cura, etc.

Ad decimum quod inittitur super auctoritate Bacon, dicentis, 'quod illa que fuerunt bene translata sunt modo corrupta', sicut, inquit, 'patet per totam Bibliam et philosophiam'.[66] Ad istud

---

1135–6 corrumpendo . . . predixi] *added in upper margin and keyed to text MS* 1140 textibus] *corr. from* textubus *MS*   1160 Mʳ *or possibly* Mᶜ *in MS; letters -r- and -t- are often similar in this script*   1161 et] eciam *canc.,* et *add. MS*   1167 *letter erased before* inittitur

---

[64] Augustine, *De doctrina christiana*, II 11 (*PL* 34. 42–3).

himself, I reply that the conclusion does not follow, because he would be understood by people who know logic in its original language, like himself. So now, when we talk in the vernacular of *Consequences*, or *Obligations*, or *Insolubles*, etc., varying some Latin terms, we are understood without difficulty, as I have just said; though not by ordinary country people without long habituation. However, we are talking now about preaching the gospel to the people, not about the liberal arts.

Bacon's final argument for his case is that there is 'a vast vocabulary of terms in foreign languages in theological and philosophical texts which cannot be written down, or put forward, or understood by anyone ignorant of those tongues, and that this is necessarily the case, because these ideas were expressed in their original language, and the translators could not find adequate words in Latin'. I agree that the point is well made that translations which rely on too many circumlocutions are not very good, and that in these cases it is necessary to borrow many terms from the original language, especially in the liberal arts; but translating them is not our present concern. In confirmation he cites the words of St Augustine in book 2 of *De doctrina christiana*, chapter 2, that 'there are certain words in particular languages which cannot be rendered into another tongue: words which signify an emotion, rather than a distinct conceptual statement', such as *racha* or *hosanna*. A wise translator, he says, leaves these words untranslated, as did Jerome, the most experienced of translators.[64] But it was not on those grounds that Jerome believed himself open to criticism: as he confesses in the *Prologus Galeatus*, he was painfully aware that he had not changed anything himself from the *hebraica veritas*, but nothing would prevent one of the copyists from translating a word that another scribe had left untranslated.[65] We have an example of that in the Hebrew word *amen*, where Mark, chapter 12, has '*Amen* I say unto you, that this poor widow has cast more in, than they all', while Luke in chapter 21 translates the word 'verily I say unto you, etc., that this poor widow has cast more than anyone'. We should note that St Augustine remarks that these interjections express no particular idea, but *amen* expresses an emotion. These are not, however, our primary concern.

The tenth argument depends upon the words of Bacon that the texts 'which were once well translated are now defective', which is obviously the case, he says, 'of the whole of the Bible and of natural science'.[66] My response to that was made in another question above,

---

[65] Jerome, *Prologus Galeatus* (PL 28. 557–8).

[66] Roger Bacon, *Opus tertium*, c. 25; ed. Brewer, *Rogeri Bacon opera*, I. 92–3.

superius est responsum in alia questione, ubi translacio Ieronimi ab   1170
202rb ista calumpnia fuerat excusata, ubi reddebatur | racio sufficiens quare
non oportet in talibus adhibere fidem ipsi Bacon. Presertim cum
dicat beatus Augustinus in epistola ad Fortunatum, et ponitur in
Decretis Di^e.9, *Neque enim*, per hunc modum: 'neque enim per quo-
rumlibet disputaciones quamuis katholicorum et laudatorum homi-   1175
num, uelud scripturas kanonicas habere debemus, ut nobis non liceat
salua honorificencia que illis debetur hominibus, aliquid in eorum
scriptis improbare atque respuere, si forte invenerimus quod aliter
senserint quam ueritas habet, diuino adiutorio uel ab aliis intellecta
uel a nobis'.⁶⁷ Hec Augustinus. Ex istis patet quod saluo honore   1180
persone, possumus sentenciam suam respuere, sentencie probabi-
liori adherendo, quod eciam pro presenti facimus ipsi Bacon. Quod
autem addit Bacon pro causa dictorum, 'quod nec scimus scribere, nec
legere, nec proferre'.⁶⁸ Si intelligat ista perfecte, conceditur sibi illud,
sicut erramus in scribendo Jhesus cum istis literis *I.h.c.*, cum non sit   1185
aspiracio in hoc nomine Ihesus; scribitur enim, ut dicit Alexander
Neckam, per ista tria elementa Greca *iota, eta, sima* apice superposito,
que tantum ualent aput nos sicut *I.e.s.* cum titulo. Erramus enim hic
ignorantes figuracionem Grecorum. Et sic *Christus* scribitur cum tribus gramatibus Grece figuracionis *chi, ros, sima* apice superposito, que   1190
ualent aput nos, *c.r.s.* Dicunt eciam magistri, ut reffert Alexander,
Irael esse dicendum et non *Israel*, sed parum, inquit, sunt instructi
in Hebraica lingua qui sic loquntur, conceditur igitur sibi quod in
eiusmodi a primeua consuetudine declinamus. Sed quando ulterius ex
isto sic concludit et per consequens perit uerus intellectus, negetur   1195
illud sequi, eque enim verum intellectum de re signata habemus, et
idem per uocabula ipsa intelligimus, quod et ipsi qui longe melius
tam scribere nouerant quam proferre.⁶⁹

Ad vndecimum dicitur quod solum concludit quod imperitus aliquis potest in transferendo de facili aberrare; peritus igitur et ad   1200
hoc dispositus non exponit se periculo, nisi forte obtrectatorum, de
quibus Ieronimus crebro conqueritur, sed propterea sanctum propositum non dimisit.

Ad duodecimum quando sic arguitur, secundum doctorem de Lira
super capitulum 14^m, ad Romanos, contra caritatem fraternam uide-   1205
tur esse, quod aliquis non dimittat ad tempus de hiis, que potest licite
dimittere, ad uitandum scandalum simplicium, qui opinantur illa esse

---

1183 Bacon quod *MS*   1184–5 ista . . . scribendo] *add. by corrector in margin, keyed*
to text MS   1187 Neckam] *corrector altered third letter, adding in margin* neckam *for*
clarity MS   1188 *letters* -tel- *are written above the letters* -tu- *of* titulo *in a darker*
ink MS   1193 loquntur] *corr. from* loquntúr

where I defended Jerome's translation from that charge and gave good reasons to doubt Bacon's own authority in the matter. It is confirmed by the words of St Augustine in his letter to Fortunatus, which is in the *Decreta* at distinction 9, *Neque enim*: 'for we should not treat the arguments even of reputable and catholic persons as we treat the canonical scriptures, for we are free, with all due respect to these persons, to disagree with and to reject anything in their writings, were we to find their opinion at variance with the truth as either we or others have understood it with the help of God'.[67] So says Augustine. So therefore, with due respect to Bacon, we may reject his opinion on this occasion and embrace a more credible view. Bacon adds in justification that 'we do not know how to write, or read, or expound' [the languages].[68] If we understand that as not knowing how to do so perfectly, I agree; we are in error, for instance, in writing the name Jesus with the letters *IHC*, as there is no aspirate in the name of Jesus; it is written, as Alexander Neckham tells us, with the Greek characters *iota, eta, sigma* with a sign above, which would work out for us as *I, E, S* with a mark of abbreviation. Our error arises from ignorance of the Greek alphabet. Again, *Christus* is written with the three Greek characters *chi, rho, sigma* with a sign above, which in our transliteration is *C, R, S*. The masters say, so Alexander reports, that we should say *Irael*, not *Israel*, as those who are not proficient in Hebrew spell it, and it must be admitted that in this respect we do not measure up to our predecessors' standards. But when he goes further and states that true understanding is lost in translation, I deny that it follows, for we have just as much real understanding of the subject, for we understand it through words, as do those who know far better how to write them than to explain them.[69]

I reply to the eleventh argument that it only shows that an un-learned translator can easily fall into error; the learned and prepared translator is not exposed to that peril, or only in the eyes of his detractors, of whom Jerome frequently complained, but did not on account of them give up his holy task.

On the twelfth point, on which it is argued according to Dr Lyra's comment on Romans, chapter 14, that it would seem to be against fraternal charity for someone not to give up for the time being those practices which he can legitimately give up, to avoid scandal to simple souls who believe that they are not lawful, until they are more fully

---

[67] *Decretum Gratiani*, pars 1 dist. 9.10 (ed. Friedberg, 1. 18), quoting Augustine, *Epistola ad Fortunatianum episcopum* (ep. 148) (*PL* 33. 629).

[68] Roger Bacon, *Opus tertium*, c. 25; ed. Brewer, *Rogeri Bacon opera*, 1. 92.

[69] Alexander Nequam, *Corrogationes Promethei*, in Bodl. MS Bodley 550, fol. 12va.

illicita, quousque super hoc plenius informentur; istud conceditur.[70]
202va Et signanter dicit doctor, *ad tempus*. Ad tempus | enim sunt satis licita
dimittenda, sicut verbum predicacionis ad tempus certis ex causis satis 1210
rationabiliter subticetur, quod tamen propterea non debet perpetuo
subticeri. Si tamen conformare nos uellemus errori omnium eciam
si magni et multi uideantur in ecclesia dicencium, malum bonum et
bonum malum, de facili incideremus in hereses periculosissimas et
errores: sicut olim accidit de Templariis, de quibus reffert Parisien- 1215
sis tractatu suo contra *Exempciones*, quod negabant Christum esse
verum Deum, et quod induxerunt de nouo receptos ad ordinem ad
hoc negandum, et ad conspuendum in cruce atque alia multa enormia
que enarrare longum foret.[71]

Ad tredecimum quando ex isto quod sacra scriptura esset in uul- 1220
gare translata concluditur quod daretur occasio mulieribus predicandi
in uulgari, negetur consequencia; sicut enim dicit Doctor de Lira
prout est superius allegatum, 'in primitiua enim ecclesia benedicciones et cetera omnia fiebant in uulgari', non tamen dabant occasionem
mulieribus predicandi, si enim accipiant ex aliquo tali occasionem 1225
delirandi.[72] Quid nobis qui ob hoc non sumus increpandi qui ea facimus que debemus. Sicut dicit Augustinus in epistola 113ª ad Publicolam, 'Absit', inquit, 'ut illud quod propter bonum aut licitum facimus
aut habemus si quid per hoc preter nostram uoluntatem cuiquam
male acciderit nobis imputetur. Alioquin nec ferramenta domestica et 1230
agrescia sunt habenda, ne quis ex eis uel se uel alterum interimat; nec
arbor est plantanda ne quis se inde suspendat, nec fenestra facienda
ne per hanc se quisque precipitet. Et quid plura comemorem quid est
in usu hominum bonum ac licitum vnde possit pernicies irrogari.'[73]

Ad 14m quando sic asseritur illud est \il/licitum quod tolleret 1235
honorem debitum bonis presbiteris. Conceditur, sed cum dicitur
quod hoc verisimiliter fieret si sacer textus foret in uulgare translatus, tunc enim quilibet rusticus docere presumeret, hoc negetur,
nisi forte intelligatur de uxoribus et filiis—istos enim licet eis docere
iuxta scienciam sibi datam. Nam \de/ uxoribus dicit Apostolus, Iª 1240
Cor.14°[:35], 'Si quid autem uolunt addiscere, domi viros suos interrogent'. Tobit eciam, 1°[:9], scribitur de sancto Tobia quod 'cum
factus esset vir, accepit uxorem Annam de tribu sua, genuitque ex
ea filium, nomen suum imponens ei quem ab infancia timere Deum
docuit et abstinere ab omni peccato'. Et rursum Daniel 13°[:3], dici- 1245
tur quod parentes Zuzanne cum essent iusti, erudierunt filiam suam

---

1211 tamen] *originally* quodque cum, -que cum *canc.,* tamen *add. MS*
1214 *originally* periculosissimos, *second* -o- *canc.,* -a- *add. MS*   1234 v *(?)*
written above v- *of* vnde   1241 viros] virosos *MS*

---

[70] Lyra, *Postilla in epistolam ad Romanos* 14:21.

informed on the matter, I agree.[70] But the doctor expressly says, *for the time being*. They can be given up, legitimately enough, for a while, as a preacher's words might be suspended for the time being for good enough reasons, but none the less they should not be suspended permanently. But if we wish to pander to the error of all those who say that good is evil and evil good, then even though many great personages in the Church are saying it, we would easily fall into extremely dangerous heresies and errors: as once happened to the Templars, who, according to Parisiensis in his tract against *Exemptiones*, denied that Christ was truly God and impelled their new members to do the same, and to spit upon the Cross and to perform many other enormities too numerous to mention.[71]

To the thirteenth argument, that if holy scripture were available in the vulgar tongue, this would give an opportunity to women to preach in the vernacular, I reject the consequence; as Dr Lyra (cited above) says, 'blessings and the like were given in the vernacular in the primitive church', but this afforded no occasion for women to preach, even if they were willing to take it as a pretext for folly.[72] We should not be reproved for doing what we ought to do. As Augustine says in his letter 113 to Publicola, 'God forbid that the things we do and have for good and lawful purposes should be blamed if they inadvertently cause harm to someone. Otherwise we might have to do without domestic utensils and farming implements, in case somebody uses them to kill himself, or somebody else; no tree should be planted in case people hang themselves from it, and no window should be installed in case they throw themselves out. There are any number of good and proper things we use which could inflict harm.'[73]

The fourteenth argument proposed that what causes good priests to lose the respect due to them is unlawful. I agree, but when it is asserted next that this is bound to happen if holy writ were translated into the vernacular, because then every bumpkin would take it on himself to expound it, I disagree. If this were a reference to wives and children, it is indeed lawful for women to teach them what they have learnt themselves. The Apostle says in 1 Corinthians, chapter 14, 'If they will learn anything, let them ask their husbands at home'. In the first chapter of Tobit, we read of the holy Tobias that 'when [Tobit] was come to the age of a man, he married Anna of his own kindred, and of her he begat a son [Tobias], gave him his name, and taught him from his infancy to fear God and to abstain from all sin'. And we read in the book of Daniel, chapter 13, that Susanna's parents were just, and taught their daughter according to the law of Moses. The

---

[71] Giles of Rome, *Liber contra exemptos*, c. 21; pr. (Rome 1555), fol. 16ra, commonly attributed to 'Parisiensis' in Oxford manuscripts.

[72] Lyra, *Postilla in epistolam ad Corinthios* 14:10.

[73] Augustine, *Epistola ad Publicolam* (ep. 47) (*PL* 33. 187).

secundum legem Moisi. Precipitur eciam ab ecclesia compatribus paruulorum quatenus doceant baptisatum oracionem dominicam |
202vb cum simbolo. Vnde Augustinus super Johanne omelia 51ᵃ in fine sic scribit: 'Cum auditis, fratres, dicentem Dominum, "vbi ego sum, 1250 illic et minister meus erit", nolite tantummodo bonos episcopos et clericos cogitare. Eciam uos pro modulo uestro ministrate Christo, bene viuendo, elemosinas faciendo, nomen doctrinamque eius quibus potueritis predicando, ut vnusquisque paterfamilias eciam hoc nomine agnoscat paternum affectum sue familie se debere. Pro Chri- 1255 sto et pro vita eterna, suos omnes moneat, doceat et hortetur, corripiat, impendat beniuolenciam, exerceat disciplinam. Ita in domo ecclesiasticum et quodammodo episcopale implebit officium, ministrans Christo ut in eternum sit cum ipso.'⁷⁴ Hec Augustinus. Multa siquidem talia possemus adducere ad probandum quod non solum 1260 licet laicis instruere vxores, filios et familiam iuxta scienciam sibi datam, sed eciam quod ad hoc ex debito cure domestice obligantur. Vnde quod mulieres docere debeant, patet per Apostolum ad Titum 2[:3–4], ubi docet Tytum quatenus hortetur anus, ut sint 'bene docentes ut prudenciam doceant'. Super quo Doctor de Lira bene 1265 inquit, docentes non in publico, sed in secreto minores mulieres.⁷⁵

Si autem laici usurpent sibi officium docendi, quod solis sacerdotibus debetur, per prelatos ecclesie ab hoc compesci debent. Nec ex patula publicacione legis Dei in uulgari ad sic docendum occasio eis datur; quin pocius tollitur quoniam ibidem possunt contrareum 1270 apertissime intueri, precipitur enim ibidem quod quilibet stet in gradu suo, quod omnia honeste et secundum ordinem fiant; quod vnus quisque in ea uocacione qua uocatus est ita permaneat, itaque quod non transgrediamur terminos antiquos quos posuerunt patres nostri. Rursum in lege sub anathemate prohibetur aliene potestatis 1275 vsurpacio, infinitaque possunt in scriptura reperiri ex quibus laici essent disuasi ad vsurpandum officium sacerdotum; sed nullatenus prouocati pocius si quidem ex celacione scripturarum quam ex earum deteccione essent ad presumpcionem inclinati, que utrobique humilitatem laudat et presumpcionem condempnat. 1280

Ad quindecimum patet responsio ex hiis que dicta sunt in responsione ad 13ᵐ et 14ᵐ argumenta. Et ad confirmacionem cum dicitur, si simplices intelligendo Latinum ex hoc ut plurimum usurpant sibi officium docendi, sed ex malicia uoluntatis quanto magis si Biblia esset in uulgare translata, hic dicitur quod simplices ex hoc quod 1285

1264 ut *erased after* sint   1270 eius *canc. before* eis *MS*

---

⁷⁴ Augustine, *Tractatus in euangelium Iohannis, tract.* 51 (*PL* 35. 1768).

⁷⁵ Lyra, *Postilla in epistolam ad Titum* 2:3–4.

church entrusts to godparents of young children the task of teaching them the Lord's prayer and the creed. So Augustine writes at the end of his 51st homily on John: 'Brethren, when you hear the Lord saying, "where I am, there shall also my servant be", do not imagine only good bishops and clergy. You too should minister to Christ in your own way, by living virtuously, giving alms and witnessing to his name and his teaching before whomever you can, and let the head of every family too in his name embrace the paternal affection which he owes to his household. For Christ and for eternal life, he should admonish all his dependents, instruct them, encourage them, chide them; he should show them good will and correct their faults. He will then be officiating in his own house rather as a bishop in the church, and will be serving Christ to be with him in all eternity.'[74] So says Augustine. We could find many other texts to show not only that it is lawful for laymen to teach their wives, their children and their household the doctrine which has been vouchsafed to them, but that it is their domestic obligation. So the Apostle affirms women's duty to instruct in the second chapter of his epistle to Titus, where Titus is informed how older women should instruct their charges and be 'teachers of good things', who 'teach [the young women] to be sober'. As Dr Lyra well puts it, they should teach younger women privately, not in public sight.[75]

But if the laity usurp the office of the teacher, which is the prerogative of priests alone, they should be restrained by the prelates of the church. The full publication of God's word in the vernacular does not, however, give them any opportunity to do so; instead, by impelling them to consider the opposite position very openly, they will learn that all persons should hold to the station in life to which they are called, so that things can be done in a decent and orderly way; that everybody has his calling in life and he should be content with that, and therefore we should not transgress the ancient limits which our fathers have laid down. The seizure of another person's authority is repeatedly anathematized in law, and there are countless passages in scripture in which the laity is warned not to assume the office of priest; but they are certainly not going to be encouraged in this presumption by texts which both condemn it and endorse humility, though they might be more inclined to it by the concealment of scripture than by its disclosure.

The response to the fifteenth point is the same as to points 13 and 14. As a rider to the additional argument proposed, that if simple souls by learning Latin attempt to usurp to themselves the office of teacher, how much more would their evil will be able to effect if the Bible were available in the vernacular, I reply that though they may

Latinum intelligunt, non vsurpant sibi docendi officium sed ex mali-
203ra cia uoluntatis, sicut nullus ex fide infusa credo errat, | sed ex falsa
coniectura quam ex proprio deffectu elicit. Isti enim sic arguentes
uidentur duo timere: primum videlicet, quod populus esset nimis
pronus ad docendum; secundum, quod esset nimis intelligens in   1290
scripturis. Sed utinam isti sic ymaginantes animaduerterent historiam Num.xj[:26], ubi sic habetur, 'remanserunt autem in castris
duo viri, quorum vnus uocabatur Eldab, et alius Medab, super quos
requieuit spiritus; nam et ipsi descripti fuerant, et non exierant ad
thabernaculum: cumque prophetarent in castris. Cucurrit puer et   1295
nuncciauit Moisi, dicens, "Eldab et Medab prophetant in castris".
\Statim/ Iosue filius Nun, minister Moisi, et ellectus a pluribus ait,
"Domine mi Moises, prohibe eos!" At ille, "Quid", inquit, "emularis
pro me? Quis tribuat ut omnis populus prophetet, et det eis Deus spiritum suum!"' Non enim uidentur esse opinionis Moisi, qui gratu-   1300
lando sapienciam et intelligenciam, et sapienciam populi peroptauit,
Deuteron.4to[:6], dicens, 'Hec est enim sapiencia uestra et intellectus
coram populis, ut audientes vniuersi precepta hec dicant, en populus
sapiens et intelligens gens magna.'

Quo contra nostri pro ignorancia populi zelantes dicerent vice   1305
uersa: 'hec est enim stulticia uestra et cecitas coram populis, ut
audientes vniuersi precepta hec dicant, en populus stultus et ignarus,
gens infima'. Non enim oportet tantum timere ne populus excellat in
sciencia, sed longe plus de ignorancia: testante propheta, 'populus',
inquit 'meus periit eo quod non habuit scienciam'. De illis etenim   1310
rebus que perfeccionem difficultatemque sapiunt, non est multum
formidandum ne qui de nimis facili talia aggrediantur. Sic enim dicit
Ieronimus contra Iouinianum, 'noli metuere ne omnes virgines sint;
difficilis res est virginitas, et ideo rara quia difficilis: "multi uocati,
pauci ellecti". Cupere plurimorum est perseuerare paucorum, vnde et   1315
grande premium eorum qui perseuerauerint. Si omnes virgines esse
possent, nunquam et Dominus diceret, "qui potest capere, capiat".
Et Apostolus in suadendo trepidaret dicens, "de virginibus autem
preceptum Domini non habeo".' [1 Cor. 7:25].[76] Hec Ieronimus.
Verumtamen sicut Deus aliquando retrahit dona propter ipsorum   1320
abusum, sicut patet Luce 19°[:20] de illo qui habuit mnam repositam
in sudario; conformiter prelati discrecionis oculo possunt precipi-
tes et effrenes refrenare, ne zelum suum quamuis pium impetuose
prosequantur. Ad hoc siquidem inter cetera dantur prelatis claues

1290 secundum] 2° MS   1306 uestra] *possibly* nostra; ura *with a macron over the
entire word in MS*   1313 *the first five letters of* Iouinianum *are written over the erased
text;* et a... (?) *written above*

---

[76] Jerome, *Aduersus Iouinianum*, I 36 (PL 23. 259).

learn Latin, they do not thereby usurp the office of teacher unless they have bad intentions, as nobody, I believe, falls into error out of the faith they have absorbed, but only from false assumptions arising from their own failings. People who argue thus seem to fear two things: first, that ordinary people might be more tempted to teach; second, that they might become more knowledgeable in the scriptures. But those who worry about that should remember the story in the 11th chapter of the Book of Numbers, where we read, 'there remained two of the men in the camp, the name of the one was Eldad, and the name of the other Medad, and the spirit rested on them; and they were of them that were written, but went not out unto the tabernacle: and they prophesied in the camp. And there ran a young man, and told Moses, and said, "Eldad and Medad do prophesy in the camp". And Joshua the son of Nun, the servant of Moses, one of his young men, said, "My Lord Moses, forbid them!" And Moses said unto him, "Do you envy for my sake? Would God that all the Lord's people were prophets, and that the Lord would put his spirit upon them!"' They fail to share the view of Moses, who was pleased at their wisdom and understanding, and welcomed the wisdom of the people, saying in chapter 4 of Deuteronomy, 'This is your wisdom and your understanding in the sight of the nations, which shall hear all these statutes, and say, surely this great nation is a wise and understanding people'.

By contrast, our zealots say the very opposite about the ignorance of the people: 'this is your foolishness and blindness in the sight of the nations, which shall hear all these statutes, and say, surely this base nation is a foolish and ignorant people'. But we should not so much fear their superior knowledge, but much more their ignorance: as the prophet says, 'my people perish, for they have no knowledge'. They know the perfection and the difficulty of these mysteries, so there is no danger they will get there too easily. As Jerome says in his tract against Jovinianus, 'fear not that not everyone should be a virgin, for virginity is a difficult thing, and therefore rare: "many are called, but few are chosen". Many aspire, but few persevere, and great is the reward of those who do. If everyone could be a virgin, the Lord would not have said, "let him that is able to receive it, let him receive it". And the Apostle would not have trembled to urge it when he said, "now concerning virgins I have no commandment of the Lord".'[76] So says Jerome. However, God will sometimes take his gifts back because they are being abused, as we see in Luke, chapter 19, about the man who kept a talent laid up in a napkin; so prelates with the eye of discretion can hold back the headlong and unrestrained behaviour of those admittedly well intentioned zealots who rush ahead impetuously. And as they have the power to bind and

potestasque ligandi et soluendi, quatenus ex nimio impetu proceden- 1325
tes iam refrenent, moderate uero incedentibus laxent habenas et quod
maius est, torpentes stimulent, ut procedant que omnia in humanis
actibus solent usualiter euenire, etc.

Ad sedecimum ex illo Ieronimi quod omnis heresis orta est a
203rb feminis, concluditur | quod si mulieres haberent sacrum canonem in 1330
uulgari, promciores essent ad hereses excogitandas.[77] Negatur consequencia. Ymo sequitur quod longe promciores essent ad hereses eui-
tandas, iuxta illud Iohannis 6[to][:63], 'verba que ego loquor, spiritus
et uita sunt'. Ymo uerba sacre scripture meditata, lecta et inspecta,
sunt singulare antidotum contra infectiuam pestilenciam hereseos. 1335
Immo signanter dicit sapiens, Prouer.4[to][:20], 'fili mi, asculta sermones meos, et ad eloquia mea inclina aurem tuam. Ne recedant ab
oculis tuis; custodi ea in medio cordis tui', et subditur pro causa, 'uita
enim sunt invenientibus ea'. Et in euidenciam huius sentencie, beatus
Ieronimus scripsit ad sanctas mulieres bene circa uiginti octo magnas 1340
epistolas, in quibus sunt satis alte questiones, grauesque difficultates.
Mulieres igitur, sicut et cetere persone, iuxta qualitates suas sunt
tractande, eisque sicut ceteris de Christi familia est mensura tritici
spiritualis erroganda. Arceantur itaque indisciplinate mulieres, eru-
dianturque deuote mulieres, et tangant saltem fimbriam uestimenti 1345
Christi in historia, quatenus taliter contingentes sanari possint cum
emoroissa a fluxu inconstancie et fragilitatis et ignorancie muliebris.
Et istud bene notat Ieronimus in epistola ad Athletam de institucione
filie, et est epistola 87[a], vbi sic: 'pro gemmis et serico, diuinos codices
amet, quibus non auri et pellis Babilonie vermiculata pectora, sed ad 1350
fidem placeat emendata et erudita distinctio. Discat', inquit, 'primum
Psalterium, hiis se canticis aduocet, et in Prouerbiis Salemonis eru-
diatur ad uitam. In Ecclesiaste consuescat que mundi sunt calcare.
In Iob virtutis et paciencie exempla sectetur. Ad ewangelia transeat,
nunquam ea positura de manu. Apostolorum Actus, et epistolas tota 1355
cordis imbuat voluntate. Cumque pectoris sui celarium opibus locu-
pletauerit, mandet memorie prophetas, et Penthateucum, et Regum,
Paralipomenon libros, Esdre quoque Ester uolumina. Sine periculo
vltimo discat Cantica Canticorum; ne si in exordio legerit, sub carnalibus, spiritualium nupciarum epitalamium non intelligens, uulne- 1360
retur.'[78] Consimilem sentenciam scribit in epistola ad Demetriadem

1336 singulariter *canc.*, signanter *add. MS*   1341 epistolas] *written over erasure of
an illegible word MS*   1343 erudiende *add. above* tractande *in a hand different from the
main scribe MS*   1344 Mulieres qualiter erudiri debent et informari in libris legendis
*written in red, in margin, but not keyed to text; presumably a note summarizing the content of
the section MS*   1346 possunt *canc.*, possint *in margin MS*   1359–60 carnalibus]
carnalia *used apparently as a neuter noun ('carnal matters')*

---

[77] Jerome, *Epistola ad Ctesiphontem aduersus Pelagium* (*ep.* 133) (*PL* 22. 1152–3).

to loose, as well as holding back those who are running too fast, they can relax the reins for those who are proceeding at an easy pace, and better still stir up sluggish people, so that human life can proceed normally.

It is argued in the sixteenth point from Jerome's remark that all heresies start with women, so if women had the sacred canon in the vernacular, they would be even more ready to think up heresies.[77] I disagree with the conclusion. What does follow is that the scriptures would be far more effective in averting heresy, for as we read in the 6th chapter of John, 'the words that I speak unto you, they are spirit, and they are life'. Certainly the words of scripture, when pondered, read and considered, are a singular antidote against the infectious plague of heresy. Indeed, the wise man says clearly in the 4th chapter of Proverbs, 'my son, attend to my words; incline your ear to my sayings. Let them not depart from your eyes; keep them in the midst of your heart'; and he adds, 'for they are life unto those that find them'. And in evidence of this view, St Jerome wrote about twenty-eight long and wholesome letters to holy women, in which he raised quite elevated matters, and discussed serious difficulties. So women, like men, should be instructed according to their abilities, and like the rest of Christ's family, they should receive a measure of spiritual nourishment. So women without discipline should be restrained, but serious women should be educated, so that, as in the gospel, they can at the very least touch the hem of Christ's garment, as the [Bible] story has it, and, as far as may be, cured of womanly inconstancy and frailty and ignorance as of an issue of blood. Jerome puts it well in his letter to Laeta on the education of her daughter, which is letter 87: 'instead of jewels and silks, let her love books of the scriptures, and not their gilding, or Babylonian parchment, or arabesque patterns, but their correct text and accurate punctuation'. He says 'she should begin with the Psalter and attend to the Psalms, and she should learn the Proverbs of Solomon as a rule of life. She should learn by getting to know Ecclesiastes that the things of this world are to be despised. She should follow Job's example of virtue and patience. Then she should go on to the Gospels, and never let them out of her hand. Let her willingly and with her whole heart drink in the Acts of the Apostles, and the Epistles. When she has filled the storehouse of her heart with all these treasures, she should commit to memory the prophets, the Pentateuch, the Books of Kings and Chronicles, the Book of Ezra, and the Book of Esther. Finally she may read the Song of Songs without danger; she should not read it earlier, when, not understanding it as the love song of a spiritual marriage, she might be harmed by its carnal language.'[78] He writes in the same vein in his letter 75 to the virgin Demetrias: 'may the sequence of the sacred

---

[78] Jerome, *Epistola ad Laetam de institutione filiae* (*ep.* 107) (*PL* 22. 876).

uirginem, et est epistola 75ᵃ, ubi sic: 'te ordo instruat celestis historie, nunc sanctum Dauid oblectet canticum, nunc sapientia erudiat
Salomonis, nunc ad timorem Domini incitent dicta prophetarum,
nunc ewangelica et apostolica perfeccio te Christo in omni sanctitate 1365
coniungat. Que paranda sunt, memorie penitus insere, eaque iugi
meditacione conserua.'⁷⁹ Hec Ieronimus.

Ad 17ᵐ cum sic arguitur, prophanum et detestabile uidetur fauere
203va hereticis | eos ve fouere, aut eis in aliquo condescendere vnde eorum
presumpcio extolleretur. Hoc conceditur, et cum sic subsumitur, si 1370
sacer canon transfereretur in uulgare, hoc fieret, hoc negetur. Dicit
enim Apostolus, Gall.4°[:18], 'quod bonum est emulemini in bono
semper'; si enim aliqui mali habeant aliquas condiciones bonas, non
debemus illas respuere sed amplecti. Non enim debemus ieiunium
contempnere quia phariseus ieiunabat bis in sabbato, nec decimas 1375
condempnare ex hoc quod phariseus decimas dedit omnium que pos-
sidet; nec rapinam aut adulterium comittere quia phariseus a talibus
abstinebat. Vnde beatus Augustinus libro *De vnico baptismo* prope
finem, 'in ipsa', inquit, 'vnitate arree dominice, nec propter bonos
laudandi sunt mali, nec propter malos deserendi sunt boni. Ut in 1380
vno homine, nec propter illud quod in eo integrum est, accipienda
est peruersitas, nec propter illud quod in eo peruersum est, negari
debet eius integritas. Quia in Iudeorum iniquitate retinetur ueritas
[resurrectionis mortuorum, et in Gentilium iniquitate detinetur veritas unius Dei, qui condidit mundum; et in eorum iniquitate qui cum 1385
Christo quia non colligunt, spargunt, detinetur veritas qua in ejus
nomine pellunt spiritum immundum; et in templorum sacrilegorum
iniquitate inventa est veritas] que collebant ignotum deum; et in
demonum iniquitate inventa est ueritas, qua confessi sunt Christum.
Et in hereticorum iniquitate inventa est ueritas non negandi baptismi 1390
sacramentum.'⁸⁰ Hec Augustinus.

Ad decimum octauum quando sic asseritur, pari euidencia qua
sacer textus esset transferendus in uulgare, et totum missale, manualeque sacramentorum cum toto seruicio ecclesiastico possent sic
transferri. Negetur assertum quamuis enim omnia ista ut dicetur 1395
licite possent transferri, non tamen sequitur quod a pari cuius racio
est: nam ex congruencia ordinis naturalis, alique operaciones sunt
apropriate vni sexui, que ab alio remouentur, nisi a maiori necessitate

1384–8 *a long passage of Augustine omitted probably by haplography; for the sense argued,
it is supplied here from the modern edition* 1397 con *canc. before* congruencia *MS*
1398 alio] *originally* alia, -a *canc.,* -o *add. MS*

---

⁷⁹ Pelagius, *Epistola ad Demetriadem uirginem* (PL 30. 32), commonly attributed to
Jerome.
⁸⁰ Augustine, *De unico baptismo*, c. 18 (PL 43. 612–14).

historical books inform your mind, may the Psalms of David delight you, and the wisdom of Solomon make you wise; may the words of the prophets fill you with the fear of the Lord, and the perfection of the gospels and the apostles join you to Christ in all holiness. Plant inwardly in your memory the things which need to be kept in readiness, and maintain them there in good order by meditation.'[79] So says Jerome.

It was argued in the 17th point that to favour heretics, to support them and aid them in anything which would increase their presumption, seems a wicked and detestable thing to do. I agree, but when the further point is made, that this would be the result if the sacred canon were translated into the vernacular, I disagree. The Apostle says in the 4th chapter of Galatians that 'it is good to be zealously affected always in a good thing'; for if particular evil people have some good traits, we should not reject the good traits but embrace them. We should not reject fasting because the Pharisees fasted twice on the Sabbath, nor tithes because they gave away a tenth of their possessions; and we should not commit robbery or adultery because the Pharisees abstained from them. As St Augustine says towards the end of his book *De unico baptismo*, 'in the unity of the Lord's court, the wicked should not be praised because they have some good qualities, nor should the virtuous be thrown over because they have their faults. We should not accept a particular individual's wrong-headed behaviour because in some respects he is blameless, nor overlook his good qualities because of what is bad in him. So the Jews in their wickedness preserved the truth [of the resurrection of the dead; and the Gentiles in their wickedness retained their belief in the one God, who created the world; and in the wickedness of those who gathered not with Christ, but scattered instead, the truth remained by which they cast out an unclean spirit; and the destroyers of the temple retained the truth in that they] worshipped the Unknown God; and in the wickedness of the devils, the truth is found that they acknowledged Christ. And in the wickedness of the heretics, the truth of their not denying the sacrament of baptism remains.'[80] So says Augustine.

In the 18th argument it is asserted that the whole missal, the manual of the sacraments and the entire office of the church should be translated on the same grounds as the Bible. I disagree. All these books, as will be shown, could lawfully be translated, but not on the same grounds as the Bible: for in the harmony of the natural order, there are some operations which are appropriate to one gender but should not be imposed on the other, unless for urgent reasons and

pro urgente. Sicut ut plurimum non iungimus uaccas plaustris, ubi
boues sunt impromptu. Hoc tamen aliquociens factum est: sicut   1400
habetur primo Reg.6to [1 Kgs. 6:7] capitulo de vaccis que traxe-
runt plaustrum in quo ponebatur archa Domini, posset eciam modo
fieri satis racionabiliter defficientibus bobus ad arandum; conformiter
viri deputantur ad opera bellica, mulieribus ab inde excusatis; legimus tamen in Guydone, *De bello Troyano*, quod Pantisilia cum suis   1405
domicellis Amazonibus magnam rem bellicam fecerant in vlcionem
Hectoris contra Pirrum.[81] Conformiter dico in proposito, ministracio
sacramentorum deputatur sacerdotibus, et alicorum certe sacramentorum solis sacerdotibus absolute, puta confeccio eukaristie, extrema
vnccio, aliquorum vero episcopis solis, puta confirmacio et ordi-   1410
num celebracio, et in nullo casu laicis. Quod ergo laici habeant ista
203vb translata in uulgari, quorum ad|ministracio non solum regulariter,
verum eciam vniuersaliter, ad solos pertinet sacerdotes, longa lataque
disparitas ad hoc quod habeant uitam Christi et eius doctrinam iuxta
fidele exemplar interpretata in uulgare. Quoniam autem ista prefata   1415
transferri possint ad deuocionem fidelium excitandam, si hoc verisimile uideretur prelatis, non uideo quam liceret. Sic enim factum
erat in ecclesia primitiua, prout est superius allegatum ex doctore
de Lira, ubi dicit quod in primitiua ecclesia benedicciones et cetera
omnia fiebant in uulgari. Vnde et dominus Ardma\ca/nus nono libro   1420
De questionibus Armenorum, capitulo 1°, ubi querit an consecracio
in omni lingua possit fieri, sic respondet: 'nemo enim Christianus
dubitat quin ita vere consecratur in vna lingua sicut in alia, quoniam sic fecerunt apostoli, et sic facere tradiderunt. Matheus enim
ewangelium scripsit in Hebraico, et Iohannes in Greco, et Marcus in   1425
Ytalico; et Paulus epistolam ad Corintheos, in qua de ista consecra-
cione fit mencio, eciam scripsit in Greco, et singuli in illis linguis
in quibus scripserunt, non dubium, consecrare docuerunt. Vnde',
inquit, 'constat in singulis linguis consecracionem posse fieri. Ymo
uidetur quod lingue omnes ad hoc erant date apostolis, sicut legitur   1430
Actuum 2° capitulo, ut modum consecracionis huius sacramenti, et
alia salutis documenta, singulis nacionibus singularum linguarum
traderent exercenda.'[82] Hec dominus Ardmachanus. Uidetis igitur
quantum faciat ille doctor eximius pro sentencia nostra, presertim
cum liber ille vnde allegacio trahitur, editus erat in curia Romana,   1435
ibique approbatus; ut audiui adeo quod post eius examinacionem
declaratum erat eciam nec errorem in ibi repertum fuisse; quod si

---

1405 tamen *corr. from* tum   guydone *with another* -u- *written above* -uy- *MS*

---

[81] Guido delle Colonne, *Historia destructionis Troiae*, XXVIII; ed. N. E. Griffin (Cambridge, MA, 1936), 214–17.

in dire necessity. We do not normally yoke cows to carts when oxen are available. But it can sometimes happen: when we read in the 6th chapter of the first Book of Kings [*sc.* Samuel] about the milch kine that pulled the cart in which the Ark of the Lord was placed, we can see that it was a reasonable thing to do, as there were no oxen for ploughing; in the same way, men are recruited for operations of war, but women are excused; nevertheless we read in Guido [de Colonna], *De bello Troiano*, that Penthesalea and her Amazon maids fought mightily in Hector's revenge upon Pyrrhus.[81] Accordingly I say to the question, that the administration of the sacraments is entrusted to priests, and indeed in the case of some sacraments, the eucharist and extreme unction, exclusively to priests without exception—and some, confirmation and ordination, only to bishops—and may not be performed by the laity. There is a very great difference, there-fore, between the laity having a vernacular translation of rites which are not only usually but invariably performed by priests, and having the life and teaching of Christ faithfully translated into the vulgar tongue from a correct exemplar. If the gospel were translated so as to stimulate the devotion of the faithful, and if it appeared plausible to prelates, I cannot see that it would not be lawful. And it was done in the primitive church, as stated above on the authority of Dr Lyra, that at that time blessings and similar prayers were always given in the vernacular. And so Armachanus in the 9th book of *Summa de questionibus Armenorum*, chapter 1, asks whether the consecration [of the eucharist] can be pronounced in any language, and he replies: 'no Christian can doubt that it can be consecrated just as well in one language as in another, since the apostles did so, and passed on the practice. Matthew wrote his gospel in Hebrew, John in Greek, and Mark in Italian; and Paul wrote the epistle to the Corinthians, in which he mentions the consecration of the eucharist, in Greek, and each of them, undoubtedly, taught how to consecrate in the language in which he wrote. Whence', he continues, 'it is clear that they could consecrate in their own languages. Furthermore, it seems that in all the tongues with which the apostles were endowed, as we read in chapter 2 of Acts, the mode of consecration of the eucharist, and other teachings necessary to salvation, were conveyed to every man in his own tongue, in which he was born, for them to put into practice.'[82] So says the lord Armachanus. You can see how much support that great doctor gives to my view, especially as the book in which his opinion is expressed was written up in the Roman curia, and there given the seal of approval; indeed, so I have heard, it was examined and declared free of any error; which, if true, makes it

---

[82] Richard Fitzralph ('Armachanus'), *Summa in questionibus Armenorum*; pr. (Rome 1512), fol. 66ra.

verum fuerit, patet nostram sentenciam nedum per ecclesiam pri-
mitiuam appropriari approbatamque esse, verum eciam ab ecclesia
moderna auctoritate curie Romane roboratam existere.   1440

Ad 19ᵐ, ubi ex translacione scripture sacre posita in uulgari, concluditur quod minueretur deuocio fidelium et potissime laicorum,
qui magis deuote cantant non intellecta quam intellecta. Negatur
hoc sequi, quoniam vt apparuit beato Paulo contrarium, sicut patet
prima Cor.14°[:14], ubi dicit, 'nam si orem lingwa, spiritus meus 1445
orat, et mens mea sine fructu est. Quid ergo', inquit, 'est michi?
Orabo spiritu, orabo et mente; psallam spiritu, psallam et mente.'
Quasi diceret, si orem et non intelligam que dico, affectus meus
fortassis in Deum eleuatur, sed mens mea et intellectus meus sine
fructu relinquitur. Concludit igitur, 'orabo spiritu, orabo et mente'; 1450
id est orabo tam affectu quam intellectu, et psallam, id est cum
melodia orabo, non solum spiritu sed mente, tamquam excellen-
cius | oraturus. Sunt igitur, quantum ad propositum pertinet, tres
modi orandi. Vnus videlicet quando quis orat in aliquo ydiomate,
ipsum nequaquam intelligens, et iste modus est bonus, et in lai- 1455
cis tollerabilis, sed in sacerdotibus scandalosus: vnde uulgariter in
prouerbium uertitur quod sacerdos legens, et que legit non intelligens, est similis garule pice maledicenti sibi ipsi. Secundus modus
est quo aliquis orando que loquitur intelligit \per modum/ simplicis
gramatici legentis prophecias, aut horas canonicas decantantis, \et/ 1460
hic certe modus, nulli sensato dubium, longe excellencior est priore.
Sed tercius modus est quando orans non solum loquitur ydioma
ipsumque intelligit, sed insuper spiritualem intelligenciam eorum
que orando dicit percipit. Ideoque dicit Apostolus ubi supra [1 Cor.
14:12], 'quoniam emulatores estis spirituum, querite vt habundetis ad 1465
edificacionem ecclesie. Et ideo', inquit, 'qui loquitur lingua, oret vt
interpretetur'. Quasi dicat modicum est scripturam sacram in aliquo
ydiomate loqui, primo modo uel secundo supradictis, nisi eciam sic
loquens sciat uerborum sentenciam spiritualem, et ideo oret homo ut
interpretetur tamquam illud quod longe excellencius est. Dicit igitur 1470
Apostolus ubi supra [1 Cor. 14:1], 'emulamini spiritualia carismata ut
dona, magis autem ut prophetetis'.

Ad vigesimum quando sic asseritur quod sancti et apostoli non
leguntur scripsisse aut transtulisse nisi in ligwam gramaticatam, vnde
et in Grecum uulgarium non transtulerunt, si per linguam non gra- 1475
maticatam linguam uulgarium intelligamus. Planum est quod falsum
assumitur, sicut patet ex multis precedentibus et potissime ex dicto
domini Ardmachani allegato in responsione ad 18ᵐ argumentum,

204ra

1444 vt] add. above the first letter of apparuit MS   1466 vt] et canc., vt
add. MS

obvious that my view was not only embraced by the primitive church, but is approved as true by the modern church as well, buttressed by the authority of the court of Rome.

In the 19th point it is argued that the devotion of the faithful and the laity in particular, who sing an unintelligible chant more fervently than words they can understand, would cool if holy scripture were translated into the vernacular. I do not agree that the conclusion follows, since it seems contrary to the words of St Paul in chapter 14 of 1 Corinthians, 'for if I pray in an unknown tongue, my spirit prays, but my understanding is unfruitful. What is it then?', he continues, 'I will pray with the spirit, and I will pray with the understanding also; I will sing with the spirit, and I will sing with the understanding also.' This is as if he were to say, if I pray, and do not understand what I say, my emotions might perhaps rise toward God, but my mind and understanding are left barren. So he concludes, 'I will pray with the spirit, and I will pray with the understanding also'; that is, I will pray with both the emotions and the mind, and I will sing, that is, I will pray with a melody not only in the spirit but in the mind, and thus pray more fruitfully. For so far as relates to the present point, there are three ways of praying. The first is to pray in a language which is not understood at all. This is a good way, tolerable among the laity, but disgraceful for priests: in the words of the common proverb, a priest who reads but cannot understand what he reads is like a chattering magpie cursing itself. The second way is to understand what is said in prayer like a simple grammar pupil reading prophecies, or chanting the canonical hours, and no sensible person will deny that this is a much better way than the first. But the third way is to pray, not only speaking and understanding the language of the prayer, but attaining a spiritual understanding of what is being said. So as the Apostle puts it in the passage just quoted, 'for as much as you are zealous of spiritual gifts, seek that you may excel to the edifying of the church. Wherefore', he continues, 'let him that speaks in an unknown tongue pray that he might be understood'. That is to say, to speak holy writ in some [unknown] tongue in the first or the second way is only of limited value, unless the speaker knows the spiritual meaning of the words, and so a man should pray that he might understand in that sense, which is far better. So the Apostle says, 'follow after charity, and desire spiritual gifts, but rather that you may prophesy'.

On the 20th point, it is proposed that we do not read that the saints and apostles wrote or translated into any but structured languages, and so they did not translate into demotic Greek, if by unstructured languages we understand the vernacular. It is obvious that this is a false assumption, as is shown by several points made above and especially by the words of Fitzralph cited in the response to the

quia dicit quod Marchus scripsit in Ytalico, et manifestum est pro
processu suo quod per Ytalicum non intelligit Latinum. Quod autem   1480
dicitur quod apostoli non scripserunt in Greco uulgarium, hoc est
ualde dubitabile, ymo oppositum est verisimiliter estimandum. Dicitur enim Actuum 4°[:13] quod principes populi et seniores 'uidentes Petri constanciam et Iohannis, comperto quod homines essent
sine litteris et ydiote, admirabantur'; non enim est verisimile quod   1485
sciuerint sciencias liberales, et per consequens nec gramaticam, et
sic ita uerisimile est aut fortassis verisimilius quod Iohannes scripsit
in Greco uulgarium sicut Marcus scripsit in Ytalico, ut dicit dominus Ardmachanus. Nec mouet quod Grecum uulgarium modo longe
discrepet ab \ex/emplari beati Iohannis apostoli, quoniam sic est   1490
in multis uulgaribus linguis, quod pro processu temporis notabiliter permutantur, sicut patet de Anglico nostri temporis et temporis
sancti Bede. Si autem beatus Iohannes scripserat in Greco clericali
204rb non contendo: hoc enim bene | poterat esse ad demonstrandum
philosophis gentilibus quod spiritus, ubi uult, spirat scienciam et   1495
uirtutes. Nec quantum michi uidetur ex toto sapit ueritatem, quod
lingue uulgares non sunt gramaticate. Est enim gramatica habitus recte loquendi, recte pronuncciandi, recteque scribendi; certum
ydioma nec gramatica secundum genus determinat sibi aliquod certum ydioma. Ideo secundum species variatur, sicut patet aput Gre-   1500
cos et Latinos, probabile est ergo quod quod libet ydioma fixum
habet gramaticam sibi apropriatam; quamuis talis gramatica non sit
in scripto tradita: sufficit enim in minus famosis ydiomatibus quod
industria congrue loquendi et scribendi in illis sit tantum memorie comendata. Vnde beatus Augustinus 2° *De doctrina Christiana*,   1505
loquens de congruitate, sic inquit: 'quid est igitur integritas locucio-
nis, nisi consuetudinis conseruacio loquencium veterum auctoritate
firmata?'[83] Possunt ergo esse in Anglico, sicut in Gallico, congruitas
et incongruitas modo suo et per consequens gramatica correspon-
dens. In Anglico enim possumus predicare ewangelium sicut iacet,   1510
sicut patet ex dicto domini Lincolniensis superius allegato.[84] Sed quis
prohibebit sic in Anglico predicatum a prouido scriptore Anglicis
litteris comendari?

Ad 21^m cuius uis stat in isto quod translacio scripture in uulgare
foret inutilis, quia nec proficeret clericis neque laicis, respondetur per   1515
interempcionem illius quod assumitur. Proficeret enim clericis non
multum scientibus de Latino, et potissime sacerdotibus et curatis
rusticanis, monialibus, et aliis deuotis viris et mulieribus; possunt

---

1485 ydiote] *originally* ydiomate, -ma- *canc. MS*   1493 clericali, -li *rewritten*
MS   1503 in¹] *originally* ut, *corr. to* in *MS*   1511 Sed] quod *canc.,* sed *add.*
MS   1516 illius] eius *canc.,* illius *add. MS*

18th argument, where he says that Mark wrote in Italian, and it is clear from the context that by Italian he did not mean Latin. As to the idea that the apostles did not write in demotic Greek, this is a very dubious notion, and the contrary is much more likely. We read in the 4th chapter of Acts that when the rulers and elders of the people 'saw the boldness of Peter and John, and perceived that they were unlearned and ignorant men, they marvelled'; it is inconceivable that they knew the liberal arts, and therefore were ignorant of grammar, and so it is all the more likely that John wrote in demotic Greek just as Mark wrote in Italian, as Fitzralph says. It does not matter that modern demotic Greek has diverged considerably from the language of St John the Apostle, since many vernaculars change markedly in the course of time, as is obvious in the case of our own English language compared with that of the Venerable Bede. I am not arguing whether St John wrote in the Greek of clerks: he may very well have done so, to show pagan philosophers that the spirit, when it wanted to, could inspire both knowledge and morals. Nor, taking a broad view, does it seem to me that the idea that vernacular languages are not structured is true. Grammar consists in the habit of speaking, pronouncing and writing a particular language correctly; grammar as a general property is not identical to the grammar of any particular tongue. So it varies in its particular manifestations, as is evident among the Greeks and Latins, and it is probable that any stable language has its own particular grammar; even if that grammar is not passed on in writing: it is enough, in the case of less prestigious languages, that the practice of speaking and writing them correctly is at least committed to memory. As St Augustine says in the 2nd book of *De doctrina christiana*, speaking of appropriate language, 'so what is correct usage, except preserving the way of talking established by inherited authority?'[83] Correct and incorrect usage can be detected in their own way in English as in French, and so the language has a corresponding grammar. We can preach the gospel in English just as it stands, as the words of Grosseteste cited above confirm.[84] But who would forbid what is preached in English to be written down in English characters by a careful writer?

The point of the 21st argument is that translation of scripture into the vernacular would be useless, profiting neither clerks nor laity. In reply I refute the premise. It would indeed be useful to clerks with a limited knowledge of Latin, especially to rural clergy and parish priests, to nuns, and to other devout men and women;

[83] Augustine, *De doctrina christiana*, II 13 (*PL* 34. 44).
[84] Robert Grosseteste, *Sermo, Scriptum est de Leuitis*, in Bodl. MS Bodley 801, fol. 194v.

enim per huiusmodi uulgare prompcius deuenire ad cognicionem
legis Domini immaculate animas conuertentis. Possunt eciam per 1520
uulgare multum adiuuari ad prompcius intelligendam scripturam
traditam in Latino, sicut multi per sacram scripturam in Gallico
iuuantur ad intelligendum eandem in Latino, et econtra, prout a
pluribus est expertum. Prodest eciam pro honesta temporis deduc-
tione, ubi alias occupati essent in romanciis vanis et frequenter fal- 1525
sis, et in quibus eciam aliquociens ministratur materia peculancie
scurilitatis aliarumque stulticiarum sine fine; a quibus non audiui
multos predicatorum modernorum disuadere, quod cum longe maius
Christianum foret quam simpliciter disuadere ne ewangelium Ihesu
Christi legeretur populo in uulgari. Ymo quantum prodesse posset, 1530
non est nobis certum, presertim cum iam tempus immineat in quo
204va uiris apostolicis tacentibus, fortassis faciet Deus | merito peccatorum
nostrorum lapides conclamare.

Ad 22^m cuius uis stat in isto, quod habita translacione in uulgari,
essent secreta mistica indignis reuelata, dicitur hoc negando, si gene- 1535
raliter intelligat laicalem populum indignum, secreta enim mistica
secundum sanctorum sentenciam nec in Latino, nec in Greco, nec
in uulgari ydiomate sunt indignis pandenda, sermone uel scriptura:
intelligendo per indignos illos qui reddunt se indignos ut eis panda-
tur verbum Dei, tales videlicet qui contradicunt uerbo Dei ipsum- 1540
que blasfemant, quales erant Iudei quibus Actuum 13°[:46] dixerunt
apostoli, 'uobis oportebat primum loqui uerbum Dei; sed quoniam
repellitis illud et indignos uos iudicatis eterne uite, ecce conuerti-
mur ad gentes'. Ideo signanter Dominus, predicatores designaturus,
Mt.10[:11] eis precipit per hunc modum, 'in quamcumque autem 1545
ciuitatem intraueritis, interrogate quis in ea dignus sit'. Quem textum pertractat Origenes, et ponitur in *Decretis*, 43d *In mandatis*, ubi
sic: 'in mandatis habemus, ut venientes in ciuitatem discamus prius
quis in ea dignus sit, ut aput eum cibum sumamus. Quanto magis
oportet nosse quis qualisve sit, cui immortalitatis uerba credenda 1550
sunt, solliciti enim esse debemus ne margarithas nostras mittamus
ante porcos. Sed ob alias causas utile est uiri huius habere noticiam.
Si enim sciam quia in hiis, in quibus non potest dubitari quod bona
sunt, emendatus est et inculpabiliter, hoc est si sobrius, si misericors,
si iustus, si mitis et humanus est, que utique bona nullus ambigit, 1555
tunc consequens uidebitur ut ei, qui optinet bona virtutum, eciam
quod deest fidei, et sciencie conferatur, et in quibus maculari uita eius
uidebatur, que est in reliquis probabilis, emendetur. Si uero in hiis
que palam sunt, peccatis inuolutus permanet et inquinatus, non me

---

1543–4 conuertimur] *originally* conuertimus, -us *canc.,* -ur *add. MS* 1558 uero]
originally uero sunt, sunt *canc.*

for through the vernacular they can more readily gain knowledge of the immaculate law of God which transforms souls. Further, with the help of the [written] vernacular they can more readily come to understand the text of the Latin Bible in front of them, as many people have found a French Bible useful in understanding the Latin, and vice versa, as numerous witnesses can attest. Besides it would be a better use of their time, when otherwise they would be busy reading silly romances, which often mislead them and provide them with wanton and scurrilous matter and endless other stupidities; from reading which I have not heard many modern preachers discouraging them, though it would be a much more Christian thing to do than simply to discourage them from reading the gospel to the people in the vernacular. Indeed, how much it would profit them cannot be known to us, especially as the time is now coming when, if the preachers of the faith hold their peace, then God perchance may make the very stones of our sins cry out.

The 22nd argument asserts that with the scriptures rendered in the vulgar tongue, secret mysteries would be revealed to the unworthy. I deny this, if, by the unworthy, lay people in general are intended, because secret mysteries, as the saints understood them, should not be revealed to the unworthy either in Latin or in Greek or in the vernacular, whether verbally or in writing: defining the unworthy as those who have disqualified themselves from receiving the word of God, by speaking against it and blaspheming it, like the Jews to whom the Apostles said in chapter 13 of Acts, 'it was necessary that the word of God should first have been spoken to you; but seeing you put it from you, and judge yourselves unworthy of everlasting life, we turn to the Gentiles'. So in Matthew, chapter 10, the Lord charged the preachers he was about to appoint figuratively in this way, 'and into whatsoever city you shall enter, inquire who in it is worthy'. Origen discusses this text, as we read in the *Decretum*, distinction 43 *In mandatis*, in these words: 'we find among these commandments, that we should discover when we arrive in a city who in it is worthy, and take refreshment with him. So we should be even more determined to find out to what persons, and to what kind of persons, we should entrust the words of everlasting life, for we must be careful not to cast our pearls among swine. There are other reasons, however, why it is useful to have information about an individual. If I would like to know that he is without fault or blame in matters about which there can be no question as to what is good, that is, is he sober, merciful, just, gentle and kind, qualities which admit no ambiguity, then it is likely that he as a man who exhibits these qualities may, even if he has no faith, have knowledge imparted to him, and may probably be corrected in the other respects in which his life may not be blameless. But if he remains caught up in an

oportet aliquid de secrecioribus et remotis diuine sciencie proloqui,   1560
sed magis protestari eum, et conuenire eum ut peccare desinat et
actus suos a viciis emendet.'[85] Hec Origenes. Sed pro dictis Dio-
nisii est notandum, quod in tempore suo erant diaconi deputati ad
abigendum penitentes, ac eciam paganos infideles nondum conuer-
sos ab inspeccione sacrorum, illos quidem quia nondum reconciliati   1565
fuerant, et ideo tamquam indigni repellebantur, istos uero ne derisui
et contemptui haberentur sacramenta Christi aput gentiles ydolatras.
Non enim reputauit Dionisius populum laicalem communicandum
cum indignis; presertim cum uocet ipsum in *De ecclesiatica ierarchia*
populum speculativum, cui ex opposito actiue corespondent sacer-   1570
dotes, sicut penitentibus diaconi corespondent.[86]

204vb   Et reuera timeo, si propter indignitatem uite et | ruditatem con-
ceptuum laici ab inspeccione sacre scripture repellerentur ut indigni,
nimis magna pars cleri staret extra fores, quod euidenter possumus
concludere ex singulari contemptu studii legis Christi, necnon ex   1575
effranata superbia, invidia, torpore, auaricia, symonia \et/ aliis spur-
ciciis, que plus solito pululant in clero nostro, ut timetur, quam ab
ante ea pululcount. Quando enim Christus venit in terram, longe
peruersiores comperit pontifices, scribas et phariseos, qui de sorte
cleri fuerant, quam inuenerat populares. Prout ex decursu ewangelii   1580
satis patet, sed specialiter ex illo Iohannis 7°[:45–9], vbi pontifices et
pharisei uolebant quod ministri eorum apprehendissent Christum,
ubi sic habetur, 'venerunt ministri ad pontifices et phariseos, et dixerunt eis, "Quare non aduxistis eum?" Responderunt ministri, "Nunquam sic locutus est homo sicut hic homo loquitur." Responderunt   1585
ergo eis pharisei, "Numquid et uos seducti estis? Numquid aliquis
ex principibus credidit in eum aut ex phariseis? Sed turba hec que
non nouit legem maledicti sunt."' Vtrum autem Christus veniens in
terram sic inveniret, nouit ipsemet qui cordium est scrutator.

Ad auctoritatem uero scripture, ubi precipitur quod 'bestia si teti-   1590
gerit montem, lapidabitur', per \quod/ hoc concluditur quod eximie
scripturarum difficultates non debent plebi propalari. Istud potest
sane concedi, et specialiter de illis ad que non sunt abiles, puta deuocionibus et religionibus, in diuinis de attributis et ydeis, de relacione
nature humane ad uerbum, de accidentibus sine subiecto, infinitisque   1595

1560 diuine] de onus *canc.*, diuine *add. MS*   1572 et *repeated at folio break MS*
1575–5 ex ineffranata *with expunction marks under* in- *MS*   1593–4 -u- *canc. in*
deuocionibus *and add. above the line MS*

---

[85] *Decretum Gratiani*, pars 1 dist. 43.2, *De mandatis* (ed. Friedberg, 1. 155), citing under
the name of Origen the letter (*ep.* 3) attributed to Clement of Rome, and taken from the
Pseudo-Isidorian Decretals, a concoction of the mid-ninth century. The letter is ed. P.
Hinschius, *Decretales Pseudoisidorianae et Capitula Angilramni* (Leipzig 1863), 52–60; cf.
59 for this passage.

openly sinful and impure life, then I should not say anything about the more mysterious and abstruse aspects of holy knowledge, but should bear witness against him, and summon him to give up his sins and desist from his vicious activities.'[85] So says Origen. But it may be noted as to Dionysius cited above, that in his time there were deacons whose task it was to prevent penitents, and even infidel pagans who had not yet been converted, from gazing on holy things, and keep them away as unworthy in case the idolatrous heathen should hold up the sacraments of Christ to derision and contempt. So Dionysius did not associate lay people with the unworthy; and indeed in his *De ecclesiastica ierarchia* he would call them the attendant people, as distinct from the corresponding active role of priests, just as deacons correspond to penitents.[86]

Moreover, I have to say, if the laity are to be kept away as unworthy to gaze upon holy things because of their improper lives and crude ideas, then much too large a body of the clergy should stand outside the barriers too, as we can see with our own eyes, from their extraordinary contempt for the pursuit of God's law, their unrestrained pride, their envy, their laziness, their greed, their simony and other abominations which flourish, I fear, more rankly in our time than they ever did before. When Christ arrived on earth he found the high priests, scribes and Pharisees, who belonged to the clerical order, much more wicked than the people. This is clear throughout the gospels, but in particular in the 7th chapter of John, where the high priests and the Pharisees desired their servants to seize Christ, and we read, 'then came the officers to the chief priests and Pharisees, and they said unto them, "Why have you not brought him?" The officers answered, "Never man spoke like this man." Then answered them the Pharisees, "Are you also deceived? Have any of the rulers or the Pharisees believed in him? But this people who know not the law are cursed."' Whether Christ will find them so when he arrives on earth, only he knows who is the searcher of hearts.

It is asserted, on the authority of the text which lays down that 'if so much as a beast touch the mountain, it shall be stoned', that the considerable difficulties of [interpreting] the scriptures should not be laid bare to the people. I can soundly agree with that, particularly in the case of subjects with which they are less familiar, for instance devotions, acts of piety, the divine attributes and divine ideas, the relation of human nature to the [incarnate] word, accidents without a subject, and countless others to which even those who have been

[86] Pseudo-Dionysius, *De ierarchia ecclesiastica*, trans. Robert Grosseteste (ed. Chevallier, *Dionysiaca*, 2. 1401).

aliis, ad que ex longinquo tempore philosophia politi cum graui studio et laboris uehemencia, vix sufficiunt palpitando attingere. Sed ex isto non conuenienter concluditur quod plane scripture historie uita Christi, eius miracula et doctrina, non possunt plebi enarrari in uulgari sicut iacent, et a peritis uiris litteris uulgaribus comendari, 1600 si enim dicatur quod populus de facili errare poterit nisi talia explanentur. Explanentur ergo eis per prelatos et curatos, qui ex officio tenentur eis panem ewangelicum frangere, et fragmenta supplere, difficultates que capacitatem popularium excedunt aput se recondere. Iste etenim modus faciendi figurabatur ex forma faciendi in 1605 duplici conuiuio Christi, prout a sanctis mistice exponitur. Ad illud autem quod a Crisostomo allegatur patet solucio ex precedentibus: erat enim Herodes infidelis et dolosus intrusor et tyrannus, et per 205ra consequens indignus erat ut sibi apperirentur scripture mistica, | et illa precipue ex quorum reuelacione apperiretur sibi introitus ad suas 1610 nequicias exequendas.

Ad 23^m cum sic arguitur quod plus obesset quam prodesset non est licitum, sed plus officeret quam prodesset talis translacio si fieret, sicut uidetur iamdudum in gente nostra, ubi numerosa heresum multitudo per libros Anglicanos in populum est dispersa, a 1615 quibus uulgus semel infectum irreuocabile perseuerat. Respondetur: concedo consequenciam, et negando minorem cuius racio patet superius in responsione ad 21^m argumentum. Sed pro euidencia minoris in argumento tacta, dico quod nichil probat contra propositum principale, sicut enim ex infinitis heresibus scriptis in Latino non 1620 potest concludi quod ewangelium non debeat scribi in Latino; sed pocius oppositum ad conuincendum videlicet falsos contra ewangelium scriptitantes, conformiter in proposito magis modo prodesset quam alias ewangelium in uulgari scribi ad manifeste conuincendum contra ewangelium susurrantes. Deleantur igitur tales tractatus, 1625 quotquot fuerint, \et/ multo amplius si fuerint in Latino, quoniam talis sermo cancrosus ex vi lingue incomparabiliter lacius diffundi posset quam in nostro Anglico exaratus, qui ultra terminos maris Britannici non posset facilius se diffundere, etc.

Ad 24^m quando sic arguitur, concessis huiusmodi translacionibus 1630 in uulgare, approbabili omnes ordines omnesque religiones ecclesie sancte Dei despectui haberentur, negetur hoc sequi tunc: enim hoc secutum fuisset in ecclesia primitiua, quando benedicciones et cetera omnia fiebant in uulgari, quod non est verum. Nec iterum in tempore Bede quando talem translacionem ipse fecit, et ab ante scribit enim 1635 Beda, libro 3°, capitulo 26°, prout recitat eum Cestrensis in sua

1603 supplere] supple *at line break* MS   1609 scripture] *originally* scriptura, -a canc., -e add. MS   1618 argumentum] *originally* articulum, -ticulum *canc.,* -m *add.* MS

honed in philosophy for a very long time, and after intensive study and Herculean labour, cannot approach without trembling. But it does not really follow that the simple stories of the Bible, the life of Christ, his miracles and teaching, cannot be told to the people in the vernacular just as they are, and be committed to writing in the vulgar tongue by learned men, so long as they were warned that people could easily fall into error unless the stories were explained. So they should be explained by prelates and parish priests, who are bound by virtue of their office to break the bread of the gospel, and to complete the fragments, and to resolve among themselves the difficult questions which are beyond the people's capacity to understand. This process was prefigured in the form of celebrating the Lord's Last Supper in two kinds, as the saints expound it in the mystical sense. All this explains the passage cited from Chrysostom above, for Herod was a faithless and deceitful usurper and tyrant, and therefore unworthy to have the scriptures with their mystical meanings revealed to him, particularly as the revelation would have been the starting point of his wicked slaughter.

In the 23rd point it is argued that things which hinder more than they help are unlawful, and that a translation [of the Bible], if it were made, would certainly be an obstacle, as experience has shown for some time now among our own people; for a great number of heresies have spread among the people through books in English, and having once infected them persist irreversibly. In reply I agree that the conclusion would follow, but deny the minor premise for the reason given in the response to the 21st point. In reply to the evidence produced in support of this premise, I say that it proves nothing to the point, since it cannot be argued that the gospel should not be written in Latin just because there are countless heresies written down in Latin; in fact it has the opposite effect of convincing the deceitful people writing away in contradiction of the gospel, and accordingly to have it written in English would at present be much more effective than otherwise in visibly persuading people who murmur against it. For these tracts, however many of them there are, would be much more destructive if they were in Latin, since their corrupt message would be incomparably more widely spread, due to the scope of the language, than when it is expressed in our own English tongue, which cannot very easily be diffused across the English Channel.

I deny the 24th point, when it is argued that if translations [of the Bible] into the vulgar tongue were permitted, every order of the holy church of God and every religious order would in all probability be held in contempt: for then it would have happened in the primitive church, when blessings and similar prayers were said in the vernacular, but it did not. Nor did it happen in Bede's time, when he translated the scriptures himself; and Ranulf Higden quotes him

cronica, libro 5°, quod circa annum domini 669: 'erat tunc temporis magna cura doctoribus seruire Deo, non seculo, cordi non ventri, qua propter religionis habitus in magna erat veneracione; ita ut clericus et monachus libenter susciperetur et ab itinerantibus benediccio illorum posceretur. Nec eis alia adeundi uicos causa fuit quam predicandi, baptisandi, et animas curandi gracia, nec aliquas possessiones ad construenda monasteria nisi a potestatibus oblatas quasi coacti susciperent.'[87] Hec Beda. Quod enim clerus noster est plus solito in despectu, absque dubio est ab exigencia peccatorum. Uideat enim homo Devteronimum, c[m] 27[m] et 28[m], et plane uidebit quod omnia mala que ut plurimum hominibus infliguntur, eueniunt merito peccatorum. Nonne dicit Dominus, Mt.5°[:13], suis discipulis: 'Vos estis sal terre; quod si sal euanuerit, in quo salietur? Ad nichilum', inquit, 'ualet | ultra nisi ut mittatur foras et conculcetur ab hominibus.'

Quod autem additur pro causa dictorum, quod tunc predicatores mendicantes essent minus necessarii, cum quilibet laicus esset impromptu predicator, dicitur quod hoc non sequitur, ymo si comunitas laicorum esset eque sciens cum comunitate fratrum mendicancium, ad huc essent ipsi fratres multum necessarium ad multitudinem infidelium conuertendam. Nec oportet tantum timere de tam plenaria conuersione populi, cum Christus uere prophetet Mt.10[:23], dicens discipulis suis per hunc modum, 'amen, dico uobis non consumabitis ciuitates Israel, donec veniat filius hominis'. Animaduertite queso quid dicat Bacon in epistola ad Clementem: 'lex', inquit, 'Dei deberet legi pueris, ut asuescerent semper ad ueritatem fidei, et maxime libri planiores, et magis morales utriusque testamenti, sicut eciam aliqui audiunt Bibliam uersificatam. Sed melius esset vt audirent et construerent ewangelium in prosa, et epistolas et libros Salomonis, scilicet quia illa scilicet uersificata Biblia truncat omnia et nichil ualet; nam primo debet homo instrui in hiis que sunt ad salutem anime, ut semper asuescat proficere in melius—et propter hoc Iudei a iuuentute primo adiscunt legem Dei. Et quia passus est bonus et aliqualiter facit ad propositum, recitabo que dicit consequenter Boecius inquit in libro *De disciplina scolarium:* docet quod pueri \primo/ instruendi sunt in libris Senece. Et Beda exponit quod hoc dicit quia primo sunt docendi in moribus, quia libri Senece sunt morales. Sed non sic instruuntur, sed \in/ insaniis et fabulis Ouidianis et ceterorum poetarum, vbi omnes errores in fide et moribus

---

1647 plurimum] pluium *canc.*, plurimum *add. MS*   1652 necessarii] *originally* necessariia, -a *canc. MS*   1655 vel debet esse *add. in margin and linked with a red line to* necessarium, *perhaps in a different hand MS*   1663 vt] si *canc.*, vt *add. MS*

---

[87] Higden, *Polychronicon*, V 18 (ed. Babington & Lumby, 6. 118), quoting Bede, *Historia ecclesiastica gentis Anglorum*, III 26 (*PL* 95. 164).

writing before then, in book 3, chapter 26, about the year A.D. 669: 'at that time there was a strong desire for teachers to serve God, not the world, the heart not the belly, and as a result the religious habit was held in great veneration; a clerk or a monk was readily welcomed and travellers would ask for their blessing. Their only occasion for visiting places was for the sake of preaching, baptizing and the cure of souls, and they would not accept any property for building a monastic house unless more or less compelled to as offerings from the powerful.'[87] So says Bede. That the modern clerk usually is held in contempt is indubitably the consequence of his sins. Look at Deuteronomy, chapters 27 and 28, and you will see plainly that all the evils which are so often visited on the human race are the just reward of sinners. 'Are you not', says the Lord to his disciples in Matthew, chapter 5, 'the salt of the earth? And if the salt have lost his savour, wherewith shall it be salted? It is thenceforth good for nothing', he continues, 'but to be cast out and trodden under foot of men.'

The additional argument made in support of the point, that mendicant preachers would then become less necessary, as every layman would become an instant preacher, does not follow, especially since, even if the body of the laity were as knowledgeable as the mendicant friars, the friars themselves would still be absolutely essential for the task of converting the vast number of people without faith. They should not fear so much the mass conversion of the people, since Christ truly prophesied in Matthew, chapter 10, saying to his disciples, 'you shall not have gone over the cities of Israel, till the Son of Man be come'. I ask you to note what Bacon says in the Letter to Clement: 'the law of God', he says, 'should be read to boys, to make them familiar with Christian truth, especially the simpler and the more prescriptive books in each Testament, as some people even hear the Bible turned into verse. But it would be better that they should hear and construe the gospel, the epistles and the sapiential books in prose, as the versified Bible abbreviates the text and is without value; for a man should first be taught the truths necessary to salvation, and then he can make constant progress to better things—for this reason the Jews learn the law of God from their youth up. And because the passage is well expressed and to some extent supports the argument, I will tell you what Boethius next recommends in his book *De disciplina scolarium*: he teaches that boys should first be instructed in the works of Seneca. Bede explains why: boys should first learn the rules of conduct, and Seneca's works are about the moral order. But this is not how they are taught now: they learn nonsense, and the fables of Ovid and other poets, in which all kinds of errors of faith and morals

proponuntur. Nam multitudinem deorum ibi audiunt, et quod homi-   1675
nes et stelle sunt et alie creature; de uita futura errores infiniti uul-
gantur, tam de uita bonorum quam malorum; et omnis supersticio
pro religione inuenitur, et omnis morum corrupcio. Et ideo iuuenes
concipiunt malos mores a iuuentute, et quando temptauerunt, semper crescunt in eis. Et inde accidit quod sunt inhabiles ad ueritatem   1680
sciencie magnificam, quia scriptura dicit quod "in maliuolam animam
non intrabit sapientia, nec in corpore subdito peccatis" [Wisd. 1:4].
Et anima deturpata peccatis est sicut speculum rubiginosum et uetus,
in quo non possunt species rerum apparere, ut pulchre dicit Algazel
in *Logica*, et anima ornata uirtute est sicut speculum nouum et pol-   1685
litum, in quo apparent clare rerum ymagines. Et ideo', inquit, 'quia
uulgus nescit hanc scienciam a iuuentute, homines habent animas
obscuras et excecatas, quod numquam possunt proficere, nisi in uanis
et falsis et malis cauillacionibus, et magnis infeccionibus sapiencie.'[88]
Hec Bacon ibidem.   1690

Et si hic arguas *contra hominem*, dicendo iampridem Bacon reli-
queras, et iterum eum allegas, respondeo et dico quod hoc non debet
205va alicui sensato inconueniens | apparere, sic enim pene fit cum omnibus
doctoribus quod in aliquibus sustinentur, et aliquociens relinquntur,
prout circumspecti scolastici satis norunt. Ecce uides quod quantali-   1695
bet publicacio legis Christi, non facit ordines ecclesiasticos despectui
haberi, sed pocius irregularis et scandalosa uita nostra.

Ad aliud autem quod additur in argumento quod procedente translacione iam dicta, possessionatis eorum regule in lingua uulgarium
explanate, eis in faciem obicerentur, dicitur quod bene uiuentibus   1700
nunquam possent sancte deuoteque regule in ignominiam obici, si
autem male uiuentibus talia obiciantur, ad uerecundiam imputent
culpe sue. Signum igitur manifestum est yppocrisis quod uolumus
boni uideri, cum simus mali; si enim pueri essemus, profecto calump-
nias hominum nequaquam metueremus. Propterea Seneca de uer-   1705
borum copia ad beatum Paulum apostolum scribit notabile uerbum
ad propositum: 'tunc', inquit, 'felicem te esse iudica, cum poteris
in publico uiuere. Uix quemquam inuenies qui posset aperto hostio
uiuere; bona consciencia turbam aduocat, mala autem in solitudine

1676 sunt *is followed by* dii *in modern editions of Bacon's text:* 'men and stars are divine'
1691–1 reliqueras] *originally* relinqueras, -n- *canc.* MS   1697 haberi] *originally*
habere, -e *canc.,* -i *add.* MS   1699 lingua] *originally* linguam, -m *canc.* MS
1709 solicitudine MS

[88] Roger Bacon, *Opus tertium*, c. 15 (ed. Brewer, *Rogeri Bacon opera*, 1. 54–5), citing
pseudo-Boethius, *De disciplina scolarium* (ed. O. Weijers (Leiden 1976), 100–101),
pseudo-Bede, *Sententiae* (*PL* 90. 991), and Algazel (al-Ghazāli), *Logica* (pr. (Venice
1506), fol. 1va–b).

are set out. They hear all about a great many gods, and that they are men and stars and other creatures; countless errors proliferate about the life to come for the righteous as well as the wicked; every kind of superstition takes the place of religion and every kind of corruption substitutes for morals. So young people get into bad habits at an early age, and once they have tried them out, they always grow into them. The result is that they are unable to appreciate the splendid truth opened up by reason: as the Bible says, "into a malicious soul wisdom shall not enter; nor dwell in the body that is subject unto sin". The soul corrupted by sin is like an old, rusty mirror in which images cannot be reflected, as Algazel elegantly puts it in his *Logica*, while the soul adorned with virtue is like a new, polished mirror in which you can clearly see the form of things. And so', he continues, 'as people fail to learn these things in their youth, they have dark and filthy souls which can only make any progress in silly, false, evil trivialities and in worse contamination of wisdom.'[88] So says Bacon.

If you were to argue *ad hominem*, saying that I rejected his view earlier in the argument, and then I cite him again, I say in reply that this should not seem unreasonable to any sensible person, since it is the case with virtually every doctor that one sometimes agrees with them and sometimes disagrees, as prudent schoolmen very well know. And you can see that however widely the law of Christ is spread abroad, this is not what brings the ranks of the clergy into contempt, but rather our improper and disgraceful way of life.

A further argument made in support of the point is that if the rules of the monastic orders concerning possessions were set out in the popular tongue, they would be used to confront [the regular clergy]. I reply that the holy and devout rules of monks who live honestly could never be held in contempt, but if fault were found with monks who do not, then those monks should blame their humiliation on their own conduct. If we wish to appear virtuous while being in reality evil, that is a manifestation of hypocrisy; whereas if we were still children, we would certainly not have any fear of general disapproval. On this, Seneca, writing to St Paul the Apostle on loquacity, makes a notably apposite point: 'so', he says, 'consider yourself happy that you can live in the public eye. You can find hardly anyone who lives with an open door; a good conscience welcomes company, but a bad conscience worries in troubled solitude. If what you do is honourable,

anxia et solicita est. Si honesta sunt que facis, omnes sciant; si turpia, 1710
quid reffert neminem scire cum tu scis?'[89] Hec Seneca.

Ad vltimum autem quod in argumento ponitur, quod scolasticis
multa argumenta fierent racione talium translacionum tam in speculatiua quam in morali. Hic dicitur quod quamuis inscios et ignaros
rudesque politicos talia contristarent, tamquam non habentes vnde 1715
talibus satisfaciant; instructorum tamen in lege Dei, ingenia per hoc
exacuerentur, spiritus reuiuiscerent, et viuacius sacram scripturam
ruminarent. Si enim laici humiliter petant questiones ad eorum salutem pertinentes, ordinat eis remedium diuina scriptura, Deut.32[:7],
dicens: 'interroga patres tuos et anuncciabunt tibi; maiores tuos et 1720
dicent tibi'. 'Parati', inquit Petrus, prima Petri 3°[:15], 'semper ad
satisfaccionem omni poscenti uos racionem de ea, que in uobis est
fide et spe'. Si enim presumptuose et pompatice talia mouerint,
debent eos instar Christi silencium imponentis Saduceis ex scripturis
convincere; si autem sint ceci et ignari, non uideo aliud nisi quod 1725
Christus dicit, Mt.15°[:14], 'si cecus ceco ducatum prestiterit, ambo
in foueam cadunt'.

Ad uigesimum quintum cuius uis stat in isto quod tracta huius
translacione in communem, lingua Latina uilesceret et finaliter sopi-
retur. Negetur hoc sequi, ymo sicut patet ex precedentibus. Multi per 1730
suum uulgare essent adiuti ad Latinum longe facilius intelligendum
quam per ante, sicut ex crebra experiencia est compertum. Illi enim |
205vb qui ex translacione sacre scripture in uulgare timent casum lingue
Latine, sunt pene in \capitulo/ maniacorum quorum quidam ut fertur credunt celum cadere, alii uero mare defficere; quorum iudicio 1735
non est sensati se comittere. Quod autem uulgare vnius terre in alia
terra crescat seu decrescat nichil facit contra propositum.

Ad 26[m] cum sic arguebatur non est licitum fieri quod prelati
uellent pariter condempnare, sed uerisimile quod prelati quamcumque talem translacionem condempnarent. Ergo etc. Respondetur 1740
negando minorem; non enim est verisimile quod prelati taliter facerent, presertim cum a tempore ecclesie primitiue usque in presens
fuerunt nonnulle tales translaciones in uulgari, nusquam propterea
condemnate, sed pocius approbate, sicut aliqualiter ex prioribus est
ostensum, etc.   1745

1715 vnde] non *canc.*, vnde *add.* MS   1721 Parati] *originally* paratires, -res
canc. MS   1729 communem] *abbreviated in* MS *to* con[am], *possibly* consequentiam
1735 mare] *the scribe added a more clearly shaped letter* -r- *above the third letter*

---

[89] Seneca, *Epist.mor.* 43.3–5 (ed. L. D. Reynolds, *L. Annaei Senecae ad Lucilium Epistulae morales* (Oxford 1965; repr. 1966)). This text appears in Oxford, Merton College,
MS 297 in a collection of Seneca's letters preceded by the pseudonymous preface of Jerome
to the supposed letters of Seneca to St Paul; if Ullerston had been using this or a similar
manuscript his misattribution is easy to explain.

let everyone know; if it is dishonest, what matters it that no one knows, as long as you know yourself ?'[89] So says Seneca.

The final argument is that on the basis of a biblical translation, schoolmen will have to answer endless arguments on speculative and moral questions. I reply that these questions will give grief to the ignorant and unlearned, and to those with only a crude understanding of the world, in so far as they lack the means to remedy their ignorance; but if they were educated in the law of God, it would sharpen their understanding, revive their spirit and give life to their meditations on holy scripture. If the laity humbly seek answers to questions which concern their own salvation, holy scripture provides a remedy for them, as we read in the 32nd chapter of Deuteronomy: 'ask your fathers, and they will show you; your elders, and they will tell you'. Peter says in chapter 3 of his first epistle, 'be ready always to give an answer to every man that asks you a reason for the faith and hope that is in you'. If they were to raise the matter presumptuously or arrogantly, then they should be shown the truth from the scriptures, like Christ imposing silence on the Sadducees; but if they are invincibly ignorant, I see nothing for it but Christ's words in the 15th chapter of Matthew, 'if the blind lead the blind, both shall fall into the ditch'.

The 25th point was that with a biblical translation in common use, the Latin language would decay, and then go to sleep. I deny that this conclusion follows, on the ground stated above. A lot of people have been assisted to a better understanding of Latin than they had before by their own vernacular, as common experience shows. People who think the translation of the Bible into the vernacular would lead to the disappearance of Latin, are just about as crazy as the madmen whom we are told believe the sky is about to fall, or the sea is about to dry up; no sensible person would embrace their opinions. Whether the vernacular of one country is used more or used less in another is not relevant to the argument.

The 26th argument was that it is unlawful to do what prelates will seek to condemn, and that it is very likely that they would condemn any translation of the Bible. I deny the minor premise; it is very likely that they would not condemn it, especially as there have been numerous translations into the vernacular from the primitive church up to our own time, which have never been condemned as translations, but actually approved, as I have shown in another context above.

Ad 27^m quando sic arguitur illicitum est promulgari quod multitudo peritorum clericorum illicitum iudicaret; sed approbabili numerositas legistarum vna cum tota religiosorum concione iudicaret quamlibet talem translacionem esse illicitam. Ergo etc. Hic qualitercumque sit de maiore, negatur minor tamquam minus probabilis 1750 sapientibus, que Dei sunt; non enim habent probabilitatem, ut ita loquar, nisi per locum a stulticia credit, enim aliquis fortassis non habens cerebrum bene dispositum, aut aliter zophismate dyaboli circumuentus, quod digniores ecclesie sic sentirent. Secundum quod dicit Salomon, Ecclesiastes 10[:3], 'in via stultus ambulans cum ipse 1755 insipiens sit, omnes stultos estimat'. Et nimirum quoniam ut dicit Crisostomus, omelia 33^a, exponens illud Mt.21[:23], 'In qua potestate hec facis?': Omnis homo secundum se estimat alterum; nec potest ipse melius sentire de aliquo, quam ipse sentit de ipsomet'. Et exemplificat, 'Ecce', inquit, 'fornicarius neminem estimat castum, item 1760 castus non facile de fornicario suspicatur; superbus neminem putat humilem, humilis neminem credit superbum'.[90] Hec Crisostomus.

Ad 28^m cum sic arguitur, illicitum est aliquod tale promulgatum esse, nisi prius fuerit approbatum, sed non inuenitur qui talia approbarent. Ergo etc. Conceditur consequencia et negatur minor. 1765 Inuenitur enim tota Trinitas talia approbasse, cuius approbacionis ueritas manifeste patuit in die Pentecostes, quando Spiritus Sanctus missus erat in discipulos, tribuens eis facultatem omnibus linguis loquendi, ubi habuerunt medium promptissimum transferendi seu interpretandi in habitu, postea uero predicando per totum orbem 1770 transferebant in actu; et aliqui uocaliter translata in scriptis uulgaribus | red\e/gerunt adeo, quod benedicciones et cetera omnia fiebant in uulgari in ecclesia primitiua, prout patet per doctorem de Lira. Nec deffuit approbacio, quoad premissa \expressa/ aut saltem interpretatiua, usque in hodiernum diem, etc. 1775

Ad 29^m cum sic arguitur illicitum est inducere prophanas vocum nouitates, sed hoc verisimiliter fieret, habitis huiusmodi translacionibus in uulgari. Ergo etc. Conceditur consequencia et negatur minor. Non enim prohibet Apostolus vocum nouitates simpliciter, ut dicit Glosa communis, sed prophanas, scilicet que sunt contra religionem, 1780 ut est *ypostasis*, que uox habet se et ad personam et ad substanciam. Alie, inquit, nouitates non sunt uitande, sunt enim doctrine religionis congruentes uerborum quedam nouitates, sicut ipsum nomen *Christianum*, quod quando dici ceperit, scriptum est, in Anthiochia enim primum post Ascensionem Domini appelati sunt *Christiani*, 1785

206ra

1748 tota] *originally* tata, -a- *canc.*, -o- *add. MS*   1772 redegerunt] *originally* redigerunt, -i- *canc.*, -e- *add. MS*   1784 est] est enim *MS*

---

[90] Pseudo-Chrysostom, *Opus imperfectum super Matthaeum*, hom. 31 (*PG* 56. 797–8).

The 27th argument was that it is not lawful to publish something that the majority of the more learned clergy consider to be unlawful; and in all probability the greater number of lawyers and the whole body of the regular clergy would consider a vernacular translation unlawful. Whatever may be the case with the major premise here, the minor is to be denied as less probable in respect of the wise and godly; for they would not hold it probable, so to speak, unless someone gives credit to an argument from folly, for instance someone not well in their head, or another led astray by false arguments of the devil, that the more worthy churchmen would think like this. As Solomon says in the 10th chapter of Ecclesiastes, 'when the fool walks by the way, his wisdom fails him, and he thinks everybody is a fool'. This is borne out by Chrysostom in his 33rd homily, explaining the text in Matthew, chapter 21, 'By what authority do you do these things?': 'Everyone judges other people in the light of himself; he cannot think better of another person than he thinks of himself'. He continues, 'A fornicator, for instance, thinks nobody chaste, and a chaste person is slow to think anyone a fornicator; a proud man thinks nobody is humble, and a humble man thinks nobody is proud'.[90] So says Chrysostom.

The 28th argument is that it would be unlawful to bring out a translation of the scriptures unless it has first been approved, and we do not find that it has been approved. I agree with the reasoning, but deny the minor premise, for the whole Trinity has approved it; as was clearly shown on the day of Pentecost, when the Holy Spirit entered into the disciples and conferred on them the gift of speaking in every tongue, so that they instantly had the ability to appear to translate and expound, and afterwards they were translating in practice, preaching throughout the world; and some of them then reduced to writing the words they had spoken in the vernacular, which became blessings and other prayers in the vulgar tongue in the primitive church, as Dr Lyra tells us. And approbation of these things, either explicitly or at least by implication, did not cease, up to the present day.

The 29th argument is that it is unlawful to introduce profane new language, which would undoubtedly happen in translations in the vernacular. I agree with the argument but deny the minor premise. The Apostle does not forbid any neologisms at all, as the ordinary gloss points out, but profane new words, that is, words contrary to orthodox belief, for instance *hypostasis*, a word which has the sense of both person and substance. Other new words, the gloss continues, need not be avoided, since some neologisms are compatible with orthodox belief. The word *Christianus* itself is an example: it was written as soon as it was spoken, since, as we read in the Acts of the Apostles, they were called *Christiani* in Antioch immediately

sicut legitur in Actibus Apostolorum. Aduersus iniquitatem Arria-
norum nomen nouum patres *homousion* adinvenerunt, quod est vnius
eiusdem que substancie. Nam si omnis nouitas prophana esset, non
a Domino diceretur [John 13:34], 'mandatum nouum do uobis', nec
testamentum appellaretur nouum, nec cantaret vniuersa ecclesia can- 1790
ticum nouum.[91] Hec Glosa.

Ad 30[m] et ultimum quando sic asseritur, admissa tali translacione,
sequitur quod ewangelium omnibus populis indifferenter esset promulgatum. Quamuis enim posset per distinccionem concedi, sicut
fortassis alias apparebit, negatur hoc sequi, bene tamen concedi- 1795
tur quod ewangelium debet omnibus populis promulgari. Prout
ipsemet Christus dicit, Mt.24°[:14], 'predicabitur hoc ewangelium
regni in vniuerso orbe in testimonium omnibus gentibus, et tunc
veniet consumacio'. Et ideo signanter propter illam consumacionem
accelerandam quam omnes expectamus, pro qua eciam tota ecclesia 1800
in oracione dominica orat, dicens 'adveniat regnum tuum'. Precepit Christus discipulis suis, Mr. vltimo [16:15], dicens, 'ite, predicate ewangelium omni creature'. Debet igitur ewangelium omnibus
populis promulgari, quod inter ceteros optime notat Ieronimus super
isto uersu Psalterii [Ps. 86:6], '"Dominus narrabit in scriptura popu- 1805
lorum et principum, horum qui fuerunt in ea". Non dixit, qui *sunt*
in ea. Dominus narrabit, et quomodo narrabat? Non uerbo, sed in
scriptura. In cuius scriptura? [In] populorum. Non sufficit, sed eciam
principum dicit. Et quorum principum? Qui *sunt* in ea, non dixit
hoc, sed qui *fuerunt* in ea. Videte igitur quoniam scriptura sancta 1810
sacramentis plena est. Legimus apostolum Paulum; legimus Petrum;
et legimus illum dicentem, "an experimentum eius queritis, qui in
me loquitur Christus". Et quod Paulus loquitur, Christus loquitur
[Matt. 10:40]: "qui enim uos recipit, me recipit". Dominus igitur
206rb noster atque saluator | narrat nobis et loquitur, "in scripturis princi- 1815
pum suorum Dominus narrabit, in scriptura populorum", in scripturis sanctis, que est scriptura populis omnibus, hoc est ut omnes
intelligant quod dicit, hoc est, sic scripserunt apostoli, sic dixerunt
apostoli, sicut et ipse Dominus, hoc est per ewangelia sua locutus
est, non ut pauci intelligerent, sed ut omnes. Plato scripsit in scrip- 1820
tura, sed non scripsit populis, sed paucis, uix enim intelligunt tres
homines. Isti uero hoc est, principes ecclesie et principes Christi,
non scripserunt paucis sed vniuerso populo.'[92] Hec Ieronimus ibidem. Quamuis igitur ewangelium ut refertur sit omnibus populis
promulgandum, differenter tamen, istis grossius et sensibilius, illis 1825

1808 *erasure before* populorum *with traces of three minims MS*   1822 uero] enim
canc., uero *add. MS*

---

[91] *GO* Tim. 6:20 (vol. 4, p. 412).

after the Ascension of the Lord. The fathers invented the new word *homoousion*, which is one and the same as substance, to counter the wickedness of the Arians. If all novelty were profane, the Lord would not have said 'a new commandment I give unto you', the New Testament would not be called new, and the Church universal would not sing unto the Lord a new song.[91] So says the gloss.

The 30th and last argument proposes that if the Bible were translated, the gospel would be available to everybody without distinction. Although I might agree with this in one sense, as may be explained elsewhere, I deny that the conclusion follows, though I willingly allow that the gospel should be made available to everybody. As Christ says in Matthew, chapter 24, 'this gospel of the kingdom shall be preached in all the world for a witness unto all nations; and then the end shall come'. So the whole church figuratively prays for that, to bring on the end which we all await, in the words of the Lord's prayer, 'thy kingdom come'. Christ charged his disciples in the last chapter of Mark, saying, 'go you into all the world, and preach the gospel to every creature'. So the gospel should be available to everybody, as Jerome notes very appositely in this verse of the Psalter among others: '"the Lord shall tell in the writings of the people and the elders, of those who were in her". He does not say, which *are* in her. The Lord will tell, and how will he tell? Not verbally, but in writing. In whose writing? In the people's writing. That is not enough: he says the writing of the elders as well. And which elders? He does not say those who *are* in her, but *were* in her. You can see that holy scripture is full of hidden mysteries. We read the Apostle Paul; we read Peter; and we read Paul saying, "since you seek a proof of Christ speaking in me". And what Paul says, Christ says: "he that receives you, receives me". So our Lord and Saviour tells us, and says, "in the writings of his elders, the Lord will tell in the writings of the people", in holy scripture, which is scripture for all people, that is so that all can understand what he says, which is, so wrote the apostles, so spoke the apostles, just as the Lord himself spoke, that is through the gospels, not to be understood by the few, but by everyone. Plato wrote his own scripture, but for the few not for the many, and barely three men understand him. But they, that is the elders of the church and the elders of Christ, wrote not for the few but for all people.'[92] So says Jerome. So although as he says the gospel is to be published for everyone, it should be published in different forms, more roughly

[92] Jerome, *Super Psalmum LXXXVI* (PL 26. 1083–4).

uero subtilius et eminencius; istis ut doceant et tradant aliis; illis
ut doceantur et adquiescant doctoribus. Istud signanter notat Crisostomus, omelia 38ª, ubi sic: 'sicut enim paterfamilias cellarium aut
uestiarium non habet expositum cunctis, sed alium. Sed alios quidem habet in domo qui dant, alios autem qui accipiunt. Sic in domo   1830
Dei, alii sunt qui docent, alii qui adiscunt.'⁹³ Istud eciam bene notat
Doctor de Lira, exponens illum textum, Mr.4°[:11], 'uobis datum
est scire misterium regni Dei, illis autem qui foris sunt, in parabolis'.
Ita scribens, 'sacra', inquit, 'scriptura hoc habet proprium quod sub
vna litera habet plures sensus, quorum aliqui sunt patenciores, et alii   1835
magis latentes; et ideo', inquit, 'in parabolis Christi turbe capiebant
sensum magis patentem, non autem latentem, sed de tali intellectu
docebat Christus apostolos ad partem.' Hec Doctor. Dicitur enim
ubi supra, 'talibus multis parabolis loquebatur verbum, prout poterant audire', quod exponens Theophilus dicit, 'quoniam turbe erant   1840
indocte, a consuetis nominibus instruit eas, scilicet per similitudinem
rerum sensibilium que erant eis cognite.'⁹⁴

Aliam causam reddit Crisostomus super Mt. omelia [31], exponens illud Mt.13°[:10], 'Quare in parabolis loqueris illis?': 'Si', inquit,
'omnes homines intelligunt bonum et malum, non tamen omnes   1845
habent graciam cognoscendi misterium regni, non est culpa Dei non
dantis, sed hominis non querentis nec eciam festinantis, nec laboran-
tis ut mereatur accipere. Si enim generalem scienciam boni et mali
transigisses, bene iuste merebaris hanc spiritualem, que pro remu-
neracione bone uoluntatis aut operum datur.'⁹⁵ Et sic quibusdam   1850
interpositis, 'Iudei enim, qui habuerunt legem et uixerunt secundum
legem, addita est eis noticia Christi; qui enim legem habentes non
habuerunt, quia nec uixerunt secundum legem, ablata est \ab/ eis
206va eciam ipsa lex quam habebant, | et nichil aput eos de lege reman-
sit, nisi sola scriptura librorum, omnis legis obseruancia pereunte.   1855
Sic enim et Christianis eueniet; qui enim uere habent Christum,
uiuentes secundum Christi precepta, dabitur illis regnum, ut iam
non credant absentem Christum, sed uideant presentem. Qui autem
habentes Christum non habent, quia non uiuunt secundum Christi

---

1843 omelia *followed by blank MS*

⁹³ Pseudo-Chrysostom, *Opus imperfectum super Matthaeum*, hom. 44 (*PG* 56. 881).

⁹⁴ Lyra, *Postilla in Marcum* 4:11, citing 'Theophilus', i.e. Theophylact of Ochrid, *Commentariae in Marcum* (*PG* 123. 535–6) from Aquinas, *Catena aurea in Euangelia*, ed. A. Guarienti, 2 vols (Turin 1953), I. 464.

⁹⁵ Pseudo-Chrysostom, *Opus imperfectum super Matthaeum*, hom. 31 (*PG* 56. 797). This passage is much abbreviated in Ullerston and differs significantly from the *PG* text, unlike two subsequent passages that are close. The text of *Opus imperfectum* was highly variable, with significant differences between English and continental manuscripts, including in

and intelligibly for some, more subtly and finely for others; for some so that they might learn and pass it on to other people; for others, so that they can be taught, and can satisfy their teachers. Chrysostom points this out figuratively in his 38th homily: 'as the head of the household does not allow everyone access to his storeroom or his wardrobe, but allows them into other rooms. He has some people in the house who give things out, and others who take them. So in the house of God, there are some who teach, and others who learn.'[93] Dr Lyra notes this well on the text in Mark, chapter 4, 'unto you it is given to know the mystery of the kingdom of God, but unto them that are without, all these things are done in parables'. On this he writes, 'holy scripture has the characteristic that one text can have many senses, some of which are clearer, and others more recondite; and so', he continues, 'the crowd understood the more obvious sense of the parables, but not the hidden meaning, and this is the meaning that Christ taught the disciples separately.' So says Dr Lyra. Expounding the text in the same chapter, 'with many such parables spoke he the word unto them, as they were able to hear it', Theophilus says, 'since the crowd was uneducated, he taught them in words familiar to them, that is, through the likeness of things they knew and could perceive.'[94]

Chrysostom gives another reason in a homily on Matthew, on the text in chapter 13, 'Why do you speak unto them in parables?': 'If', he says, 'everybody understands good and evil, but not everybody possesses the grace of knowing the mysteries of the kingdom, that is not the fault of God's not giving it to them, but of their own failure to seek it out and hasten it, and their want of trying to deserve the gift. For if you were to acquire a general knowledge of good and evil, you would well and properly deserve this spiritual knowledge, which is given as a reward for a good will and good works.'[95] And so he adds, on the text which follows, 'for the Jews, who had the law and lived according to it, knowledge of Christ was given to them; for those who, though they had the law, gave it up, and did not live according to it, the law which they had was taken from them, and nothing of it remained to them except only the written text, as they had ceased to observe it at all. So will it happen to the Christians; for those who truly have Christ and live according to his commandments, will be given the kingdom, so that they might not believe Christ to be absent now, but see him to be present. But those who, having Christ, have given him up and do not live according to his commandments,

the number of the homilies (note the gap in Ullerston where the number of the homily should have been). See J. van Banning, *CCSL* 87B (1988).

precepta, tollitur ab eis eciam hoc ipsum quod uidentur agnoscere 1860
Christum, ut credant antichristo, aut certe ut condempnati in die
iudicii, separati de parte Christianorum, eciam hoc ipsum perdant
quod videntur Christi, cum infidelibus deputati.'⁹⁶ Hec Crisostomus.
Et consequenter eadem omelia, exponens illud [Matt. 13:13] 'ideo in
parabolis loquar illis, quia uidentes non uident', ita ait: 'non enim 1865
quia Christus in parabolis loquebatur ideo illi, uidentes, non uidebant, sed quia, uidentes, non uidebant ideo illis in parabolis loquebatur. Ecce, uiderunt mirabilia Moisi: numquid uere uiderunt? Si enim
uere audiuissent, utique uixissent secundum legem, et credidissent in
eum quem prophetabat lex. Uiderunt et ea mirabilia; sed non uiden- 1870
tes, non uiderunt. Si autem uidissent ea, et profecissent in eis; et sic
ideo non dedit eis Deus oculos fidei, ut uideant diuina mirabilia Christi. Audiant nec viva uerba eius, ne similiter contempnant Christum,
cognoscentes, quemadmodum contempserunt et legem habentes.'⁹⁷
Hec Crisostomus ibidem. 1875

Alia eciam potest esse causa, videlicet, propter facilitatem addi-
scendi, que convenit ex parabolis; tradit enim Aristoteles, 3 *Retho-*
ricorum, quod si uelimus scire quid facit locucionem dellectabilem,
debemus hoc supponere tamquam principium, quod faciliter addiscere est quoddam dellectabile. Cum ergo omnia nomina, qualiter- 1880
cumque accepta, significent aliquid, quecumque elloquia faciunt nos
faciliter addiscere sunt dellectabilissima. Huiusmodi autem nomina
continere debent quantum ad lingwam quamdam extraneitatem, quia
si sint propria et nichil extraneitatis continent, cum talia sciamus,
non faciunt nos addiscere. Hec Philosophus ibidem in sentencia, et 1885
exemplificat Philosophus in hac materia de hac methaphora: senectus
et calamus perdiderunt florem; hoc est tam senes quam dediti studio
florem, id est dellectacionem sensibilium amiserunt.⁹⁸

Alie eciam cause possent asignari quas pretereo pro presenti. Ad
hoc igitur quod dicit doctor de Lira, quod uulgaribus turbis et pha- 1890
riseis incredulis non est concessum secreta ecclesie militantis intelligere, non propterea dictum est quod ewangelium non diceretur
populo in uulgari, sicut iacet, nec eciam quod eis non exponeretur;
sed quod primo non exponantur eis sensus scripture subtilissimi.⁹⁹
\Ymo/ secundum quod in deuocione et intellectu crescerent, secun- 1895
206vb dum hoc essent eis | scripture exponende, quod patet per textum

1860 eis, *originally* eo *with expunction marks under the letter* -o- *and* -is- *written above it*
MS   1873 viva] *originally* invia, viva *add. above the line MS*   1883 extrametatem
corr. to extraneitatem *MS*

⁹⁶ Pseudo-Chrysostom, *Opus imperfectum super Matthaeum*, hom. 31 (*PG* 56. 797–8).
⁹⁷ ibid. (*PG* 56. 798).
⁹⁸ Aristotle, *Rhetorica*, 3.10, trans. Moerbeke (*AL* 31. 1–2, 298=Bekker 1410b).

even the appearance of knowing Christ shall be taken from them, as they believe in Antichrist, and are doubtless condemned at the day of judgement, separated from the body of Christians, deprived even of the appearance of belonging to Christ, and cut off with the unbelievers.'[96] So says Chrysostom. And further on in the same homily, on the text 'therefore I speak to them in parables, because they seeing see not', Chrysostom says, 'it was not because Christ spoke to them in parables that they, seeing, saw not, but because they, seeing, saw not that he spoke to them in parables. Look, they saw the miracles of Moses: but did they really see? If they had really heard, they would doubtless have lived according to the law, and believed in him who was prophesied by the law. And they saw the miracles but, unseeing, they saw not. If, then, they had really seen, they would also have gone forward through them; so God on that account did not give them the eyes of faith to see the wonders performed by Christ. They may not hear his living words, lest in the same way they, knowing, despise Christ, somehow both having the law and holding him in contempt.'[97] So says Chrysostom.

There might be another reason why it was better to speak in parables: because it made learning easier; for Aristotle teaches us in the third book of the *Rhetoric* that if we want to know what makes discourse agreeable, we should take it as a guiding rule that learning something easily is an agreeable thing. As all names, wherever they come from, will signify something, so whatever expressions will teach us most easily will be most agreeable. Names which we know from an unknown language should contain some exotic feature, since if they were purely literal and contained no distinctive element, we would know them already and would learn nothing from them. This is Aristotle's opinion, and he gives a metaphor as an example: old age and stubble have lost their flower; that is, old men like bookworms have no flower, that is, they have no pleasure in the senses.[98]

Further reasons might be adduced which I shall pass over at present. But it does not follow from the words of Dr Lyra, that the mysteries of the church militant are not open to the understanding of the uneducated masses or unbelieving Pharisees, that the gospel should not be revealed to the people in the vernacular just as it stands, nor does it follow that it should not be explained to them; but it does mean that the most subtle senses of scripture should not at first be expounded to them.[99] As their devotion and understanding grows, so should the scripture be explained to them, as the text which follows

[99] Lyra, *Postilla in Matthaeum* 13:11.

sequentem ubi supra, 'qui', inquit, 'habet, dabitur ei [Matt. 13:12] et
habundabit'; super quo doctor de Lira, 'habentibus deuocionem et
fidem, ut Christi discipulis, datus est intellectus uerus sacre scripture,
ut habetur Luce vltimo [24:45], "apperuit illis sensum ut intellige- 1900
rent scripturas"'.[100] Debent ergo scripture primo proponi populis
grosso modo, deinde eis exponi, et eis potissime qui absque expo-
siccione non sufficiunt intellectum spiritualem carpere. Quod bene
notat Augustinus, super Iohannem omelia prima, *In principio*, ubi
sic: 'animalis', inquit, 'homo non percipit ea que sunt spiritus Dei, et 1905
in turba caritatis uestre sunt multi animales, qui non possunt erigere
se ad spiritualem intellectum; et animalis homo non percipit hoc
"in principio erat uerbum", etc. Quid igitur silebimus, fratres, hinc?
Quare ergo legitur, si silebitur? Aut quare auditur, si non exponatur?
Si non intelligitur? Itaque quoniam esse non dubito in numero vestro 1910
quosdam, a quibus possit non solum expositum capi, sed antequam
exponatur, intelligi, non fraudabo eos qui possunt capere. Qui loquitur, dicit quod potest; nam dicere ut est, quis potest? Audeam dicere
forsitan nec ipse Iohannes dixit ut est, sed ut ipse potuit: quia de
Deo homo dixit, et quidem inspiratus a Deo, sed tamen homo. Dixit 1915
aliquid; si non inspiratus esset, dixisset nichil; quia uero inspiratus
homo, non totum quod est dixit, sed quod potuit homo, dixit.'[101]
Hec ille. Ecce habemus hic plane ab Augustino quod istud deitatis
sacramentum maximum, 'in principio erat uerbum'. De quo beatus
Ieronimus in epistola ad Paulinum, 'hoc', inquit, 'doctus Plato nesci- 1920
uit; hoc Demoscenes ignorauit'.[102] Uolebat non solum populis esse
legendum, sed ab eis intelligendum, ipsisque exponendum.

   Aliter ut audeo dicere Anglicus noster Beda, non inmerito venerabilis appellatus, nunquam ausus fuisset atemptasse transferre ewangelium Iohannis in Anglicum sicut fecit, nisi non solum licitum hoc 1925
fuisset, verum eciam et expediens, vnde cum iste Beda vnus nedum de
ellectissimis viris nacionis nostre fuerat, sed eciam sanctissime con-
uersacionis fuerat. Miror quo ausu auderet quispiam in quo scintilla
timoris diuini relinqueretur, reputare factum suum illicitum in hac
parte, presertim cum, ut recitat Cestrensis in cronica sua, libro 5, 1930
capitulo 24°, quod tante auctoritatis erat, quod per epistolam Gregorii pape invitatus erat, 'ut Romam veniret ad enodandum aliquas
nuper emersas questiones'. 'Ubi', inquit Cestrensis, 'aduertendum est

---

1901 populis] scripturis *canc.*, populis *add. MS*   1909 s *canc. before* aut *MS*
1917 quod est] quo est *MS*   1930 5] ij°, *with* 5 *written above MS*

---

[100] ibid. 13:12.
[101] Augustine, *Tractatus in euangelium Iohannis*, tract. 1 (*PL* 35. 1379).
[102] Jerome, *Epistola ad Paulinum presbyterum* (*ep.* 53, 'Frater Ambrosius') (*PL* 22. 543).

that cited above shows, 'for whosoever has, to him shall be given, and he shall have more abundance'; on which Dr Lyra comments, 'a true understanding of scripture is given to those who had devotion and faith, like Christ's disciples, as we read in the last chapter of Luke, "then opened he their understanding, that they might understand the scriptures"'.[100] So the scriptures should first be put before the people in a simple form, and then explained to them, and expounded above all to those who, without explanation, lack the spiritual understanding to grasp it. Augustine expresses it well in his first homily on John, *In principio*: 'animal man cannot perceive things which pertain to the spirit of God, and there are many in the crowd encompassed by your charity who are bound to be animals and who are unable to rise to a spiritual understanding; animal man cannot understand the text "in the beginning was the word", and so on. So should we be silent, brothers, on that account? If we say nothing, how will the text be read? And how shall it be heard, if it is not explained? [And how will it be explained, if it is] not understood? So since I have no doubt that there are some among you by whom the text could not only be grasped when explained, but understood before it is explained, I will not defraud those who can understand [though I fear my words will flow over the ears of those who are unable to grasp it. By the mercy of God perhaps it will turn out well enough for all that everyone who can, should understand. For] he too that speaks, says only what he can; for who can tell it as it really is? Indeed I dare say that even John did not tell it as it really is, but so far as he could: as he was a man speaking about God, and although inspired by God, he was still only a man. He said something; if he were not inspired, he would have said nothing; but even a man inspired could not say the whole truth, but said what a man could say.'[101] So says Augustine, giving us clearly his view on that great mystery of the Deity, 'in the beginning was the word'. Jerome says in his letter to Paulinus, 'the learned Plato knew nothing of this; Demosthenes was ignorant of it'.[102] He desired not only that it be read to the people, but understood by them and explained to them.

Besides, I dare say that our own English Bede, not undeservedly termed the venerable, would never have dared, nor attempted, to translate the gospel of John into English had it not only been lawful to do so, but useful as well, since Bede was not only one of the most distinguished men of our race, but a man of very holy life. I am amazed that anyone with a trace of the fear of the divine left in him should dare to consider his action in this case unlawful, especially as we learn from book 5, chapter 24, of Ranulf Higden's chronicle that his authority was such that he was summoned to Rome by a letter from Pope Gregory, 'to elucidate some questions which had recently been raised'. 'It should be noted here', Higden continues, 'how highly

quanti pensus sit ille a curia, quo Romana sublimitas ad elucidandas
207ra questiones indigeret; quanti eciam pendend\us/ sit | a nobis ex modo 1935
viuendi et docendi. Non enim poterat seruire viciis qui mentem suam
sic consumeret in scripturarum exposicionibus', et sequitur paucis
interpositis, 'ewangelium Iohannis lingua Anglica interpretatus est,
sic inquiens "discite, filioli, dum uobiscum sum; nescio enim quam-
diu subsistam".'[103] Hec Cestrensis. 1940

Adducant omnes aduersarii publicacionis legis Christi tam planum et manifestum et autenticum testimonium ad probandum quod
simpliciter illicitum sacram scripturam literis uulgaribus exarari, si
possint. Et credo firmiter quod non reperient. Notandum insuper
quod beatus Augustinus in prefata auctoritate dicit sic: 'Qui loquitur, 1945
dicit quod potest? Nam dicere ut est, quis potest? Audeam dicere,
forsitan nec ipse Iohannes dixit ut est.'[104] Hec Augustinus. Ex quo
intelligit quod quamuis Iohannes ewangelista in nulla lingua possibili
pro statu uie[105] potuit absolute exprimere diuini uerbi sacramentum,
propter excellenciam rei substrate, non tamen tacuit, sed dixit quo- 1950
modo potuit, et quod dixit in scriptis redegit; et si dicas, eciam, sed
nunquam in uulgari, hoc nescis, sed nulla uis de isto. Nusquam tamen
legis, vbi ipse aut aliquis sanctorum patrum usque in presentem diem
murmurauit aut prohibuit sacram scripturam in uulgari ydiomate
conscribi. Ymo si bene aduertas, dominus noster Ihesus Christus, qui 1955
ewangelizare pauperibus missus est ex testimonio prophetali, scripsit ewangelium suum per ydioma uulgare in mentibus discipulorum
et turbarum. Sed quis, si non aduersarius publicacionis ewangelice,
audeat dicere quod sic mentibus exaratum non licuisset in ydiomate
popularium literis designari, propter faciliorem cognicionem Domini 1960
saluatoris ac per hoc veritatis accendende? Cognicio etenim alicuius
est efficacissimum medium ipsum dilligendi, presertim cum impo-
sibile sit aliquid dilligi nisi cognitum, testante beato Augustino, 8°
De trinitate, capitulo 16°, ubi sic: 'Quis dilligit quod ignorat? Quasi
diceret nullus. Scire enim aliquid et non dilligi potest, dilligi autem 1965
quod nescitur, quero quomodo possit? Quare si non potest, nemo
dilligit Deum antequam sciat.'[106] Hec Augustinus. Et si dicas quod
ex isto bene sequitur quod licet ewangelium predicare, exponere seu
declarare, sed nullo modo ipsum literis laicis exarari, tum quia lingue

---

1934 o written above -o in quo for clarity MS   1935 fol. 207r–v has a slight fold
running vertically through 207ra and vb; the letters affected are supplied here without notice
unless there is doubt about the word in question   1951 redegit] legible in the MS is
redegi, but the letter -t- may be concealed in the fold of the folio

---

[103] Higden, Polychronicon, V 24; ed. Babington & Lumby, 6. 224.

[104] Augustine, Tractatus in euangelium Iohannis, tract. 1 (PL 35. 1379).

[105] 'pro statu vie', 'on the basis of his state of life', 'because of the condition of the path
[of life]'.

regarded he was at the Curia for solving problems which even the excellence of Rome could not sort out; and we should regard him just as highly for his way of life and mode of teaching. For he could not accommodate the defects in explaining the scriptures which occupied his mind', and he adds, a little further on, 'he expounded the gospel of John in the English language, saying "learn, my children, while I am with you, for I don't know how long I will still be here".'[103] So says Higden.

Let all the opponents of the dissemination of Christ's law produce, if they can, clear, open and genuine proof that it is plainly unlawful to write down holy scripture in the vernacular. I firmly believe that they will be unable to do this. Let me remind you of what St Augustine says in the passage quoted above: 'Does not he that speaks, says only what he can? For who can tell it as it really is? I dare say that perhaps John himself could not tell it as it is.'[104] So says Augustine. By this he meant that although John the evangelist could not, in this life,[105] fully express in any possible language the mystery of the divine word, because of the sublime character of the subject, he did not, nevertheless, remain silent but put it as well as he was able, and then put it in writing; and if you say, that may be, but never in the vernacular, you do not know this, and the argument has no force. Nowhere in the law will you find that John or any of the holy fathers up to the present criticized or forbade the writing of holy scripture in the vulgar tongue. Our Lord Jesus Christ, you should well note, who was sent to convert the people by the testimony of the prophets, wrote his gospel in the vulgar tongue in the minds of the disciples and the crowds. Who but an opponent of the gospel's propagation would dare to declare it unlawful, that what had thus been implanted in their minds should be put into writing in the language of the people, to promote knowledge of our Lord and saviour and to light up the truth? For knowing a person is the most effective path to loving him, especially as it is not possible to love anything without knowing it, as Augustine avers in book 8, chapter 16 of his *De Trinitate*: 'Who can love what he does not know? Nobody. It is possible to know something and not to love it, but how, I ask, can one love the unknown? Nobody can love God without knowing him.'[106] So says Augustine. You may say that while it does indeed follow from this that the gospel may lawfully be preached, expounded and made manifest, but may not be written down in the language of the laity, because vernaculars are very often

---

[106] Augustine, *De trinitate*, VIII 4 (*PL* 42. 543).

uulgares sunt ut plurimum inperfecte; tum quia non sunt gramati- 1970
cate, et tum propter errorem in quem posset populus de facili incidere; et postremo ne prebeatur eis uia de articulis fidei disputandi,
quod sub anathemate est prohibitum *Extra de hereticis*, in Sexto,
Quodcumque, ubi sic, 'iubemus quoque ne cuiquam laice persone
207rb liceat publice uel priuatim de fide katholica disputare. Qui | vero 1975
contrafecerit excommunicacionis vinculo innodetur.'[107] Hec Decre-
talis. Ex isto dicto tuo vna cum dicto \domini/ Linconiensis superius
allegato, ubi dicit quod licet nudum textum ewangelii predicare, patet
manifestissime non proteruo quod licet ipsum nudum ewangelium
in uulgari ydiomate scriptitari, nec propter imperfeccionem ydioma- 1980
tis debent ydonei desistere; quin cum debitis circumstanciis modo
legant nudum ewangelium, modo predicent, modo exponant, modo
scribant ad edificacionem populi in uulgari. Quin, prout superius
allegaui ex beato Ieronimo in *De optimo genere interpretandi*, sufficit
transferre de sentencia in sentenciam, modo paucioribus uocabulis, 1985
modo pluribus, modo per circumlocucionem, secundum quod Spiritus Sanctus mouerit suos ad loquendum et scribendum magnalia
in diuersis ydiomatibus, eciam si numquam gramaticata fuerint ad
mentem sic loquencium.[108] Nec de errore popularium oportet tantum
timere, sicut superius declaraui, quin ymo infinitum plus de multi- 1990
tudine numerosa gramaticorum simplicium aliorumque, politicorum
insculptorum credencium totam scripturam mendaciis esse plenam,
propter troporum ignoranciam et sciencie theoloice irrecuperabilem
ignoranciam. Propter quam aput plebem sopiendam uellent ewangelium et legem Christi \a/ populis occultari, ne legis Dei ignari que- 1995
madmodum non solum sunt, sed semper esse proponunt a populis
reputentur. Quod si tamen dellectarentur in studio legis Christi sicut
in rebus aliis mundum concernentibus profecto, non adeo murmu-
rarent, sed pacienter tollerarent ac eciam congauderent. Alia eciam
potest esse causa, quam tangit Crisostomus, omelia 38ª, exponens 2000
illud Mt.23°[:13], 've uobis scribe, pharisei et yppocrite, qui clauditis
regnum celorum', etc.; ita scribens, 'uult enim Dominus ostendere
sacerdotes Iudeorum omnia auaricie causa facere; qui per scripturas quidem cognoscebant Christi aduentum, considerabant autem
quoniam si Christus creditus fuisset, consuetudo sacrificiorum offe- 2005
rendorum fuerat extinguenda'. Et sic quibusdam interpositis, 'magis

1971 tum *replaces a crossed-out word* MS   1986 secundum] sed *canc.,*
secundum *add.* MS   1998 profecto] *originally* profacto, -a- *canc.,* -e- *add.*
MS   2003 auaricie] *originally* amaritudine, -maritudine *canc.,* -uaricie *add.* MS
2004 quidem] *originally* qui donum, donum *canc.,* -dem *add.* MS

[107] *Liber Sextus decretalium*, V tit. 2 *De hereticis*, c. 2 *Quicumque* (ed. Friedberg, 2.
1070).

inadequate; because they are not structured languages, and therefore can cause the people to fall very easily into error; and, finally, to avoid giving occasion for them to debate the articles of faith, which is prohibited and anathematized in *Extra de hereticis*, in the Sext, *Quodcumque*, where we read, 'we ordain, further, that no lay person may dispute about the catholic faith, in public or in private. Whoever contravenes this will incur the penalty of excommunication.'[107] So say the Decretals. Taking this opinion of yours together with the remark of the lord Robert Grosseteste cited above, that it is lawful to preach the plain text of the gospel, it is absolutely clear that it is lawful for a careful person to write down the plain gospel in the vulgar tongue, and that suitable persons should not desist from the task because of the limitations of the language; but that, in the right circumstances, they may sometimes read the plain gospel text, sometimes preach it, sometimes expound it, and sometimes write it in the vernacular to edify the people. It is enough, as Jerome says in the passage cited above from *De optimo genere interpretandi*, to translate sense for sense, sometimes in fewer words, sometimes in more, and sometimes in circumlocutions, as the Holy Spirit might move his servants to speak and write on sublime matters in different tongues, even if they were not structured languages in the minds of those who were speaking them.[108] One should not worry too much about popular errors, as I have argued above, but infinitely more about the vast number of elementary pupils and others, formed public figures, who believe that the whole of scripture is full of lies, because of their unfamiliarity with figures of speech and invincible ignorance of the science of theology. This has come about from their desire to tranquillize the people by hiding the gospel and the law of Christ from them, so that the people will not think them ignorant of God's law, although they not only are ignorant of it but intend to remain so. If they were to apply themselves to the study of Christ's law as assiduously as they do the things of this world, they would not now complain about it, but patiently put up with it and even take pleasure in it. There might be another reason for it, which Chrysostom mentions in his homily 38 on the text in Matthew, chapter 23, 'woe unto you, scribes and Pharisees, hypocrites, for you shut up the kingdom of heaven', and so on; on which he writes, 'God wishes to show that the high priests of the Jews did everything for avarice; for they indeed knew of the advent of Christ through the scriptures, but thought that if Christ were believed, the practice of offering sacrifices would cease'. A little further on he adds, 'they much preferred the law to remain

---

[108] Jerome, *Epistola ad Pammachium de optimo genere interpretandi* (*ep.* 57) (*PL* 22. 572).

enim cupiebant ut, lege manente, in vsu essent sacrificia, quibus ipsi ditabantur, non Deus, quam, lege cessante, sacrificia iusticie venirent in vsum, quibus Deus dellectabantur et homines iustificabantur'. Et multis interpositis ad propositum ita scribitur, 'modo heretici sacer- 2010 dotes claudunt ianuam ueritatis, sciunt enim quoniam si manifesta fuerit ueritas, eorum ecclesia non est, et ipsi de sacerdotali dignitate 207va ad | humilitatem venient popularem'.[109] Hec Crisostomus. Si autem nostri sic se habeant hiis diebus, nouit Deus!

Istud tamen quod premissum est videlicet de publicacione legis 2015 Christi in quocumque ydiomate est cum moderamine faciendum, ut superius dictum erat. Quod bene notat dominus Altissiodorensis in prologo suo super Primum, ubi declarat quod oportet paulatiue exercitari in articulis fidei. Pro quo declarando adducit auctoritatem beati Augustini in primo libro *Soliloquiorum*, paulo ante finem sic 2020 dicentis: 'sunt nonnulli oculi tam sani et rigidi, quod se mox ut aperti fuerint in ipsum solem sine ulla trepidacione conuertant. Hiis quoddammodo sanitas est nec doctore indigent, sed sola fortasse amonicione, hiis credere, sperare, amare satis est. Alii uero quando- que uehementer uidere desiderant, fulgore feriuntur, et, eo non uiso, 2025 sepe in tenebras cum dellectacione redeunt, quibus periculosum est, quamuis talibus ut sani recte dici possint, uelle ostendere quod ad huc uidere non ualent; igitur exercendi sunt prius, et eorum amor utiliter differendus et enutriendus. Primo enim quedam eis demon- stranda sunt que non per se lucent, sed per lucem uideri possunt, 2030 ut uestis, aut paries, aut aliquod horum. Deinde quod non per se quidem, sed tamen per illa plenius effulget, ut argentum, aurum et similia, nec cum ita radiant, ut oculos ledant. Tunc fortasse terrenus iste ignis modeste demonstrandus est, deinde sidera, deinde luna, deinde aurore fulgor et albescentis celi nitor; in quibus siue cicius, 2035 siue tardius, seu per totum ordinem, siue quibusdam contemptis, pro sua quilibet ualitudine asuescens; sine trepidacione et cum magna uoluptate solem uidebit. Tale aliquid sapientibus nec acute iam tamen uidentibus magistri optimi faciunt; nam ordine quodam ad eam peruenire bone discipline officium est; sine ordine autem vix cre- 2040 dibilis facilitatis.'[110] Hec Doctor. Uolebant igitur omnes sancti noti- ciam creatoris ad omnes populos peruenire, quod bene notat beatus Ieronimus, epistola cxii[a] ad Eliodorum, vbi sic: 'ante resurrectionem

2040 vix] quis *canc.,* vix *add. MS*   2043 *Gonville and Caius fragment begins here; its variants are recorded below with siglum G; only the recto of the fragment is sufficiently well preserved to make collation possible*

[109] Pseudo-Chrysostom, *Opus imperfectum super Mattheum*, hom. 44 (*PG* 56. 881–2).

[110] William of Auxerre, *Summa aurea*; ed. J. Ribaillier, 5 vols (Paris 1980–87), I. 17, citing Augustine, *Soliloquia*, I 13 (*PL* 32. 881–2).

and sacrifices, which enriched them and not God, to continue, than the law to be superseded and sacrifices according to the order of justice, which pleased God and justified men, to take their place'. After several further points he continues, 'now heretical priests close the door of truth, for they know that if the truth were made manifest, their church would cease to be and they would exchange their priestly dignity for the humble status of the people'.[109] So says Chrysostom. God only knows if our own clergy find themselves in this position in our own time!

The foregoing case for the propagation of Christ's law in any language should be applied with due deliberation, as I have already pointed out. The lord William of Auxerre makes the point well in his prologue to the first book of the Sentences, where he says that one should proceed gradually on the articles of faith. He cites the authority of Augustine's *Soliloquies*, toward the end of the first book: 'there are some eyes which are so strong and direct that they soon adjust themselves to look straight at the sun itself without any fear. Their strength is such that they need no teacher, only a little advice perhaps, and it is enough for them to believe, to hope and to love. There are others who greatly desire to see, but are blinded by its brilliance, and so being unable to see, return with relief into the shadows. Although they can be said to see straight like strong eyes, it is dangerous for them if you try to show them what they are not yet strong enough to see; they should be first trained, and their desire usefully protracted and nourished. To begin with they should be shown things which do not shine with their own light, but can be seen by light, like cloth, or a wall, or similar things. Then they should look at things which, while they have no light of their own, shine more brightly in the light, like silver or gold and things like that, but do not dazzle them and harm the eyes. Next they should look a little at earthly fire, and after that at the stars, then the moon, and then at the brightness of the dawn and the glow of the whitening sky; either looking very quickly or gazing for longer, whether with deliberation, or more boldly, adjusting to the strength of the particular eye; and then it can look upon the sun without fear and with great joy. The best masters do something like this for wise persons who nevertheless do not see very well; for the best practice in teaching is to get there step by step; but without method, it can hardly be achieved.'[110] So says Augustine. So the saints desired with one mind to bring knowledge of the creator to all people, as St Jerome well points out in his letter to Heliodorus: 'before the resurrection,

notus tantum in Iudea erat Deus. Absque noticia etenim Creatoris
sui, omnis homo pecus est. Nunc uero post passionem Christi et 2045
resurreccionem eius, cunctarum gencium uoces et littere Christum
sonant. Taceo de Hebreis, Grecis, Latinisque, quas naciones fidei sue
in crucis tytulo Dominus dedicauit.'III Ecce quomodo Ieronimus |
207vb plane ponit, quod non solum littere Hebree, Grece et Latine post
resurreccionem Christum sonant, verum eciam cunctarum gencium 2050
littere Christum sonant. Dicit enim uoces et littere Christum sonant
in signum quod non solum in uocibus linguarum suarum Christum
predicant, sed eciam legem eius litteris lingue sue comendabant, quatenus lex Dei non solum uocibus singularum gencium propalaretur,
verum eciam earum literis, ut fixius foret memorie comendata, per 2055
hoc enim deuocio crescere potest in cordibus fidelium. Vnde et beatus
Ieronimus in prologo super Baruch, 'que enim alia potest esse uita
sine sciencia scripturarum, per quam eciam ipse Christus agnoscitur,
qui est uita credencium?'112 Istud si quidem dilligenter aduertentes,
olim deuoti laici totum auisum suum ad sciendum scripturas sanc- 2060
tas applicuerunt. De quorum vno refert beatus Gregorius, omelia
15ª: 'quod cum nequaquam litteras nouerat scripture sancte, sibi-
met codices emerat, et religiosos quosque in hospitalitate suscipiens,
hos coram se legere sine intermissione faciebat. Factumque est ut,
quantum ad mensuram propriam, plene sacram scripturam disce- 2065
ret, cum, sicut dixi, funditus litteras ignoraret.'113 Hec Gregorius. Si
enim dominus Ihesus Christus, peregre proficiscens ab hoc mundo,
tradidit seruis suis bona sua, vnicuique videlicet secundum propriam
uirtutem, per quorum usum laudabilem possunt regnum celeste adi-
pisci, quis prohibere potest fidelem seruum eius, cui Dominus dedit 2070
talentum interpretacionem videlicetsermonum eius in uulgare, ne sic
transferat in uulgare? Cum talis spiritu Dei actus, non minus possit
aliud loqui, quam Dominus in ore eius posuerit; quam propheta
gentilis Balaam, qui dixit, ut habetur Numeri 23°[:12], 'num aliud
possum loqui nisi quod iusserit Dominus?' Et hoc idem senciendum 2075
est de illis qui habent industriam aquisitam ad consimilia peragenda,
que et omnia alia ad sui laudem perficere nos concedat Ihesus Christus, qui sine \fine/ viuit et regnat. Amen.

1. Licitum est transferre legem Christi in liguam nostram Angli-

2045 pecus] *this word is unclear in G*   2049 *see above, l. 1934 for fold affecting*
this column   2052 linguarum] singularum G   2053 predicant] predicabant
G   2054 lex] *om.* G   2055 fixius] fiximus *canc.,* fixius *add.* MS   comendata]
comendata traderetur G   2058 sine] aut *canc.,* sine *add.* MS   sciencia] scienciarum
G   2060 auisum *with a nasal mark above* -a- G   2066 litteras] litteris G
2067 hoc *om.* G   2068 videlicet *add. in margin* G   2069 celeste] celorum G
2078 Amen *is followed by an abbreviation for* quod *and* p. *in G, presumably* quod patet
2079 *the nine propositions are numbered in G, but not in MS 4133*

God was known only in Judaea. Without knowledge of his creator, man is but a beast. But after Christ's passion and resurrection, the voices and writings of all peoples ring out with his name. I am not speaking of the Hebrews, Greeks or Latins, those peoples whom the Lord dedicated to the faith by the title of the crucifixion.'[111] Note how Jerome distinctly says that not only the writings of the Hebrews, Greeks and Latins ring out with his name, but the writings of all peoples. He says that their voices and writings ring out with his name as a sign that they preached about Christ in their own languages not just orally, but committed his law to written form in them, in so far as the law of God was not to be propagated only in the spoken form of every nation's tongue, but in their writing, so that it could be committed more easily to memory, and thus devotion could burgeon in the hearts of the faithful. So Jerome further says in his prologue to Baruch, 'what other life could there be without knowledge of the scriptures, through which Christ himself is known, who is the life of the faithful?'[112] Careful readers will note that at one time the devout laity gave all their attention to learning holy scripture. St Gregory mentions one such in his homily 15: 'as he had no knowledge at all of the written form of holy scripture, he bought manuscripts for himself and invited some monks into his household, and had them read the text to him ceaselessly. As a result he was able to learn them thoroughly, as far as was appropriate to his station, although he was, as I just said, completely illiterate.'[113] So says Gregory. If the Lord Jesus Christ, about to depart from this world, gave up his property to his servants, that is to say, to each according to his talents, by using which each could laudably achieve the kingdom of heaven, who could forbid his faithful servant, to whom the Lord gave the gift of translating his words into the vernacular, from using his gift? A translator, moved by the spirit of God, could do no less than to say what the Lord has placed in his mouth; as the heathen prophet Balaam said, as we read in the 23rd chapter of Numbers, 'must I not take heed to speak that which the Lord has put in my mouth?' And those should think likewise who have taken the trouble to achieve similar things, which have been allowed us to achieve to his praise by the Lord Jesus Christ, who lives and reigns for ever. Amen.

    1. It is lawful to translate the law of Christ into our own English

---

[111] Jerome, *Epistola ad Heliodorum* (*ep.* 60) (*PL* 22. 591).

[112] Jerome, *Epistola ad Paulam de alphabeto hebraico Psalmi CXVIII* (*ep.* 30) (*PL* 22. 443).

[113] Gregory the Great, *Homiliae XL in euangelia*, hom. 15 (*PL* 76. 1133–4).

canam. Patet ex hoc quod sic transferre nullo precepto Domini pro-   2080
hibetur.

2. Non minus licitum est Anglorum genti habere sacram scripturam in uulgare suum translatam quam Gallicis, Teutunicis, Wan-
dalicis seu Armenis. Patet ista ex paritate libertatis gentis Anglicane
cum ceteris nacionibus.   2085

3. Sicut licuit Ricardo heremite, trium linguarum principalium
periciam non habenti, transferre Psalterium in uulgare, ita licet aliis
parem ydoneitatem habentibus et eodem spiritu Dei ductis. Patent
ista ex hoc quod de similibus simile est iudicium.

4. Sicut difficultas circa opera uirtuosa non facit ea inagressibilia,   2090
ita difficultas transferendi scripturam in uulgare non arguit huiusmodi translacionem inpossibilem. Patet hec per hoc quod 'regnum
celorum vim patitur, et uiolenti rapiunt illud'.

5. Non obstantibus multiphariis rerum naturalium proprietatibus,
tropis, equiuocis et sinomomis, potest sacra scriptura transferri a   2095
sentencia in sentenciam in uulgare. Patet ista per hoc quod crebro a
sanctis patribus sic est factum.

6. Non solum licitum est sed expediens est talia transferre in linguam maternam ad profectum exiliter litteratorum et laicorum, quibus uerisimile est eos bene uti. Patet ista per hoc quod 'operandum   2100
est bonum ad omnes', Gall.6to[:10].

7. Sicut predicacionis uerbi Dei, ministracionis sacramentorum
ecclesie exercicium est taxandum per sanum concilium prelatorum, ita
eciam de usu translacionis quamlibet licite est censendum. Patet hec ex
fidelitate et prvdencia serui [Luke 12:42–43] 'quem constituit Domi-   2105
nus super familiam suam, ut det illis in tempore tritici mensuram'.

8. Si que sint ecclesie secreta que non sunt pandenda laicis in
Latino, talia a forciori in uulgare translata non sunt laicorum stu-
diis comendanda. Patet ista ex prouidencia uiri nobilis qui dedit vni
seruorum nouem talenta, alii vero duo, alii uero vnum.   2110

9. Sicut non est perdendus iustus cum impio, ita opuscula Anglicana, laudabiliter conscripta, non sunt dampnacioni obnoxa. Patet
ista per hoc quod 'nichil dampnacionis hiis que in Christo Ihesu'
[Rom. 8:1]. Amen, etc.

Explicit tractatus Magisgtri Ricardi Vllerston, doctoris in theologia,   2115
de translacione sacre scripture in vulgare, editus ab eodem Oxon'
anno domini 1401.

2086 licuit] licui G   2095 text on the recto of the Caius fragment ends at this point;
the verso is mostly unreadable, apart from the colophon   sinomomis] originally sinonomiis,
second -n- canc., -m- add.; first -i- canc. MS   2103 ita] ista crossed out, ita add.
in margin MS   2106 mensuram followed by ar^r (?) or M^r MS   2112 obnoxa]
possibly obnoxia MS   2115 colophon supplied from G   2116 translacione] line
break after tran-; the rest is partly unreadable   2117 anno] partly unreadable

tongue. This is proved because there is no precept of the Lord which prohibits translation.

2. It is no less lawful to have holy scripture in the vernacular for the English people than it is for the French, Germans, Wends or Armenians. This is proved by the freedom enjoyed by the English equally with other nations.

3. As it was lawful for Richard the Hermit, who had no knowledge of the three main learned languages, to translate the Psalter into the vernacular, so it is equally lawful for others who have the same degree of knowledge and the same divine inspiration. This is proved on the principle that the same circumstances lead to the same conclusion.

4. The difficulty of performing good works does not make them impossible to attempt, and so the difficulty of translating the Bible into the vernacular does not make that task impossible. This is proved by the text of Galatians, chapter 6, 'the kingdom of heaven suffers violence, and the violent take it by force'.

5. In spite of the multiple particular properties of things which occur in nature, the expressions, the equivocal meanings and the synonyms, holy scripture is capable of being translated into the vulgar tongue sentence by sentence. This is proved because it has often been accomplished by the holy fathers.

6. It is not only lawful but useful to translate scripture into the mother tongue concisely, for the profit of both the educated and the laity, who are likely to use it to good purposes. This is proved by the text of Galatians, chapter 6, 'let us do good unto all men'.

7. As the wise counsel of prelates should govern the preaching of God's word and the administration of the sacraments, so should they oversee the lawful use of translations. This is proved by the fidelity and wisdom of the steward whom the Lord 'made ruler of his household, to give them their portion of wheat in due season', etc.

8. If there are mysteries of the church which should not be revealed to the laity in Latin, *a fortiori* they are not translated into the vernacular and given over to the perusal of laymen. This is proved by the providence of the nobleman who gave nine talents to one servant, two to another, and one to a third.

9. As a just man should not be lost with an unjust man, so tracts in English which are admirably composed should not be liable to be condemned. This is proved by the text 'there is no condemnation to those which are in Christ Jesus'. Amen, etc.

Here ends the treatise of Master Richard Ullerston, doctor of theology, on the translation of Holy Scripture into the vernacular, published by him in Oxford in the year of our Lord 1401.

WILLIAM BUTLER

Contra translacionem anglicanam

Against Translation into English

Oxford, Merton College, MS 68, fols. 199ra–204vb

Frater Gulielmus Butler: Contra translacionem anglicanam

. . . intellexisse scripturam sacram et eam false composuisse, et multa secundum illum sensum falsum disputasse in libro *De moribus ecclesie catholice.* Textus enim in quo errauit erat iste: 'Quoniam propter te mortificamur tota die', vbi translacio Septuaginta interpretum secundum Augustinum habet 'Quoniam propter te morte afficimur tota 5 die', et codex lectus ab Augustino sic habuit solum 'Quoniam propter te afficimur tota die'.[1] Si constat quod libri, si multiplicarentur, essent mendosi, qui cito legentes inducerent ad errorem, ergo, periculosum esset tales libros scribi. Sed forsan pariformiter argueret quis libros in Latino non esse legendos, cum equaliter contingeret fore falsos. Huic 10 dico, quod ecclesia ordinauit vniuersitates in quibus docetur scriptura et scribuntur libri, qui si falsi sunt, facile possunt corrigi; que policia non potest comode seruari stante multiplicacione tanta populi. Nec debent prelati hoc admittere, quod singuli ad libitum eorum legunt scripturam in Latinum translatam, quia sicut experiencia satis docet, 15 hoc fuit multis modis occasio incidendi in hereses et errores. Non est ergo politicum ut quicunque, vbicunque, quantumcunque voluerit se det feruenti studio scripturarum.

Item forsan aliquis diceret quod scriptura sacra perlecta saltem reficeret gustum affectus pro qualibet eius particula secundum sen- 20 sum litteralem. Sed contra hoc arguit beatus Augustinus, libro *De moribus ecclesie*, artem tradens in disputando procedendi.[2] Dicit sic: nature ordinem habere se, ut, cum dicimus, rationem precedat auctoritas; ne racio infirma forsitan iudicetur, ideo hoc efficacius suadeo auctoritate. Nam scribens Augustinus, epistola 39 ad Paulinum, de 25 iudicio Dei occulto, quo quosdam approbat ad salutem, quosdam reprobat ad penam, tandem capit textum ad Coll.[2:18], 'nemo vos seducat', etc., de quo textu Paulinus quesierat; et notabiliter dicit, 'Dixisti', inquit Augustinus, 'ista obscura tibi esse, sed nec ego', inquit, 'sine caligine intelligo, atque utinam', inquit Augustinus, 'pre- 30 sens de me ista quesisses, nam in sensu quem mihi in his verbis habere uideor, adhibenda est quedam pronunciacio in uultu et modo

TITLE: Buttiler contra translacionem anglicanam *MS*   10 non] nam *MS*   13 comode] comede *MS*   19 perlecta] plecta *MS,* perlecta *Deanesly* 23 ordinem] ordi *at line break MS,* ordinem *Deanesly*   25 Paulinum] Paulum *MS,* Paulinum *Deanesly*   29 nec] nunc *MS*   30–31 presens] prius *MS,* praesens *Deanesly*   31 quesisses] quesisset *MS,* quaesisses *Deanesly*   in sensu] incensu *MS,* in sensu *Deanesly*

---

[1] Augustine, *Retractationes* (PL 32. 592), citing his *De moribus ecclesiae catholicae* (PL 32. 1317). The passage begins in the midst of Augustine's acknowledgement of citing Ps. 43:22 incorrectly, which he attributes to faulty codices.

William Butler, OFM: Against Translation into English

[. . . Augustine to have wrongly] understood holy scripture and organized [the text] incorrectly, and to have argued several points on
the basis of that misunderstanding in his book *De moribus ecclesiae
catholicae*. The text about which he made the error was this: *Quoniam
propter te mortificamur tota die* ('Because for thy sake we are killed all
the day long'), where the version of the Septuagint translators, as
Augustine had it, read *Quoniam propter te morte afficimur tota die*
('Because for thy sake we suffer death all the day long'), and the
manuscript read by Augustine had only *Quoniam propter te afficimur
tota die* ('Because for thy sake we suffer all the day long').[1] If we can
agree that books, if multiplied, carry misleading texts which straight
away draw their readers into error, then it is dangerous to have such
books copied. But perhaps, similarly, it could be argued that books in
Latin should [not] be read either, as they might be equally erroneous.
I reply to this, that the Church has established universities in which
scripture is taught and books are copied, which if erroneous can easily
be corrected; but this course cannot conveniently be followed if too
many people are involved. Prelates should not allow that individuals
may read the Bible in Latin translation at will, for experience shows
clearly enough that this leads people to fall into all kinds of heresy
and error. So it is not prudent that anybody anywhere, and as often
as they wish, should engage in the intensive study of scripture.

Then someone might argue that the reading of holy scripture
would at least refresh the disposition and desire to know its com-
ponent parts according to the literal sense. But Augustine argues
against this in his book *De moribus ecclesiae*, where he is teaching
the way to proceed in argument.[2] He says that the order of nature
is so arranged that, as we say, authority comes before reason; since
reason might be considered unsound, one persuades people more
effectively through authority. For writing to Paulinus (letter 39) on
the hidden judgement of God, by which he elects some to salvation
and condemns others to punishment, Augustine comes to consider
the text in the Epistle to the Colossians, 'let no man beguile you',
etc., about which Paulinus had enquired; and he says distinctly, 'You
have said that this passage is mysterious to you; nor do I understand
it clearly, and I wish that you were here to ask me in person, for in
the sense which these words seem to me to have, they rely on a facial
expression and tone of voice, which cannot be conveyed in writing,

[2] Augustine, *De moribus* (PL 32. 1311).

vocis, qui exprimi litteris non potest ut ex aliqua parte aperiatur, quod ideo fuit obscurius quia non recte, ut estimo, pronunciatur'.[3] Cum ergo Paulino instructo in diuinis litteris non potuit Augustinus 35 exponere scripturam in hiis, quomodo a rudibus talibus scriptura sic lecta posset intelligi? Sed aliquem sensum ab eis non cognitum intelligere deberent, et tunc non reficeret gustum, sed pocius duceret in errorem.

Item Augustinus Memorio episcopo, epistola 55, dicit quod ali- 40 que scripture difficile intelliguntur, si non assit qui disputancium posset separare personas, et pronunciando sonare morulas uerborum et sillabarum, ut omnis exprimatur sensus, quia proferunt aurium si feriantur genera numerorum. Cum ergo in libro Ecclesiastis Salomonis, in quo connectuntur persone sapientes et insipientes, et sic per- 45 sone virtuose et viciose, et sententie harum sunt commixte, sic quod difficile sit perito theologo illas sentencias sic ab invicem distinguere; cum ergo Augustinus consulat Memorio | episcopo ut non legat sine doctore libros Ecclesiastici, ne ipsum legisse peniteat sic desit qui personas distinguit, qui sonat morulas sillebarum, cum desit talis 50 expressio, qua sensum aurium feriant genera numerorum.[4] Conformiter consulendum est wlgari populo ne scripturam sacram legere cupiant, sed sint secundum Iacobi [Jas. 1:19] concilium 'veloces ad audiendum', et non presumptuosi aliquatenus ad loquendum.

199rb

Confirmatur, secundo, hec ratio per Aristotelem, 2° *Ethicorum*, 55 sic dicentem: opus morale, inquit, suscipimus non contemplacionis gratia, scilicet, ut sciamus, sed ut boni fiamus.[5] Sed dicta est sacre scripture ad alias scripturas, quia ipsa non accipit verum et bonum, sed uerum ut bonum, et nedum ut bonum morale, sed ut bonum gratuitum; ergo talis scriptura est accipienda ut boni fiamus, et sic 60 sciamus ut boni fiamus gratuite. Ergo cum, teste Ieronimo, aliquit latet in voce quod non latet in cortice littere; ut patet epistola 33[a], que est de omnibus diuine historie libris, in qua exhortatur Paulinum ad addiscendum, et maxime per auditum.[6] Et hoc per exempla Pauli, qui didicit ad pedes Gamalielis [Acts 22:3], qui postea adiit discipulos 65 in Ierusalem ut videret Petrum, vbi misterio ebdomadis et ocdoadis

---

38 intelligere deberent *add. Deanesly*   41 intelligitur, si *Deanesly*   42 sonare] seruare *MS*   43 aurium] aurum *MS,* aurium *Deanesly*   44 numerorum] minerarum *MS,* numerorum *Deanesly*   51 aurium] aurum *MS,* aurium *Deanesly* numerorum] nimeriarum *MS*   53 cupient *corr. to* cupiant *MS*   58 non] *uncertain;* non *Deanesly*   62 littere] *preceded by* scripture *underdotted MS*

---

[3] Augustine, *Epistola ad Paulinum* (*ep.* 149) (*PL* 33. 639).

[4] Augustine, *Epistola ad Memorium episcopum* (*ep.* 101) (*PL* 33. 369).

[5] Aristotle, *Ethica*, trans. Robert Grosseteste, 2.2 (*AL* 26/3. 397=Bekker 1103b).

[6] Jerome, *Epistola ad Paulinum presbyterum* (*ep.* 53, 'Frater Ambrosius') (*PL* 22. 541–2).

to clarify their meaning to some extent, and so the text is difficult to understand because, I think, it is not correctly enunciated'.[3] So if Augustine could not explain holy writ to Paulinus who was learned in the scriptures, how could this text be understood by uncultivated people? They would be forced to give it some alien meaning, and then it would not refresh their appreciation of it, but lead them into error.

Again, Augustine says in letter 55 to Bishop Memorius, that a written text is difficult to understand, if there is not someone present who can sort out the different roles of the participants in the discussion, and by speaking out loud sound the quantities of the words and syllables, so that every sense which strikes the ear is expressed when particular measures are sounded. So therefore in Solomon's book of Ecclesiastes, in which wise and foolish persons are linked together, and virtuous and vicious persons too, and their sayings are mixed, it is difficult for a learned theologian to distinguish one [voice] from another; and so Augustine advises Bishop Memorius not to read that book without a teacher, to avoid disappointment on reading it in the absence of someone who can distinguish the different voices, and can enunciate the intervals of the syllables, for otherwise the meaning conveyed to the ears by the distinctive measures would be lost.[4] Accordingly, ordinary people should be advised not to aspire to read holy scripture, but to follow the counsel of James and be 'swift to hear', rather than rashly presume to expound it.

This line of reasoning is confirmed by Aristotle in the second book of the *Ethics*, who says, we undertake the study of moral philosophy not as a matter of contemplation, in order to know, but to become good.[5] But this applies to holy scripture in relation to other writings, because it does [not] receive the true and the good, but the true as the good, and not as moral good, but good as a free gift; and therefore we should receive scripture to become good, and so we should know it to become freely good. So as Jerome says, something is hidden in the spoken word but not in the rind of the written text; this is in letter 33, which is about all the books of sacred history, and where he exhorts Paulinus to study, above all, by listening.[6] He adduces the example of Paul, who learned at the feet of Gamaliel, and then went up to the disciples in Jerusalem to see Peter, where the future preacher to the Gentiles was to be instructed in the mystery

futurus gencium predicator instruendus.[7] Et quilibet habens zelum feruidum animarum pocius deberet consulere ut wlgus addiceret per auditum, pocius quam legendo; quia ergo secundum Ieronimum, audire sit medium melius perueniendi ad sacre scripture noticiam 70 quam scripturam legere, cum proclamet philosophia quod in paucioribus uia sit maior. Cum via audiendi sit melior, securior, atque expedicior quam via legendi, propter paucitatem mediorum tenendam, debet via legendi prohiberi et uia audiendi sepissime hortari.

Sed forte obicit quis, quod licet audire sit melius, parum intelligere 75 wlgaribus sit bonum. Hic dico, quod leccio est inductiua in errorem pocius quam auditus, quod sic ostendo, nam Augustinus epistola 58ᵃ, describit errorem, dicens: 'Non mihi uidetur aliquem errare, cum aliquis nescire se scit, sed cum putat se scire quod nescit'.[8] Set sic putare accidit per legere cicius quam per audire; ergo legere periculosum est, 80 saltem wlgari populo. Item Augustinus Ps. 59 ad hoc notat, 'Auditui meo', inquit Psalmista, 'dabis gaudium et leticiam, et exultabunt ossa' [Ps. 50:10]. Constat namque ibi, secundum mentem beati Augustini, quod iste textus fuit dictus in persona humilium illuminandorum, et nota quod non dixit *lectioni nec dabis gaudium et leticiam*, sed 85 *auditui*.[9] Cum ergo gaudium et leticia non lectioni scripture, sed ipsius scripture auditui sunt commissa, tenere tantum illam uiam est ipsis laicis magis tutum; nam dato quod populus legeret ad alium sensum, qui non est scripture, de scriptura haberet. Tunc secundum Augustinum, epistola 69 ad Maximam feminam, esset de his sicut 90 de illis qui ferramentis medicinalibus puniuntur, 'que utique non ad uulnerandum sed ad sanandum sunt facta'; sic, secundum mentem Augustini, scripture sunt ordinate ad sanandum non ad perimendum.[10] Ferrum ergo scripture sacre non debet dari inperito cirrurgico, ne propter artis inpericiam mors sequatur; cauere ergo summe debent 95 pontifices infulati, qui legere, qui predicare debent scripturas, ne vnde perueniret vtilitas, inde proueniat mortis calamitas.

Secundo, arguo contra assercionem prefatam ex radice defec-
199va tus intellectus humane. | Nam tradit venerabilis doctor Halys, prima parte *Summe*, distinccione 2ᵃ, articulo 3°, humane nature 100

79 scit] sit *MS*, scit *Deanesly*   81 notat] notas *followed by a space MS,* notans *Deanesly*   87 illius *canc.*, ipsius *MS*   94 cirrurgico] crrurgico *MS* 98 *blank for capital, guide letter* s *MS*

---

[7] 'The mystery of the sevens and the eights' is obscure, either in its precise differentiation or in its overall context. Butler is not always an accurate reporter of his authorities, but here he keeps very close to Jerome, following the story of Paul's consultation in Jerusalem with Gamaliel, Acts 22:3 (*PL* 22. 541): 'Hoc enim mysterio hebdomadis et ogdoadis, futurus Gentium praedicator instruendus erat'. It is perhaps possible that Jerome is referring to the liturgical eight-day week (the octave) as distinct from the normal secular week.

of the sevens and the eights.[7] Whoever has a burning zeal for [the cure of] souls should resolve to teach the people by having them hear, rather than read; for according to [Jerome], hearing is a much better means of getting to know holy scripture than reading, since it is a rule of philosophy that the broader way goes through fewer stages. Hearing is a better, safer and more convenient procedure than reading, because it goes through fewer stages, so the way of reading should be prohibited and the way of hearing consistently adopted.

It may be objected that although it is better to hear [holy writ], is it a good thing for ordinary people to understand too little? I reply to this, that reading more readily leads to error than listening, and I show this by reference to Augustine's letter 58, where he describes error in these words: 'It does not seem to me that someone errs when he knows he is ignorant [of something], but when he thinks he knows something which he does not'.[8] This happens more quickly when people read than when they listen; therefore reading is dangerous, at least for ordinary people. So Augustine notes on Psalm 59, 'Make me to receive joy and gladness from my hearing, that the bones may rejoice', and here he is clear in his mind, that this text is spoken in the voice of the humble, who are to be enlightened, and observe that he says *joy and gladness from my hearing* not *reading*.[9] Since joy and gladness are the reward of hearing scripture, not reading it, this way is very much safer for the laity; for given that people will read another, non-scriptural meaning into it, they will hold that their interpretation is in the Bible. Moreover, according to Augustine's letter 69 to the lady Maxima, it would be like someone being punished with a surgical brace, 'which was not intended to harm but to heal'; in his view, scripture was instituted to heal, not to destroy.[10] The iron of scripture should not be issued to an incompetent surgeon, in case his lack of skill leads to death; so prelates in their insignia of office should take great care over who should read and who should preach the scriptures, lest death is the unfortunate result of their attempt to be useful.

I argue secondly against that idea on the ground of the inadequacy of the human mind. The venerable doctor Hales teaches in the first part of his *Summa*, distinction 2, article 3, that human understanding

---

[8] Augustine, *Epistola ad Hesychium de fine saeculi* (*ep.* 199) (*PL* 33. 924).

[9] Augustine, *Ennarrationes in Psalmos*, 50:10 (*PL* 36. 593–4).

[10] Augustine, *Epistola ad Maximum* (*ep.* 264) (*PL* 33. 1085).

intelleccionem in duobus deficere propter originalem potencie corrupcionem, nam deficit in his que verissime sunt et maxime sunt intelligibilia, et in hiis que minime sunt, et minime intelligibilia essent,
ut patet, inquit, de esse motus et temporis; et ideo, inquit, sicut
sensus deficit in extremis, scilicet maxime sensibilibus et minime   105
sensibilibus; ita intellectus obtenebratus deficit. Et ideo Aristoteles
ponit, intellectum nostrum se habere ad perfectissima nature sicut
se habet ad solem oculus uespertilionis.[11] Propter ergo originalem
corrupcionem prouenientem ex peccato Ade, corruptus est noster
modus intelligendi; et secundum postillatorem Petrum Iohannem   110
super Genesim prius, nota nature fuerunt prius nota Ade in statu
innocentie, ita quod noticia racionis deriuacione speciei dimisit dis-
cursum racionis.[12] Nam Adam, per combinaciones qualitatum, nouit
quod combinacio variaret gradum specificum, et quod determinaret
hoc in tali specie ad diuersa indiuidua; sed adueniente corrupcione   115
intellectus, iam non est nobis cognoscibilis effectus per causam in
contingentibus, sed cognoscimus causam per effectum. Hiis premissis, premittenda sentencia est beati Augustini in sua *Dialectica*, quod
duo sunt inpedimenta veritatis, ne ueritas capiatur, scilicet 'obscuritas
et ambiguitas, inter que hoc interest, quia in ambiguo plura se osten-   120
dunt, quorum quid pocius accipiendum sit penitus ignoratur, sed in
obscuris parum aut nihil quod attendatur apparet'. Et exemplificat
Augustinus, dicens quod 'vbi parum est quod apparet, tunc obscurum
est ambiguo similiter: [veluti si quis ingrediens iter, excipiatur aliquo
bivio, vel trivio, vel etiam, ut ita dicam, multivio loco, sed densi-   125
tate nebulae nihil viarum quod est, eluceat; ergo a pergendo prius
obscuritate tenetur. At ubi aliquantum rarescere nebulae coeperint,
videtur aliquid, quod utrum via sit an terrae proprius et nitidior color
incertum est: hoc est obscurum ambiguo similiter.] Dilucessente celo
quantum oculis satis est, iam omnium uiarum deduccio clara est, sed   130
qua pergendum sit non obscuritate set ambiguitate dubitatur. Huius
obscuri tria sunt genera, vnum quod sensui patet sed animo clausum
est, sic patet de uidente malum pictum Punicum et non nouit malum
Punicum; anima tunc talis', inquit Augustinus, 'nescit cuius rei pic-
tura sit. Alterum genus obscuri est, vbi res animo pateret, nisi sensu   135

---

112 racionis] roris *MS*, rationis *Deanesly*   124–29 *MS omits a long passage necessary
for the understanding of Butler's argument; it is here supplied from PL 32*   130 satis]
satus *MS*, satis *Deanesly*   135 pateret, nisi] patet vbi *MS*, pateret nisi *Deanesly*

---

[11] Alexander of Hales, *Summa theologica, tractatus introiti* 2.3; ed. Fratres Minores, 4
vols (Quaracchi 1924–48), I. 19, citing Aristotle, *Metaphysica*, 2.1, trans. Jacobus Veneticus
(*AL* 25/1. 36=Bekker 993b)).
[12] Peter John Olivi, *Super Genesim*, III 7, in Paris, Bibliothèque nationale de France,
MS lat. 15559, fol. 28va–b; Rome, Biblioteca Apostolica Vaticana, MS Ottoboni lat. 694,
fol. 34vb.

is doubly defective because of the corruption of its powers by original
sin, since it is inadequate as to things which are the most true and
the most intelligible, and as to those which are furthest from truth
and least intelligible, as for example, he continues, the essence of
motion and time; and so the senses are inadequate at both ends of
the spectrum, as to the most and as to the least perceptible things;
and thus the intellect is obscured. And so Aristotle says that the
human mind is to the most perfect things of nature as is the eye of a
bat to the sun. [11] Our mode of understanding is thus disordered by the
original corruption deriving from the sin of Adam; and according to
the commentator Peter John [Olivi] on the first chapter of Genesis,
the things known to nature were originally known to Adam in the
state of innocence, so knowledge derived from its species replaced
knowledge through reason. [12] For Adam knew, through the combination of qualities, that the combination would alter the degree of
the species, and that he could determine this within a given species
with respect to its different individuals; whereas after the corruption
of the [human] mind, in contingent things an effect is no longer
knowable for us through its cause; we know a cause through its effect.
On this basis, St Augustine's opinion in his *Dialectics* may be considered, that there are two obstacles to truth which prevent it being
grasped, namely 'obscurity and ambiguity, on which we can note that
in ambiguity several things present themselves, between which we
are entirely without means of choosing, whereas in obscurity little or
nothing of relevance can be discerned'. Augustine gives an example,
remarking that 'where there is little visibility, the obscure is like the
ambiguous: [for instance someone going on a journey comes upon a
parting of the ways in two, three or several directions, but the dense
fog prevents any of them from being seen clearly; then obscurity at
first prevents him from proceeding. But then the fog begins to lift a
little, and something is visible; the brighter light leaves it uncertain
which is the right way over the ground: then the obscure is like the
ambiguous.] As the sky lightens, giving enough visibility, all the
ways forward are in plain view, but which is the right way is in doubt
not through obscurity but through ambiguity. There are three kinds
of obscurity, one which is open to the senses but closed to the mind,
for instance someone seeing a painted pomegranate, not knowing it is
a pomegranate; but his mind knows not what the picture portrays',
says Augustine. 'In another kind of obscurity, an object is present

clauderetur, sicut est homo pictus in tenebris. Tertium genus obscuri
est quando res sensui absconditur, et, si sensui nudaretur, nihil tamen
animo eueniret. Quod genus omnium est obscurissimum.'[13] Huius
exemplum est, secundum Augustinum, quod cum inperitus 'de malo
punico, malum Punicum in tenebris cogeretur cognoscere'. Conse- 140
quenter Augustinus dicit duo fore genera ambiguitatum: 'primum
est in hiis que dicuntur, alter enim est in his que scribuntur. Ut si
quis audiret *acies*, siue legeret, ignoraret aut sit militum acies, ferri, vel
oculorum. Si quis vero legat scriptum, verbi gracia, *leporem*, dubitabit
de penultima an sit media correpta siue sillaba producenda.' Cum 145
ergo in scriptura ista concurrunt inpedimenta, quantumcunque quis
legat in obscuris et ambiguis prout exemplificat Augustinus, in uia
non graditur cognicionis. Cum ergo populis sit difficilis intellectus
et scriptura sacra sit plena ambiguis et obscuris, ymmo, secundum
Dionisium, sacris poeticis informacionibus, quomodo, queso, foret 150
eorum legere medium in via cognicionis sentencie scripture sacre?
Relinquitur ergo, quod uulgarem populum in scriptura sacra legentem non est medium deducens eos in noticiam eiusdem scripture,
et propter hoc solum consulitur in oppositum oppinantibus, scilicet,
199vb ut propter maiorem | agendorum cognicionem promouerentur ad 155
practicam spiritualem memorie accione.

   Confirmatur racio philosophice, nam, secundum Philosophum,
pauci sunt vigentes acumine intellectus, et ideo ponit, 3°*Rethorice*,
quod quanto maior est populus tanto minor vel remocior est intellectus.[14] Ergo, licet politicum fuisset, quod populus uulgaris, quando 160
pauci de lingua fuerint ad fidem conuersi in quacunque nacione fuisset, quod tunc sacram scripturam legisset; non tamen sequitur quod
modo in eadem nacione foret sic politicum, ut omnes modo chate-
zizati fide possent conformiter scripturam perlegere. Et si inuenia-
tur quod aliquis doctor approbatorum seu canonizatorum scripturas 165
sacras alicui populo transtulerit legendas, uel eis legere consulerit,
non sequitur modo quod sic staret politicum. Quia indubio verum
est, quod dicit Philosophus, quod quanto maior est populus tanto
remocior est intellectus. Cum ergo optimum medium ad cognoscen-
dum Deum sit de Deo cogitare, et ipsum Deum suppliciter exorare, 170
et plus perficiunt christiani per hec duo media quam per leccionem
siue per auditum, ut in epistola 48 ad Paulinam, *de uidendo Deo*, docet
limpidius Augustinus—mihi uidetur—quod consulere populum ad

136 pictus] uinctus *MS*, pictus *Deanesly*   139 Augustinum] Augustinus *MS*
141 primum] Io^m *MS*   143 audiret] an audiret *MS*   156 accione] accionis
MS   167 verum] vnum *MS*

[13] Augustine, *Dialectica*, cc. 7–8 (*PL* 32. 1414–15).
[14] Aristotle, *Rhetorica*, 3.12, trans. William de Moerbeke (*AL* 31/1. 306=Bekker 1414a).

in the mind, but closed to the senses, such as a man painted in the dark. . . . The third kind of obscurity arises when an object is hidden from the senses, and, since it does not impinge on the senses, is not present in the mind either. This is the most obscure of all.'[13] Augustine's example is a man, unaware of the pomegranate, who is obliged to recognize it in the dark. He goes on say that there are two kinds of ambiguity: 'one is in the spoken word, and the other in the written word. So if someone either hears, or reads, the word *acies*, he does not know whether it refers to a line of soldiers, a line [or edge] of a sword, or a line of sight. If he reads the written word *leporem*, for example, he will be in doubt whether the penultimate syllable is formed [from *lepos*, charm, or *lepus*, a hare].' So since these difficulties accumulate in the written text, in so far as someone reads these obscurities and ambiguities which Augustine adduces, he will not progress in knowledge. As ordinary people find understanding difficult and as holy scripture is full of obscurities and ambiguities, and furthermore, according to Dionysius, of holy poetical concepts, how, I ask, would reading furnish their means of knowing holy scripture? It follows then, that having ordinary people read the Bible is not the way to bring them to the knowledge of scripture, and on this ground alone I would advise those who disagree, that [people] should be induced to gain greater understanding [of scripture] by spiritual practice through the working of memory.

The argument is confirmed philosophically, since according to Aristotle, few people flourish by the sharpness of their intellect, and so he argues in the third book of the *Rhetoric* that the larger the populace, the lesser and the remoter their understanding.[14] It may have been advisable that ordinary people, at a time when few of any nation who spoke the same language had been converted to the faith, should read holy scripture; but it does not follow that it would be desirable now, in any particular country, that all who have been catechized in the faith could accordingly study the Bible. If it were established that some doctor among those approved or canonized [by the Church] had translated holy scripture for a particular people to read, or had admonished them to read it, we should not infer that it would still be desirable now. Undoubtedly the one principle stands, as the Philosopher says, that the larger the populace the remoter their understanding. Since the best way of knowing God is to meditate on him, and to pray fervently to him, and Christians perfect profit more by these two methods than by reading or listening, as Augustine says very clearly in his letter 48 to Paulina, *de videndo Deo*; and— so it seems to me—that to urge the people to these two ways, to

hec duo media, scilicet cogitare et orare, foret concilium sanius quam
consulere quod scriptura wlgariter translata tradenda sit laicis.[15]   175
Tercio, principaliter arguo contra prefatam assertionem ex radice
disposicionis ierarchie angelice create. In qua materia sic procedam,
primo, requiram quomodo acta sit reuelacio in angelis ierarchie disposicionis causa; quo habito, et supposito communiter dato a doctoribus quod perfeccio, pro statu uie ecclesie militantis, sumatur   180
et attendi habeat penes conformitatem ad ecclesiam triumphantem, concludam oppositum opinantis predictam sepius assercionem.
Primo, qualiter fiat reuelacio, siue a supprema ierarchia siue a sibi
subordinato ierarca? Conclusio est Augustini, quod semper fuit actu
voluntatis superioris relato ad purgatum per actum huiusmodi col-   185
lustrandum. Nam disputat et tenet gloriosissimus Augustinus, epistola 48°, *de videndo Deo*, ad Paulinam, qualiter Deus, suppremus
ierarca, sit visibilis, qualiter inuisibilis a creatura: 'si queris', inquit,
'si Deus a nobis uideri possit, respondebo', inquit Augustinus, 'quod
ipse potest, quia in verissima scriptura legitur, "beati mundo corde,   190
quoniam ipsi Deum uidebunt" [Matt. 5:8]. Et si queris quomodo
uidetur a me Deus inuisibilis, et', inquit Augustinus, 'Deum esse
inuisibilem natura, voluntate tamen visibilem, quia uidetur ab alico
quando vult et cui uult, nam plurimis', inquit Augustinus, 'non qualis
sed quali specie illi placuit.'[16] Ex qua sentencia liquet Deum esse   195
uisibilem a creatura non natura, sed sua voluntate. Iam qualiter angeli
sint uisibiles est breuiter disserendum, pro quo dicit Augustinus, 12
Super Genesim ad litteram, declarans quomodo occulte miscetur spiritus malus cum spiritu hominis; et exemplificat de uno arepticio qui,
in quadam solempnitate paganorum, peractis sacrificiis agnitisque   200
phantasticis, saltando et ludendo, dixit coram omnibus, 'in silua',
inquit, 'iuxta nos posita hac nocte quidam a leone perimetur', ad
cuius cadauer spectandum tota hec turba est confluxura, et locum
huius solempnitatis totaliter desertura; quod et contigit. Et consequenter subiungit Augustinus, quod hec est differentia inter uisio-   205
nem hominum et uisionem spirituum, quod spiritus, etsi nolimus,
2oora nos uident, nos autem, inquit Augustinus, ymagines ex|istentes in
eis nosse non possumus nisi nobis ostendantur. 'Nam, ut estimo',
inquit Augustinus sic, 'habent spiritus in potestate eorum occultare
ymagines in eis existentes spiritalibus modis, sicut nos interiectis   210

176 *blank for capital, guide letter* t *MS*   177 angelice] anglice *MS,* angelicae
Deanesly   create] creature *MS,* creatae *Deanesly*   178 quomodo] q°, *possibly* quo
MS   reuelacio *om. MS*   179 causa *om. MS*   183 supprema] suppreme
MS, supprema *Deanesly*   184 Augustini] Augustinus *MS*   187 Deus] deum
MS, Deus *Deanesly*   suppremus] supprema *MS*   202 perimetur] permetur *MS,*
perimetur *Deanesly; minim omitted at line break*   204 consequenter] communiter
MS, consequenter *Deanesly*   206 nolimus] volimus *MS,* nolimus *Deanesly*

meditate and to pray, would be sounder advice than to propose that the Bible be translated into the vernacular for the laity.[15]

I argue thirdly, and particularly, against that proposition from the premise of the organization of the created angelic hierarchy. On this I will proceed, first, by considering how [revelation] is effected among angels [in relation to] the arrangement of the hierarchy; and then, assuming in common with the doctors that perfection, for the church militant on earth, is and can only be achieved by conformity with the church triumphant, I will conclude in an opposite sense to the proponent of this frequently cited assertion. First, how is revelation effected, by the highest order [of angels] or by an order subordinate to it? My answer is that of Augustine, that it is always effected by an act of will of the superior power and associated with the purification which that act will bring about. The glorious Augustine argues and maintains, in his letter 48 to Paulina, *de videndo Deo*, in what way God, the supreme hierarch, is visible and in what way invisible to creatures, that 'if you ask whether God can be seen by us, I will reply that he can, as we read in the very true words of scripture, "blessed are the pure in heart, for they shall see God." And if you ask how the invisible God is seen by us, I will add that God is invisible by nature, but visible by his will, as he is seen by some when he will and by those whom he wishes to see him, and by many of them not as he is but in the particular guise he pleases.'[16] It is clear from these words that God is visible to creatures not by his nature, but by his will. Again, how angels are visible is briefly discussed by Augustine in the twelfth book of his literal commentary on Genesis, where he discusses how an evil spirit may be hidden in a human spirit; he gives an example of a man possessed by a spirit who in some pagan ceremony, after sacrifices had been offered and phantasms invoked with dancing and frolicking, speaks out in front of everybody, saying that 'in the wood just by us someone will be killed by a lion tonight', and the whole company will go to see the corpse, leaving the ceremonial ground quite deserted; and then it turns out just that way. And Augustine adds that this is the difference between the vision of men and the vision of spirits, that the spirits see us, whether we like it or not, but we cannot see their images unless they are shown to us. 'For I believe', he says, 'that spirits have the power to hide their appearance in spiritual ways, just as we hide our bodies behind intervening objects to avoid being seen

[15] Augustine, *De uidendo Deo* (*ep.* 147, *ad Paulinam*), c. 15 (*PL* 33. 613).
[16] ibid. c. 6 (*PL* 33. 606–607).

obstaculis quibusdam nostra corpora, ne aliorum oculis uideantur,
abscondimus'.[17] Hec Augustinus. Ex qua sententia satis claret quod
spiritus solum illuminat ex libera eleccione proprie voluntatis; ex
istis arguitur, sic noto gratia argumenti, Raphaelem, angelum ordinis
inferioris qui debet illuminari de vero sibi obscurum per Gabrielem,   215
archangelum ordinis superioris. Et arguit sic, in ista ierarchia ecclesie triumphantis, illuminacio passura Raphaelis totaliter dependet
a voluntate Gabrielis in ordine causali creato. Sed ierarchia ecclesie
militantis sequi debet ierarchicam disposicionem ecclesie triumphantis, ergo illuminacio passiua uiantium de ordine inferiori dependere   220
debet complecte a volitiua uiancium in ordine superiori. Sed constat
quod legere scripturam vulgaliter translatam est actus imperatus a
voluntate illuminandi illius qui est ordinis superioris, et non elicitur
neque inperatur a volitiua persone inferioris ordinis. Ergo talis actus,
qui est legere, repertus in inferiori, per sacramenta tantummodo pur-   225
gato, ierarchie celesti penitus est informis.

Confirmatur ratio purgandi per sacramentum a labe peccati ori-
ginalis, uel actualis mortalis contracti, est magis necessarium ad
salutem quam talem purgatum sacram scripturam cognoscere per
lecturam; set non contingit aliquem purgare se per sacramenta; sed   230
purgatur semper per personam distinctam, baptizantem in sacramento baptismi; et tunc sic, quod personam absoluentem, qui actum
purgandi rerum pure voluntarie exercet, conformiter tamen ad inten-
cionem legislatoris. Ergo conformiter purgatus sed non illuminatus
illuminari debet per operacionem voluntariam persone illuminantis,   235
qui ut sic est ordinis superioris; et ideo christianissimi principes et
sanctissimi presules predicatoribus quasi suis lluminationibus, et ut
sic eis superioribus, honorem antiquitus exhibebant.

Confirmatur ratio sic secundo, et noto statum uie angelorum ante
confirmacionem in beatitudine, et quero ab opinante scripturam   240
sacram uulgariter translatam debere tradi laicis ad legendum, cur
debet hoc fieri? Si dicat, prout puto talem dicere velle, quod tunc
inferiores possent quando uellent cognoscere eis utilia ad salutem,
et inflammancia affectum ad religiosissimam pietatem, et ego per
idem noto vnum latentem angelum ordinis inferioris excitatum ad   245
maiorem trinitatis deifice congnicionem, et continentem maiorem
obiecti beatifici fruicionem; et quero, si angeli superioris ordinis
permittant angelos inferioris ordinis speciales habere libros, in quibus per spiritualem lecturam siue specialem possent cognoscere talia

---

239 statum] statuu *with macron over* -uu *MS*   245 inferioris *om. MS,* inferioris
Deanesly, note p. 408.

---

[17] Augustine, *Super Genesim ad litteram,* XXII 47–8 (*PL* 34. 473).

by others'.[17] So says Augustine. It is quite clear on this view that a spirit only manifests itself by the free choice of its own will; and it follows from this, I may point out for the sake of the argument, that Raphael, an angel of a lower order who needs a truth hidden from him to be revealed by Gabriel, an archangel of a higher order. So he argues that in the hierarchy of the church triumphant, the passive illumination of Raphael is completely dependent on the will of Gabriel in the created causal order. But the hierarchy of the church militant should follow the hierarchical order of the church triumphant, and so the passive illumination of people on earth of a lower order should entirely depend on the will of people on earth of a higher order. It is agreed that to instruct someone to read scripture translated into the vernacular is a willing act of revelation by someone of a [higher] order, which is not brought about, nor commanded by the will of a person of a lower order. So the act of reading [scripture] on the part of a person of a lower order, albeit purified by the sacrament, is entirely repugnant to the celestial hierarchy.

This argument is confirmed in that sacramental absolution from the stain of original sin, or of mortal sins which have been committed, is more necessary to salvation than a person absolved knowing holy scripture through reading; but nobody absolves themselves through the sacraments; they are absolved by a separate person, baptizing them in the sacrament of baptism; and then the person absolving them from their sins is performing a purely voluntary act, in accordance with the intention of the law. So by analogy an absolved but not enlightened person should be informed by the voluntary operation of the person making the revelation, who is, as such, of a higher order; in this way, in the past, the most Christian princes and the holiest prelates would honour the preachers who brought them enlightenment, and were therefore their superiors.

The argument is further confirmed, bearing in mind the standing of angels before they are established in beatitude, if I ask of the proponent of translating holy scripture into the vernacular for the laity to read, why should this be done? If he were to reply, as I think he would like to reply, that then people of lower standing could when they wished learn things useful for their salvation, which would encourage their disposition to fervent piety, then I bring up the case of an angel of a [lower] order secretly desiring a greater knowledge of the divine trinity, and therefore a greater enjoyment of the object of beatitude; and ask, whether angels of a higher order would allow those of a lower order to have special books through which they would learn by spiritual or special reading things which

inflammancia affectum, sine reuelacione aliqua ordinis superioris, uel 250
non permittunt? Si dicatur quod non sunt huiusmodi libri speciales,
sed tantummodo illuminantur per revelacionem ierarchie eis prelatorum, tunc, cum Deus disposuit ad se primum principium reducere
infima per media, et ita ecclesiam militantem per triumphantem,
200rb cur debet aliquis murmurare quod nostri | intronizati pontifices non 255
permittunt suis infimis lecturam sacre scripture per cognicionem
inflammancium ad pietatem, cum hoc in celesti ierarchia, vbi uidetur esse conformis, nullatenus sic repertum? Et rogo, multitudinem
terrestris patrie tales lecturas non permittant in ecclesia militante,
quousque doceatur per aliquos sufficienter, quod sic est in ecclesia 260
triumphante; et ad sic supplicandum auctoritate beati Ieronimi, que
ponitur inter epistolas beati Augustini 59, et est ad Marcellinum
et Anapsichem, moneor vehementer.[18] 'Si', inquit Ieronimus, 'iuxta
oratorem, [silent leges] militum inter arma, [quanto magis] studia
scripturarum?' Que studia, secundum Ieronimum, incidere indigent 265
librorum multitudine, silencio, librariorum sedulitate, securitate et
ocio dictancium. Cum ergo tanta uel maior sit occupacio populi in
agris colendis, in animalibus nutriendis, seruiciis inpendendis quanta
sit occupacio militum in armis, quomodo, queso, inter tot varia non
nisi silerent studia scripturarum? Uidetur ergo bonum Ieronimum 270
wlgari populo laicali non committere studia scripturarum.

Quarto, arguo contra prefatam assertionem ex radice singula-
ritatis colleccionis legis euangelii. Docet enim Crisostomus *Super
Mattheum opere imperfecto*, omelia prima, qualem mundi corde non
indigent auxilio litterarum; sed oportet uitam prebere puram, ut gra- 275
tia spiritus sancti pro libro fieret nostris animabus. Et consequenter
deducit quod 'Noe et Abrahe et filiis eius, et Iob et Moysi non per
litteras loquebatur, sed ipse per seipsum', illorum inueniens mentem
puram; et contra dans causam, quare in his Deus Moysi legem dedit,
notabiliter ita scribit: quoniam, inquit, in malicie profundum populus 280
ceciderat Hebreorum, tunc itaque fieret quod littere et tabule fierent.
Sed hoc, inquit, non factum sanctis ueteris testamenti, neque hiis
qui in nouo, sed cessante causa, cessat effectus. Cum ergo rationaliter malicia refrenata fuit, causa quare Hebreis fuit lex data in
scripto, ut patet ex [*blank*] Crisostomo, cum populus christianus 285
iam sit infrenatus laude diuina, iuxta idem scripture, 'infrenabo te

---

259 terrestris] celestis *MS*   264 silent leges *missing from MS, supplied*   quanto
magis *missing from MS, supplied*   269 tot] tor *MS*   272 *blank for capital, guide
letter* q *MS*   274 imperfecto] perfecto *MS,* imperfecto *Deanesly*   281 ceciderat]
crederat *MS,* inciderat *Deanesly*   283–4 rationaliter malicia] rationabilitatis mali-
ciarum *MS*   285 *blank space sufficient for a short word MS*

---

[18] Jerome, *Epistola ad Marcellinum et Anapsychiam* (ep. 126) (*PL* 22. 1086).

dispose them [to fervent devotion], without any revelation by angels of a higher order, or would they not allow this? If he replies that there are no such special books, and they are only enlightened though the revelation of the order set above them, then, since God has ordained as a first principle that lower creatures should be brought back to him through intermediate creatures, and so to bring back the church militant through the church triumphant, why should anyone complain that our enthroned prelates do not permit their inferiors to read holy scripture and acquire knowledge which excites them to devotion, when no such thing is found in the celestial hierarchy, to which the hierarchy of the church seems to conform? And I ask, they do not allow reading [scripture] to the multitude on earth in the church militant until they have been sufficiently informed by [competent] persons, because that is the case in the church triumphant; and I strongly advise anyone who asks to do so to heed the authority of St Jerome in his letter to Marcellinus and Anapsyches, which is letter 59 among the letters of St Augustine.[18] 'If', says Jerome, 'according to Cicero, [the laws are silent] on the battlefield, [how much more] the study of scripture?' For study of this kind, according to Jerome, they lack the many books, the silence, the help of librarians and the security and leisure for dictating. As people work as hard or more in cultivating the fields, feeding the animals, and fulfilling the service they owe as do soldiers in arms, how, I ask, faced with so many different tasks, can they without ceasing to perform them study the scriptures? So it seems right to Jerome not to put ordinary lay people to study the Bible.

Fourth, I argue against that assertion on the ground of the uniqueness of the body of evangelical law. Chrysostom teaches us in the first homily of his *Opus imperfectum in Matthaeum* that the pure in heart need no help from texts; they should offer a pure life, so that the grace of the Holy Spirit acts like a book in our souls. He goes on to infer that 'God did not speak to Noah, or to Abraham and his sons or to Job or Moses, by means of writing, but directly in himself', finding them of pure mind; and by contrast, explaining why he gave the Law to Moses in written form, he distinctly says that the people of the Hebrews had fallen into a pit of wickedness, and he therefore ordained that they should receive it in writing and on tablets. But this was not done for the holy men of the Old Testament, nor yet for the New Testament, for when the reason for it disappeared, so did the effect. When their evil was put under reasonable restraint, the reason why the law was given to the Hebrews in writing could accordingly cease to operate, as Chrysostom makes clear; for the Christians were restrained by the praise of God, as we read in chapter 48 of Isaiah, 'for my praise will I refrain for you'. It was more appropriate that the

laude mea', Ysa.48[:9], rationabiliter cessare debet effectus, scilicet, scriptura legis. Et ad conformitatem noue legislacionis maxime congruum est offerre tabulas cordis, et ideo consequenter addit Crisostomus: non, inquit, apostolis dedit legem scriptam Deus, sed pro 290 libris promittebat se daturum esse gratiam Spiritus Sancti, 'ille enim rememorabit vobis', Jo.14[:26].¹⁹ Et Paulus inquit, hanc excellenciam demonstrans dicebat, 'non nos suscepisse legem [in tabulis lapideis sed] in tabulis [cordis] carnalibus' [2] Cor.[3:3]. Declarat differentiam lacius noui et veteris testamenti, notans quomodo lex vetus 295 scripta fuit in tabulis, et quando et vbi; pro quibus dicit quod vetus dabatur post Egipciorum destruccionem, in heremo in monte Syna, in fumo et igne ascendente a monte, buccina sonante, tonitruis et coruscacionibus existentibus; sed in nouo, inquit, testamento non sic, neque, inquit, in heremo, neque in monte, neque in fumo, in tenebris 300 nebule et fulgure, sed incipiente die, in domo omnibus considentibus, cum multa mansuetudine omnia contingebant; quia, inquit, irrationabilibus et effrenatis necesse erat indigencia fantasie, solitudinis, montis, buccine, et aliorum, exaltacionibus et persuacionibus, neque huiusmodi, inquit, erat necessitas. Nam etsi ibi sonitus factus est, 305 hoc non propter apostolos, | sed propter presentes Iudeos, propter quos et lingue ignis uise sunt, et horum dans rationem subuertit: sed, inquit, Iudei post ista uisa dixerunt, 'musto pleni sunt isti' [Acts 2:13]. Multo magis si nichil uidissent hec utique dixissent, et post pauca subiecit quod apostoli non descendebant tabulas ferentibus in 310 manibus sicut Moyses; set ipsum in mente ferentes textum sancti libri et legem, per gratiam animati, tria milia, quinque milia, ymmo orbis terrarum attraxerunt populos Deo, loquentibus omnibus aduenientibus per linguas eorum. Ex quo processu satis liquet quod lex gratie non conferebatur in Christo legiferis ministris, nec ab illis 315 communicabatur nisi aduenientibus linguis.

    Concordat cum hoc quod Dei sapientia humanata, cum esset ex tempore duodenis, reperitur in templo, in medio doctorum, audiens et interrogans, sed tunc in lege utique legens, docens per hoc ad Domini legem accedere volentes debent ad medium doctorum acce- 320 dere, et non omnium doctorum docencium in templo; sed uidete ad quales actus debent procedere, quia tantummodo ad audiendum et interrogandum, secundum Christi exemplum, quia hoc a Christo pro cursu etatis nullatenus est exemplatum.

(left margin: 200va, at line 306)

293–4 in tabulis lapideis sed *missing from MS, supplied*   294 cordis *missing from MS, supplied*   305 huiusmodi] vnius hore *MS* ascendebant titulos *MS,* descendebant tabulas *Chrysostom MS*   310 descendebant tabulas] ascendebant titulos *MS,* descendebant tabulas *Chrysostom*   312 animati] animanti *MS*

¹⁹ John Chrysostom, *Opus perfectum in Matthaeum,* hom. 1 (*PG* 57. 13–15).

new dispensation should be put forward in tablets of the heart, and so Chrysostom goes on to say that God did not give the apostles a written law, but promised that instead of books he would give them the grace of the Holy Spirit, as in the 14th chapter of John, 'he shall bring all things to your remembrance'.[19] And Paul said, bearing witness to this fine truth, that 'we have not received the law in [tablets of stone, but in] fleshy tablets [of the heart]'. He points out the difference between the Old and the New Testaments at greater length, remarking that the old law was written on tablets, and when, and where; he says that the old law was handed down after the destruction of the Egyptians, in the wilderness on Mount Sinai, in smoke and fire rising from the mountain, to the sound of the trumpet, and amid thunder and lightning; but this was not the case with the new law, which was not put forward in the wilderness nor on a mountain, nor in smoke, nor in darkness and flashes through the clouds, but at daybreak, in a house where everybody was sitting down together in an atmosphere of great calm; for there was no need of things of that kind, phantasms or solitude, or the mountain, or the trumpet and the rest of it to excite and convince the irrational and the unrestrained. Even though there was a sound [from heaven], it was not for the sake of the apostles, but for the Jews who were present, for whose sake the tongues of fire were also seen, and [the apostle] explaining it in the second chapter of Acts turns the reason for them upside down, saying that having seen these things the Jews said: 'these men are full of new wine'. They would certainly have said much more had they not seen these things, and after a while would reproach the apostles for not descending from heaven carrying the tablets of the law like Moses; but they, carrying the contents of the holy book and the law in their minds, and moved by grace, brought over to God three thousand, five thousand, indeed people of the whole world, and they spoke in their own tongue to all who were present. In is clear enough from all this that the law of grace was not handed down by Christ to his servants bearing the law, and that it was only communicated verbally to the people who were there.

In accordance with this, the wisdom of God in human form, when he was twelve years old, is found in the temple in the midst of the doctors, listening and asking questions, and then indeed reading the law; and so he taught those who were willing to assent to the law of the Lord to come into the midst of the doctors, but not into the midst of all the doctors teaching in the temple; notice therefore what they should do among the doctors, that is, they should only listen and ask questions, following Christ's example, for Christ at that age offered no example [of a teacher].

Patet ergo singularitas collacionis euangelii quia non dabatur in 325
scripto, ex quo sic arguo: sapientissimus legislator optime cunta
secundum tempora disponebat, et noticiam legis gratie non nobis
nominauit per scripturam, sed tantummodo per gratiam. Ergo
modus iste communicandi legem per prudentissimum legislatorem
est securus, ymmo securissimus, et tempori gratie congruentissimus. 330
Sed modus lectionis est alius modus a modo prefato, ergo ille modus
legendi in laicis non est admittendus, ratione alicuius perfectionis.
Sed ad oppositum ab oppinantibus ponitur iste modus ratione
perfectionis cognicionis, ergo ex consequenti racione alicuius perfectionis. Ergo cum iste modus non sit modus traditus a legislatore 335
perfectissimam legem tradente, sequitur quod conclusio ad illam
perfeccionem est inutilis, sic quod ad eandem perfeccionem sine
illo modo de communi lege quis poterit deuenire. Confirmatur
per argumentum valentem. Religio communis christiana est
perfectissima, quia a perfectissimo legislatore congnoscente quid 340
maxime est commodum subdito, et maxime diligit subditum;
et ideo, inquiunt, si priuata religio contra communem aliquid
perfectionis apponeret, sequeretur quod iste priuate religionis
institutor foret latore legis communis sapiencior, vel in volendo
subdito commodum ei foret magis affectus: quorum nullum est 345
dandum. Per idem arguo eis modus quo populus participat fuit
perfectissimus, ergo, per argumentum eorum, quilibet alius modus,
qui non est ille, est superfluus; sed modus ille quem tradit prefata
assercio non est modus legislatoris, ergo est quoad omnem rationem
perfeccionis signabilem superfluus et dimmittendus. 350

Quinto, arguo contra prefatam assercionem per subtilitatem ipsius
scripture spiritalis artificii, et contra vnum, quod ita dicunt assertores prefati, qui, ut mihi relatum est, nedum esse utile et conferens scripturam uugaliter translatam a populo legi, ymmo quod utile
foret et conferens, quod exposiciones sanctorum doctorum wlgari- 355
ter transferri et a populo legi. Ut potest confirmari hec racio tamen
secundum Gregorium, 2[3] *Moralium*, dicentem quod sancta mater
ecclesia sit cum Christo vna persona; et in scriptura fuit multa que
intelligenda sunt, secundum doctrinam Ticonii in suis regulis, neces-
2oovb saria, | et maxime ad cognoscendum transitum a capite ad aliquod 360
membrum.[20] Et nisi foret transitus, contingeret error; cum, per

327 legis] regis *MS*, legis *Deanesly*   333 ab *om. MS*   334 ergo ex] ergo ex
non sit, non sit *canc. MS*, ergo ex *Deanesly*   350 dimmittendus] dimitus (?) *MS*,
dimmittendus *Deanesly*   351 *blank for capital, guide letter* q *MS*   353 nedum]
ne dum *MS*   354 utile fo, *repetition at line break MS*   357 2] 20 *MS*

---

[20] Gregory, *Moralia super Iob*, XXIII 1 (*PL* 76. 251); cf. Augustine, *De doctrina christiana*, III 31–2 (*PL* 34. 82–3). Despite holding Donatist views, Tyconius was much ad-

Clearly then the unique character of the transmission of evangelical [law] is that it was not handed over in writing, and on this basis I
argue that the wisest of legislators arranged everything in due season
in the best possible way, and he did not communicate knowledge of
the law of grace to us through writing, but only through grace. It follows that this way of communicating the law by the most prudent of
legislators is safe, indeed the safest possible, and the most appropriate
to the age of grace. But the way of [communicating it by] reading
is a quite different way from this, and so it is not to be allowed to
the laity, on the grounds that the first way is the perfect one. But
to the contrary my opponents urge the way [of communicating it
by the written text] on the ground of the perfection of knowledge
which it brings, and so as a consequence by reason of the perfection
of this other way. But since this way is not the way adopted by the
legislator handing down an entirely perfect law, it follows that the
conclusion as to the perfection [of knowledge] is pointless, in that
anyone could acquire that perfection in ordinary religious practice
without this way [of communicating the Gospel]. It is confirmed
by a formidable argument. The common Christian religious practice
is entirely perfect, because it was ordained by the most perfect of
legislators as the most suitable for the one who is a subject, and a
subject whom he especially loves; and therefore, they say, if a private
religious order adds any form of perfection in opposition to the common practice, it would follow that the founder of that religious order
was wiser than the legislator of the common religion, or had a greater
desire in wishing what was best for the willing subject: none of which
can be true. I [on the other hand] argue on the same ground that
the way in which the people receive the law is entirely perfect, and
so on my opponents' premise any other way at all besides this way is
superfluous; and the way [of communicating the Gospel] which they
propose is not the mode of the legislator, and is therefore unnecessary
on any determinable ground of perfection, and should be discarded.

Fifth, I argue against that assertion on the ground of the subtle
spiritual artistry of scripture, and against one particular point, as
those who maintain that assertion, so I am told, believe that it would
be useful and convenient not only for scripture to be translated into
the vernacular to be read by the people, but the expositions of the
holy doctors as well. My case against this is buttressed by the remark
of Gregory in chapter 23 of the *Moralia*, that holy mother Church is
one person with Christ; in scripture there are many necessary meanings, following the rules of Tyconius, which must be understood, and
especially the transference [of meaning] from the head to a member
[of the body].[20] Unless this transference is taken into account, error

mired by Augustine as an interpreter of scripture. His rules were incorporated by Augustine into *De doctrina christiana*, and from there became a regular element in medieval
biblical exegesis.

possibile, sententiam priorem a capite, a quo fit transitus, adtribuit
sententiam de membro, et tunc crederetur secundam sentenciam de
capite ab equaliter sicut primam. Tunc talis credulitas tenderet in
errorem, quia sic legens illam sententiam crederet sic dictam esse de 365
capite Christo, que solum dicitur de membro.

Item, aliqua sententia dicitur de corpore Christi vero, cui con-
nectitur sententia de corpore Christi mistico, legens ergo vtramque
sententiam, putans utramque verificari de corpore Christi vniformi-
ter sumpto, prolabitur in errorem; sed legere exposiciones sanctorum 370
preseruat a casibus huiusmodi sic legentem. Ergo legere expositiones sanctorum erit omnino utile. Sed contra hoc arguitur per sentenciam domini Altissidiorosensis super 3^m *Sententiarum*, articulo
3°, quod ingressi in tabernaculum inuoluerunt vasa tabernaculi, sic
involuta traderent Coathitis, qui non uiderent, inquit, nec tange- 375
rent vasa tabernaculi, in signum quod simplicibus non licet per-
scrutari archana Dei; quia talis, inquit, perscrutator 'opprimetur a
gloria' [Prov. 25:27].^{21} Contigit dupliciter uidere Deum: vno modo
per fidem, et sic licet cuilibet; alio modo per scrutinium, et hoc
tantummodo licet perfectis. Sed non est magis scrutinium de Deo 380
quod cognoscendo expositiones doctorum beatorum, in variis sensibus idem veritatis lumen ostendencium. Ergo inperfectis de genere
hoc non licet, et ideo, inquit doctor, consequenter signanter dictum
est quod quinque milia plebis percussa sunt, quia plebi, inquit, non
licet Deum uidere per scrutinium. 385

Hoc idem ostendit Origenus *Super Leuiticum*, libro 4°, parte 4^a,
tractans de veste sacerdotali, vbi notat quod alia veste sacerdos vteba-
tur in exitu ad populum, et alia dum esset in misterio sacrificiorum.
Hoc, inquit, Paulus faciebat, scientissimus pontificum et sacerdotum sapientissimus, qui cum esset in cetu perfectorum, tanquam 390
inter sancta sanctorum positus, et stola perfeccionis indutus. Dicebat, 'sapientiam loquimur inter perfectos' [1 Cor. 2:6]; sapientiam,
inquam, non huius mundi, neque quisque principum huius mundi
cognouit. Sed ad populum exiens mutat stolam et alia induitur longe
inferiori quam illa, et dicit, 'nihil aliud iudicaui me scire inter vos, nisi 395
Ihesum, et hunc crucifixum' [1 Cor. 2:2]. Videns ergo, inquit Origenes, quomodo mutat stolam, quomodo aliis utpote perfectis preparat
cibos, sed docens alios inferiores lacte potat ut paruulos, alios oleribus

362 adtribuit] ad ad, *repeated at line break MS*, adtribuat *Deanesly*   371 preseruat]
preserua *MS*, praeservat *Deanesly*   372 utile] inutile *MS*, utile *Deanesly, p. 411*
n. 7   374–5 sic involuta] sunt portanda *MS*   387 sacerdotali] sacordotali *MS*
397 preparat] reparat *MS*, praeparat *Origen, Deanesly*

---

^{21} William of Auxerre, *Summa aurea*, IV 7 q.3; ed. J. Ribaillier, 5 vols (Paris 1980–87),
4. 171.

will ensue; for instance, attributing the meaning appropriate to the head from which it is transferred, to the member, and then believing it (to apply to the member) in the same sense that it first had for the head. Such credulity leads to error, as the reader of this text will think a meaning which refers only to the member is true of the head, who is Christ.

Again [it could be argued that] someone reading a text which refers to the actual body of Christ, where the meaning is linked to the mystical body of Christ, faced with both meanings, might think both applied equally to the actual body of Christ assumed into heaven, and fall into error; whereas reading the expositions of the saints would preserve him from this sort of mistake. Reading the expositions of the saints is therefore highly useful. But against this one can adduce the view of the lord William of Auxerre in the third book of the *Sentences*, article three, that [Aaron and his sons] went in to the tabernacle and covered the vessels, and handed them covered to the Kohathites, who, he says, should neither see the vessels nor touch them, in token that it is not lawful for ordinary people to gaze upon the mysteries of God; whoever does look upon them will be 'crushed by their glory'. [21] There are two ways to see God: one way is by faith, and that is open to anybody; and other is by close study, and that is only lawful for the perfect. But no study of God is closer than knowledge of the expositions of the holy doctors, who shine the light of truth upon the various senses [of scripture]. So these things are not lawful for those who are imperfect by nature, and so, adds the doctor, it was figuratively said that five thousand of the people were struck down, because it was not lawful for the people to gaze upon God by close study.

Origen proves the same point in book 4 of his commentary on Leviticus, part 4, where he discusses priestly vestments, and notes that a priest wears one sort of vestment when he goes out to the people, and another in the mystery of sacrifice. This, says Origen, is what Paul did, the most knowledgeable of prelates and the wisest of priests, who when he was in the company of the elect, that is in the holy of holies, wore the stole of perfection. He said, 'we speak wisdom among them that are perfect'; and I say, he knew wisdom, which was not the wisdom of this world, nor of the princes of this world. But when he went out to the people he took off his stole and was vested in a stole of lesser quality, and says, 'I determined not to know anything among you, save Jesus, and him crucified'. So, says Origen, seeing how he changes his stole, and how he prepares food for the others, the elect, but when he is teaching lesser folk he will feed them with milk like children, or with green vegetables like the

nutrit ut infirmos. Et quod idem fecerit Christus ostendit, dicens:
ipse autem pontificum pontifex, Ihesus, primo hoc fecerit, et ista 400
discipulis imitanda reliquit, nam euangelium refert de eo, 'quia in
parabolis loquebatur ad turbas, et sine parobola non loquebatur eis',
seorsum autem soluebat ea discipulis. Uides ergo quomodo docuit ea
ipse, aliis indumentis vti debere pontifex cum procedit ad turbas, et
aliis cum perfectis et eruditis ministrat.[22] Ex quibus patet Origenem 405
velle sentire quod ipsi sacri pontifices et sacerdotes carent communi
potestate communicandi scripturas ipsis, et hoc quocunque modo;
et cum putam illos in ierarchia ecclesiastica priuilegiari, nec ex auctoritate aliquis posse vltra pontificem, videtur tunc quod nulli liceat
turbe communicare scripturam sacram ab eis legendam. 410

Huic sentencie concordat venerabilis doctor de Lyra super Acta,
21 capitulo, dicens quomodo in populo Iudeorum aliqui maiores
scripturas legis et prophetarum scientes, et aliqui minores, scilicet
20ira layci | wlgares, scientes tantum necessaria ad salutem. Nam per omne
sabatum legebatur, Moyses, id est decalogus datus Moysi, prout dicit 415
Paulus ad Hebreos [9:19], sed subtilitates scripturarum et dicta prophetarum prefati laici ignorabant. In cuius, inquit, signum, Herodes
sciscitabatur a scribis de natiuitate Christi, et non a populis, quia fuit
secretum prophetale.[23] Hec Lyra. Cum ergo locus natiuitatis pertinet
ad articulum fidei de propinquo, et tamen hoc non debuit scire popu- 420
lus, ex consequente nec alias circumstancias de aliis credendis siue
fidendis. Sed nihil continetur in scriptura sacra nisi substantia fidei,
decem mandata decalogi, uel predictorum multiformes circumstan-
cie, ut patet ex passu superius declarante quare quatuor fuit sensus
scripture.[24] Consequens est ut ipsi laici scripturas cum doctorum 425
exposicionibus minime debeant legere, cuius tamen oppositum ponit
opinio prelibata.

Amplius confirmatur, nam ipsi Moysi legitur Deus dedisse tabulas
continentes mandata, et non dedit populo tabulas illas legendas. Et
scripture faciunt mencionem quod sacerdotes legerunt coram populo 430
in libro legis distincte et aperte ad intelligendum, sed non asserit
scriptura quod populus unquam legerit in libro Moysi. Et tamen, per
istos assertores et omnes rectiloquos, sacra scriptura sufficiens est de
utilibus ad salutem: tamen modum istum, suple, quod populus legat

411 Acta *om. MS*   412 in in *at line break MS*   420 et et *at line break MS*
422 fidendis] fiendis *MS*   nihil *preceded by* data decalog *canc. MS, error due to eye-skip*
428 moyses *canc. before* ipsi *MS*

---

[22] Origen, *Super Leuiticum*, hom. 4, trans. Rufinus (*PG* 12. 441).
[23] Nicholas de Lyra, *Postilla in Acta apostolorum* 10:35; the reference to Herod may be
a tendentious interpretation of Lyra, *Postilla in Matthaeum* 2:5.

sick. Origen shows that Christ did the same: Jesus, the high priest among priests, did this first, and left his disciples to imitate him, for the gospel says of him, 'with parables spake he the word unto the multitude, but without a parable, spake he not unto them'; and when they were alone, he expounded all things to his disciples. You can see how he himself taught these things, that a prelate should wear one set of vestments when he goes out to the people, and another when he ministers to the elect and the learned.[22] It is clear from all this that Origen wishes to convey that holy prelates and priests lacked the ordinary authority to reveal the scriptures to the people in any form; and since I hold the members of the ecclesiastical hierarchy are privileged, but that none of them can exercise any authority except that of their priesthood, it seems that none of them is permitted to open up holy scripture to be read by the people.

The venerable Dr Lyra agrees with this opinion in his commentary on [Acts?], chapter 21, remarking that among the Jews some prominent people knew the law and the prophets, and others of lower standing, that is the laity, know only what was necessary for salvation. For as Paul says in Hebrews, Moses, that is the ten commandments given to Moses, was read on every Sabbath day, but the laity were ignorant of the subtleties of scripture and the sayings of the prophets. As a sign of this Herod enquired of the scribes about the birth of Christ, not of the people, because it was a prophetic secret.[23] So says Lyra. Now, as the place of the nativity is closely related to an article of faith, and nevertheless it was not for the people to know, it follows that other circumstances of other articles of faith and belief are equally secret. But in scripture there is only the substance of the faith, the ten commandments of the Decalogue, and the infinite variety of circumstances incidental to them, as is clear from the passage above explaining why there are four senses of scripture.[24] So the laity hardly needs to know the scriptures or the doctors' exposition of them, contrary to the opinion already asserted.

This can be further confirmed, as we read that God gave to Moses the tablets containing the commandments, and not to the people to read for themselves. And the scriptures tell that the priests read from the book of the law before the people clearly and openly, so that they could be understood, but nowhere say that the people ever themselves read from the book of Moses. For both my opponents and all right-thinking people, scripture contains everything useful for salvation: but it says nothing about this way of reading it, that is,

[24] In the lost section at the beginning?

in aliquo ydiomate uel translacione, scriptura non expressit. Miror 435
quomodo predictum modum utilem voluit asserere, ex quo minime
colligitur ex scriptura.

Tercio confirmatur ratio per Raby Moysen, *De duce neutrorum,*
libro secundo, capitulo 10, ponentem quod sapientes prohibebant
plana legis populo ne pandarentur, quia illa plana vel inducunt mali 440
quam pessimam cognicionem, vel in errorem, vel incredulitatem
malam in veritatem creatoris, vel in elacionem omnimodam et nega-
cionem principatuum legis. Et subnectit, 'necessarium est', inquit,
'cuilibet scienti aliquid de his quod non reuelet populo, sicut expo-
suimus; sapientes dixerunt a principio libri usque adhuc quod "gloria 445
Domini est celare verbum"' [Prov. 25:2].²⁵ Ex quo doctoris passu
patet quod idem ex sententia doctoris Origenis et Lyre quod non
solum populo non est intimandum de relacionibus originalibus, de
attributis, uel de accidentibus eukaristie, ut exemplificat assertor opinionis contrarie, ymmo quod non est licitum intimare populo per 450
predicacionem multa plana legis; nam si scripturam haberent quam
legere scirent, tunc in disputacionem legis de facili possent prorupere,
quod summe prohibet ius ciuile.²⁶ Nam, ut patet in epistola Inno-
cencis pape ad Senonensem et Remensem archiepiscopos, et eorum
suffraganeos, et ad Bernardum, abbatem de Claravalle (et epistola 33 455
inter epistolas beati Bernardi), scripserat quomodo Marcianus, laicus
christianissimus tamen imperator, tempore predecessorum eiusdem
Innocencii, prohibuit ne clericus uel militaris uel cuiuscunque con-
dicionis de fide christiane publice tractare tenetur in posterum. Hec
ille.²⁷ Nam secundum ius ciuile, si talis miles est, milicia priuari 460
debet; homo priuatus et liber, de urbe expellatur conpetenti sup-
plicio subdendus; hec *De summa trinitatis et fide catholica*, capitulo
*nemo.*²⁸ Istis testimoniis non abest ius canonicum sed constanter ei
occurrit, prebens osculum pacifice veritatis, statuens quod laicis de
fide disputans publice uel priuate excommunicandus; *extra de hereti-* 465
cis, cap. *quicunque,* libro 6°.²⁹ Ex quibus omnibus testimoniis mihi
201rb uidetur sequi, quod propter subtilitatem | litteralis artificii ipsius
sacre scripture, et hec per doctorum plana testimonia, quod sacra
scriptura nec pro parte eius plana, nec pro parte eius obscura, nec
cum doctorum approbatorum exponentibus quomodolibet a wlgari 470
populo sit legenda.

---

448 originalibus] originbus *MS,* originalibus *Deanesly*   454 archiepiscopos]
axchiepiscopos *MS*   462 *trinitatis*] trintatis *MS*

---

²⁵ Moses Maimonides, *De duce dubiorum,* II 30; pr. *Rabi Mossei Aegyptii Dux seu Director Dubitantium aut Perplexorum* (Paris 1520), fol. 59v.
²⁶ This appears to be a reference to Ullerston's answer to his 22nd point, where he
cited philosophical topics unsuitable for lay discussion, 84–6.1592–7.

that the people should read it in some vernacular or in translation. I am amazed that [my opponent] wants to assert that this is a useful way, as it can hardly be based on anything in scripture.

The argument can be confirmed in a third way, through the remark of Rabbi Moses Maimonides in the second book of *De duce neutrorum*, chapter 10, that wise men did not allow the literal sense of scripture to be revealed to the people, because the literal sense either impels them to know evil in the worst possible way, or provokes them to error, or to wicked disbelief in the truth of the creator, or to every kind of pride, or to deny the authority of scripture. And he adds, 'any person with knowledge [of scripture]', he says, 'must not reveal anything in it to the people, as we have already written; wise men have said from the beginning of scripture until now that "it is the glory of God to conceal a thing"'.[25] In this passage of Rabbi Moses it is clear that he shares the opinion of the doctors Origen and Lyra that not only should the people be spared knowledge of original relations, of [the divine] attributes or the accidents of the eucharist, as the proponent of the opposite opinion specifies, but the people must not be informed through preaching of many aspects of the literal sense; for if they had a text of scripture which they know how to read, arguments about its meaning could easily break out, which the civil law particularly forbids.[26] For, as we read in the letter of Pope Innocent to the archbishops of Sens and Rheims and their suffragans, and to Bernard, abbot of Clairvaux (which is letter 33 among the letters of St Bernard), Marcian, a layman but a very Christian emperor, forbade, in the time of Innocent's predecessors, any clerk, knight or anybody else in whatever capacity to argue in public about the Christian faith. So says Pope Innocent.[27] According to civil law, an offender, if a knight, is to be deprived of his military status; if a free private citizen, he is to be expelled from the city and subjected to punishment, as we find in [the Code], chapter beginning *nemo* of the title *Summa trinitatis et fide catholica*.[28] Further evidence can be found in canon law, which provides many instances, displaying peaceful truth with a gentle touch while laying down that laity who argue about the faith in public or in private will be excommunicated; as appears in the Sext, *extra de hereticis*, chapter beginning *quicunque*.[29] On all this evidence it seems to me that the subtle artistry of the literal sense of scripture, on the clear witness of the doctors, precludes the reading of the Bible by ordinary people, either in its literal or in its more hidden senses, not even with the commentaries of doctors however much approved by the Church.

[27] Innocent II, *Ep.* 1547 (to the archbishops of Sens and Rheims; *PL* 179. 516).

[28] *Codex*, 1.1.4; ed. P. Krueger, 3 vols (Berlin 1954), 2. 6.

[29] *Sextus*, 5.2.2 (ed. Friedberg, 2. 1068).

Sexto et vltimo, in hac materia arguo contra sepedictam assercionem ex radice coadunacionis corporis Christi mistici. Nam apostolus Paulus, ad Coll., primo [:24], vocat corpus Christi ecclesiam militantem, dicens: 'adimpleo ea que desunt pascionum Christi in carne   475
mea pro corpore Christi, quod est ecclesia'. Et ad Ephes., capitulo primo [:22], hoc idem dicit de Christo, quod 'Deus pater dedit ipsum in caput supra omnem ecclesiam, que est corpus Christi'; et [1] ad Cor.12, c.[:12], enumeratis divisionibus gratiarum spiritus sancti, ita dicit: 'sicut vnum corpus est et multa habet membra, omnia autem   480
membra, cum sint multa, vnum corpus sunt; ita et Christus. Etenim', inquit Paulus, 'in vno spiritu omnes baptizati sumus vnum corpus, siue Iudei siue Gentiles, siue serui siue liberi' [1 Cor. 12:12–13]. Et sequitur ibidem, 'Si totum corpus oculus, vbi auditus? Si totum auditus, ubi odoratus? Nunc autem', inquit Paulus, 'posuit Deus membra   485
sicut voluit. Quod si omnia membra essent vnum, tunc corpus', inquit Paulus, 'vbi est?' [1 Cor. 12:17–19] Et idem Paulus ad Romanos 12[:4–5], 'Sicut in vno corpore multa membra habemus, omnia membra autem non eundem actum habent, ita multi vnum corpus sumus in Christo, singuli autem alter alterius membra'. Ex quibus testimoniis   490
apostolicis irrefragabilibus patet, omnes per baptismum Christi et ecclesiam renatos cum distinctis actibus correspondentibus distinctis membris, concurrere per vnionem spiritus Dei in vnionem corporis Christi mistici; ex qua sententia catholica omnes fideles, renati sacramento baptismi, sunt membra Christi. Noto tunc membra Christi   495
comparata manibus, dorso, toraci, ventri et intestinis, cruribus, pedibus, et articulis, et sic de ceteris per A, et noto omnia membra comparata ecclesie in eodem corpore per B, et arguitur sic: ista distincta membra signata per A non possunt in actum convenientem oculis. Sed litteras legere est actus appropriatus oculis, ergo, secundum sen-   500
tentiam apostoli, non possunt competere membris signatis per A. Sed totus populus christianus wlgaris est aggregatus ex membris signatis per A, ergo ex radice coadunacionis corporis Christi mistici, iuxta mentem apostoli, sequitur populum vvlgarem textum sacre scripture legere nullatenus sic debere.   505

Confirmatur quia, dato quod sic, facio argumentum Apostoli [1 Cor. 12:17], 'Si totum corpus oculus, vbi odoratus, vel vbi pes?' Sed si pedes, qui sunt populus, scire legem deberent, tunc pedes essent oculi; uel pedes et oculi eundem actum haberent, contra apostolum ex vtraque parte, ergo et assercio est contra apostolum. Et supplico   510
reuerenciis uestris, ut secundum regulam racionis de ista practica iudicetis, an foret vtile conueniens librum ad legendum porrigere

472 Sexto] *blank for capital, guide letter* s *MS*   478 supra] sicut *MS,* supra *Deanesly*   508 tunc tunc *MS*   511 ut] et *MS*

Sixth and last, I argue against this much cited proposition on the ground of the unity of the mystical body of Christ. The apostle Paul in his epistle to the Colossians, chapter 1, calls the church militant the body of Christ: 'I fill up that which is behind of the afflictions of Christ in my flesh for his body's sake, which is the church'. In chapter 1 of his epistle to the Ephesians, he says the same thing of Christ, that 'God gave him to be the head over all things to the church, which is his body'; and in the first epistle to the Corinthians, chapter 12, after going through the different graces of the Holy Spirit, he says: 'for as the body is one and has many members, all the members of that one body, being many, are one body; so also is Christ'. He goes on, 'For by one spirit are we all baptized into one body, whether we be Jews or Gentiles, whether we be bond or free'. Then he continues, 'If the whole body were an eye, where is the hearing? If the whole were hearing, where is the smelling? But now God has set the members every one of them in the body, as it has pleased him. And if they were all one member, where is the body?' And in chapter 12 of the epistle to the Romans Paul says, 'For as we have many members in one body, and all members have not the same office, so we, being many, are one body in Christ, and every one members one of another'. It is clear from all these unimpeachable testimonies that everyone reborn through the baptism of Christ and through the church, with distinct functions corresponding to different members of the body, comes together, through the unity of the Spirit of God, in the communion of the mystical body of Christ; and by this catholic doctrine all the faithful, reborn by the sacrament of baptism, are members of Christ. If I denote the members of Christ compared with the hands, back, chest, stomach, intestines, legs, feet, joints and all the rest by the letter A, and the members of Christ compared to the church in the same body by the letter B, I infer that these distinct parts of the body cannot perform the function appropriate to the eye. But to read a written text is a function appropriate to the eye, and so, following the apostle's doctrine, this function cannot be performed by the members denoted by the letter A. But the whole mass of ordinary Christians corresponds to the members signified by the letter A, so on the ground of the unity of the mystical body of Christ, according to the apostle's interpretation, it follows that the people should by no means read the text of holy scripture.

In confirmation of this, given the above, I put forward the argument of the apostle, 'If the whole body were an eye, where is the smelling, or where is the foot?' But if the feet, that are the people, should read the scriptures, then the feet would be eyes; or the feet and the eyes would have the same function, contrary to the apostle's argument in either case, and therefore the proposition is contrary to the apostle's argument too. I beg your reverences that you will judge it reasonable if I ask about this example, whether or not it would be useful or appropriate to produce a book to be read by the foot, or the

pedi vel pedis articulo, uel non? Si decreueris quod non, tamen sub
zelo animarum hoc agere conentur prefati articuli assertores, queso
ut omnes articuli a tali incongruo iam declinent! Nam si ita bene pes 515
uel articulus pedis legeret sicut oculus, tunc corpus Christi misticum
euacuaretur in sua composicione ab illa caritatiua, et paternali, ac
201va celica armonia que ei | inesse deberet, ut patet ex apostoli sententia
superius iam discripta.

Veruptamen qualiter hec membra corporis Christi mistici habet 520
nutriri docet Crisostomus, Grecorum eximius, *Opere inperfecto
super Mattheum*, omelia 31 [*on Matt. 21:10–13*], notabiliter, per
hunc modum, notans quod plus quam illic venit in templum
Dei, sicut, dicit Crisostomus, medicus ingrediens ad infirmum,
statim de stomacho interrogat et eum componere festinat, quia, si 525
stomacus sanus fuerit, est validum ipsum corpus. Ita, si sacerdocium
integrum fuerit, ecclesia florescit, et, si corruptum est, omnium fides
marcida est. Et subnectit: sicut, inquit, stomachus recipiens cibum
coquid eum in seipso et per totum corpus dispergit, sic sacerdotes
accipiant scienciam per scripturas de Deo, et meditantes apud se toto 530
populo subministrant. Et sicut ministrante stomacho vnumquodque
membrum suscipit nutrimentum et conuertit secundum naturam
membri, ut puta quod suscipit iecur totum et sanguinem; sic,
que ascendunt ad pulmonem, fleumata, quod suscipit fel totum,
efficitur bilis; quod in mamillis, efficitur totum lac; sed, inquid, per 535
sacerdotes in ecclesia verbum omnes suscipiunt, vnusquisque tamen
conuertit illud secundum proprium cor. Ita ut idem verbum in rectis
cordibus procedat ad uitam, et in peruersis cordibus suscitet ad
iracundiam. In aliis operatur dileccionem dulcissimam, id est, lac, in
aliis fleumata, id est, odia nociua totaliter expuenda. Et consequenter 540
exponens hunc textum 'ex ore infancium perfecisti laudem' [Ps. 8:3],
distinguitur inter pastum per miraculum et pastum per scripturam,
ita docet ad propositum pertinenter: lac, inquit, sine labore et
opere dencium manducatur, et manducantem sua suauitate delectat.
Sic miraculum nec laborem videntibus inponunt, sed uidentes 545
admiracione delectantur, et ad fidem nos molliter inuitant. Panis
est perfeccionis doctrina et iustitie, quam accipere non possunt
nisi sensus exercitati fuerint circa spiritualia: quoniam qui audit
necesse habet se tractantibus discutere et meditari, de quibusdam
spiritualibus dentibus molere, vnde et lex ruminancia animalia 550
munda wlt esse [*cf.* Deut. 14:6]. Et sicut, inquit Crisostomus,
si infanti dederis fragmentum panis, quia angustos dentes habet,
suffocatur amplius quam nutritur; sic homini imperfecto in fide et

---

521 *Opere om. MS*   535 bilis] bibit *MS*, bilis *Deanesly*   553 imperfecto]
perfecto *MS*, imperfecto *Chrysostom*

toe? If you determine that it would not, and the proponents of the toe should persevere in their zeal for souls, I ask all toes to refuse to do anything so absurd! For if a foot or a toe could read successfully like an eye, then the composition of the mystical body of Christ would be deprived of the kindly, paternal, celestial harmony which should inhere in it, as is implicit in the doctrine of the apostle set out above.

The excellent Greek doctor Chrysostom, moreover, distinctly teaches us how in his view the members of the mystical body of Christ are nurtured, in his commentary on Matthew, homily 31, noting that he not only went into the temple of God like a physician visiting a sick man, but first examined the stomach and promptly took action to heal it, since, if the stomach were healthy, the whole body is strong. So if the priesthood is sound, the church flourishes, but if it has been corrupted, the faith of the whole church withers away. Then, he adds, just as the stomach takes in food, digests it within itself and disperses it throughout the body, similarly, priests take in knowledge of God through the scriptures, reflect upon it, and pass it on to all the people. And as digestion in the stomach sustains each particular member with nourishment, converting it all, according to the nature of each part of the body, into the liver for instance, or the blood; what rises to the lungs becomes phlegm, what sustains the gall-bladder becomes bile; what goes into the breasts is all converted into milk—so, in the church, Chrysostom continues, the word sustains everyone through the priesthood, and each person converts it according to his particular character. So the same word will confer life on well-ordered dispositions, and excite disordered temperaments to anger. It will produce the milk of human kindness in some, and in others the phlegm of destructive hatred, which should be utterly spat out. In his exposition of the text 'out of the mouths of babes you have crafted praise', he distinguishes between nourishment through miracles and nourishment through scripture, and teaches us something relevant to the issue: milk is swallowed without effort and use of the teeth, and its gentleness gives pleasure to its consumer. Likewise, a miracle demands no effort from those who see it; the onlookers are gratified by the spectacle, and this encourages us to an easy faith. But bread is the teaching of perfection and equity, which cannot be ingested unless the senses have been trained in spiritual matters: the recipient needs to discuss them with his teachers and to think about them, to chew them over in his teeth, and so scripture encourages ruminant animals to be cleansed. If, he continues, you give a piece of bread to an infant whose teeth are weak, it chokes him more than it nourishes him; equally, if you impart the higher mysteries to a man not yet perfect

puro sensibus si alciora misteria volueris dicere, eius angusta fides
magis scandalizatur quam edificatur. Set si viro perfecto dederis lac, 555
quod fauces eius delectat, membra tamen non confortat; sic, si ei
miracula ostendis, delectantur quidem aspectu, sed nihil proficit ad
edificacionem aut noticiam ueritatis.[30] Hec Crisostomus. Ex qua sentencia patet quod sacerdocium solum pro toto populo doctrinam
201vb hauriet, a quo sicut a stomacho sunt nutrimentum ac|cepturi. 560

Quia multi opinantur litteram sacri codicis posse reficere, audiant
sententiam Augustini *Super Iohannem*, omelia 9ª, declarantis
quomodo hoc fuit inicium signorum, quod Christus in nupciis
mutauit aquam in uinum. 'A prophetie dispensacione', inquit
Augustinus, 'nulla tempora cessauerunt. Vinum', inquit, 'in aqua 565
quodamodo latet; sic', inquit Augustinus, 'si in prophetiam
Christus non intelligatur, ipsa prophetia aqua erit. Lege', inquit
Augustinus, 'omnes libros propheticos non intellecto Christo, quid
tam incipidum fatuumque inuenies? Sed intellige Christum, et
non solum sapit quod legis sed eciam inebriat, mutans mentem a 570
corpore, ut preterita obliuisceris in ea que autem sint extendaris'
[Phil. 3:13].[31] Hec Augustinus. Quod autem eunuchus Candacis
regine Ethiopum quo et eunucho, ut testatur Ieronimus, non fuit
Ieronimus sanctior ymmo nec eo studiosior, ut patet in epistola
33, cum interrogaretur an intelligeret que legerentur, respondit et 575
'Quomodo', inquit, 'possum, nisi aliquis me docuerit?'[32] Et cum
sic Augustinus, prophetia est quid incipidum, ymmo fatuum, cum
pro cognomine habeat nomen pincerne, cuius est bonum uinum
diligere.[33] Cernam membra corporis Christi mistici iam inebriati
in parte uidetur eadem membra aqua insipida, id est, populum 580
christianum, pro quadam collacione spirituali reficere, sed hec facere
nituntur, qui corticem littere intellectum difficilem ad legendum
populo consulunt. Ego uero pedibus uel manibus ad legendum
libros offerre nolo, nec eis ad manducandum quibus non nutriantur
porrigo. Sed purgare stomachum corporis Christi mistici exhortor in 585
Domino, asserens cum Crisostomo hoc esse potestissimum medium,
vt sub capite Christi eius corpus misticum nullatenus infirmetur, sed
in sanitate Dei perpetuo conseruetur. Ex quibus omnibus plane patet
quod ego grosse senserim de translacione scripture in quecumque
wlgaria, contra affirmacionem eius simplici via occurrens. Quarum 590
prima est ex allectiua condicione sacre scripture; secunda est ex

556 fauces] faucos *MS*   584 nolo] volo *MS,* nolo *Deanesly*

---

[30] Pseudo-Chrysostom, *Opus imperfectum super Matthaeum*, hom. 38 (*PG* 56. 839, 843).
[31] Augustine, *Tractatus in euangelium Iohannis*, tract. 9 (*PL* 35. 1459).
[32] Jerome, *Epistola ad Paulinum presbyterum* (*ep.* 53, 'Frater Ambrosius') (*PL* 22. 543–4).

in faith or pure in disposition, their weak faith will be scandalized, not edified. But if you were to give milk to a grown man, it may soothe his throat, but it would not nourish any of his parts; similarly, if you show him miracles, you may give pleasure to his sight, but in no way would you edify him or enhance his knowledge of the truth.[30] So says Chrysostom. It follows from his teaching that only the priesthood can expound the faith to all the people to receive like nourishment to the stomach.

All those who believe that the literal sense of holy writ can refresh [the soul] should attend to the words of Augustine in his 9th homily on John, explaining that the first of the signs was when Christ, at the wedding feast, changed the water into wine. 'There has been no age', he says, 'without the dispensation of prophecy. The wine was somehow latent in the water; but if Christ is not discerned in a prophecy, that prophecy will be water. Read all the books of the prophets without understanding that Christ [is intended], and do you not find them insipid and pointless? But understand Christ in them, and the text not only has a savour but actually intoxicates you, releasing the mind from the body, so that you forget those things which were behind and reach forth unto those things which are before.'[31] So says Augustine. Jerome tells us in his letter 33 that he was himself no holier nor more learned than the eunuch of Queen Candace of the Ethiopians, who when asked [by Philip] whether he understood what he read, replied 'How can I, except some man should guide me?'[32] And so if—as Augustine puts it—a prophecy is an insipid thing and deeply pointless, then one should take as one's surname the name of a butler, whose job it is to seek out the good wine.[33] I will see that the members of the mystical body of Christ, that is, the Christian people, now somewhat inebriated it seems with tasteless water, are restored with some spiritual refreshment, a task which those who prescribe for them the reading of the nearly in-comprehensible husk of the literal sense [of scripture] will struggle to perform. I have no wish to offer the feet and the hands books to read, nor to provide them with food which cannot nourish them. But I do urge you in the Lord to purge the stomach of the mystical body of Christ, as I agree with Chrysostom that this is the indispensable means by which, under the headship of Christ, his mystical body, far from being weakened, will be preserved in the perpetual health of God. From all I have said it will be very clear what I think in general about the translation of scripture into any vernacular: I simply oppose that proposition. The first ground is the alluring character of holy

---

[33] On Butler's pun on his own name, a convention in a *principium* address, see the introduction, pp. xxxvi, xli.

defectiua intellectione humane nature; tercia est ex ierarchica disposi-
cione angelice creature; quarta ex singularitate collacionis legis euangelii, quinta ex subtilitate scripture litteralis artificii; sexta est ex
condicione coadunativa concurcionis membrorum corporis Christi 595
mistici. Hec sunt dicta cum omni reuerencia oppositum mihi opinancium, uires cognicionis mee nimium excedente, absque inpacti-
uorum verborum misera garrulitate.

Explicit determinacio fratris et magistri Willelmi Buttiler ordinis
minorum, regentis Oxonie. Anno domini M°CCCC° primo. 600

596 oppositum] omni *MS,* oppositum *Deanesly*   598 garrulitate] christianitate
MS, garrulitate *Deanesly, p. 418*

scripture; the second is the defective understanding of human beings; the third is the hierarchical arrangement of the angelic order; the fourth is the uniqueness of the body of evangelical law; the fifth is the subtle artistry of the letter of scripture; the sixth is the combination in unity of the members of the mystical body of Christ. I say this with all reverence for my opponents, who far outmatch me in the strength of their knowledge, and with no unpleasant outpouring of offensive language.

Here ends the determination of Friar and Master William Butler of the order of friars minor, regent master of Oxford, in the year of the Lord 1401.

THOMAS PALMER

*De translacione scripture
sacre in linguam anglicanam*

*On the Translation of
Holy Scripture into English*

Cambridge, Trinity College,
MS B. 15. 11, fols. 42vb–47va

Thomas Palmer *De translacione scripture sacre in linguam anglicanam*

42vb 1°. Utrum sacra scriptura in liguam Anglicanam uel in aliam barbaricam sit transferenda, et quod sic videtur, nam licet illam predicare et docere, igitur et scribere, et hoc in omni lingua eis nota, qui ad seruandam illam et obseruandam obligantur. Multi Anglici uel barbarici sunt huiusmodi. Igitur, etc. 5

2°. Sic, omnis lex recte viuendi aliquibus tradita, que confert uitam obseruatoribus et mortem transgressoribus, est in lingua eis nota habenda. Sacra scriptura est huiusmodi. Igitur, etc. Iohannis 5[:39], 'scrutamini scripturas in quibus putatis vitam eternam'.

3°. Sic, scriptura librorum inuenta est \in/ remedium obliuio- 10 nis, ad iuuandam memoriam, quia labilis est memoria hominis; sed tradere sacram scripturam obliuioni, in qua tota lex recte viuendi continetur veteris et noui testamenti, est maxime periculosum. Igitur illa in vulgari nostro propter labilitatem memorie est habenda, et sic in illa est transferenda. 15

4°. Sic, nullus recte obligatur ad obseruandum legem aliquam ignotam; sed vtraque lex, noua et antiqua, est vulgo ignota quousque in vulgari habeatur, quia vulgus nullam aliam intelligit nisi propriam et vulgarem. Igitur vulgus non obligatur ad sacram scripturam obseruandum: ideo licet vulgo habere illam translatam in linguam suam 20 quam solam intelligit.

5°. Sic, iam habetur in Hebraico, Greco, Latino, Caldaico et Gallico, et iam necessarium est Anglicum et barbarum habere illam sicut

43ra predicti; | igitur eque est habenda a nobis in Anglico sicut et illis in vulgari suo. 25

6°. Sic, dicitur quod Beda venerabilis totam scripturam transtulit in linguam Anglicam, ne lingua sua barbarica videretur, quod non fecisset nisi licuisset. Igitur, etc.[1]

7°. Sic, quilibet tenetur vitare peccatum mortale; quod non potest nisi cogitando quale peccatum sit mortale; quod sciri non potest a 30 laicis nisi per doctrinam in lingua propria et vulgari, cum nullam aliam intelligat. Igitur etc.

8°. Sic, non solum tenemur scire que sunt fugienda sed etiam que timenda, que credenda, que sunt facienda, que sunt speranda et alia sacramenta quecumque omnia, que necessaria sunt ad salutem. Igitur 35

TITLE: Palmer de translacione scripture sacre in linguam barbaricam *MS; for title adopted here see p. cxxiii.* 1 1° *om. MS* 10 in remedium] *originally* obremedium, ob *canc.,* in *add. MS* 11 memoriam] memoria *MS,* memoriam *Deanesly* 23 illam] illa *MS,* illam *Deanesly*

Thomas Palmer, OP: On the Translation of Holy Scripture into English

1. The question is whether holy scripture should be translated into English or any other vernacular language. It seems that the answer is yes, because it is lawful to preach it, to teach it, and therefore to write it, and in every language known to those who are bound to respect it and observe its precepts. Many English and barbarian peoples fall into that category.

2. Again, every rule of right living laid down for particular people, which gives life to those who observe it and imposes death on those who flout it, should be available to them in a language which they know. Holy scripture is one such rule: for, in the 5th chapter of John, 'search the scriptures for in them you think you have eternal life'.

3. Again, books in writing were invented to help the memory, as a remedy for forgetfulness, as the memory of man is faulty; but to let holy scripture, in which the whole of the Old and the New Testaments' rule of right living is contained, fall into oblivion is especially dangerous. It should therefore be available in our vernacular as a prompt to faulty memory, and so should be translated into that tongue.

4. Again, nobody is obliged to observe a law which is unknown to them; but both the old and the new law are unknown to ordinary people unless they are available in the vulgar tongue, as they know no other vernacular but their own. So they are not obliged to observe holy scripture [unless] it is lawfully translated into the only language they know.

5. Again, [the Bible] can already be read in Hebrew, Greek, Latin, Aramaic and French, and now it needs to be available to the Englishman and barbarian in the same way; it should be just as available to us in English as it is to others in their own vernacular.

6. Again, we learn that the Venerable Bede translated the whole of scripture into English, so that his language would not be deemed barbarian, which he would not have done had it not been lawful.[1]

7. Again, everyone is obliged to avoid mortal sin; but nobody can do this without knowing which sins are mortal; and this can only be known by lay people through being instructed in it in their own language, since they know no other.

8. Again, we are obliged to know what must be rejected and what must be avoided, what must be believed, what must be done, what must be hoped for and all other sacraments whatever, which are necessary for salvation. It is therefore lawful for you to have it

[1] Thomas Aquinas, *In Politica*, I 22; ed. R. M. Spiazzi, *S. Thomae Aquinatis Doctoris Angelici In libros Politicorum Aristotelis expositio* (Turin 1951), 8).

licet tibi habere hoc in scriptis, et hoc in vulgari tuo, quia nullam aliam linguam intelligis; igitur sic curati tenentur predicare, et populum eis subiectum informare de necessariis ad salutem. Secundum illud Marci vltimo [16:15], 'Predicate euangelium omni creature'.

[9.] Sic, multi in casu sunt muti, et aliqui surdi, qui in scientia non 40 possunt vti vocibus sed scripturis. Igitur licet propter tales habere totam sacram legem in scriptis.

10°. Sic, que habentur in vulgari et in lingua eis nota magis mouent ad deuocionem, ad Deum laudandum et diligendum; igitur in tali lingua sunt habenda. 45

11°. Sic, omne quod licet mihi loqui licet mihi scribere; sed vtramque legem licet mihi predicando, disputando, defendendo loqui; igitur licet eam scribere. Nichil valet eam scribere in lingua ignota; igitur scribenda est in lingua nobis nota, ut in vulgari nostro.

12°. Sic, posset contingere quod nullus Latinus esset inter barbaros 50 et Anglicos propter guerras uel inimicicias capitales, et dato quod esset, et nullus eorum sciret linguam nostram, et sic nec interpretari illam posse nobis, sicut si vnus Hebreus uel Grecus esset inter Latinos ignorans Latinam, nulli posset interpretari in lingua nostra. Igitur nisi haberemus sacram scripturam in vulgari nostro, non erit nobis 55 via possibilis ad sciendum illam, et cum obligamur ad illam faciendum quia obligamur ad illam obseruandam. Igitur irremediabiliter essemus astricti ad peccandum.

13°. Sic, 'quecunque scripta sunt ad nostram doctrinam scripta sunt' [Rom. 15:4]; sed modicum valet scriptura ad nostram doctri- 60 nam, nisi fuerit scripta in lingua quam intelligimus, sola talis est vulgare nostrum. Igitur, etc. |

43rb 14°. Sic, scriptura ignota non intellecta modicum valeret ad correcionem nostram, sed 'quecunque scripta sunt ad nostram correctionem scripta sunt' [1 Cor. 10:11]. Igitur cum tantum scriptura in 65 vulgari nostro tradita est nobis vtilis, et ad correctionem nostram vtilis, igitur scriptura sacra, cum sit nobis vtilis et tam necessaria in vulgari nostro, habenda est in scriptis.

15°. Sic, 'necesse est impleri omnia que scripta sunt', Ioh.2[:17],² igitur necesse est inpleri omnia que scripta sunt nobis in vulgari 70 nostro in Anglico, quia hoc sunt aliqua scripta, sicut ea que scribuntur in Latino, Greco uel Hebreo; et si necesse est omnia

39 Math' MS, Marci Deanesly   40 MS has no section 9; the two sentences here are perhaps the relic of a longer section abbreviated by eye-skip. The sections that follow go on from 10.   Sic] sed MS, sic Deanesly   41 scripturis] scripturas MS   58 peccandum] Deanesly read praecavendum and suggested emendation to praevaricandam—a possible lectio difficilior?

---

² A paraphrase rather than quotation.

in writing, and in your own vernacular as you understand no other tongue; and so those with cure of souls are obliged to preach these things, and to instruct those in their care of the things necessary for salvation. Accordingly we read in the last chapter of Mark, 'Preach the gospel to every creature'.

[9.] Again, many are, as fate would have it, mute, and some are deaf, and are unable to make use of voices in matters of learning, but instead depend on writings. So for these reasons it is lawful to have available the whole Bible in writing.

10. Again, [the scriptures] available in the vernacular and in the language known to [the people] move them to greater devotion, to praise and to love God; so they should be available in the popular tongue.

11. Again, everything which it is lawful for me to put into spoken words is lawful for me to write down; but it is lawful for me to expound both the Old and the New Testament, by preaching, disputing and defending them; it is therefore lawful to write them down. There is no point in writing them in an unknown language; so they may be written in a language known to us, such as our own vernacular.

12. Again, it could happen that because of wars and major conflicts no Latin speaker remained among the English and barbarian nations, and if it were the case that none of them knew our language and could not interpret their own for us, like a Hebrew or a Greek, living among the Latins, who knew no Latin, and so could not translate for us any part of scripture. In that case, unless we had holy scripture in our own vernacular, there would be no possible way for us to get to know it, as we are obliged to do since we are bound to observe its rules. We are therefore bound absolutely to avoid this situation.

13. Again, 'whatsoever things were written aforetime were written for our learning'; but there would be no virtue in writing it for our learning unless it were written in a language which we understand, the only one of which is our vernacular.

14. Again, scripture, if unknown and not understood would do nothing to amend our conduct, but 'whatsoever things were written, were written for our admonition'. But since scripture given to us in the vernacular is useful to us and useful for our admonition, it is useful and indeed necessary in our vernacular, and should be available in writing.

15. Again, 'all things which are written must be fulfilled' as we read in the second chapter of John's gospel, [2] and therefore all things must be fulfilled which are written for us in English in our own vernacular, because some things are written in this [language], just like those which are written in Latin, Greek and Hebrew; and if

scripta in Anglico impleri, necesse est omnia scripta in Anglico esse.

16°. Sic, Deutero.6[:5–9] sic scribitur de lege, 'Audi, Israel: Domi- 75
nus deus tuus unus est; diliges Dominum Deum tuum ex toto corde
tuo, scribe uerba hec, que precipio tibi hodie in corde tuo; narrabis
ea filiis tuis et meditaberis sedens in domo tua, ambulans in itinere;
scribes ea in limine et hostiis domus tue'; igitur, eadem ratione, in
libris Anglicanis.   80

17°. Sic, Deutero.31[:25–7], postquam Moyses scripsit uerba legis
huius in volumine, decem mandato Domini, precepit Leuitis, dicens,
'tollite librum illum et ponite in latere arche federis Domini, ut sit
ibi contra te in testimonium'. Igitur, conformiter, licet nobis habere
legem nostram in vulgari nostro; confirmatur, quia tam necessarium 85
est nobis Anglicis et aliis barbaris habere legem nostram in vulgari
nostro, sicut Hebreis, Grecis aut Latinis in suo, ut eam sciamus et
obseruemus, cum nullam aliam intelligimur, exceptis paucis litteratis.

18°. Sic, secundum regulam rationis, omnia intelligimur esse con-
cessa, que expresse non sunt prohibita; sed non inuenitur in tota 90
sacra scriptura prohibitum quod ipsa sic transferatur in ydioma barbaricum.

Igitur propositum. Pro autoritate nota distinctionem 26, *qualiter*.[3]

1. Ad oppositum, etc. Nulla vulgo inutilia sunt in vulgari nostro
habenda, quia nocerent plus quam prodessent. Sed multa in scriptura 95
sunt huiusmodi; Hugo de Vienna *Ecclesiastici* tertio: inutilia non sunt
\in/uestiganda neque habenda neque scribenda; ut quare musca aut
43va pules tot habet pedes, et | camelus tantum quattuor, et homo tantum
duos.[4] Item: 'reprobatio quod fuit precedentis mandati propter infirmitatem et invtilitatem eius' [Heb. 7:18]. Sed quod est reprobatum 100
non est in vulgari non habendum uel scribendum, quia esset causa
erroris. Igitur, etc.

2°. Non omnis ueritas est scribenda in Anglico, quia multe sunt
inutiles; sed omnis ueritas continetur in sacra scriptura secundum
Lollardos, quia continet primam ueritatem que continet omnes alias 105
ueritates.

3°. Sic, multa sunt occultando et non populo ostendendo, ne
nota et vsitata vilescerent; vnde dicit Carnocensis super primum

76 unus *add. Deanesly*   78 sedens] edens *MS*, sedens *Deanesly*   94 *marginal
heading* Ad oppositum   96 sunt huiusmodi] *uncertain;* sunt huiusmodi *Deanesly*
99 mandati] mandata *MS*, mandati *Deanesly*

---

[3] Apparently a marginal note incorporated into the text; the reference is unidentified.
[4] Hugh of St Cher, *Postilla in Ecclesiasticum* 3:22; pr. *Postilla in totam Bibliam*, 7
vols ([Basel 1498–1502]), unpaginated.

all things which are written in English must be fulfilled, they must necessarily be written in English.

16. Again, we read about the law in the 6th chapter of Deuteronomy, 'Hear, O Israel: the Lord your God is one God; you shall love the Lord your God with all your heart, and these words, which I command you this day, shall be in your heart; and you shall teach them diligently to your children, and shall talk of them when you sit in your house, and when you walk by the way; and you shall write them upon the posts of your house, and on your gates'; and therefore, by the same token, in English books.

17. Again, we read in the 31st chapter of Deuteronomy, that after Moses had written the words of this law, that is the ten commandments of the Lord, in a book, he commanded the Levites, saying, 'take this book and put it in the side of the ark of the covenant of the Lord, that it may be there for a witness against you'. Accordingly, it is lawful for us to have the law in our own vulgar tongue, and this may be confirmed as it is just as necessary for us English and other barbarian peoples to have our law in our own vernacular, as it is for the Hebrews, Greeks and Latins in theirs, so that we can learn it and observe it, since, apart from a few literate people, we know no other.

18. Again, following the rule of reason, we understand that all things are allowed, which are not expressly prohibited; but in the whole of scripture we find no prohibition on translating it into a vernacular language.

Note for an authority on this proposition, distinction 26, *qualiter*.[3]

Arguments on the opposite side:

1. Nothing which is of no popular use should be available in our vernacular tongue, because it would do more harm than good. But there are many things [of this kind] in scripture, as Hugh [of St Cher] says on the 3rd chapter of *Ecclesiasticus*: useless topics are not to be enquired into or set out or written down; such as why flies or fleas have so many feet, while camels have just four, and human beings only two.[4] Again: 'for this commandment is indeed annulled, as weak and unprofitable'. But what has been annulled should neither be set out nor written down, because it would be a source of error.

2. Not all truths should be written in English, as many are of no use; but all truth, according to the Lollards, is contained in holy scripture, as it has in it the first truth, in which all others are included.

3. Again, many things should be hidden away and not shown to the people, to avoid cheapening them by familiarity and over-exposure; Carnotensis says accordingly on the first *Confitemini* that the gold

Confitemini quod si in lamina aurea mitre sopremi pontificis scri-
bebantur quattuor littere magni nominis Dei in tetragramaton, *ioth*, 110
heo, wach, hoth sine apicibus, cum ne notum esset vulgo magnum
nomen Dei, quia sic per illud frequenter et horribiliter iurassent,
sicut non faciunt christiani, et multipliciter inhonorassent.[5] Illi enim
apices diuersitudine a tergo, pro et ex vtraque parte per et si debite
erat apposite, illis litteris significabunt *hia, haue, hia, houem*, que 115
dictiones in Latino significant *qui est, qui erat, et qui venturus est.*
Igitur conformiter, cum multa de scriptura in honore sint habenda,
expedit ut a vulgo occultentur ne vilescant.

4°. Sic, nulla habenda sunt in vulgari que simplicibus essent occasio et causa erroris, quia facilius potest vulgus duci in errorem. Sed 120
multa de scriptura in vulgari nostro translata, male intellecte, ducerent simplices in errorem; nam si Arrium, Sabellium, Nestorium et
Frontinum et alios hereticos difficultas illius ducat in errorem, et a
forciori simplices in errorem ducerent!

5°. Sic, nulla sunt reuelanda aliquibus qui non sunt talium capa- 125
ces; sed multarum difficultatum sacre scripture non sunt tales laici
capaces. Igitur saltem talia in vulgari nostro non sunt scribenda;
ideo Ecclesiastici 3°[:25–6], 'plura sunt supra sensum hominum', id
est transcendunt intellectum et rationem, et 'multos supplantauit
43vb suspicio', id est fidei fun|damentum subripuit et a ueritate deiecit 130
in errorem: 'alciora te ne quesieris' [Ecclus. 3:22]. Et 'qui scrutator
est magestatis oprimetur a gloria', Prouer.25[:27].

6°. Sic, illa que diminuerent meritum fidei simplicium non sunt eis
in vulgari tradenda. Huiusmodi sunt multa in scriptura, vnde Ecclesiastici 3°[:23], 'multa abscondita sunt a Domino tibi'; ubi Hugo in 135
glossa reddit causam: 'propter', inquit, 'meritum fidei, quia secundum Gregorium, fides', inquit, 'non habet meritum cum humana
ratio probat experimentum'.[6] Contra tunc noceret clericis respondet
taliter si non aliter traderent.

7°. Sic, stultum est solicitum esse circa illud quod sine periculo 140
ignoratur; sed multa sacre scripture sine periculo a simplicibus igno-
rantur, quia transcendunt ingenium eorum. Non igitur oportet soli-
cite illa scribere in vulgari.

110 esset vulgo magnum nomen dei quia sic per illud frequenter *all canc. before* nominis
dei *MS*   111 note *canc. before* apicibus *MS*   120 vxorem *canc. before* errorem
MS   138 experitum *canc. before* experimentum *MS*   143 soli|te *at line break*
MS, sollicite *Deanesly*

---

[5] Unidentified. The passage does not occur in the commentaries of either Ivo of
Chartres junior ('Carnotensis') or Gilbert of Poitiers on the psalm *Confitemini* (104);
see discussion on p. lix, note 135.

[6] Hugh of St Cher, *Postilla in Ecclesiasticum* 43:36; Gregory, *Homiliae XL super euangelia*, hom. 26 (*PL* 76. 1198).

plate on the mitre of the chief priest has written on it four letters in a tetragrammaton, *ioth*, *heo*, *wach*, *hoth* without the vowel points, so that the great name of God should not be known, and should not be dishonoured time and again, as Christians do not, in frequent and horrible oaths.[5] For these vowel points, if they were properly placed among the letters in their particular ways on the back, front and each side, would read *hia*, *hawe*, *hia*, *houem*, which means in Latin *qui est, qui erat, et qui venturus est*, who is, who was, and who will come again. So accordingly, as there are many things in scripture which should be held in honour, they are rightly concealed so that they are not vulgarized.

4. Again, nothing should be open to ordinary people which might cause uneducated minds to fall into error, for it would make it easier for the people to be led into error. But there are many things in scripture which, imperfectly understood in translation into our vernacular, would lead such people into error; for if its difficulties could lead Arius, Sabellius, Nestorius and Frontinus into error, how much more easily would it do the same for simple folk!

5. Again, nothing should be revealed to people who are not capable of grasping it; and the laity is not capable of grasping the many difficulties of holy scripture. For that reason these difficult passages should not be written down in our vernacular; as we read in the 3rd chapter of Ecclesiasticus, 'many things are beyond human understanding', that is, they transcend the mind and the reason, and 'many are deceived by their own vain opinion', which takes away the root of their faith and hurls them from truth into error: 'seek not out the things which are too hard for thee'. As we read in the 25th chapter of Proverbs, 'men who search their own glory shall be crushed by it'.

6. Again, anything which lessens the merit of ordinary people's faith should not be available to them in the vernacular. There are many such passages in scripture, and so we read in the 3rd chapter of Ecclesiasticus, 'the Lord has hidden many things from you'. Hugh [of St Cher] gives the reason in a gloss: 'this is because of the merit accrued by faith, since according to Gregory faith has no merit when human reason finds a proof'.[6] Then to the objection that this could be harmful to clerks, he responds that they should teach in that way if there is no other way.

7. Again, it is not sensible to take trouble with things that can safely remain unknown; but many things in holy scripture are unknown to ordinary people without any danger to them, as they are beyond their understanding. So it is not prudent to go to the trouble of writing them down in the vernacular.

8°. Sic, multa per preceptum Dei sunt occulta, non sunt in vulgari scribenda, quia sic possent contra preceptum primum omnibus   145
esse nota; sed multa misteria communicata subtilioribus et sapientibus prohibentur scribi, ne nota fiant simplicibus. Vnde Apok.10[:4],
'signa', scilicet, 'absconde que locuta sunt septem tonitrua', id est
misteria Dei, secundum glosam; 'et noli ea scribere', id est in publico
denunciare. Cuius rationem ponit ibi Gorram: quia infidelibus, fetore   150
malitie agittatis, blasphemie plusquam edificacionis materia esset.[7]
Prouer.[2]3[:9], 'in auribus insipiencium ne loquaris; quia despicient
doctrinam eloquii tui'; et Dani.12[:4], 'tu, Daniel, claude significa-
ciones et lingua libera usque ad tempus'.[8]

9°. Sic, aliqua sunt simplicibus nimis ardua, et nimis difficilia,   155
et alta, non sunt simplicibus communicanda. Nam Paulus discipulus
scribit [1 Cor. 3:1–2], 'Tanquam paruulus in Christo vobis lac potum
dedi, non escam; nondum enim poterant, sed nec nunc quidem potestis. Adhuc enim carnales estis.' Prima Cor.[2:14] sequitur, 'animalis
homo non percepit ea que Dei sunt'.   160

10. Sic, illa que simplices nollent obseruare, sed vellent pocius
propter duriciem sectam christianam spernere, non sunt admit-
tenda neque scribenda in nostro vulgari; vnde et Bygaius super illud
Apoc.10:[4], 'que locuta sunt septem tonitrua, noli ea scribere'. In
inicio fidei, donec predicatores sancti, videntes infirmitatem gen-   165
cium ad fidem veniencium, non sunt ausi austeriora eis Christi pre-
cepta committere; ne for|te duritia preceptorum territi, non auderent
44ra
ad fidem Christi suscipiendam accedere.[9] Et, ut videretur, sic fecerunt apostoli, Actis 15[:28–9]: 'placuit Spiritui Sancto et nobis nichil
inponere vobis oneris', id est conuersis ad fidem de gentibus, 'nisi   170
ut abstineatis vos ab ymolacione simulacrum et sanguine, suffocato
et fornicacione'. Igitur duriora legis non sunt infirmis scribenda et
reuelanda.

11°. Sic, secreta non sunt extraneo reuelanda: Prouer.2[5:9], 'secretum extraneo ne reueles', et Ysa.24[:16], 'secretum meum michi';   175
sed tantum amicis meis [John 15:15], 'vos nunc dixi amicos; quia
quecunque audiui a patri meo, notam feci vobis'. Igitur talia secreta

---

144 multa *add. Deanesly*   152 3] 13 *MS*   159 Cor.2] Cor 3 *MS*   animalis]
animal *MS*   165 videntes] videte *MS,* videntes *Deanesly*   166 eis] *uncertain;*
eis *Deanesly*   174 Prouer 21 *MS*

---

    [7] Nicholas Gorran, *Postilla in Apocalypsin* 10:4; pr. Gorran, *In Acta Apostolorum, Jacobi,
Petri, Johannis et Iudae canonicas epistolas et Apocalypsin Commentarii* (Antwerp 1620),
233.
    [8] Dan. 12:4, 'Tu autem Daniel claude sermones, et signa librum usque ad tempus
statutum'.
    [9] Berengaud, *Expositio super septem uisiones libri Apocalypsis,* c. 10 (*PL* 17. 865).

8. Again, [many things] are concealed by God's precept, and are not to be written in the vernacular, as thus they could become known generally, contrary to this primary precept; many mysteries imparted to subtler and wiser minds are not to be written down, in case they become known to people of a cruder understanding. Hence we read in the 10th chapter of the Apocalypse, 'seal up those things which the seven thunderclaps have uttered', which the gloss interprets as the mysteries of God, 'and write them not', that is, reveal them to anyone. [Nicholas] Gorran gives the reason: these matters would give the faithless who are excited by the stench of evil more occasion for blasphemy than for edification.[7] As the 13th chapter of Proverbs puts it, 'speak not in the ears of a fool; for he will despise the wisdom of your words'; and the 12th chapter of Daniel, 'you, Daniel, shut up the words and seal the book, even to the time of the end'.[8]

9. Again, some things are too high, too difficult and arduous for ordinary people, and should not be imparted to them. As the disciple Paul says, 'I have fed you with milk, and not with meat, as unto babes in Christ; for hitherto you were not able to bear it, neither yet now are you able. For you are yet carnal.' And in the 2nd chapter of the first epistle to the Corinthians he says, 'the natural man receives not the things which are of God'.

10. Again, the precepts which ordinary people would not want to observe, and which would cause them to reject the Christian fellowship because they are too hard, should not be received into or written down in our vernacular; as Berengaud says on the text in the Apocalypse, 'those things which the seven thunderclaps have uttered, write them not'. In the early days of the faith, holy preachers, seeing the weakness of gentile converts, drew back from imposing Christ's more austere precepts; for they might be too alarmed by the difficulty of these precepts to come forward and embrace the faith of Christ.[9] It seems the apostles did the same, in the 15th chapter of Acts: 'for it seemed good to the Holy Spirit and to us to lay no greater burden on you', that is, on Gentiles converted to the faith, 'so long as you abstain from pollutions of idols, and from fornication, and from things strangled, and from blood'. So the harder points of the law should not be written down or revealed to weaker brethren.

11. Again, secrets should not be revealed to an outsider: we read in the 25th chapter of Proverbs, 'discover not a secret to another', and in Isaiah, 'my secret unto me'; but to my friends, 'I have called you friends; for all things which I have heard of my father, I have made known unto you'. So secrets are not to be written down for

non sunt extraneis, simplicibus Deum ignorantibus, scribenda, quia
ea legere posset eque inimicus sicut amicus.

12°. Sic, illa que scripta non prodessent sed nocerent scribere vulgo   180
non deberent, quia essent contra Christi caritatem; sed talia sunt
multa. Iob 9[:28], 'verebar omnia opera mea', antecedens patet de die
mortis, de peccatis, de predestinacione et reprobacione.

13°. Sic, caritas est, palam fieri nolle quod noceat agnoscenti; sed
multa in scriptura nocerent simplicibus, quia nocerent hereticis valde   185
intelligentibus. Igitur talia non sunt eis scribenda.

14°. Sic, omnis transgressio noue legis est peccatum mortale, pro
cuius figure transgressione mors debebatur in lege veteri. Sed Aaron
et filii, videntes quod erant in sanctuario et voluta morerentur, vnde
Num.4[:15–20]: 'cumque involuerent inuoluta, et non tangunt vasa   190
sanctuari, ne moriantur. Nolite perdere populum Caat de medio
Leuitarum; sed hoc facite eis ut viuant, et non moriantur, si tetigerint
sancta sanctorum. Aaron et filii eius intrabunt, et deponent onera
singulorum, et diuident quot portare quis debeat; alii nulla curio-
sitate videant que sunt in sanctuario postquam inuoluant, alioquin   195
moriantur.' Hec fuit figura quod nulli laici in noua lege deberent
uidere secreta et sancta involuta in sanctuario sacre scripture, de quo
sanctuario Psal.72[:16]: 'estimabam ut cognoscerem hoc, labor est
ante me, donec intrem in sanctuarium Dei, et intelligam in nouissimis
eorum'. Vbi glosa interliniaris, ordinantur enim qui ineffa|bilia sacra-   200
menta contigerunt, et promoti in sacerdocii gradum, ut filii Aaron,
id est sacerdotes quibus omnia aperta et nuda videre concessum est,
vnde bonis sanctis viri percussi sunt, qui viderunt archana Domini,[10]
et legis capitulo sexto de plebe.[11] Et alia figura Deutero.2[2:6–7]: 'Si
in terra uel in arbore nidum auis inueneris, et matrem pullis desuper   205
incumbentem, non tenebis eam cum pullis, sed abire pacieris, ut
bene sit tibi et longo viuas tempore'. Que figura secundum Gregorium significat, quod sensus litteralis, qui est quasi mater aliorum
sensuum, allegorie et anagogie, dimitti debet, et pulli eius retinere,
quia 'littera occidit, spiritus autem viuificat' [2 Cor. 3:6].[12] Quomodo   210
igitur simplices illiterati, uel sola grammatica instructi, illos pollos
trium sensuum ignorantes, non errarent habentes matrem, id est
litteralem sensum, tamen de pullis non curantes?

44rb

186 non] *uncertain;* non *Deanesly*   188 fugit *canc. before* figure *MS*
191 Nolite] nolente *MS*   192 facici *canc. before* facite *MS*   202 aperta
et] et aperta *MS*   203 viri] vrri *MS,* viri *Deanesly*   204 et legis capitulo sexto
de plebe] et 50 de plebe legis sexto *MS*   204 Deutero 24 *MS*

---

[10] *GO* Num. 4:5 (vol. 1, p. 285).

[11] 'et legis . . . plebe' is apparently a marginal note incorporated in the text; perhaps a
reference to the *plebs* of the Kohathites, Num. 4:4 or 7:9.

outsiders, simple folk who know nothing of God, for an enemy could read them just as well as a friend.

12. Again, texts which would not benefit but do harm to ordinary people should not be written down, because that would be contrary to the charity of Christ; but there are many such. As Job says in chapter 9, 'I am afraid of all my sorrows', clearly referring to the day of his death, his sins, to predestination and reprobation.

13. Again, it is charitable not to desire open harm to people whom we know; but many things in scripture would do harm to simple folk, because they would do harm to [those who would become] heretics by taking hold of them intensely.

14. Again, every transgression of the new law is a mortal sin, and transgression of its prefiguration in the old law deserved death. But Aaron and his sons, seeing the things which were in the sanctuary and spread about, tarried there, as we read in the 4th chapter of Numbers: 'and when they had covered [the vessels], then [the sons of Kohath shall carry them, but] shall not touch the vessels, lest they die . . . Cut not off the tribe of Kohath from among the Levites; but do thus unto them, that they may live, and not die, when they approach unto the holy of holies. Aaron and his sons shall go in, and appoint them everyone to his service and to his burden; but they shall not go in to see when the holy things are covered, lest they die.' This text prefigured [the precept that] no lay person in the new dispensation should see the mysteries and the holy things covered in the sanctuary of holy scripture, of which we read in Psalm 72: 'when I thought to know this, it was too painful for me, until I went in to the sanctuary of God; then understood I their end'. On this the interlinear gloss says, those who touched the ineffable mysteries are ordained, and promoted to the ranks of the priests, like the sons of Aaron, that is priests who are allowed to see everything openly and without cover, as a result of which men were struck down by what was good and holy because they had seen the secret things of God,[10] and you can read about that people in the sixth chapter [of Numbers].[11] And there is another prefiguration in the 24th chapter of Deuteronomy: 'If a bird's nest chance to be before you in the way in any tree, or on the ground, and the dam sitting upon the young, you shall not take the dam with the young, but shall let her go, that it be well with you and that it prolong your days'. This signifies, according to Gregory, that the literal sense, which is, as it were, the mother of the other allegorical and anagogical senses, should be set aside, and its young retained, since 'the letter kills, but the spirit gives life'.[12] How then can ordinary illiterate people, or people who have only learnt grammar, avoid error, not knowing the young birds of the three senses [of scripture], having only the mother or literal sense and caring nothing for the senses hatched from it?

---

[12] Unidentified.

15°. Sic Ezech.47[:3–5], 'Vir qui habebat funiculum in manu sua mensus est mille cubitos, et transduxit me per aquam usque ad 215 genua, et iterum mensus est mille, et transduxit me per aquam usque ad renes; et mensus est mille, et veni ad torrentem quem non potui transire; quoniam intumuerunt aque profunde torrentis, qui non potest transuadari'. Quem textum exponit Gregorius de sacra scriptura, et in prologo ponit *Moralium*: divinus sermo sicut miste- 220 riis exercet prudentes, sic plerumque superficie simplices refouet.[13] Habet in publico vnde paruulos nutriat, seruat in secreto vnde mentes sublimium in admiracione suspendat; quasi quidam quippe fluuius est planus et altus, in quo agnus ambulet et elephas natet. Ex istis patet quod scriptura sacra in aliqua sui parte est ita difficilis quod 225 comprehendi a uiatoribus perfecte non potest, quare non \\est communicanda simplicibus in vulgari.

16°. Sic, misteria fidei non sunt communicanda simplicibus, nec// scribenda; patet Apok. X°[:4]: 'signa', id est, absconde misteria fidei, 'que locuta sunt septem tonitrua, et noli ea scribere' in publicum, 230 deueniant et in materiam blasphemie pocius quam in edificacionem conuertantur, ut dicit Gorran. Ideo Math.7[:6]: 'nolite sanctum dare canibus'.

44va   17°. Sic, Paulus [2 Cor. 12:4] 'audiuit archana | verba que non licet homini loqui', que non erant alia quam diuina misteria in sacra 235 scriptura contenta, que continet omnia. Igitur non licet illa scribere.

18°. Sic, causa putatur quare Iudei interfecerunt Christum fuit quia docuit eos intelligere sacram scripturam spiritualiter; quia 'littera occidit, spiritus autem viuificat' [2 Cor. 3:6]; et quando aliqui discipulorum abierunt retrorsum, dixit [John 6:64] 'uerba que ego loquor 240 spiritus et uita sunt'. Spiritualiter intellecta uitam efficiunt eternam. Vnde pro causa mortis eius allegabant, dixit, 'quia possum destruere templum corporis sui', Ioh.2°[:21] et Math.26[:61]. Quomodo igitur non errarent simplices ydiote circa scripturam, si eam haberent in vulgari? Nonne modo, propter malum intellectum Lollardorum 245 et simplicium gramaticorum, solum intelligentes Christi discipulos illam spiritualiter et exponentes persequntur?[14] Constat quod sic.

218 intumuerunt] intimuerunt *MS,* intumuerunt *Deanesly*   221 plerumque] *uncertain;* plerumque *Deanesly*   223 quippe] *uncertain;* quippe *Deanesly* 244 simplicium gramaticorum et solum intelligentes *all canc. before* scripturam *MS*

---

[13] Gregory the Great, *Moralia in Iob*, c. 4 (PL 75. 515).

[14] Perhaps a reference to Lollard heckling during orthodox sermons, of which the reception of Richard Alkerton's London sermon in autumn 1406 is an example. For a summary of the 'scandal' and of its perpetrator's career, see the introduction to the first of the two texts in A. Hudson (ed.), *Two Wycliffite Texts: the Sermon of William Taylor 1406, the Testimony of William Thorpe 1407*, EETS 301 (1993), xvii–xxv.

15. Again, we read in the 47th chapter of Ezekiel, 'The man that had the line in his hand measured a thousand cubits, and brought me though the waters up to the knees, and again he measured a thousand, and brought me through, and the waters were up to the loins; and he measured a thousand, and it was a river I could not pass over; for the waters were risen, a river that could not be passed over'. Gregory expounds this text of holy scripture in the prologue to his *Moralia*: the word of the Lord exercises the wise with mysteries, but refreshes the simple with the surface meaning.[13] Its public face nourishes the children, while privately it holds the minds of the wise in wonder; the water is smooth and deep, in which the lamb can paddle and the elephant can swim. It is clear from these words that scripture is too difficult in some parts to be perfectly understood in this world, and so should not be imparted to ordinary people in the vernacular.

16. Again, it is clear from the words of the 10th chapter of the Apocalypse that the mysteries of the faith are not to be imparted to simple folk, or written down: hide the mysteries of the faith, that is 'seal up those things which the seven thunderclaps uttered, and write them not' in public, in case they are changed to the matter of blasphemy rather than to any edification, as Gorran says. And note too the 7th chapter of Matthew: 'give not that which is holy unto the dogs'.

17. Again, Paul 'heard secret words, which it is not lawful for a man to utter', which were no other than the divine mysteries contained in scripture, which embraces all things. So it is not lawful to write them down.

18. Again, the putative reason why the Jews killed Christ was that he taught them to understand holy scripture spiritually; for 'the letter kills, but the spirit gives life'; and when some of the disciples went back, he said 'the words that I speak unto you, they are spirit, and they are life'. Spiritually understood, they bring eternal life. So they alleged as a reason why he should die that he said, 'I am able to destroy the temple of my body', as we read in the 2nd chapter of John and the 26th chapter of Matthew. How then could simple folk not be in error over scripture, if it is available to them in the vernacular? Do they not now, as a result of the misinterpretations of the Lollards and of simple grammar pupils, harass the disciples of Christ who understand and expound the text only in its spiritual sense?[14] Everyone agrees that this is the case.

Pro responsione in hac materia uolo ponere alias ueritates, quarum prima est illa:

[1.] Sacra scriptura in omni ydiomate et lingua quoad aliquam 250 eius partem est habenda. Probatur, omne necessarium omni homini ad salutem est in lingua sibi nota habendum, ne tradat illud obliuioni quod tenetur scire et obseruare sub pena dampnacionis eterne. Huiusmodi sunt multa in sacra scriptura contenta, prima Cor.14[:19], 'In ecclesia volo quinque uerba sensu meo legi, ut alios instruam, 255 quam [et] decem milia uerborum'; ubi Gorran dicit, illa quinque uerba esse que sunt fugienda, patet septem peccata mortalia; que sunt timenda, videlicet infernales poene; que sunt credenda, in simbolo contenta; que sunt facienda, x mandata; et que sunt speranda, premia eterna.[15] Omnia ista sunt necessaria ad salutem. Igitur hec et 260 consimilia in vulgari sunt habenda et scribenda. Pro illa ueritate sunt multa argumenta, pro parte affirmatiua questionis adducta.

2ª ueritas. Non tota sacra scriptura est in omnem linguam et linguagium transferenda. Probatur hec per argumenta ad partem negatiuam adducta, et iterum, sic. Sacra scriptura in multis locis saluari non 265 potest aliquando incongruitate et falsitate, nisi per figuras et regulas gramaticales, | sicut ostensum est in quodam tractatu quem uidi: in quo erant omnes figure gramaticales, et declarate et quotate, ubi per eas sacra scriptura in partibus suis sit ab errore seruata et defensata. Igitur in nullam linguam que regulatur regulis et figuris gramatica- 270 libus est ipsa transferenda. Probatur consequentia quia, si in lingua illis figuris regulata transferretur, esset erronea nisi illis figuris saluaretur; igitur in aliam linguam que illis non regulatur translata, esset erronea, quod non per illas excusaretur. Dicitur forte quod alie lingue per regulas, proprietates et figuras gramaticales regulantur. Contra, 275 '*barbarismus* est vicium, quod constat in coniunccione litterarum, et sillabe uel sillabarum induccione, uel earum accentibus, quo vicio barbari maxime solent vti';[16] sed dicit *Catholicon* de tropis, quod *metaplasmus* excusat *barbarismum*, qui est vicium diccionis; *scema*— *scolocismum*,[17] qui est vicium orationis; et tempus inproprietatem 280 sillabe excusans.[18] Sed hee figure non inueniuntur in Anglico, nec

44vb

---

258 infernales poene] in *followed by a blank in MS,* infernales poenae *Deanesly* 260 in simul *canc. before* omnia *MS* 269 sit] sic *MS* seru (?) *canc. before* seuata 272 transferretur] *uncertain;* transferretur *Deanesly* 281 ex *canc. before* excusans *MS*

---

[15] Nicholas Gorran, *Postilla in epistolam primam ad Corinthios* 14:9; pr. Gorran, *In omnes divi Pauli Epistolas* (Antwerp 1617), 228.

[16] Uguccione da Pisa, *Deriuationes*; ed. E. Cecchini, 2 vols (Florence 2004), 2. 116.

[17] *Metaplasmus* is the alteration of a word by addition, subtraction or transposition; *solecismus* is a grammatical mistake.

In my response to this question I would like to put forward some propositions, of which the first is this:

1. Some part of holy scripture should be available in every language or idiom. We can prove this, because everything necessary to salvation should be available to all persons, and in the language they know, so that they do not consign to oblivion what they are obliged to know and to observe under pain of eternal damnation. Many of these are contained in holy scripture, as we read in 1 Corinthians, chapter 14, 'Yet in the church I had rather speak five words with my understanding, that by my voice I might teach others too, than ten thousand words in an unknown tongue'; on which Gorran says, these five words are what must be avoided, that is the seven deadly sins; what must be feared, eternal damnation; what must be believed, which is in the creed; what must be observed, that is the ten commandments; and what must be hoped for, eternal life.[15] All these are necessary to salvation. So these and similar materials should be available in the vulgar tongue. There are many arguments which could be adduced for the affirmative side of the question.

2. The second proposition is this: not all of holy scripture should be translated into any language or dialect. We can prove this by reference to the points made on the negative side of the argument, and again as follows. Several texts in holy scripture can only be rescued from inconsistency and untruth by recourse to figures of speech and grammatical rules, as a treatise I have seen explains: it had all the figures of grammar set out and exemplified, through which the various parts of holy scripture can be justified and acquitted of error. It cannot therefore be translated into any language which is not controlled by the rules and forms of grammar. The consequence follows, that if [it were translated] into a language controlled by these forms, it would contain error unless its [original] forms were preserved, and so if it were translated into another language, not controlled by [rules and forms of grammar], it would [definitely] contain error, because it would not be justified by these conventions. It might be objected that other languages are controlled by grammatical rules, characteristics and forms. But against that, '*barbarismus* is a fault, which consists in joining up letters and introducing one or more syllables or their accents, a fault to which vernacular speakers are particularly prone';[16] but the *Catholicon* says about tropes, that *metaplasmus* [the alteration of a word by addition, subtraction or transposition] excuses *barbarismus*, which is a fault of speech; *scema* excuses *solecismus* [grammatical mistake],[17] which is a fault of prose; and metre excuses the wrong use of a syllable.[18] But these figures are not found in English or in

---

[18] ibid. 2. 768, 1111. A popular medieval encyclopedia, the *Catholicon* of Johannes de Janua (1286), drew, among other sources, on Uguccione's *Deriuationes*, and may have been Palmer's immediate source.

in ydiomate barbarico; probatur quod alique figure habent. Similiter circa medias sillabas, alique circa ultimam, alique addende, alique auferende litteras uel sillabas, ut patet in *Catholicon*; et pro maiori parte dicciones Anglie sunt monasillabe, sicut *ston, bon, non, don, gon,* 285 *man, that, math, rat*. Igitur in istis monasillabis non habent locum tales figure gramaticales, nec possunt oraciones et propositiones ab incongruitate et falsitate per eas saluari.

2°. Si proprietates vnius lingue per regulas grammaticales regu- late non possunt seruari in lingua etiam eisdem regulis regulata, a 290 forciori ille proprietates non possunt seruari in lingua barbarica non regulata illis regulis gramaticalibus. Sed proprietates lingue Latine, que regulantur, ut constat, regulis gramaticalibus, non possunt ser- uari in Greco linguagio, quod est regulis gramaticalibus regulatur. Vnde post propheciam Sibille, quam Ysidorus in sermone *De natali* 295 subiungit, hec de natiuitate, passione, resurreccione et secundo eius aduentu dicta sunt, ut si quis in Greco capita eorum versuum dicere voluerit, inueniet *Ihesus Christus Yos Thou Sothor*,[19] quod in Latinum 45ra translatis eisdem uersibus apparet [*blank*] quod | Grecarum litte- rarum proprietates potuit non adeo obseruare.[20] Hec ille. Quomodo 300 igitur proprietates lingue possent in Anglico uel in lingua barbarica, que regulis gramaticalibus minime regulatur, obseruari, non video.

3°. Sic, orationes, dictiones, proposiciones, sillabe multe non pos- sent plectro lingue formari, nec litteris Latinorum alphabeti sil- labicari, sed balbuciendo et de gutture euomendo, quasi granitus 305 porcorum uel rugitus leonum exprimendo. Quomodo igitur in lin- gua tali possent regule gramaticales fieri et proprietates obseruari non video. Littere sufficientes deficiunt ad exprimendum et sonan- dum Anglicum nostrum; in cuius argumentum alie littere minime contentis in alphabeto Latinorum sunt inuente ad exprimendum et 310 sonandum Anglicum nostrum: patet *h*,[21] ad exprimandum *ha, horo* et consimilia; et de *ȝow* ad expressionem talium: *ȝeȝyth, ȝonge, ȝor*; et de *þorn* ad expressionem talium: *þero, þat, þorwe, þenne* et huiusmodi.

5ª. Sic, non solum deficit lingua Anglicana in litteris, sed etiam

299 *blank space within a line* MS　　　sunt credenda *all canc. before* grecarum *MS*
301 lingua anglico *MS, with expunction marks under 'lingua'*　　　309 minime] *crossed* m *with superscript* a *MS*, minime *Deanesly*　　　311 h *with superscript* c *('hoc'?)* MS, *see note to translation*　　　ad ad *MS*　　　314 *there is no section 4 in MS*

[19] An approximation of Greek *Ἰησοῦς Χριστός Υἱός Θεοῦ Σωτήρ*, 'Jesus Christ Son of God Saviour'.
[20] This reference is presumably taken from a manuscript similar to Rome, Biblioteca Apostolica Vaticana, MS Reginensis lat. 125, where a sermon *de natali domini* is attributed to Isidore of Seville (it is actually from his *De officiis ecclesiasticis*, I 25), and followed, after some other sermons on the same topic, by *versus Sibyllae de judicio extremo*. The text of the verses is in Augustine, *De ciuitate Dei*, XVIII 23 (*PL* 41. 579).

any vernacular, which is established by the fact that they do have some figures [of speech]. [They do] the same with middle syllables, or indeed final syllables, by adding or taking away letters or syllables, as appears in the *Catholicon*; and the majority of English words are monosyllables, like *ston*, *bon*, *non*, *don*, *gon*, *man*, *that*, *math*, *rat*. There is, therefore, no place in these monosyllables for figures of grammar, and so the speeches and statements [of scripture] cannot be rescued from inconsistency and untruth.

Secondly, if the characteristics of a language governed by grammatical rules cannot be retained even in another language governed by the same rules, *a fortiori* they cannot be retained in a vernacular language which is not governed by those rules. But the characteristics of the Latin language, which is governed as everyone agrees by rules of grammar, cannot be retained in Greek, which is also governed by rules of grammar. So after the Sybil's prophecy, which Isidore appends to his sermon *De natali*, the words are applied to the nativity, passion, resurrection and second coming of Christ, and if anyone were to spell out the initial letters of the verses, he would get *Iesus Christus Yos Thou Sothor*;[19] and if these verses were translated into Latin it would appear as [*blank*], since [in Latin] the characteristics of the Greek letters are not retained.[20] So says Isidore. I fail to see how these characteristics of the Greek letters could be rendered in English or any other vernacular, which are hardly governed at all by the rules of grammar.

Thirdly, many [English] forms of speech, expressions, statements and syllables cannot be shaped on the tip of the tongue, or spelt out with the letters of the Latin alphabet, without stammering or clearing the throat, like the grunts of pigs or the roaring of lions. I cannot see how the rules and properties of grammar can be respected in this language. There are no adequate letters to express and reproduce the sound of our English tongue, and as a result other letters not part of the Latin alphabet have been invented to express and to represent our English: *h*,[21] for instance, to express *ha*, *horo* and so on; and *ȝow* to represent sounds like this: *ȝeȝyth*, *ȝonge*, *ȝor*; and *þorn* to represent sounds like *þero*, *þat*, *þorwe*, *þenne*, etc.

Fifthly [*sic*], English is not only deficient in letters [of the

---

[21] The spelling appears to be *hᶜ* in the manuscript. According to the *Oxford English Dictionary*, Middle English form of the letter name 'ache' points to late Latin forms '*accha*', '*ahha*', or '*aha*'.

in diccionibus: nam pro notissimis diccionibus et communissimis in   315
lingua Latina non sunt nomina neque dicciones in Anglico correspondentes; patet de istis transcendentibus, *ens, substantia, accidens*;
et etiam de predicamentis, *quantitas, qualitas, relacio, habitus,* et *posi-
cio, accio, passio, quando* et *vbi.* Sic de *fallaciis,* sicut de *equiuoca-*
cione, amphibolia, quibus non correspondent in Anglico dicciones;   320
non obstante quod illa lingua plus aliis utitur monasillabis, sed vix
per circumlocucionem exprimi possunt in eadem.

6°. Sic, si tota sacra scriptura sit in Anglicum uel in linguam
barbaricam transferenda, aut igitur de uerbo ad verbum, aut de sentencia ad sentenciam. Non primo modo, quia multe dicciones Latine   325
non habent dicciones in Anglico correspondentes, sed tantum per
circumlocuciones exprimi possunt in vulgari nostro, cuius sunt *legio,*
666 et *lustrum,* quod est spacium 5 annorum.[22] Similiter multe partes
scripture saluari non possunt ab incongruitate et falsitate nisi per
figuras gramaticales, que non habent locum in lingua Anglicana, ut   330
45rb ostensum est igitur, si translacio fieri debet de Latino | in Angli-
cum, non posset in lingua illa ab incongruitate et falsitate saluari.
Nec translacio debet fieri de sententia ad sententiam, quia sententia eiusdem littere Latine est apud diuersos diuersa; in quem igitur
sensum transferri debet ignoratur. Dicet forte quis, quod habeat sen-   335
sum litteralem, moralem, allegatum et anagogicum, transferri tamen
debet quoad sensum litteralem; contra, sensus litterales sunt diuersi
secundum opiniones diuersorum, et stat argumentum sicut prius.

7°. Sic, 70 interpretes nunquam nisi ieiuniis et orationibus peractis
transferrent, et tamen, dicit Ieronimus, frequenter errauerunt, sicut   340
Ieronimus hoc idem de seipso confitetur. Quomodo igitur generaliter
simplices, solum linguam unam et vix eam intelligentes, in transferendo non errarent?

3ᵃ ueritas. Sacra scriptura non debet omni publicari quoad omnia,
nec ab omnibus occultari quoad aliqua. Probatur nam Beda dicit,   345
'misteria fidei christiane non passim pandenda sunt, ne vilescant,
nec probis claudenda, ne in totum lateant'.[23] Item angelus precepit Iohanni, Apo.10[:4], 'quod vides in libro scribe', sed 'que locuta
sunt septem tonitrua, noli ea scribere'. Igitur aliquibus est scribenda,
aliquibus non publicanda, secundum diuersitatem parcium. Similiter   350

---

316 nomina neque dicciones] neque latina dicciones, *with expunction marks under*
'*latina' MS*   339 peractis] pussis, *with abbreviation mark over -i MS,* peractis
Deanesly, possibly piissimis   342 linguam unam *om. MS*   346 passim] possim,
followed by contie *with a bar over the letters* -ie *MS*

---

[22] Cf. Rev. 13:18.
[23] Bede, *In Apocalypsin,* X 3 (*PL* 93. 161).

alphabet], but in expressions as well: there are no nouns or phrases in English corresponding to some very well known and commonly used Latin terms, for instance abstractions such as *ens, substantia, accidens*, and categories too, *quantitas, qualitas, relatio, habitus*, and *positio, actio, passio, quando* and *ubi*. The same is true of *fallacia, equivocatio, amphibolia*, which do not have a corresponding term in English; although that language is richer than others in monosyllables, these terms can barely be rendered by a circumlocution.

Sixthly, if the whole Bible were translated into English or [another] vernacular, it would need to be translated either word for word, or sense for sense. It could not be done word for word, because many Latin terms have no corresponding English term and would have to be rendered entirely in circumlocutions, such as *legio, 666*, and *lustrum*, which means a period of five years.[22] On the same ground many texts of scripture can only be preserved from inconsistency and untruth by the use of figures of grammar which do not exist in English, as we have shown, and therefore, in a translation from Latin into English, they could not be rescued from untruth or inconsistency. Nor could scripture be translated sense for sense, for the meaning of the same Latin text varies with the different senses, and it would not be clear in which sense it should be translated. It might be objected that although the text has a literal, moral, figurative and anagogical sense, only the literal sense should be translated; but against that, there are various literal senses, according to different interpretations, and so the argument stands.

Seventhly, the seventy translators [of the Septuagint] would never begin their translations until they had prayed and fasted, and they were still frequently in error, according to Jerome, who admits he was just as mistaken himself. So how can simple people, most of whom know only one [language] and barely understand that, not fall into error?

3. Holy scripture should not be revealed in every particular to anyone, nor should it, in some respects, be hidden from everyone. This can be shown from the words of Bede, who says that 'the mysteries of the Christian faith should not be revealed indiscriminately for fear of cheapening them, nor should they be hidden from upright people, to avoid their final oblivion'.[23] Again, the angel admonished John in Apocalypse chapter 10, 'what you see, write in a book', but 'those things which the seven thunderclaps uttered, write them not'. So there are things, which should be written down for some, but not revealed to others, depending on what parts [of scripture] they are.

Paulus 2ª Cor.12[:4], 'audiuit archana que non licet homini loqui'; igitur nec scribere ea licet.

4ª ueritas. Sacra scriptura non est malis totaliter communicanda, voce uel scriptura, probatur Math.7°[:6], 'nolite sanctum dare canibus'; et Gorran super illo Apok.10[:4], 'noli scribere que locuta sunt 7 tonitrua', quia infidelibus, inquit, furore malitie agitatis blasphemie pocius quam edificacionis materia esset.[24] Vnde Prouer.23[:9], 'in auribus insipiencium ne loquaris, quia despicient doctrinam eloquii'.

5ª ueritas. Licet ipsa sit reuelanda, tamen aliquando ad tempus est occultanda; probatur Daniel 12[:4]: 'Tu, Daniel, claude sermonem, et signa librum usque ad tempus; pertransibunt plurimi et multiplex erit scientia'.

6ª ueritas. Aperienda est amicis Dei et claudenda inimicis; probatur per glosam, Apok.10[:4], 'noli ea scribere', inquit ut amicis pateant et noli ea scribere ut inimicos lateant; et in euangelio [John 15:14–15], 'vos | autem dixi amicos meos, quecumque audiui a patre meo, nota feci vobis'.

7ª ueritas. Secreta Dei celanda sunt a simplicibus et non omnibus manifestanda; probatur Ysa. 24[:16], 'secretum meum mihi, et secretum meum, ue . . .'; 'extraneo ne reueles' [Prov. 25:9]; Prouer.25, capitulo 2, 'gloria Dei celare verbum'.

Octava ueritas. Magis difficillima ad intelligendum, et que excedunt intellectum simplicium, non est scripture demandandum eis, ne in errorem inducantur; probatur quia [Ecclus. 3:22], 'alciora te ne quesieris', que scilicet transcendunt intelligencie tue rationem; quia Prouer.25[:27], 'qui scrutator magestatis opprimetur a gloria'. Sicut maxima claritas obtendit visum, sed nimia perscrutacio secretorum Dei obtendit intellectum, et ideo non plus sapere quam oportet; secundum Apostolum, 'quia bestia que tetigit montem, lapidabitur', Hebre.12[:20].[25] Bestia est intellectus humanus simplicium, et mons simplicitas scripturarum; et 'plura sunt supra sensus hominum' et transcendunt rationem et intellectum: Ecclesiastici 3°[:25] et sequitur, 'multa abscondita tibi sunt a Domino'.

9ª ueritas. Multa sunt abscondita a simplicibus, et eis non reuelanda, propter meritum fidei augendum. Probatur per Gregorium, quia fides non habet meritum ubi humana ratio prebet

353 scriptura] *uncertain;* scriptura *Deanesly*   361 sermonem] sernomen *MS*
373 *Octava*] 4ª *MS*   379 montem lapidabitur he. 12 *all canc. before* dei *MS*
obtendit] obte|d' cat *MS*

---

[24] Nicholas Gorran, *Postilla in Apocalypsin* 10:4; pr. Gorran, *In Acta Apostolorum, Jacobi, Petri, Johannis et Iudae canonicas epistolas et Apocalypsin Commentarii* (Antwerp 1620), 233.
[25] A quotation also used by Ullerston, at 12.197–8.

Likewise Paul says in 2 Corinthians, chapter 12, he 'heard unspeakable things, which it is not lawful for a man to utter'; and which, therefore, it is not lawful to write.

4. Holy scripture should not be wholly revealed to evildoers, either verbally or in writing, as is shown in the 7th chapter of Matthew, 'give not that which is holy unto the dogs'; and Gorran says on Apocalypse, chapter 10, 'those things which the seven thunderclaps uttered, write them not', because it provides [more] material for the infidels to blaspheme in their raging malice than for the edification [of the faithful].[24] As we read in the 23rd chapter of Proverbs, 'speak not in the ears of a fool, for he will despise the wisdom of your words'.

5. Although scripture should [in general] be revealed, there are times when it should be restricted, as is shown in the 12th chapter of Daniel: 'But you, Daniel, shut up the words, and seal the book; many shall pass away, and knowledge shall be multiplied'.

6. That [the scriptures] should be open to the friends of God and closed to his enemies is shown by the gloss on the text in the 10th chapter of the Apocalypse, 'write them not', which says that this was to keep them open to friends and hidden from enemies; on which we read in the gospel, 'I have called you friends, for all things which I have heard of my father, I have made known unto you'.

7. The mysteries of God should be hidden from simple folk and not revealed to everybody, as we read in the 24th chapter of Isaiah, 'my secret unto me, and my secret unto me, woe . . .', and 'discover not a secret to another', and in the 25th chapter of Proverbs, 'it is the glory of God to conceal the word'.

8. [The parts of scripture] too difficult to comprehend, which are beyond the understanding of simple folk, should not be entrusted to them, in case they fall into error, as is shown by the text 'seek not out the things which are too hard for you', that is, which are beyond your reason and understanding; for we read in the 25th chapter of Proverbs, 'men who search their own glory shall be crushed by it'. As intense brightness obstructs your vision, so too much probing the mysteries of God obstructs your understanding, and therefore we should know nothing more than is appropriate; as the Apostle says in the 12th chapter of Hebrews, 'if so much as a beast touch the mountain, it shall be stoned'.[25] By the beast we should understand the human mind of simple folk; by the mountain, the simplicity of the scriptures; 'many things are above the apprehension of the mind of men', and they transcend reason and understanding: as the text in the 3rd chapter of Ecclesiasticus continues, 'many things are hidden from you by the Lord'.

9. Many things are hidden from simple folk, and should not be revealed to them, to increase the merit due to their faith. This is clear from the words of Gregory, that faith has no merit when

experimentum, et Hugo de Vienna super illo Ecclesiastici 3°[:23],
'multa sunt abscondita tibi a Domino', in glosa *Propter*, inquit, meri-
tum fidei.[26]   390

10ᵃ veritas. Nimis ardua ad obseruandum non erunt simplicibus tradenda. Probatur nam Paulus propter eandem causam scribit discipulis: 'Tanquam paruulis in Christo lac potum vobis dedi,
non escam; nondum enim poteratis sicut nec nunc quidem potestis.
Adhuc enim carnales estis', 1ᵃ Cor.[3:2]. Similiter Berengarius super   395
illo Apok.10°[:4], 'que locuta sunt 7 tonitrua, noli ea scribere'. 'In
inicio', inquit, 'fidei, predicatores sancti, videntes infirmitatem gencium ad fidem ueniencium, non fuerunt ausi eis austeriora precepta
committere; ne forte duricia preceptorum territi non auderent ad
fidem Christi sustinendum accedere'.[27] Sic enim fecerunt apostoli,   400
Actus 15[:28], vbi sic: | 'spiritui sancto et nobis nichil inponere vobis
oneris, nisi ut abstineatis vos ab immolatis, et sanguine suffocato, et
a fornicacione', dixerunt apostoli conuersis de gentibus ad fidem.

11ᵃ ueritas. Vana simplicibus et inutilia non sunt eis manifestanda,
pro illo Ecclesiastici 3°[:22], 'in vacuis rebus noli scrutari multiplici-   405
ter, et in multis operibus eius non eris curiosus'; ubi Hugo de Vienna
in postilla, in rebus vacuis, id est, in eis quorum scientia non est
vtilis, ut quod musca et pulex tot pedes habent, et camelus tantum
quattuor, et homo solum duos.[28]

12ᵃ ueritas. Laicis vtilia ad salutem et non alia de sacra scriptura   410
sunt eis tradenda; probatur Ecclesiastici 3[:22–23], 'alciora te ne quesieris, et forciora te non scrutatus fueris; sed que precepit tibi Deus,
illa cogita semper; et in pluribus operibus eius non sis curiosus'.
Deutero.6[:5–9], 'Hec sunt precepta et cerimonie atque iudicia, que
mandauit Dominus Deus uester; Audi Israel, et obserua que precepit   415
Dominus Deus tuus: diliges Dominum Deum tuum ex toto corde, et
ex tota anima tua, eruntque uerba hec que ego precipio tibi hodie in
corde tuo, et narrabis ea filiis tuis, et meditaberis sedens in domo tua
et ambulans in itinere, dormiens atque consurgens, et ligabis quasi
signum in manu tua; eruntque et mouebuntur inter oculos tuos;   420
scribesque ea in limine et hostiis domus tue'. Ecce quot scribenda
erunt precepta in populo. Vana et inutilia sunt vitanda, ad Titum
3°[:8–9], 'De hiis uolo te confirmare, ut currant in bonis operibus

45vb (marginal)

---

395 cor 13 *MS*   398 austeriora] exteriora *MS*   404 manifestanda] manife-
standam *MS*   411 3] 30 *MS*   412 et se *canc. before* te *MS*   et deut° 6 *all*
canc. before sed *MS*   418 sedens] sedes *MS, sedens Deanesly*

---

[26] Gregory the Great, *Homiliae XL super euangelia*, hom. 26 (*PL* 76. 1198); Hugh of
St Cher, *Postilla in Ecclesiasticum* 43:36; pr. *Postilla in totam Bibliam*, 7 vols ([Basel 1498–
1502]), unpaginated.

human reason finds a proof, and Hugh [of St Cher] glosses the text of Ecclesiasticus, 'many things are hidden from you by the Lord', that this is for the merit due to faith.[26]

10. [Precepts] which are too hard to observe should not be communicated to simple folk. This is evident from what Paul writes to his disciples on the matter, in 1 Corinthians, chapter 13: 'I have fed you with milk, and not with meat, as unto babes in Christ; for hitherto you were not able to bear it, neither yet now are you able. For you are yet carnal.' Likewise, Berengaud says on the text in the Apocalypse, 'those things which the seven thunderclaps have uttered, write them not', and 'in the early days of the faith, holy preachers, seeing the weakness of gentile converts, drew back from imposing Christ's more austere precepts; for they might be too alarmed by the difficulty of these precepts to come forward and embrace the faith of Christ'.[27] It seems the apostles did the same, for we read in the 15th chapter of Acts that they said to Gentiles converted to the faith, 'for it seemed good to the Holy Spirit and to us to lay no greater burden on you, so long as you abstain from pollutions of idols, and from fornication, and from things strangled, and from blood'.

11. Pointless and unnecessary things should not be put before simple folk, in accordance with the 3rd chapter of Ecclesiasticus, 'ponder not too much on empty questions, and be not curious in unnecessary matters'; as Hugh [of St Cher] says in his comment on this, [there are] pointless questions, on which knowledge is useless, such as why flies or fleas have so many feet, while camels have just four, and human beings only two.[28]

12. What is useful for the salvation of the laity should be put before them, but not other parts of holy scripture, as is shown by the words of the 3rd chapter of Ecclesiasticus, 'seek not out the things that are too hard for you, neither search the things that are above your strength; but what is commanded of you, think on them always; and be not curious in unnecessary matters'. As we read in the 6th chapter of Deuteronomy, 'Hear, O Israel, the Lord your God is one God; you shall love the Lord your God with all your heart, and these words, which I command you this day, shall be in your heart; and you shall teach them diligently to your children, and shall talk of them when you sit in your house, and when you walk by the way; and you shall write them upon the posts of your house, and on your gates'. Note how many injunctions upon the people are to be written down. As we read in the 3rd chapter of the epistle to Titus, 'These things I desire you to affirm, so that they who believe in God might be careful

[27] Berengaud, *Expositio super septem uisiones libri Apocalypsis*, c. 10 (*PL* 17. 865).

[28] Hugh of St Cher, *Postilla in Ecclesiasticum* 3:22; pr. *Postilla in totam Bibliam*, 7 vols ([Basel 1498–1502]), unpaginated.

que credunt Deo. Hec sunt bona et vtilia hominibus. Stultas autem
questiones, et geneologias, et contenciones, et inpugnas legis devita; 425
sed tales sunt nobis invtiles et uane.'

13ᵃ ueritas: Aliqua pars scripture sacre in mente non potest extra
exprimi, scripta uel voce. Probatur quia sicut iubilus mentis potest
esse tantus quod propter illius vehemenciam extra ostendi non poterit, sic est aliqua pars scripture in mente diuina, tam iocunda, quod 430
extra in voce uel scriptura non potest plene et perfecte apparere; quia
46ra 'nec oculus vidit, nec auris audiuit, | nec in cor hominis ascendit, que
preparauit Deus diligentibus se', et [1] ad Cor.2[:9]. Sed illa ueritas
non est ad propositum, quia hic loquimur de scriptura sacra nobis
tradita in canone Biblie. 435

Contra tamen predictam ueritatem, ut magis appareat, arguitur sic:

[1.] 'Qui deliquerit in vno factus est omnium reus', secundum
Iacobum [2:10]. Sed facilius propter aliquis delinquere contra legem
antiquam et etiam nouam, nisi habeantur in scriptis, cum labilis sit 440
memoria hominis. Igitur, etc.

2°. Sic secretissima Dei et difficillima sint nobis a Deo tradita, ut
articulus Trinitatis: quod vna res et vna essentia sint tres persone,
realiter dicte a qualibet earum. Quo articulo nullus est difficilior vel
secrecior, igitur difficultas uel secretum non inpediet. 445

3°. Sic, Ioh.6[:51–3], 'ego sum panis viuus qui de celo descendi: si
quis manducauerit ex hoc pane, viuet in eternum; et panis quem ego
dabo, caro mea est pro mundi uita. Litigabant igitur Iudei ad inuicem
dicentes, quomodo potest hic dare carnem \suam/ ad manducandum?
[6:60] Durus est hic sermo, quis potest eum audire? [6:66] Ex hoc 450
multi discipulorum abierunt retrorsum, et iam cum illo non ambula-
bant' [6:67]. Et [I] Ioh.2°[:19], 'ex vobis prodierunt, sed ex vobis non
erant; nam si fuissent ex vobis, permansissent [*blank*]'. Difficilima
et secretissima eis docuit, non obstante quod capere non uoluerunt,
sed ab eo recesserunt. 455

4°. Sic, Math.19°[:11–12], 'dicunt ei discipuli, si ita est, non expedit
nubere. Qui dixit eis, non omnes capiunt uerbum illud, sed quibus
datum est; sunt enim eunuchi qui semetipsos castrauerunt propter
regnum Dei. Qui potest capere, capiat.'

5°. Sic, Ioh.[16:12], 'Adhuc habeo vobis multa dicere, sed non 460
potestis portare modo. Cum autem venerit ille spiritus ueritatis,

---

425 devita] *uncertain;* devita *Deanesly*   426 uane] inane *MS*   431 audiuit]
nec in cor hominis ascendit *all canc. before* uel *MS*   433 illa] illas *MS,* illa *Deanesly*
438 *unnumbered MS*   439 propter] ppt *with abbreviation mark over the letters* -pt
MS, potest *Deanesly*   453 *blank space within a line MS*   460 Ioh 6° *MS*
adhu *canc. before* non *MS*

to maintain good works. These things are good and profitable unto men. But avoid foolish questions, and genealogies, and contentions, and strivings about the law; for they are unprofitable and vain.'

13. Some portion of holy scripture can only be expressed in the mind, not outwardly in writing or in speech. We know this is true because the exultation of the mind can be so intense that it cannot be outwardly manifested, and so some part of scripture in the mind of God can cause so much delight that it cannot be fully or completely revealed in speech or writing; as we read in the 2nd chapter of the [first] epistle to the Corinthians, 'eye has not seen, nor ear heard, neither have entered into the heart of man, the things which God has prepared for them that love him'. But this truth is not relevant to the argument, as we are speaking here of holy scripture handed down in the canon of the Bible.

But against this argument, to make the point clearer, we could argue:

1. As we read in the Epistle of James, 'he who offends in one thing is guilty of all'. But it is easier to offend against the old law, or even the new, if it is not available in writing, as the memory of man is defective.

2. The deepest and most incomprehensible mystery of God has been revealed to us by God, namely the doctrine of the Trinity: that one thing and one essence are three persons, and they are truly predicated of each person. Since no doctrine is more difficult and mysterious than this, difficulty and mystery will not obstruct [our understanding].

3. As we read in the 6th chapter of John, 'I am the living bread which came down from heaven: if any man eat of this bread, he shall live for ever; and the bread that I will give is my flesh, which I will give for the life of the world. The Jews therefore strove among themselves, saying, how can this man give us his flesh to eat? . . . This is a hard saying; who can hear it? . . . From that time many of his disciples went back, and walked no more with him.' And in chapter 2 of the first Epistle of John, 'they went out from us, but they were not of us; for if they had been of us, they would have continued [with us]'. He taught them difficult and mysterious things, even though they did not desire to understand, but departed from him.

4. And we read in the 19th chapter of Matthew, 'his disciples say unto him, if this is the case, it is not good to marry. But he said unto them, all men cannot receive this saying, save they to whom it is given . . . and there be eunuchs, which have made themselves eunuchs for the kingdom of heaven's sake. He that is able to receive, let him receive it.'

5. And in the 6th chapter of John, 'I have yet many things to say to you, but you cannot bear them yet. Howbeit, when he, the spirit

docebit vos omnem veritatem.' Igitur docebit omnem ueritatem, et secretissimam et difficillimam. Hec contra octavam [et] nonam ueritatem.

Et item similiter, si fides non habet meritum ubi humana ratio 465 prebet experimentum, tunc non expediret doctoribus studere ad fidem defendendam ratione, sequitur etiam quod melius docti in fide essent minoris meriti. Similiter Christus sublimia predicauit in diuinis, 'equalem se faciens Deo', Ioh.[5:18], propter quod Iudei querebant eum interficere. Sicut ibidem dicitur Ioh.8[:58–9]: 'dixit eis, 470 ego prin|cipium qui loquor vobis, et antequam Abraham fieret, ego sum', propter quod, ut ibi dicitur, 'tulerunt lapides ut iacerent in Ihesum', Igitur sanctum videtur dedisse canibus.

Similiter margaritas videtur posuisse ante porcos conculcandas, quando Deum se figuratum esse per manna dicebat, John 6°[:51– 475 2]: 'ego sum panis uiuus qui de celo descendi; non sicut patres vestri manducauerunt manna in deserto et mortui sunt; qui manducat hunc panem viuet in eternum'. Quam margaritam multi conculcauerunt, dicitur ibi [6:60]: 'durus est hic sermo, quis potest eum audire? Et abierunt retrorsum.' 480

Item, ex hoc quod dedit Iude proditori, qui et canis et porcus fuit, eukaristiam, qua nichil sanctius est in sacramentis; item ex hoc quod ipse alibi videtur dixisse contrarium docuisse, ut Math.10[:27]: 'quod dico vobis in tenebris, dicite in hoc lumine; et quod in aure auditis, dicite in cubiculis, predicate in tectis'. 485

Item ex hoc loco, 'nolite sanctum dare canibus', Math.7[:6], videtur quod non deberem dare eukaristiam subdito meo quem scio esse uel canem per infidelitatem, uel porcum per spurciciam peccatorum; nam si dedero, faciam contra doctrinam Christi, et, si non dedero, facio iniuriam, et cetera. Queritur in casu isto, vtrum possim ei dare 490 hostiam non consecratam loco consecrate; quod sic videtur, quia sic incedam in media via, et uitabo ambo predictam inconvenientiam, quia nec dabo sanctum canibus neque perdam peccatorem.

Item, nullo sapiente homine actore fit homo deterior; non enim illa parua culpa, ymmo tanta est, ut in sapientem hominem cadere 495 nequeant, ut dicitur 83.q.3.[29] Sed si dedero ei, fit me actore multo deterior quam fuit ante, patet 2 Cor.11[:16]. Nullo igitur modo, si sim sapiens, debeo ei dare hostiam sanctam, nec debeo ipsum prodere; relinquitur illa via media, sicut dictum est.

463 octavam et nonam] 8.9 *MS*, octavam et nonam *Deanesly*   465 item] iter *MS*, item *Deanesly*   466 non] *uncertain;* non *Deanesly*   469 Ioh 9 *MS* 471 Abraham] archana *MS*, Abraham *Deanesly*   475 quando] *uncertain;* quando *Deanesly*   483 dixisse *canc. MS*   484 auditis *om. MS, cf. Matt. 10:27*

[29] Augustine, *De diuersis quaestionibus LXXXIII*, q. 3 (*PL* 40. 11).

of truth, is come, he will guide you into all truth.' So he will teach all truth, including the most mysterious and the most difficult. This contradicts the 8th and 9th points.

Again, likewise, if faith has no merit where human reason finds a proof, there would be no point in doctors taking trouble to defend the faith by reason, and it would follow that those who were most learned in faith would have least merit. Further, Christ preached exalted truths about God, 'making himself equal with God', as we read in the 9th chapter of John, and therefore the Jews sought to kill him. We find the same in the 8th chapter: 'he said unto them, I am the beginning who speak unto you, and before Abraham was, I am', and so, it goes on, 'they took up stones to cast at Jesus'. So it seems that one may give that which is holy unto the dogs.

It seems too that pearls can be cast before swine to be trampled, since God said he was prefigured by manna in the 6th chapter of John: 'I am the living bread which came down from heaven; not as your fathers did eat manna, and are dead; he that eats of this bread shall live for ever'. And many people trampled on this pearl, as is written there: 'this is a hard saying, who can hear it? And they went back.'

Again, [the point is confirmed] in that he gave the eucharist, that which nothing among the sacraments is holier, to Judas that betrayed him, and who [was prefigured as] both dog and swine; and in that he seems to have taught the contrary [to the opposing argument] in the 10th chapter of Matthew: 'what I tell you in darkness, that speak ye in light; and what you hear in the ear, that tell ye in the bed-chambers, and preach ye upon the house-tops'.

Again, on the text in the 7th chapter of Matthew, 'give not that which is holy unto the dogs', it seems that I should not give the eucharist to my parishioner when I know him either to be a dog through faithlessness, or a swine through the foulness of sins; for if I were to give it to him, I will be acting contrary to Christ's teaching, and if did not, I would do him a [public] injustice. One may ask, in this instance, whether I could give him an unconsecrated host instead; and it seems that I could, as I would then be walking the middle way, and would avoid both these disagreeable alternatives, neither giving what is holy unto dogs nor losing a sinner.

Again, nobody becomes evil by the agency of a wise person; for [an action of that kind] is no small fault, indeed a very serious sin, and could not occur in the case of a [truly] wise person, as we read in question 3 of [Augustine's] *83 Questions*.[29] But if I give [the sacrament] to such a person, he would by my agency become more evil than he was, as we can see in the 11th chapter of [2] Corinthians. So if I am wise, I should by no means give him or hand over the consecrated host, for that would be to leave the middle way, as we have seen.

Responsio. Dicendum quod nichil inuenitur in factis uel in dictis   500
quod repugnet [*blank*] intellecte 'nolite sanctum dare canibus'
[Matt. 7:6]. Dicit enim Augustinus libro secundo *De sermone Domini
in monte* (nota ibi), vnde non debet 'sanctum dare canibus', neque
46va margaritas posuit ante porcos per se, | sed per actus solum, quia non
propter eos, sed propter alios dixit.[30]   505

Ad aliud quod obicitur de eukaristia data Iude, adhuc occultum erat
discipulis, propter quod et ei dedit etiam eukaristiam, ut dispensaturos
futuros huius sacramenti doceret quod propter occultum peccatum
non repellerent subditos suos, publice cum aliis hoc sacramentum
querentes, et hoc propter tres rationes: prima, ne talis proderetur;   510
secunda, ne scandalum generetur in cordibus aliorum videncium;
tertia, ne tales dispensatores haberent libertatem contra bonos mali-
gnandi, repellendo eos a communione et infamando eos. Quando igitur
dicitur, 'nolite sanctum dare canibus' de illis quorum crimina sunt
manifesta et notoria intelligendum dico, si ad eukaristiam trahantur; 515
uel, si de aliis, quorum crimina sunt occulta, contendat aliquis hoc
debere intelligi, tunc prohibetur non actus dandi, similiter et in omni
casu, sed voluntas; debet enim sacerdos peccatorem occultum primo
monere, si potest, ut penitentiam agat, et ad sacramentum accedat;
quod si noluerit, debet ei occulte prohibere ne communicantibus   520
publice se immisceat; quod si se immiscuerit, debet dare ei hostiam
consecratam voluntate lugubri et nolente, ut dictum est.

Ad aliud, ut dictum est [Matt. 10:27] 'predicate super tecta',
respondet Crisostomus, omelia 23, *Operis imperfecti*, quod non precepit Christus omnibus omnia dicere, quia sic contrarium huic loco   525
precepisset, sed precepit quibus oportuit cum libera propalacione, et
in aperto dicere et non in angulis, neque in tenebris, sicut dicunt doctrine suspecte.[31] Quemadmodum Christus obseruauit, Ioh.18[:20],
'ego palam locutus sum mundo'.

Ad aliud quod obicitur de eukaristia, patet quod non debet dari   530
occulto peccatori cum aliis se ingerenti hostia non consecrata, propter
duas rationes. Primo, quia ueritati nulla ficcio adiungenda est; 'quia
nulla conuentio lucis ad tenebras?', 2° Cor.6[:14]. Et per hoc probat
Augustinus, 83 q.14, quod corpus Christi non fuit fantasticum, quia

---

501 *blank space within a line MS*   524 *imperfecti*] perfecti *MS,* imperfecti *Deanesly*
529 locutus] locutum *MS,* locutus *Deanesly*   534 q. q. *at line break MS*

---

[30] 'Quod autem Dominus noster quaedam dixisse invenitur, quae multi qui aderant, vel
resistendo vel contemnendo non acceperunt; non putandus est sanctum dedisse canibus,
aut margaritas misisse ante porcos: non enim dedit eis qui capere non poterant, sed eis qui
poterant, et simul aderant; quos propter aliorum immunditiam negligi non oportebat',
Augustine, *De sermone Domini in monte,* II 76 (*PL* 34. 1301).
[31] Pseudo-Chrysostom, *Opus imperfectum super Matthaeum,* hom. 25 (*PG* 56. 761).

In response to this, I say that nothing in the deeds or words [of Christ] is incompatible with the [proper] understanding of the words 'give not that which is holy unto the dogs'. For Augustine says in the second book of *De sermone Domini in monte* (note this passage), one should not 'give that which is holy unto the dogs', nor did [Christ] cast pearls before swine in actual fact, but was only making a point, because he was not speaking to those [who could not understand him], but to others [who could].[30]

To the other objection, about the eucharist given to Judas, the [mystery of the] sacrament was still hidden from the disciples, and it was given to him as well to teach future ministers of this sacrament, that they should not turn away their parishioners because of a secret sin, when they come up for it with other people in public, for three reasons: first, to protect [the sinner] from being exposed; second, to avoid causing scandal in the hearts of the onlookers; and third, to prevent ministers taking the liberty of maligning virtuous people by refusing them communion and harming their reputation. So I maintain that the precept, 'give not that which is holy unto the dogs' applies to those whose misdeeds are open and notorious, if they wish to receive the eucharist; or if someone wishes to argue that it applies to others whose sin is not generally known, then the act of administering [the sacrament] is not forbidden too, in every instance, but the desire to administer it; for the priest should warn the secret sinner, in advance, if he can, to do penance and then receive the sacrament; but if the sinner is not willing, he should prohibit the sinner privately not to mix in public with the communicants, but if he does, the priest should give him the consecrated host sadly and reluctantly, as it were.

To the further objection, on the text 'preach ye upon the house-tops', Chrysostom replies in the 23rd homily of his *Opus imperfectum* that Christ is not enjoining them to preach everything to everyone, but is saying the opposite in this text, that they should preach freely what is appropriate, and that openly and not in a corner or in the dark, as people suspected of heresy do.[31] As Christ pointed out, as we read in the 18th chapter of John's gospel, 'I spake openly to the world'.

To the further objection on [receiving] the eucharist, an un-consecrated host should certainly not be given to a secret sinner together with others present, for two reasons. The first is that no untruth should be associated with the truth; as we read in 2 Corinthians, chapter 6, 'what communion has light with darkness?' Augustine shows this in question 14 of his *83 Questions*, saying that the body of Christ was not a phantasm, as Christ, who is truth,

ueritas Christus fallere non potest.³² Iob 13[:7], 'Numquid indiget 535
Deus vestro mendacio ut pro illo loquamini dolos?' Et ideo in sacramentis ecclesie, que sunt sacramenta ueritatis, nihil agendum est per
fictionem, precipue in sacramento eukaristie, in quo Christus totus |
46vb continetur; manifeste enim esset ficcio si hostia non consecrata daretur loco consecrate. Secundo, quia sacerdos hoc faciens, quantum in 540
se est, fieret populo circumstanti occasio ydolatrie; qui populus licet
peccatum ydolatrie non incurreret, estimans probabiliter hostiam
esse consecratam, tamen sacerdos, ex hoc ipso quod hostiam non
consecratam populo exhiberet adorandum, crimen ydolatrie incurreret. Vnde manifestum est quod in nullo casu faciendum est quod 545
hostia non consecrata exhibeatur alicui tanquam consecrata. Ex istis
patet quod illa via media non est elicienda sed abicienda, quia in
extremo consistit ueritas in proposito.
 Ad aliud scilicet, quod nullo sapiente fit homo deterior, dicitur
quod me actore non fit ille deterior, qui me inuito accipit sacramen- 550
tum, sed seipso per se, et non ego nisi per accidens et coactus.
 Ad aliud scilicet, 'fides non habet meritum',³³ verum sed si nollet
credere nisi haberet rationem pro se; et ad aliud, 'qui deliquerit in
vno factus est reus omnium' [Jas. 2:10], quia scilicet omnia remissa
per ingratitudinem reddeunt.   555
 Ad primum principale, cum sic arguitur, licet totam sacram scripturam predicare et docere, igitur et scribere, hic dico primo, negando
consequentiam, quia dictum est Iohanni Apok.10[:4], 'que locuta
sunt septem tonitrua, nolite ea scribere'; vidit tamen, audiit et intellexit ea. Secundo, nego antecedens quia Math.7[:6] dicitur, 'nolite 560
sanctum dare canibus, neque margaritas ponere ante porcos'; similiter
Paulus [2 Cor. 12:4], 'audiuit archana verba, que non licet homini
loqui', videlicet predestinacionem beatorum et reprobacionem malorum, nec sibi nec homini licet hoc loqui propter presumpsionem pre-
destinatorum et desperacionem dampnandorum. Tertio dico, quod 565
licet transferri eam liceat, non tamen in omnem linguam, quia non in
barbaricam, ut arguendo ad aliam partem ostensum est. Quarto dico,
non omnes obligantur ad obseruanciam omnium in ea contentorum,
sed tamen ad precepta, ut ibi ostensum est.
 Ad secundum principale dico quod lex recte viuendi quoad pre- 570
cepta, et quoad alia que conferunt vitam, et que ad illa necessa-
rio requiruntur est habenda, non tamen quoad alia difficillima et

³² Augustine, *De diuersis quaestionibus LXXXIII*, q. 14 (*PL* 40. 14).
³³ Gregory the Great, *Homiliae XL super euangelia*, hom. 26 (*PL* 76. 1198).

cannot deceive.[32] As we read in the 13th chapter of Job, 'Will you speak wickedly for God? And talk deceitfully for him?' So in the sacraments of the church, which are sacraments of truth, nothing must be done to deceive, especially in the sacrament of the eucharist, in which Christ is present in person; it would clearly be a deception if an unconsecrated host were to be given instead of a consecrated host. The second reason is that a priest who did this would, so far as it was in his power, be giving the people present an occasion for idolatry; although the people would not be committing the sin of idolatry, believing that the host was consecrated, but the priest would be guilty of idolatry, by holding up an unconsecrated host for the people to adore. So clearly an unconsecrated host should never be shown to anyone as if it had been consecrated. It follows that the compromise suggested must not be adopted but rejected, because the truth of the argument lies in not compromising.

To a further objection, that nobody becomes evil by the agency of a wise person, I reply that [a sinner receiving the sacrament] is not made evil by my agency, since he received it against my will, but only by his own, and by mine only as a matter of accidental circumstance, as I had no alternative.

To another objection, that 'faith has no merit [where human reason finds a proof]',[33] that is true if a person is unwilling to believe without a reason; and to another, that 'he who is guilty of one thing offends in all', that all sins which are forgiven return through the ingratitude [of the penitent].

To the first main argument [on the affirmative side of the question], that since it is lawful to preach and teach holy scripture [in the vernacular], it is therefore lawful to write it, I first of all reply by denying that it follows. As we read in the 10th chapter of the Apocalypse of John, 'those things which the seven thunderclaps have uttered, write them not'; but he has seen them, heard them and understood them. Secondly, I deny the premise through the words of the 7th chapter of Matthew: 'give not that which is holy unto the dogs, neither cast ye your pearls before swine'; and Paul, similarly, has 'heard unspeakable things, which it is not lawful for a man to utter', that is the predestination of the blessed and the damnation of the wicked, on which a man may not lawfully speak, to avoid presumption by the predestinate and despair on the part of the damned. Thirdly, it may be lawful to translate scripture, but not into every language, and not into a vernacular tongue, as has been shown in the arguments on the opposite side. Fourthly, not everybody is obliged to observe everything contained in [the scriptures], but only its precepts, as is shown in the same section.

To the second point I reply that the rule of right living according to [scriptural] precepts, and other things which confer [eternal] life and are necessary to salvation, should be available, but not other difficult

obscura. Secundo, dico quod in scripturis aliqua inueniuntur in quibus putamus uitam eternam habere, et preter illa sunt multa alia ad
que laici minime obligantur scire uel agere.   575

47ra   Ad tertium | dico concedendo quod labilis est memoria hominum,
et ideo in omni nacione scriptura est habenda in tali lingua in qua
potest transferri, ut in lingua Ebraica, Greca uel Latina; et ideo in
omni nacione requiritur quod sint clerici in aliqua lingua tali periti,
qui possunt populo per circumlocucionem scripturas interpretari.   580

Ad quartum dico quod licet vulgo per clericos sibi interpretantes habere notitiam scripture sacre, et habere omnia precepta eis
necessaria, requisita ad salutem, non tamen est eis necessarium ad
salutem habere alia difficillima et obscura et ad salutem inpertinentia.
Secundo dico, si eis omnia scire esset necessarium ad salutem, esset 585
eis ad salutem necessarium linguam talem addiscere in qua licet eam
transferre.

Ad quintum nego consequentiam, quia in linguam Ebraicam,
Grecam et Latinam ipsa potest transferri, non tamen sic potest in
omnem linguam Ebraicam, quia absque alphabeto Latinorum non   590
vtuntur neque Grecorum neque Ebreicorum, et licet vterentur illo,
non tamen expediret neque deberent omnia in illam transferri, propter quedam ante dicta.

Ad sextum, licet Beda transtulit totam sacram scripturam, tamen
illius translacionem ecclesia non acceptat, quia forte errauit, sicut 595
Ieronimus et alii fere omnes qui eam transferre presumpserunt.
Secundo dico, quod Beda non transtulit eam nisi quoad necessaria ad
salutem et quoad facilia, quia secundum se totam non potuit transferri in linguam barbaricam, ut in secunda ueritate est ostensum.

Ad septimum dico, quod aliquis potest vitare peccatum mortale, 600
licet non congnoscat illud esse peccatum mortale, per inclinacionem
ad obiectum, vnde habitus fidei non solum inclinat ad assertum ad
articulum, sed inpedit assertum ad heresim oppositam, licet ignore-
tur an sit heresis. Similiter auctor *De fide et legibus* notat, sufficit alicui
pro sententia ipso ignorante se supponat; nisi obstaret peccatum 605
aliquod illius, quo non cognosceret eam, quia Deus conscientiam
illius faceret murmurare, uel aliter inpediret ne peccaret.[34] Similiter mutus uel surdus posset uitare peccatum, licet nullam linguam
intelligeret iam.

Ad octavum concedo questionem adductam, quia licet habere in 610
vulgari omnia nobis necessaria ad salutem.

578 ppt *canc. before* potest *MS*   602 subiectum *canc. before* obiectum *MS*
604 notat] non *MS*   606 quo] *uncertain;* quo *Deanesly*

[34] William of Auvergne, *De fide et legibus*, 'De legibus', c. 1; pr. in *Guillelmi Alverni
opera omnia* (Paris/Orleans 1674), 20–22.

and obscure [parts of scripture]. Secondly, there are some things in scripture through which we hope to have eternal life, but many other things besides which the laity are hardly obliged to know or act upon.

To the third point I reply by agreeing that the memory of men is faulty, and so scripture should be available to every nation in a language into which it can be translated, like Hebrew, Greek and Latin; and so in every nation there should be clerks learned in these languages, who can interpret the scripture to the people by circumlocution.

To the fourth point I reply that it is lawful for the people to have knowledge of holy scripture through clerks who interpret it for them, and to know all the precepts which are necessary and required for their salvation, but it is not necessary for them to know other very difficult and obscure matters which are irrelevant to their salvation. Secondly, I reply that if they were obliged to know everything necessary for salvation, it would be necessary to their salvation for them to learn a language into which it was lawful for [the scriptures] to be translated.

On the fifth point I deny the consequence, in that [scripture] can be translated into Hebrew, Greek and Latin, but not that Hebrew can be translated into all languages, being without the Latin alphabet, which the Greeks and Hebrews do not use, and even if they did use it, it would not be expedient or right that everything should be translated, on grounds already stated.

On the sixth point, although Bede translated the whole of scripture, the church did not accept his translation, perhaps because he made mistakes, as Jerome did and nearly every other person who presumed to translate it. Secondly, I reply that Bede only translated the parts necessary to salvation and easier to understand, as on his own admission not everything could be translated into a vernacular language, as is shown in the second point.

On the seventh point I say that anyone can avoid mortal sin even though he does not know that it is mortal sin, through a [natural] tendency to that condition, as the habit of faith not only inclines him to assert an article [of faith], but disinclines him to the contrary heresy, even though he is unaware that it is heresy. Likewise, according to the author of *De fide et legibus*, it is enough for someone's [moral] sense that he submit himself even in ignorance; unless some sin prevents him from recognizing it, God will rouse his conscience or hinder him from sinning in some other way.[34] Likewise a dumb or a deaf person can avoid sin, although he cannot understand speech.

On the eighth point I concede the argument, for it is lawful to have in translation all that is necessary for our salvation.

Ad nonum etiam concedo questionem, quia omnia nobis necessaria ad salutem sunt habenda in vulgari, et si aliquis sit surdus et sciat
47rb legere, scribatur sibi in nomine Domini quod est si|bi necessarium ad salutem. 615

Ad decimum dico, quod non est generaliter verum, quod magis nota plus mouent ad deuocionem. Quia quandoque vetula est magis deuota quam magister in theologia, quia 'pluribus minor est ad singula sensus'.[35] Similiter, magis nota quandoque vilescunt et facilius veniunt in contemptum. Dixit Festus Paulo, 'multe littere faciunt te 620 insanire' [cf. Acts 26:24].

Ad undecimum nego assertum, propter illud Apok.10[:4], 'que locuta sunt septem tonitrua', et ratio assignata est superius, in articulo ad partem negatiuam illius dubii.

Ad duodecimum dicitur quod 'in omnem terram exiuit sonus 625 eorum' [Ps. 18:5], id est apostolorum, qui omnem linguam sciuerunt, et in omni lingua predicauerunt omnibus que erant eis necessaria saluti, secundum illud Marci vltimo [16:15], 'euntes predicate euangelium omni creature', etc. Alia curiosa scripture et ardua non oportet quod in scriptis habeantur, nisi a clericis si qui sint et inter eos, 630 id est barbaros, in lingua Latina, Greca uel Hebrea, uel alia regula et figuris grammaticalibus regulata; sine quibus tamen est salus.

Ad tertiam decimum dico, quod stat quod [Rom. 15:4] 'quecunque scripta sunt, ad nostram doctrinam scripta sunt'; licet non intelligamus ea, quia possunt interpretari nobis in lingua nobis nota et 635 probari.

Ad quartam decimum, scripta nobis ignota multum valent ad correccionem nostram, quia possunt nobis interpretari.

Ad quintam decimum, 'necesse est inpleri omnia que scripta sunt de me', dicit Christus [Luke 24:44]. Similiter necesse est inpleri 640 omnia quecunque scripta sunt ab hominibus; que, scilicet, necessaria sunt saluti, et non alia.

Ad sextam decimum, concedo quod que nobis precepta sunt, habenda sunt in scriptis, ne obliuiscantur, quia sunt necessaria saluti.

Conformiter dico ad septimam decimam: concedo quod tam 645 necessarium est barbaris sicut Grecis, Latinis uel Hebreis, habere legem christianam in scriptis, quantum ad omnia precepta in ea et que sunt necessaria saluti, non quantum ad alia secreta et difficilia, et impertinentia saluti. Etiam, licet illa esset necessaria

637 multum] multa MS

[35] H. Walther, *Proverbia sententiaeque Latinitatis Medii Aevi: Lateinische Sprichwörter und Sentenzen des Mittelalters in alphabetischer Anordnung*, 6 vols (Göttingen 1963–9), no. 21629.

On the ninth point I again concede the argument, that it is lawful to have in translation all that is necessary for our salvation, and for a deaf man who can read, what is necessary for his salvation should be written out for him.

To the tenth point I reply that it is not generally the case that when people know something better, they are moved to greater devotion. An old women may be more devout than a master of theology; and '[attention to] many things means less for each'.[35] Moreover, when things are better known they are cheapened and easily fall into contempt. As Festus said to Paul, 'much learning makes you mad'.

I reject the argument of the eleventh point, on the basis of the text in the Apocalypse, 'those things which the thunderclaps have uttered [write them not]', and because the argument is stronger on the negative side of the proposition.

To the twelfth point I reply that the text 'their sound is gone out through all the earth' refers to the sound of the apostles, who knew all tongues, and preached to everyone in every language what was necessary for their salvation, according to the words in the last chapter of Mark, 'go and preach the gospel to every creature'. It is not good for everyone to have other curious and difficult parts of scripture in writing, except the clergy if they are among vernacular speakers, and provided they are in Latin, Greek or Hebrew, or another language governed by a rule and figures of grammar; but salvation is possible without all these things.

On the thirteenth point I say that we agree that 'whatsoever things were written, were written for our learning'; but even if we fail to understand them, they can be translated and explained to us in a language we know.

On the fourteenth point I say that writings which we cannot read might do something to amend our conduct, because they can be translated for us.

On the fifteenth point, Christ says, 'it is necessary that all things which are written of me shall be fulfilled'. Likewise, all things written by men must be fulfilled; that is, all things necessary to salvation, but no other things.

On the sixteenth point, I agree that those things which are commanded of us should be available in writing, so that they are not forgotten, because they are necessary for salvation.

Accordingly, I reply on the seventeenth point: I agree that it is as necessary to barbarian peoples to have the law of Christ in writing as it is for the Latins, Greeks and Hebrews, in so far as all its precepts and those things necessary for salvation are concerned, but not the other parts, the mysteries and difficult passages and matters irrelevant to salvation. Indeed, although [the law of Christ] is necessary for

saluti, non tamen posset secundum omnem eius partem in linguam   650
barbaricam transferri, quia nulla lingua talis regulatur regulis et figuris gramaticalibus; et ideo aliunde debemus eis prouidere de notitia
scripture quam per translacionem barbaricam, dando eis donum alia-
47va rum linguarum, | sicut olim dedit conuersis ad fidem.

Ad 18° arguebatur sic, principalis causa quare non potest transferri   655
in linguam barbaricam videtur esse quod illa non regulatur regulis
gramaticalibus et figuris, cum quibus non potest sacra scriptura a
falsitate et incongruitate saluari; sed propter hanc causam non deberet
ea transferri secundum aliquam partem eius, nec quoad necessaria
saluti nec quoad alia, quia hec regule, tropi et figure sunt omnibus   660
partibus scripture sacre equevocaciones, cuius oppositum dictum est.
Ad istud dico negando quod omnibus partibus scripture sunt ille
regule, tropi et figure, equevocaciones; quia alique partes quoad sensum litteralem uerificantur sine ipsis, et alique non. Precepta autem
legis et ea que necessaria sunt saluti, aperta sunt et plana: 'iugum   665
enim meum suaue est, et onus meum leue' [Matt. 11:30]. Et que
moralia sunt quasi de iure naturali et facilia ad credendum, vnde
Ps.[92:5], 'testimonia tua credibilia facta sunt nimis', et ideo non
indiget figuris et tropis, uel aliis, a falsitate ac incongruitate saluentur,
ut alia difficilia ibidem contenta.   670

Ad honorem Dei qui est benedictus in secula. Amen. Deo gratias.

655 Ad *om. MS*   658 hanc] hac *MS,* hanc *Deanesly*

salvation, not every part of it could be translated into the vernacular, because no vernacular language is governed by the rules and figures of grammar; and therefore we should convey knowledge of scripture in some other way than by translation into a vernacular language, by giving them the gift of other tongues, as Christ once gave to those converted to the faith.

On the eighteenth point, it was argued that the chief reason why [scripture] could not be translated into a vernacular language seemed to be that the vernacular is not governed by grammatical rules and figures, without which scripture cannot be rescued from untruths and inconsistencies; but on this reasoning no part of scripture should be translated, whether necessary for salvation or otherwise, for these rules, tropes and figures in every part of scripture are equivocations, of which the opposite meaning could be taken. To this I reply that these rules, tropes and figures are not equivocations in every part of scripture; because some parts can be justified according to their literal sense, and others cannot. The precepts of the law and other things necessary for salvation are clear and unequivocal: 'for my yoke is easy, and my burden is light'. And those parts which are moral precepts belong, as it were, to natural law, and are easy to believe: according to the Psalm, 'your testimonies are very sure', and therefore need no figures and tropes or anything else to preserve them from untruth and inconsistency, or other intrinsic difficulties.

For the honour of God who is blessed for all time. Amen. Thanks be to God.

First seiþ Bois

Cambridge, Trinity College, MS B. 14. 50,
fols. 26r–30v, and New York, Pierpont Morgan
Library, MS M 648, fols. 142r–143v (N1)

The following table lists passages where the text has close parallels with Ullerston's determination (and in one case with Palmer). These are also signalled in the numbered footnotes. As the table demonstrates, the parallels peter out towards the end, as the text becomes virtually independent of Ullerston.

Bois	Ullerston/Palmer
3–13 'First . . . mater'	U 1667–90 'et propter . . . Bacon ibidem'
16–20 'For wane . . . Detronomie, 31° c°	U 483–91 'Sed qualitercumque . . . in uulgari'
20–24 'And Esdrias . . . grete wepinge'	U 493–502 'Et confirmatur . . . ad librum'
24–29 'In Deut., 32° c° . . . her sonnes'	U 1718–21 'Si enim . . . dicent tibi'
29–31 'And þus . . . and hope'	U 1721–23 'Parati . . . et spe'
36–48 'Þus þis . . . placis þe profecies'	U 1482–89 'Dicitur enim . . . Ardmachanus'
48–51 'and, of þis . . . Genesis'	U 474–77 'Et singnanter . . . omnibus etc.'
52–57 'If God . . . profite'	U 1765–73 'Inuenitur . . . de Lira'
57–62 'For as it . . . spirite'	U 1291–1300 'Sed utinam . . . spiritum suum'
67–68 'And seint Poule . . . to profecie'	U 274–76 'Et isto modo . . . interpretetur'
68–75 'also he seiþ . . . answere "amen"'	U 529–36 'Et ideo . . . Amen'
75–77 'Also, in . . . not'	P 254–57 'Huiusmodi . . . mortalia'
78–85 'Also seuenti . . . han had'	U 844–55 'Et quod . . . legit eas'
	U 583–86 'Quid, queso . . . dampnes'
	U 1112–18 'Et si dicas . . . uulgaria'
85–91 'Worschipful . . . þeraftur'	U 587–92 'Reffert enim . . . fuisset'
91–96 'It was herde . . . enmyes'	U 592–98 'Audiui nempe . . . emulorum'
96–103 'Also venerabile . . . and xxxij'	U 598–607 'Nonne credis . . . nostro Anglico'
108–12 'Also Cistrence . . . and þre'	U 607–17 ' Subsequenter scribit . . . Cestrensis'
113–22 'Also seint Thomas . . . "barbarus"'	U 1097–1106 'Dicit enim . . . ibidem'
122–35 'Also þe . . . Bibil'	U 622–40 'A\u/sculta . . . pagine'
136–40 'Also . . . þei ben'	U 618–20 'Quid eciam . . . hac parte'
140–46 'Also sire Wiliam . . . Englond'	U 644–53 'Que considerans . . . obligantur'
146–54 'But þer . . . martis'	U 694–701 'Sed eo . . . Ricardus'
154–57 'And to hem . . . eretikes'	U 1612–25 'Ad 23ᵐ . . . susurrantes'
157–64 'Also þe . . . Englische'	U 1420–29 'Vnde et . . . posse fieri'
172–78 'But ȝit . . . curiosly'	U 1473–76 'Ad vigesimum . . . intelligamus'
178–80 'But þei . . . writynge'	U 1497–1500 'Est enim . . . ydioma'
186–92 'For Ierom . . . translacioun'	U 1155–59 'Non tamen . . . translatum'

First seiþ Bois

26r Aȝens hem þat seyn þat hooli wriȝt schulde not or may not be drawun
into Engliche we maken þes resouns:

First[1] seiþ Bois, in his boke *De disciplina scolarium*,[2] þat childeren
schulde be tauȝt in þe bokis of Senek, and Bede expowneþ þis, seying
childeren schulden be tauȝt in vertues, for þe bokis of Senek ben 5
morals, and for þei ben not tauȝt þus in her ȝougþe, þei conseyuen
yuel maners and ben vnabel to conseyue þe sotil sciense of trewþe,
seyinge þe Wise Man 'wisdom schal not entre into a wicked soule',[3]
and moche þer of þe sentence of Bede. And Algasel in his *Logik*[4]
seiþ þe soule of a man is as clene myrour newe polichid, in wiche is 10
seen liȝtliche þe ymage of man. But for þe puple haþ not konynge in
ȝouþe, þei han derke soulis and blyndid, so þat þei profiten not but
in falsenes, malice and oþer vices, and moche þer of þis mater.

O, siþen heþen philosefris wolden þe puple to profeten in natural
science, how myche more schulden cristen men willen þe puple to 15
profiten in science of vertues, for so wolde God. For[5] wane þe lawe was
ȝouen to Moises in þe mounte of Synay, God ȝaf it in Ebrew for þat al
þe pupel schuld vnderstonde it, and bad Moises to rede it vnto hem to
þe tyme þei vndurstodyn it, and he rede it, as is pleyn in Detronomie,
31° c°.[6] And[7] Esdrias also redde it f\r/om morou to mydday,[8] as it is 20
pleyn in his first boke, 8° c°[9], apertily in þe stret, and þe eeres of þe
puple weren entently ȝouen þerto and pei vnderstoden it, and þis þei
m\i/ȝt not haue done but if it hadde ben redde in þer modur-tounge,
so þat þe pupel hering felle into grete wepinge. In[10] Deut., 32° c°,[11]
it is writen 'aske þi fadris and þei schullen schewe to þee, and þin 25

6 þus] this *N1*   7 conseyue] *om. N1*   10 clene] a clene *N1*   12 þei] þe
MS   16 wolde] will *N1*   17 þat] *om. N1*   18 hem] them *N1*   19 to
þe tyme] *om. N1*   þei] they playnly *N1*   is pleyn] it ys *N1*   20 redde] he redd *N1*
21 his first] the ij^de *N1*   22 entently] entenly *MS*, enten\ti/ly *N1*   23 þer] her
N1   modur-tounge] modis tong *N1*   24 wepinge] lovyng *N1*   25 writen]
wrete that the shull *N1*

---

[1] 3–13 'First . . . mater': cf. U 1667–90 'et propter . . . Bacon ibidem'.

[2] Pseudo-Boethius, *De disciplina scolarium*, ed. O. Weijers (Leiden 1976), 100–101.

[3] Wisd. 1:4.

[4] Algazel (al-Ghazālī), *Logica*, trans. Dominicus Gundissalinus; pr. (Venice 1506),
fol. ıva–b.

[5] 16–20 'For wane . . . Detronomie, 31° c°': cf. U 483–91 'Sed qualitercumque . . . in
uulgari'.

[6] Deut. 31:30.

[7] 20–24 'And Esdrias . . . grete wepinge': cf. U 493–502 'Et confirmatur . . . ad librum'.

[8] Neh. 8:1–9.

[9] Neh. 8:1–9.

[10] 24–29 'In Deut., 32° c° . . . her sonnes': cf. U 1718–21 'Si enim . . . dicent tibi'.

[11] Deut. 32:7.

26v elderis and þei schulen sei to þee'. | Also þe profete seiþ 'how many
þings he haþ seid vnto oure faderis, þei schul make hem knowen vnto
her sones, and þe sones þat scholen be borne of hem schulen rise
and schullen teche þes þings to her sonnes'.[12] And[13] þus seiþ Petre in
his first pistile: 'be ȝe redi to fulfille to eche man þat askeþ ȝouȝ in   30
resoun, in feiþ and hope',[14] and also Peter seiþ 'euery man as he haþ
taken grace mynyster he forþe to oþer men'.[15] And in þe Apocalips it
is writen: 'þe housebonde and þe wiffe seyn "come!", and he þat hereþ
seiþ he comeþ',[16] þat Crist, þat is heed of holi chirche is þe housbonde,
and parfite prechouris and doctouris, þat is þe wiffe, clepen þe puple   35
to þe weies of heuene, and iche man þat heriþ clepe oþer. Þus[17] þis
is conferm\e/de in Actus of Apostilis: þereas þe apostilis weren but
rude men and fischeris, þei legeden þe prophecies, as Peter in þe first
chapiter seid, 'þe Hooli Goost be þe mouþe of Dauid be Iudas, þat
was þe duke of hem þat token Crist', and more processe þere.[18] In   40
þe 2° c° Peter seiþ 'it is writun be þe prophete Ioel, it schal be in
þe last daies, seiþ þe Lorde, I shal schede ouȝt \of/ my spirite vpon
iche flesche; ȝoure sones and ȝoure douȝtteris schulen prophecie and
ȝoure ȝonge men schullen se viciouns', and more þer in processe.[19]
Also in þe 15 c°, James seiþ, allegginge þe profecie, 'aftur þes þings   45
I schal turne aȝene and I schal make vp þe tabernacle'.[20] And þus
þe apostilis, þat ben cleped ydiotes be scripture,[21] allegeden here and
in many oþer placis þe profecies, and,[22] of þis it is notabile þat þe
lewde puple in þe olde lawe knewe ȝe þe lawe, notwithstanding þat
God for synne hadde departed þe tunges of hem, as it is opon in þe   50
11 chapitur of Genesis.[23]

   If[24] God wole, he loueþ not lesse vs cristen men in þes daies þan
27r he | dide þe pupel in þe olde testament but better, as he haþ scheued
be þe mene of Cristis passioun and be þe newe perfite lawe ȝouen to
vs. And herfore on þe Witsondaie he ȝaf to many diuerse naciouns   55

---

28 hem corr. from hym MS   29 þus] this N1   36 clepe] shuld clepe N1
37 Apostilis] the apostelis N1   38 legeden] aleggyd N1   46 and] N1, om. MS
46 þus] thys N1   49 ȝe] om. N1   notwithstanding] not withstonding N1

---

[12] Joel 1:2–3.
[13] 29–31 'And þus . . . and hope': cf. U 1721–23 'Parati . . . et spe'.
[14] 1 Pet. 3:15.
[15] 1 Pet. 4:10.   [16] Rev. 22:17.
[17] 36–48 'Þus þis . . . placis þe profecies': cf. U 1482–89 'Dicitur enim . . . Ardmachanus'.
[18] Acts 1:16.
[19] Acts 2:16–7; Joel 2:28.
[20] Acts 15:16.   [21] Acts 4:13.
[22] 48–51 'and, of þis . . . Genesis': cf. U 474–77 'Et singnanter . . . omnibus etc.'.
[23] Gen. 11:1–9.
[24] 52–57 'If God . . . profite': cf. U 1765–73 'Inuenitur . . . de Lira'.

knowing of his lawe be on tunge, in tokene þat he wolde alle men
knewe his lawe, to his worschipe and her profite.[25] For[26] as it is writun
in þe boke of Numeri, þe 11 c°, wane Moises had choson seuenty
elder men and þe spirite of God rested on hem and þei profecieden,
twey men, as Eldad and Medad, profeciden in castelis, and on seid   60
to Moises 'sir, forbede hem', and he seide 'wat enviest þou for me?
Wo schal lette þat alle þe puple profecie, if God ȝif hem his spirite?'[27]
And in Actus of Apostilis, þe II° c°, seiþ Peter, wane he had cristened
Cornelie and his felowes repreued hym þerof for he was an heþen
man, he seid to hem 'if God haþ ȝouen to hem þe same grace þat he   65
haþ ȝeuen to vs wiche beleuen in our Lorde Iesu Crist, wo am I þat
may forbede God?'[28] And[29] seint Poule seiþ in I[a] Cor., 14° c°, 'I wole
euery man to speike with tunges; more, forsoþe, to profecie';[30] also[31]
he seiþ 'I schal preye with spirit and I schal preie with mynde',[32] þat
is, with affeccioun and with vndurstandinge, and þis is myche better   70
þan al-onli to haue deuocioun in wordes and not in vndurstanding,
and þis preueþ þe texte aftur, þat seiþ 'how schal he sei "amen" vpon
þis blessing þat wot not wat þou seiste?'[33] And on þis seiþ þe doctor
Lire 'if þe puple vnderstood þe preyour of þe prest, it schal þe better
be lade into God and þe more deuouteli answere "amen"'. Also,[34] in   75
þe same chapeter, he seiþ 'I wole raþer fyue wordes be spoken to þe
vnderstanding of men þan ten þousand þat þei[35] vnderstonden not'.[36]

---

59 þei] om. N1   63 in] in the N1   64 þerof] her of N1   73 wot] he
wot N1   77 þei] p(re)þe(?) and N1

---

[25] Acts 2:1–11.

[26] 57–62 'For as it . . . spirite': cf. U 1291–1300 'Sed utinam . . . spiritum suum'.

[27] Num. 11:25–9.   [28] Acts 11:17.

[29] 67–68 'And seint Poule . . . to profecie': cf. U 274–76 'Et isto modo . . . interpretetur'.

[30] 1 Cor. 14:5.

[31] 68–75 'also he seiþ . . . answere "amen"': cf. U 529–36 'Et ideo . . . Amen'.

[32] 1 Cor. 15:15.   [33] 1 Cor. 14:16.

[34] 75–77 'Also, in . . . not': cf. P 254–57 'Huiusmodi . . . mortalia'.

[35] 'Preye and' may have been intended, but the letter that follows 'p' with a superscript
abbreviation for 're' in N1 appears to be a thorn. The scribe uses thorn occasionally, but
rarely. He may have had difficulty distinguishing between thorn, y and yogh in his north-
ern(?) exemplar: variants and errors (some occurring repeatedly) in MS M 648 are often
in words that may have been spelt in the exemplar with these letters, e.g. 'the' instead
of 'they', 'this' instead of 'thus', 'her of' instead of 'þerof', 'þok' instead of 'ȝork'. This
requires further investigation, but is potentially interesting as evidence of the northern
circulation of Bois, usually assumed to have been disseminated in the Lollard milieu in
the south. See further S. Powell, 'The transmission and circulation of the Lay Folk's
Catechism', in A. J. Minnis (ed.), Late-Medieval Religious Texts and their Transmission.
Essays in Honour of A. I. Doyle (Woodbridge 1994), 67–84, at 77); also M. Benskin, 'The
letters ⟨þ⟩ and ⟨y⟩ in later Middle English, and some related matters', Journal of the Society
of Archivists 7 (1982), 13–20.

[36] 1 Cor. 14:19.

27v   Also[37] seuenti docturis withouten mo byfore | þe incarnacioun
translatiden þe Bibile into Greek ouȝt of Ebrew, and aftur þe ascen-
cioun many translatiden al þe Byble, summe into Greek and summe   80
into Latyne, but seint Ierom translatide it out of Ebrew into Latine, wos translacioun we vsen most. And so it was translatid into
Spaynesche tunge, Frensche tunge and Almayne, and oþer londes
also han þe Bibel in þer modur-tunge, as Italie haþ it in Latyn for
þat is þer modur-tonge, and be many ȝeeris han had. Worschipful[38]   85
Bede, in his first boke *De Gestis Angulorum*, 2° c°,[39] telliþ þat seint Os-
wold, kyng of Northehumberlond axide of þe Scottys an holi bischop
Aydan, to preche his puple, and þe kynge of hymself interpreted it
on Engliche to þe puple. If þis blessid dede be aloued to þe kynge of
al hooli chirche, how not now as wel auȝte it to be alowed a man to   90
rede þe gospel on Engliche and do þeraftur? It[40] was herde of a worþi
man of Almaine þat summe tyme a Flemynge, his name was James
Merland, translatid al þe Bibel into Flemmyche, for wiche dede he
was somoned before þe pope of grete enmyte.[41] And þe boke was
taken to examynacioun and trwly apreued; it was deliuered to hym   95
aȝene in confucioun to his enmyes. Also[42] venerabile Bede, lede be
þe spirit of God, translatid þe Bibel, or a grete parte of þe Bibile, wos
originals ben in many abbeis in Englond. And Sistrence, in his fifte
booke, þe 24 c°,[43] seiþ þe euaungelie of Ion was drawen into Engliche
be þe forseide Bede, wiche euaungelie of Ion, and oþer gospellis, ben   100
ȝit in many placis of so oolde Englische þat vnneþe can any man rede
hem, for þis Bede regnede an hooly doctor aftur þe incarnacioun
28r   seuene hundered | ȝeer and xxxij. Also a man of Loundon, his name
was Wyring,[44] hadde a Bible in Englische of norþen speche wiche
was seen of many men, and it semed too houndred ȝeer olde. Also   105
seint Poule seiþ 'if oure gospel is hid, it is hid to hem þat schal be

---

78 docturis] gret docturis *NI*   84 also] *om. NI*   it] *om. NI*   85 þer] her
NI   86 3°] ij *NI*   87 bischop] pischop *MS, bishope NI*   88 of] *om.*
NI   96 confucioun] conficioun *MS*   97 a] *om. NI*   Bibile] byble in to
enflyshe *NI*   99 d *canc. before* drawen *MS*   101 ȝit] ȝt *MS*   man] englysche
man *NI*   102 regnede regned, *second canc. MS*   104 Wyring] wering *NI*
105 fc *canc. before* of *MS*

---

37 78–85 'Also seuenti . . . han had': cf. U 844–55 'Et quod . . . legit eas'; U 583–86
'Quid, queso . . . dampnes'; U 1112–18 'Et si dicas . . . uulgaria'.
38 85–91 'Worschipful . . . þeraftur': cf. U 587–92 'Reffert enim . . . fuisset'.
39 Bede, *Historia ecclesiastica gentis Anglorum*, III 3 (*PL* 95. 119–21).
40 91–96 'It was herde . . . enmyes': cf. U 592–98 'Audiui nempe . . . emulorum'.
41 Jacob van Maerlant, *Rymbybel*; ed. J.-B. David, 3 vols (Brussels 1858–61).
42 96–103 'Also venerabile . . . and xxxij': cf. U 598–607 'Nonne credis . . . nostro
Anglico'.
43 Ranulf Higden, *Polychronicon*, V 24; ed. C. Babington & J. R. Lumby, 9 vols, RS
41 (1865–86), 6. 224.
44 No identification has been suggested, see Dove, *EAEB*, 215.

dampned',[45] and eft he seiþ 'he þat knoweþ not, schal not be knowen
of God'.[46] Also[47] Cistrence, in his sext bok, þe I c°,[48] seiþ þat Alrede
þe kynge ordined opone scolis of diuerse artes in Oxenforde and
he turnede þe best lawes into his modor-tunge, and be Sawter also, 110
and he regned aftur þe incarnacioun ei3t hundered 3eer and seuenti
and þre.

Also[49] seint Thomas seiþ þat 'barbarus' is he þat vnderstandiþ
not þat he redeþ in his modor-tunge, and þerfore seiþ þe apostile
'if I knowe not þe vertu of þe voice to wome I speike, I schal be to 115
hym barbarus, and he þat speikeþ to me barbarus, þat is to sey, he
vnderstandiþ not wat þat I sey, ne I vnderstande not wat he seiþ'.[50]
Sum men þenkyne hem to be barbaros wiche han not propur vnder-
standinge of þat þat þei reden, to answere þer\to/ in her modor-
tunge. Also he seiþ þat Bede drew into Englische þe liberal artis leste 120
Engliche men schuldon be holden barbarus: þis seint Thomas *super
primum Poleticorum, exponens hoc vocabulum 'barbarus'*.[51] Also[52] þe
grette sutil clerk Lyncolne seiþ, in a sermon þat bigynneþ '*Scriptum
est de Leuitis*', if, he seiþ, any prest seie he can not preche, oo remedie
is resyne he vp his benefice; anoþer remedie is, if he wol not þus, 125
recorde he in þe woke þe nakid tixt of þe Soundaie Gospel þat he
kunne þe groos story and telle it to his puple, þat is, if he vndurstonde
28v Latyne, and do he þis euery woke of þe 3eer, and forsoþe he | schal
profite wel, for þus preched þe Lord seyng, Iohn 6°, 'þe wordes þat
I speike to 3ou3 ben spirit and lijf'.[53] If, forsoþe, he vnderstonde no 130
Latyn go he to oon of his nei3tboris þat vnderstandiþ, wiche wole
charitabily expone it to hym, and þus edifie he his flock, þat is, his
puple. Þus seiþ Lyncolne.[54] And on þis argueþ a clerk[55] and seiþ 'if it

115 knowe] knewe *MS*   117 þat] *om. N1*   he *repeated at line break, first canc. MS*
118 barbaros] barbarus *corr. to* barbaros *MS*, seyd barbaros *N1*   119 vnderstandinge]
vnderstange *MS*   122 Poleticorum] Polecicorum *MS*   125 þus] this *N1*
126 boke *canc. before* woke *MS*   130 vnderstonde] vnderstode *MS*

[45] 2 Cor. 4:3.

[46] 1 Cor. 14:38.

[47] 108–12 'Also Cistrence . . . and þre': cf. U 607–17 ' Subsequenter scribit . . . Cestrensis'.

[48] Higden, *Polychronicon*, VI 1, ed. Babington & Lumby, 6. 354–60.

[49] 113-22 'Also seint Thomas . . . "*barbarus*"': cf. U 1097–1106 'Dicit enim . . . ibidem'.

[50] 1 Cor. 14:11.

[51] Thomas Aquinas, *In libros Politicorum Aristotelis expositio*, I 22; ed. R. Spiazzi (Turin
1951), 8.

[52] 122–35 'Also þe . . . Bibil': cf. U 622–40 'A\u/sculta . . . pagine'.

[53] John 6:64.

[54] Robert Grosseteste, *Sermo, Scriptum est de Leuitis*, as in Bodl. MS Bodley 801,
fol. 194v.

[55] Reference to Ullerston, see 36.635–7.

is leuefful to preche þe naked text to þe pupel, it is also lefful to write
it to hem, and consequentliche, be proces of tyme, so al þe Bibil'.   135

Also[56] a nobil hooly man, Richerde Eremyte,[57] drewe oon Englice
þe Sauter with a glose of longe proces, and lessouns of *Dirige* and
many oþer tretis, by wiche many Engliche men han ben gretli edified,
and if he were cursed of God þat wolde þe puple schulde be lewder,
eiþer wors, þan þei ben. Also[58] sire Wiliam Thorisby,[59] Erchebischop   140
of ʒork, did do to drawe a tretys in Englisce be a worschipful clerk
wos name was Gaytrik,[60] in þe wiche weren conteyned þe articulis of
þe feiþ, seuene dedli synnes, þe werkes of mercy and þe ten comande-
mentis, and sente hem in smale pagynes to þe comyn puple to lerne
þis and to knewe þis, of wiche ben ʒit manye a componye in England.   145
But[61] þer ben summe þat seien, if þe gospel were on Engliche, men
myʒten liʒtly erre þerinne, but wel touchiþ þis holi man Richard
Hampol suche men, expownyng þis tixte, '*ne auferas de ore meo verbum veritatis vsquequaque*'.[62] Þer he seiþ þus: 'þer ben not fewe but
many þat wolen sustene a worde of falsenes for God, not willing   150
to beleue to konynge and better þan þei ben. Þei ben liche to þe
frendes of Iob, þat wiles þei enforsiden hem to defende God, þei
offendeden greuosly in hym. And þouʒ suche ben slayne and don
myracles, | þei neuerþeles ben stynkyng martirs'. And[63] to hem þat
seien þat þe gospel on Engliche wolde make men to erre, wyte wele   155

29r

135 to] vnto *N1*   136 hooly] *om. N1*   Richerde] Ric' hampol *N1*   Eremyte]
Emyte *MS*   136 oute *canc. before* oon *MS*   138 wiche] the which *N1*
139 if] *om. N1*   schulde] they shuld *N1*   lerned *canc. before* lewder *MS*   141 ʒork]
pok *N1*   did do to drawe] did draw *N1*   142 þe] *om. N1*   143 þe feiþ] byleue
N1   147 touchiþ] couchiþ *MS*   Richard] Richad *MS*   155 Engliche] enliche
MS   to] *om. N1*

[56] 136–40 'Also . . . þei ben': cf. U 618–20 'Quid eciam . . . hac parte'.

[57] Richard Rolle's *English Psalter Commentary* (c. 1340) is ed. in H. R. Bramley, *The
Psalter or Psalms of David, and Certain Canticles, with a Tr. and Exposition by R. Rolle*
(Oxford 1884). See also H. E. Allen, *Writings Ascribed to Richard Rolle, Hermit of Hampole
and Materials for his Biography* (New York, NY, 1927), and *English Writings of Richard
Rolle, Hermit of Hampole* (Oxford 1931); and R. Hanna, *The English Manuscripts of Richard
Rolle: a Descriptive Catalogue* (Exeter 2010).

[58] 140–46 'Also sire Wiliam . . . Englond': cf. U 644–53 'Que considerans . . . obligantur'.

[59] John (not William) Thoresby, archbishop of York, 1352–73. Concerned with improving religious knowledge of the laity, he issued in 1357 an injunction summarizing in Latin
the basic principles of Christian belief for use by clergy with pastoral responsibilities
for the laity. It appears in Thoresby's register with an English version, known as *The
Lay Folk's Catechism*, that was also circulated separately, and is attributed in several
manuscripts to John Gaytryge, usually identified as a Benedictine monk of St Mary's
abbey, York.

[60] T. F. Simmons & H. E. Nolloth, *The Lay Folks' Catechism*, EETS 118 (1901).

[61] 146–54 'But þer . . . martis': cf. U 694–701 'Sed eo . . . Ricardus'.

[62] Ps. 118:43; see Bramley, *The Psalter or Psalms of David*.

[63] 154–57 'And to hem . . . eretikes': cf. U 1612–25 'Ad 23^m . . . susurrantes'.

þat we fynden in Latyne mo heretikes þan of ale oþer langagis, for þe
Decres rehersiþ sixti Latyn eretikes.[64] Also[65] þe hooli euaungelistis
writen þe gospelle in diuerse langages, as Matheu in Iudee, Marke
in Ytalie, Luck in þe partyes of Achaie and Iohn in Asie, aftur he
hadde writun þe Apocalips in þe yle of Pathomos, and al þes writun   160
in þe langage of þe same cuntre, as seiþ Ardmakan. Also Ardmakan,
in þe *Book of Questiouns*, seiþ þat þe sacrament mai wel be made in
iche comoun langage, for so, as he seiþ, diden þe apostilis.[66] But we
coueyten not þat, but prey Anticrist þat we moten haue oure bileue
in Englische. Also, we þat han moche comyned wiþ þe Iewis, knowen   165
wel þat al my3ty men of hem, in wat londe þei ben born, \3it/ þei han
in Ebrew þe Bible, and þei ben more actif of þe olde lawe þane any
Latyn man comonli, 3he, as wel þe lewde men of þe Iewes as prestis.
But it is red in comyne of þe prestis to fulfille þer prestes office and
to edificacioun of porayle þat for slouþe studieþ no3t. And þe Grekis   170
wiche ben nobel men han al þis in þer owne langage.

But[67] 3it aduersaries of trewiþ seien, wane men rehersen þat Grekis and Latyns han al in þer owne langage, þe clerkis of hem speiken
gramaticalliche and þe pupel vnderstondiþ it not. Witte þei þat þou3
a clerke or anoþer man þus lerned can sette his wordis on Engliche   175
better þan a rewde man, it foloweþ not herof þat oure langage schuld
be destried. It were al on to sei þis and to kitte oute þe tunges of
2.9v hem þat can not speke | þus curiosly. But[68] þei schulde vnderstande
þat gramaticaliche is not ellis but abite of ri3t spekyng and ri3t pro-
nounsyng and ri3t writynge.[69] But frere Tille,[70] þat seide before þe   180
buschop of Londoun, heerynge an hundrid men, þat Ierom seide he
errid in translatyng of þe Bibel, is lijk to Elymas, þe wiche wolde haue
lettid a bischope or a iuge to heere þe byleue, to wom Poule seid 'O

156 we fynden in Latyne] yn latyn we fynd *N1*   157 sixti] 66 *N1*   159 and]
om. N1   162 þe] a *N1*   164 coueyten] coueteyten *MS*   prey] *om. N1*
165 þe] *om. N1*   166 my3ty] the myghty *N1*   167 of] yn *N1*   168 þe]
om. N1   169 þer] her *N1*   171 þer] her *N1*   173 þer] her *N1*   of hem]
om. N1   174 vnderstondiþ] vnderstodiþ *MS*   it] *om. N1*   175 þus] this *N1*
on] yn *N1*   177 þe] her *N1*   178 of hem] *om. N1*   þus] so *N1*   179 abite]
the habite *N1*   180 þe] þi *MS*

[64] According to Gratian's *Decretum, causa* 24, q. 3, c. 39, *Quidam*, there were sixty-eight
Latin heresies; Friedberg, 1001–6 (Dove, *EAEB*, 216).

[65] 157–64 'Also þe . . . Englische': cf. U 1420–29 'Vnde et . . . posse fieri'.

[66] Both references are to Richard Fitzralph, *Summa in questionibus Armenorum* (Rome
1512), fol. 66ra.

[67] 172–78 'But 3it . . . curiosly': cf. U 1473–76 'Ad vigesimum . . . intelligamus'.

[68] 178–80 'But þei . . . writynge': cf. U 1497–1500 'Est enim . . . ydioma'.

[69] The passage starting at 'But 3it aduersaries. . .' and ending at '. . . ri3t writynge' is
omitted in *N1* and supplied by the same scribe at the end on fol. 143v.

[70] John Dille, provincial of the Dominican friars in England from *c.* 1404 until 1410;
see discussion at pp. cvii–cviii.

þou, ful of al trecherie and of al falace, seching to turne þe buschop
from þe beleue, þou schalt be blynde to a tyme'. Þis is writun in   185
þe Dedus of þe Apostilis, 13° c°.[71] For[72] Ierom seiþ in þe prolog of
Kyngis 'I am not knowyng to myself in any maner me to haue changyd
anyþinge from þe Ebrew trewiþ. Wel I wot', he seide, 'sum tyme þat
holy writ was false aftur þe letter'.[73] But aftur, wane Austyn hadde
writen to him and he to him aȝen, he grantid wele þat it was trewe,   190
as he rehersiþ in a pistile and in þe prolog of þe Bible, and was glad
and ioyeful of his translacioun.[74] And þerfor, wane he haþ rehersiyd
al þe bookis of þe Bibel, þane he seiþ in þe prolog of Penteteuke 'I
praie þe, dere broþer, lyue amonge þese, haue þi meditacioun in þese,
knowe noon oþer þing nor seche non oþer þing but þese'. But Ierom   195
hadde many enemyes for translating of þe Bibel, as he rehersiþ in þe
first prolog to his enemyes þus: 'whi art þou turmented be enueye?
What stirist þou þe willes of vnkunnynge men aȝens me? If it semeþ
to þe þat I haue erred in myn translacion, aske þe Ebrewes, councel
wiþ þe maisteris of diuerse citees'.[75] In þe secunde prolog he seiþ 'þis   200
we seeyn (rehersing þe sentence bifore) leest we ben seen to holde
oure pes aȝens debatouris'. And in þe same he seiþ: 'we, hasting to
30r oure contre, schullen passe wiþ | a deffe eere to þe dedely songyis of
þe mermaidens'.[76] And þus in many prologis he scorneþ his enemyes
and lettiþ not his hooly werk but seiþ: 'I seide, I schal kepe my weies   205
þat I trespas not in my tounge; I haue put keping to my mouþ wane
þe synful man haþ stande aȝens me'.[77] Þese ben þe wordes of Ierom
rehersing þe profiȝte.

Also it is knowen to many men þat in þe tyme of kyng Richerd,
whos soule God asoile,[78] into a parliment was put a bille, be assent   210
of two erchebischopis and of þe clergie, to anulle þe Bibel þat tyme
translatid into Engliche, and also oþer bokis of þe gospel translatid
into Engliche, wiche, wanne it was seyn of lordis and comouns, þe

185 is om. MS   writun] is wreten N1   187 changyd] changyng MS
191 and] om. N1   was] om. N1   195 nor seche non oþer þing] om. MS, no seche
non odyr þing N1   199 Ebrewes] Ebrew MS   202 debatouris] þe batouris
MS   211 þat tyme] om. N1   213 comouns] of comyns N1

---

[71] Acts 13:10–11.
[72] 186–92 'For Ierom . . . translacioun': cf. U 1155–59 'Non tamen . . . translatum'.
[73] Jerome, Prologue to Kings, 'Prologus Galeatus' ('helmeted prologue'); PL 28. 557–8.
[74] This reference and the following quotation 'I praie þe, dere broþer. . .' are from
Jerome, 'Frater Ambrosius tua mihi munuscula preferens', Epistola ad Paulinum (ep. 53);
PL 22. 540–49.
[75] Jerome, 'Desiderii mei desideratus accepi epistolas', Preface to Pentateuch; PL 28.
558.
[76] Jerome, Preface to Joshua; PL 28. 464.
[77] Jerome, Preface to Kings; PL 28. 558.
[78] King Richard II, d. February 1400.

good duke of Lancastre, Ion, wos soule God asoile for his mercy,
answered þerto scharpely, seying þis sentence, 'we wel not be þe refuse   215
of alle men, for siþen oþer naciouns han Goddis lawe, wiche is lawe
of oure byleue, in þer owne modur-langage, we wolone haue oure
in Engliche, wo þat euere it bigrucche'. And þis he affermede with
a grete oþc.[79]

Also þe bischope of Caunturbiri, Thomas Arrundel þat nowe is,[80]   220
seide a sermon in Westinminster þeras weren many hundred puple
at þe biriyng of quene Anne,[81] of wos soule God haue mercy, and
in his comendyngis of hir he seide it was more ioie of hir þan of
any whoman þat euere he knewe, for notwiþstanding þat sche was
an alien borne, sche hadde on Engliche al þe foure gospeleris wiþ   225
þe docturis vpon hem.[82] And he seide sche hadde sent hem vnto
him, and he seide þei weren goode and trewe,[83] and comended hir in
þat sche was so grete a lady and also an alien, and wolde so lowliche
studiee in so vertuous bokis. And he blamed in þat sermoun scharpeli
30v þe necligence of prelatis | and of oþer men, in so miche þat summe   230
seiden he wolde on þe morowe leue vp his office of chanceler and
forsake þe worlde, and þan it hadde be þe best sermoun þat euere
þei herde.[84]

215 þe] om. N1   217 þer] her N1   modur-langage] langadge N1   218 we wolone haue oure in Engliche] om. N1   220 Arrundel] of arundell N1   221 þeras]
the as N1   225 gospeleris] gospelles N1   227 and] a N1   229 so lowliche
studiee] stody so lowlich N1   in] om. N1   þat] the N1   230 miche] om. N1
232 best] lest MS, best N1

[79] See a discussion of historical accuracy of this claim in M. Jurkowski, 'The selective
censorship of the Wycliffite Bible', in ESWB, 360–81, at 365.

[80] Thomas Arundel (1353–1414), archbishop of Canterbury, 1396–7 and 1399–1414.

[81] Anne of Bohemia, first queen of Richard II, d. 1394.

[82] Possibly a reference to the Glossed Gospels; see Doctors in English. In De triplico
uinculo amoris, written c. 1382, Wyclif states that Anne of Bohemia owned the gospels in
Czech, German, and Latin; ed. R. Buddensieg, John Wiclif's Polemical Works in Latin, 2
vols (London 1883), 2. 168/9–11; Dove, EAEB, 218.

[83] Apparently an anachronistic reference to Arundel's Constitutions of 1407 requiring
episcopal approval for biblical translations (Wilkins, 1. 317).

[84] There are no other records of Arundel preaching a sermon at the funeral of Anne
of Bohemia (Dove, EAEB, 218).

Select Bibliography

Primary Sources

The use of the *Patrologia Latina* (*PL*) and *Patrologia Graeca* (*PG*) as primary text sources, whenever available, perhaps requires some justification. Two reasons, of very different origins, seem to us to speak conclusively in the same direction. Most immediately the availability of online texts for *PL* is much more predictable in academic libraries than that of a host of more modern scholarly editions; although the origins of *PL* volumes are often much anterior to those of more recent texts, a student can more readily lay hands on the work required in *PL*. The traditional rejection of *PL* in favour of other series rests on the alleged inaccuracy of Migne's texts, together with the frequent difficulty of reading its column numbers. No justification can be brought forward for the latter; but the former perhaps usefully reminds the modern reader that medieval scholars had not (save in very rare circumstances) the means to distinguish correct readings from incorrect.

The following list aims to include (a) sources repeatedly used, with cross-listing to the abbreviations; and (b) sources that could be misidentified without full referencing. Names are indexed alphabetically by forename; forenames in Latin or any other language are indexed in sequence under their English equivalents.

Alexander of Hales, *Summa theologiae*, ed. Fratres Minores, 4 vols (Quaracchi 1924–48)
Alexander Neckham, *Corrogationes Promethei*, unprinted; used here is Bodl. MS Bodley 550; for other copies see R. W. Hunt (ed. and revised M. Gibson), *The Schools and the Cloister: The Life and Writings of Alexander Nequam (1157–1217)* (Oxford 1984), esp. 131–4
Ardmacanus: *see* Richard Fitzralph
Aristoteles Latinus, ed. L. Minio-Paluello & others, 25 vols (Amsterdam 1951–)
Armachanus: *see* Richard Fitzralph
Augustine, *Opera*, PL 32–47
Bede, *Opera*: PL 90–95; *Historia ecclesiastica gentis Anglorum*, ed. B. Colgrave & R. A. B. Mynors (Oxford 1969)
Berengaudus, *Expositio super septem visiones libri Apocalypsis*, PL 17
'Cestrensis': *see* Ranulf Higden
Chrysostom: *see* John Chrysostom
Corpus iuris canonici, ed. E. Friedberg. 2 vols (Leipzig 1879–81; repr. Graz 1959)
Council of Constance: see *Magnum oecumenicum Constantiense concilium*
Dionysius, *De ierarchia ecclesiastica*, trans. Robert Grosseteste, ed. Ph. Chevallier, *Dionysiaca*, 2 vols (Paris 1937–49)
Giles of Rome, *Liber contra exemptos*, pr. Rome 1555
Glossa ordinaria: most accessible is *Biblia latina cum glossa ordinaria: Facsimile Reprint of the Editio Princeps Adolph Rusch of Strasburg 1480/81*, ed. K. Froehlich & M. T. Gibson, 4 vols (Turnhout 1992); citation here is usually to biblical book, chapter and verse and this is appropriate for all editions
Gregory, *Opera*, PL 75–78

Guido delle Colonne, *Historia destructionis Troiae*, ed. N. E. Griffin (Cambridge, MA, 1936)

Henry Knighton, *Chronicon*, ed. G. H. Martin (Oxford 1995)

Hugh of Saint-Cher, *Postillain totam Bibliam*, pr. Basel *c.* 1500

Hugh of Saint-Victor, *Didascalicon*, ed. C. H. Buttner (Washington, DC, 1939)

Huguccio: see Uguccione da Pisa

Jerome, *Opera*, *PL* 22–30

pseudo-John Chrysostom, *Opus imperfectum super Matthaeum*: *PG* 56. 611–946; also J. van Banning, *CCSL* 87B (1988), introduction to a new edition (which has not appeared), which contains valuable information about the preservation and organization of the text

John Trevisa, *Polychronicon*, trans., ed. R. Waldron, *John Trevisa's Translation of the 'Polychronicon' of Ranulph Higden, book VI*, Middle English Texts 35 (Heidelberg 2004)

——, Prefaces on translation, ed. R. Waldron, 'Trevisa's original prefaces on translation: a critical edition', in *Medieval English Studies Presented to George Kane*, ed. E. D. Kennedy, R. Waldron & J. S. Wittig (Wolfeboro, NH, 1988), 285–99

Josephus, *Antiquitates*, Latin trans., pr. *Flauii Josephi Antiquitatum Iudaicorum libri xx* (Basel 1540)

The Lanterne of Liȝt, ed. L. M. Swinburn, EETS 151 (1917)

'Lincolniensis': see Robert Grosseteste

Magnum oecumenicum Constantiense concilium, ed. H. von der Hardt, 6 vols (Frankfurt 1697–1700)

Moses Maimonides, *Dux dubitantium aut perplexorum*, pr. *Rabi Mossei Aegyptii Dux seu director dubitantium aut perplexorum* (Paris 1520)

Nicholas Gorran, *In omnes divi Pauli Epistolas*, pr. Antwerp 1617

——, *In Acta Apostolorum, et singulas Apostolorum, Iacobi, Petri, Iohannis, et Iudæ canonicas epistolas, et Apocalypsin commentarij*, pr. Antwerp 1620

Nicholas de Lyra, *Postilla litteralis super totam Bibliam*: numerous early printed editions exist, of varying reliability; Lyra's comments are usually attached to a particular biblical text and reference to this is the most helpful means of retrieval

Origen, *Super Leuiticum*, *PG* 12

'Parisiensis': *see* Giles of Rome

Petrus Johannis Olivi, *Super Genesim*, ed. D. Flood (St Bonaventura, NY, 2007); *see* Paris, Bibliothèque nationale de France, MS lat. 15559

Ranulf Higden ('Cestrensis'), *Polychronicon*, ed. C. Babington and J. R. Lumby, RS 41, 9 vols (1865–86)

Richard Fitzralph ('Ardmacanus', 'Armachanus'), *Summa in questionibus Armenorum*, pr. Rome 1512

Richard Rolle, *English Psalter*, ed. H. R. Bramley, *The Psalter or Psalms of David, and Certain Canticles . . . Exposition by R. Rolle* (Oxford 1883). See also *RP*

Robert Grosseteste ('Lincolniensis'), *Sermones* and *Dicta*, unprinted; Bodl. MS Bodley 801 used here; for other manuscripts see S. Harrison Thomson,

The Writings of Robert Grosseteste (Cambridge 1940); for his translation of *De ierarchia ecclesiastica* see above under Dionysius

Roger Bacon, *Opus tertium*, ed. J. S. Brewer, *Fr. Rogeri Bacon Opera quaedam hactenus inedita*, RS 15, 3 vols (1859); trans. R. Burke, *The Opus Majus of Roger Bacon. A Translation*, 2 vols (Philadelphia, PA, 1928)

Rosarium theologiae, ME trans., ed. C. von Nolcken, *The Middle English Translation of the 'Rosarium theologie'*, Middle English Texts 10 (Heidelberg 1979)

Seneca, *Dialogi*, ed. J. W. Basore, 3 vols (London 1928–35)

Statuta antiqua uniuersitatis Oxoniensis, ed. S. Gibson (Oxford 1931)

Thomas Aquinas, *Catena aurea in quatuor evangelia*, ed. A. Guarienti, 2 vols (Rome 1953)

——, *In libros Politicorum Aristotelis*, ed. R. Spiazzi (Turin 1951)

——, *Summa theologiae*, ed. Fratres Predicatores, *Sancti Thomae Aquinatis Doctoris Angelici (de Aquino) opera omnia iussu Leonis XIII edita* (Rome 1882–), vols 4–12

Uguccione da Pisa, *Deriuationes*, ed. E. Cecchini, 2 vols (Florence, 2004)

William of Auvergne, *De fide et legibus*, pr. Paris 1674

William of Auxerre, *Summa aurea*, ed. J. Ribaillier, 4 vols in 5 (Paris 1980–87)

William Caxton, *Opera*, ed. N. F. Blake, *Caxton's Own Prose* (London 1973)

William of Malmesbury, *Gesta regum Anglorum*, ed. R. A. B. Mynors, R. M. Thomson & M. Winterbottom, 2 vols (Oxford 1998–9)

Secondary Sources

Allen, H. E., *Writings Ascribed to Richard Rolle, Hermit of Hampole and Materials for His Biography* (New York, NY, 1927)

Bloomfield, M. W., *Incipits of Latin Works on the Virtues and Vices, 1100–1500* (Cambridge, MA, 1979)

Catto, J. I., 'The Wycliffite Bible: the historical context', in *ESWB*, 11–26

Courtenay, W. J., *Schools and Scholars in Fourteenth-Century England* (Princeton, NJ, 1987)

——, 'The London 'studia' in the fourteenth century', *Medievalia et Humanistica* 13 (1985), 127–41

van Dussen, M., *From England to Bohemia: Heresy and Communication in the Later Middle Ages* (Cambridge 2012)

Ellis, R. (ed.), *The Oxford History of Literary Translation in English*, 1: *To 1550* (Oxford 2008)

Emden, A. B., *An Oxford Hall in Medieval Times* (Oxford 1927)

Fowler, D. C., *The Life and Times of John Trevisa, Medieval Scholar* (London 1995)

Hanna, R., 'Merton College, MS. 68: production and texts', *Bodleian Library Record* 27 (2014), 129–52

——, 'Richard Rolle's *Incendium amoris*: a prospectus for a future editor', *Journal of Medieval Latin* 26 (2016), 221–61

——, 'The transmission of Richard Rolle's Latin works', *The Library*, 7th ser. 14 (2014), 313–33

Harris, R. & T. J. Taylor, *Landmarks in Linguistic Thought: The Western Tradition from Socrates to Saussure* (London 1989)

Harvey, M., 'English Views on the Reforms to be Undertaken in the General Council, 1400–18', DPhil thesis (University of Oxford 1963)

——, *Solutions to the Schism: A Study of some English Attitudes 1378–1409* (St Otilien 1983)

Hruza, K., 'Liber Pauli de Slauikouicz. Der hussitische Codex 4937 der Österreichischen Nationalbibliothek in Wien und sein ursprünglicher Besitzer', in *Handschriften, Historiographie und Recht. Winfried Stelzer zum 60*, ed. G. Pfeifer (Vienna 2002), 128–52

Hudson, A., 'The debate on Bible translation, Oxford 1401', *EHR* 90 (1975), 1–18; repr. in her *Lollards and their Books* (London 1985), 67–84

Jurkowski, M., 'New light on John Purvey', *EHR* 110 (1995), 1180–90

Kelly, H. A., *The Middle English Bible: A Reassessment* (Philadelphia, PA, 2016)

Ker, N. R., 'Wyclif manuscripts in Oxford in the fifteenth century', *Bodleian Library Record* 4 (1953), 292–3

Kraebel, A., 'The use of Richard Rolle's *Latin Psalter* in Richard Ullerston's *Expositio canticorum scripturae*', *Medium Ævum* 81 (2012), 139–44

——, 'The manuscript tradition of Richard Ullerston's *Expositio canticorum scripturae*', *Medieval Journal* 3 (2013), 49–82.

——, *Biblical Commentary and Translation in Later Medieval England: Experiments in Interpretation* (Cambridge 2020); Ullerston's life and writings are discussed by Prof. Kraebel at several points in his book, which we are grateful to have seen before publication

Kuczynski, M. P., *A Glossed Wycliffite Psalter: Oxford, Bodleian Library MS Bodley 554*, 2 vols, EETS 352, 352 (2019)

Law, V., *The History of Linguistics in Europe from Plato to 1600* (Cambridge 2003)

Levy, I. C., 'The place of Holy Scripture in John Wyclif's theology', in *ESWB*, 27–48

Linde, C., 'Arguing with Lollards: Thomas Palmer, O.P. and *De translatione scripture sacre in linguam barbaricam*', *Viator* 46 (2015), 235–54

——, *How to correct the 'Sacra Scriptura'? Textual Criticism of the Bible between the Twelfth and Fifteenth Century*, Medium Ævum Monograph 29 (Oxford 2012)

Marigo, A., *I codici manoscritti delle 'Derivationes' di Uguccione Pisano* (Rome 1936)

McFarlane, K. B., *Lancastrian Kings and Lollard Knights* (Oxford 1972)

Muller, W. P., *Huguccio: The Life, Works and Thought of a Twelfth-Century Jurist* (Washington, DC, 1994)

Powicke, F. M., *The Medieval Books of Merton College* (Oxford 1931)

Scott, K., *Later Gothic Manuscripts 1300–1490*, 2 vols (London 1996)

Seuren, P. A. M., *Western Linguistics: An Historical Introduction* (Oxford 1998)

Smalley, B., *The Study of the Bible in the Middle Ages*, 3rd edn (Oxford 1983)

——, 'John Wyclif's *Postilla super totam Bibliam*', *Bodleian Library Record* 4 (1952–3), 186–205

——, 'Wyclif's *Postilla* on the Old Testament and his *Principium*', *Oxford Studies presented to Daniel Callus*, Oxford Historical Society, new ser. 16 (1964), 253–96

Trapp, D., 'Augustinian theology of the 14th century', *Augustiniana* 6 (1956), 146–274

Walsh, K., *Richard FitzRalph in Oxford, Avignon, and Armagh: A Fourteenth-Century Scholar and Primate* (Oxford 1981)

Watson, N., 'Censorship and cultural change in late-medieval England: vernacular theology, the Oxford translation debate, and Arundel's *Constitutions* of 1409', *Speculum* 70 (1995), 822–64

Weijers, O., *A Scholar's Paradise: Teaching and Debating in Medieval Paris* (Turnhout 2015)

Whitfield, D. W., 'Conflicts of personality and principle: the political and religious crisis in the English Franciscan province, 1400–1409', *Franciscan Studies* 17 (1957), 321–62

Index of Biblical Quotations

References are to line numbers; the texts are indicated by prefixed sigla: U=Ullerston; B=Butler; P=Palmer; Bois=First seiþ Bois. The index includes all of the references noted by the scribes of the four texts and included in the editions in this volume. Unstated biblical allusions are not included. Verse numbers are supplied by reference to the modern Vulgate. In the edited text editorially supplied information is in square brackets; here, to leave the list typographically more clear, these brackets have been removed. Biblical allusions not specified by the scribes are not listed.

Index of Manuscripts

References are to page numbers.

General Index